The Beautiful and Damned

Glamour, Excess & the Heavy Price
of Desire in Roaring-Twenties Manhattan

A Modern Translation
Adapted for the Contemporary Reader

F. Scott Fitzgerald

Translated by Tim Zengerink

Table of Contents

Preface
Message to the Reader

Rebuilding the Greatest Library in Human History

Thousands of years ago, the Library of Alexandria was the heart of global knowledge — a sanctuary where the wisdom of every known civilization was gathered and shared freely.

And then, it was lost.

Now, we're rebuilding it — and you are invited to join us.

At the Library of Alexandria, we've set out to make every book available to every person on Earth — not just in print, but in every language, every format, and for every reader.

Here's how we do it:

- **Deluxe Print Editions at True Printing Cost** - Order any book as a high-quality paperback, elegant hardcover, or stunning boxset — and only pay what it costs to print. No markups. No middlemen.
- **Unlimited Access to the Greatest Works** - Enjoy thousands of timeless classics — from Plato to Shakespeare to Tolstoy — in beautiful, modern eBook and audiobook editions. Read and listen without limits — for every reader, everywhere.
- **Modern Translations for Every Language & Dialect** - We're reimagining the classics in clear, accessible language — and translating them into every dialect imaginable. Everyone deserves to understand humanity's greatest ideas.

When you visit **LibraryofAlexandria.com**, you're not just accessing books — you're joining a global movement to restore, preserve, and share the wisdom of civilization.

Join us today at LibraryofAlexandria.com

Together, we'll ensure the light of human wisdom never fades again.

With gratitude,

The Modern Library of Alexandria Team

Visit:
www.libraryofalexandria.com
Or scan the code below:

Introduction

The Jazz Age and Fitzgerald's Portrait of Decay

F. Scott Fitzgerald's *The Beautiful and Damned*, first published in 1922, stands as one of the most evocative examinations of ambition, love, and disillusionment in the Jazz Age. Often considered the darker, more introspective sibling to *The Great Gatsby*, this novel delves deep into the glamorous yet hollow world of New York's upper class, portraying the destructive effects of wealth, vanity, and relentless desire. It is a story of dreams and downfall, of a generation seeking meaning amid the glittering chaos of modernity, only to find themselves adrift in a world of moral uncertainty.

At its core, *The Beautiful and Damned* chronicles the marriage of Anthony Patch and Gloria Gilbert, a couple who embody the restless, hedonistic spirit of the 1920s. Anthony, the grandson of a wealthy businessman, is a man of privilege but little purpose. He is intelligent, cultured, and charming, but lacks ambition and a clear sense of direction in life. Gloria, his beautiful and vivacious wife, is both the love of his life and a symbol of the allure and vanity that drives their social circle. Together, they live a life of lavish parties, extravagant spending, and idle pleasures, believing that Anthony's inheritance will eventually secure their future.

However, their life of indulgence is built on a fragile foundation. Anthony's inheritance is tied up in legal battles, and as the years pass, the couple's once intoxicating love gives way to resentment, boredom, and despair. As they wait for the wealth that may never come, their lives spiral into alcoholism, financial ruin, and moral decay. Through their story, Fitzgerald paints a searing portrait of a generation intoxicated by glamour and success, yet ultimately consumed by its own excesses.

The novel is a profound exploration of the American Dream and its dark underside. While Anthony and Gloria initially appear to have everything—youth, beauty, and social status—their relentless pursuit of pleasure and wealth leaves them spiritually bankrupt. They are characters who live for the surface glitter of life, failing to cultivate the depth, purpose, or resilience needed to withstand life's inevitable challenges. In this sense, *The Beautiful and Damned* serves as both a cautionary tale and a critique of the cultural values that defined the Roaring Twenties.

Fitzgerald's own life and marriage provide a strong autobiographical undercurrent to the novel. Much like Anthony and Gloria, Fitzgerald and his wife Zelda were icons of the Jazz Age, celebrated for their beauty, charm, and extravagant lifestyle. However, beneath the surface of their glamorous public image lay tensions, insecurities, and struggles with personal ambition. In *The Beautiful and Damned*, Fitzgerald explores these themes with both intimacy and critical distance, offering readers an unflinching look at the costs of living for pleasure and fame.

When the novel was first published, it was met with mixed reviews. Some critics praised its vivid portrayal of a generation, while others found it overly pessimistic or lacking the polished structure of Fitzgerald's later works. Yet over time, *The Beautiful and Damned* has come to be recognized as a powerful exploration of love and ambition, one that captures the zeitgeist of the 1920s with remarkable precision. The novel's characters, with their flaws and contradictions, feel as relevant today as they did a century ago, reflecting timeless questions about success, happiness, and the meaning of life..

Love, Vanity, and Disillusionment

One of the central themes of *The Beautiful and Damned* is the nature of love and its entanglement with ambition, vanity, and self-interest. Anthony and Gloria's relationship begins with the intoxicating thrill of romance, but as the narrative unfolds, it becomes clear that their love is built more on physical attraction and shared hedonism than on genuine understanding or shared values. Gloria's beauty is both her greatest asset and her curse; she is worshipped for her appearance, but she also feels trapped by the fleeting nature of youth and the fear of losing her allure. Anthony, on the other hand, is drawn to Gloria's charm and vivacity but is too passive and self-indulgent to build a stable future for them.

As the story progresses, their relationship deteriorates under the pressures of financial uncertainty and unfulfilled expectations. Both Anthony and Gloria are consumed by their own egos, unable to compromise or grow together. Their marriage, which once seemed like a partnership of equals, becomes a battleground of resentment and broken dreams. Through their downfall, Fitzgerald explores the idea that love, when based on superficial desires and social ambitions, cannot withstand the trials of time and adversity.

The theme of disillusionment permeates the novel. Both Anthony and Gloria begin the story with high expectations for their future, believing that wealth and social status will guarantee happiness. However, as they face the harsh realities of life—legal battles over Anthony's inheritance, the decline of their social standing, and their own moral failings—they are forced to confront the emptiness of their aspirations. Fitzgerald masterfully captures the slow erosion of their dreams, illustrating how the pursuit of pleasure and status can lead to spiritual and emotional bankruptcy.

Another key theme is the passage of time and the inevitability of change. Gloria's obsession with her beauty and youth reflects a broader cultural preoccupation with appearances and the fear of aging. As she grows older and her looks begin to fade, she becomes increasingly desperate and disillusioned. Anthony, too, is haunted by the passage of time, as he realizes that his youthful charm and family name are not enough to secure his future. This focus on time and decay foreshadows the themes that Fitzgerald would later explore in *The Great Gatsby*, particularly the idea that all dreams are ultimately subject to the inexorable passage of time.

Fitzgerald also uses the novel to critique the materialism and superficiality of the upper class. Anthony and Gloria's social circle is filled with characters who live for parties, gossip, and fleeting pleasures, with little concern for deeper values or lasting achievements. This portrayal of the idle rich reflects Fitzgerald's ambivalence toward the world of wealth and privilege. While he was fascinated by its glamour, he also recognized its emptiness and moral decay. In *The Beautiful and Damned*, this critique is particularly sharp, as the characters' pursuit of pleasure leads not to fulfillment but to ruin.

Fitzgerald's Style and the Novel's Legacy

Fitzgerald's prose in *The Beautiful and Damned* is as lyrical and evocative as ever, filled with vivid descriptions, sharp dialogue, and moments of profound insight. He has a gift for capturing the moods and atmospheres of the Jazz Age, from the glittering allure of New York's nightlife to the quiet despair of personal failure. His writing is both romantic and cynical, reflecting the contradictions of a generation caught between the old values of the Gilded Age and the modern sensibilities of the 1920s.

One of the novel's strengths is its psychological depth. Anthony and Gloria are not merely caricatures of the idle rich; they are complex, flawed individuals whose struggles feel both personal and universal. Fitzgerald delves into their inner lives, exploring their fears, insecurities, and desires with empathy and precision. This psychological realism adds a layer of complexity to the narrative, making their downfall all the more poignant and believable.

The novel's structure, while less tightly woven than The Great Gatsby, allows for a rich exploration of character and theme. Fitzgerald moves fluidly between scenes of social gaiety and moments of introspection, creating a narrative that is both expansive and intimate. While some critics have argued that the novel lacks the formal perfection of Fitzgerald's later work, its rawness and ambition are part of its enduring appeal.

Over the years, *The Beautiful and Damned* has been recognized as an important work in Fitzgerald's canon, offering a window into both his artistic development and the cultural moment he sought to capture. The novel's portrayal of the Jazz Age—its glittering surface and dark undercurrents—remains as compelling today as it was in the 1920s. In many ways, the story of Anthony and Gloria is timeless, reflecting the universal human struggle to find meaning and happiness in a world that often values appearances over substance.

The legacy of *The Beautiful and Damned* lies not only in its cultural resonance but also in its exploration of themes that continue to resonate in modern society. The pursuit of wealth, the obsession with youth and beauty, the fragility of love, and the disillusionment that comes when dreams fail to materialize—these are issues that remain as relevant today as they were a century ago. Fitzgerald's ability to capture these themes with both elegance and honesty is what makes this novel a lasting masterpiece.

Book One

Chapter I: Anthony Patch

In 1913, when Anthony patch turned twenty-five, two years had already passed since irony, the holy ghost of this modern era, had, at least in theory, come down upon him. Irony served as the final shine on his shoes, the last stroke of the clothes brush, a kind of intellectual "There!"—but at the beginning of this story he had only reached the conscious stage. When you first encounter him, he often wonders whether he lacks honor and might be slightly insane, a disgraceful and vulgar film shimmering on the world's surface like oil on a pristine pond, these moments naturally alternating with times when he considers himself quite an extraordinary young man, completely worldly, perfectly suited to his surroundings, and considerably more important than anyone else in his circle.

This was his healthy condition and it filled him with joy, made him agreeable, and drew intelligent men and all women to him. In this frame of mind he believed that he would someday achieve some quiet, refined accomplishment that the chosen few would consider worthwhile and, moving forward, would take his place among the fainter stars in a vague, uncertain heaven somewhere between death and eternal life. Until the moment arrived for this endeavor he would remain Anthony Patch—not merely the image of a man but a clear and vibrant personality, strong in his opinions, scornful, working from his core outward—a man who understood that there could be no true honor and yet possessed honor, who recognized the false reasoning behind courage and yet remained courageous.

A Worthy Man and His Gifted Son

Anthony gained the same sense of social standing from being Adam J. Patch's grandson as he would have felt if he could trace his ancestry across the ocean to the crusaders. This was unavoidable; despite what Virginians and Bostonians might claim, an upper class built purely on money requires actual wealth from each individual member.

Now Adam J. Patch, better known as "Cross Patch," left his father's farm in Tarrytown early in 1861 to join a New York cavalry regiment. He returned home from the war as a major, dove into Wall Street, and through considerable commotion, excitement, praise, and hostility he accumulated around seventy-five million dollars for himself.

This consumed all his energy until he reached fifty-seven years of age. At that point, following a serious bout with sclerosis, he decided to dedicate what remained of his life to the moral transformation of society. He transformed into a crusader among crusaders. Following the inspiring example of Anthony Comstock, whose name he gave to his grandson, he launched a diverse array of attacks against alcohol, books, immorality, art, patent medicines, and Sunday theater performances. His mind, influenced by that subtle corruption that eventually affects all but a select few, threw itself passionately into every moral outrage of the era. From his office chair on his Tarrytown property, he waged war against the vast theoretical enemy of wickedness, a battle that continued for fifteen years. During this time, he revealed himself to be a fanatical obsessive, a complete pest, and an insufferable nuisance. The year when this tale begins found him growing tired; his crusade had become sporadic; 1861 was slowly encroaching upon 1895; his mind dwelled extensively on the Civil War, somewhat on his deceased wife and son, and barely at all on his grandson Anthony.

Early in his career, Adam Patch had married a frail thirty-year-old woman named Alicia Withers, who brought him one hundred thousand dollars and flawless access to New York's banking elite. She promptly and quite spiritedly gave birth to a son, and as though completely drained by this remarkable achievement, she thereafter withdrew into the dim confines of the nursery. The boy, Adam Ulysses Patch, grew up to become an enthusiastic club member, an expert in proper etiquette, and a skilled driver of horse-drawn carriages—at the remarkable age of twenty-six, he started writing his memoirs with the title "New York Society as I Have Seen It." When word spread about this project, publishers competed eagerly to acquire it, but after his death, the work proved to be excessively wordy and overwhelmingly boring, so it was never even privately published.

This Fifth Avenue gentleman married when he was twenty-two years old. His wife was Henrietta Lebrune, Boston's "Society Contralto," and their only child was named Anthony Comstock Patch at his grandfather's request. When the boy enrolled at Harvard, the Comstock part of his name disappeared into complete obscurity and was never mentioned again.

Young Anthony owned just one photograph of his parents together—he had looked at it so many times during his childhood that it had become as familiar and unremarkable as a piece of furniture, yet everyone who entered his bedroom found it fascinating. The picture captured a well-dressed gentleman from the 1890s, lean and good-looking, standing next to a tall, dark-haired woman holding a muff with the hint of a bustle in her dress. Standing between them was a small boy with long brown curls, wearing a velvet Little Lord Fauntleroy outfit. This was Anthony at age five, the same year his mother died.

His memories of the Boston Society Contralto were vague and filled with music. She was a woman who sang constantly in the music room of their Washington Square home—sometimes performing for guests who gathered around her, with men standing with crossed arms, balancing precariously on the edges of couches, and women sitting with hands folded in their laps, occasionally whispering to the men and always applauding enthusiastically while making delighted sounds after each performance—and frequently she would sing just for Anthony, performing in Italian or French or in a peculiar and awful dialect that she believed represented the way Southern Black people spoke.

His memories of the brave Ulysses, the first man in America to turn up the lapels of his coat, were much clearer. After Henrietta Lebrune Patch had "joined another choir," as her widower would say in a rough voice from time to time, father and son moved in with grandfather in Tarrytown, and Ulysses would come every day to Anthony's nursery and speak pleasant, strong-smelling words for sometimes as long as an hour. He was always promising Anthony hunting trips and fishing trips and visits to Atlantic City, "oh, some time soon now"; but none of them ever happened. They did take one trip; when Anthony was eleven they traveled overseas, to England and Switzerland, and there in the finest hotel in Lucerne his father died with heavy sweating and groaning and calling out loudly for air. In a state of panic, despair and fear Anthony was brought back to America, bound to a dim sadness that would remain with him for the rest of his life.

Past And Person of The Hero

At eleven years old, he was terrified of death. During six formative years, his parents had passed away and his grandmother had gradually declined almost without notice, until, for the first time since her wedding, she commanded absolute authority over her own living room for just one day. So for Anthony, life became a battle against death, which lurked around every corner. As a way to calm his anxious, health-obsessed mind, he developed the practice of reading in bed—it brought him comfort. He would read until exhaustion overtook him and frequently drifted off to sleep with the lights still burning.

His favorite hobby until he turned fourteen was collecting stamps; his collection was massive, as complete as any boy's collection could be—his grandfather foolishly believed that it was teaching him geography. Anthony maintained correspondence with about six "Stamp and Coin" companies and it was unusual for the mail not to deliver new stamp albums or packages of shining approval sheets—there was something mysteriously captivating about endlessly moving his new acquisitions from one album to another. His stamps brought him the greatest joy and he would give annoyed looks to anyone who disturbed him while he was playing with them; they consumed his entire allowance each month, and he would stay awake at night thinking constantly about their diversity and brilliant, multicolored beauty.

At sixteen, he had lived almost completely inside his own world, a boy who struggled to express himself, thoroughly un-American, and courteously confused by others his age. He had spent the previous two years in Europe with a private tutor, who convinced him that Harvard was the right choice; it would "open doors," it would provide an incredible boost, it would give him countless selfless and loyal friends. So he enrolled at Harvard—there was no other sensible option for what to do with him.

Unaware of the social hierarchy, he spent some time living alone and unnoticed in a high room in Beck Hall—a slender, dark boy of average height with a timid, delicate mouth. His spending money was quite generous. He began building a personal library by buying first editions of Swinburne, Meredith, and Hardy from a traveling book dealer, along with a faded, barely readable handwritten letter by Keats, only to discover later that he had been drastically overcharged. He transformed into an elegant fashion enthusiast, gathering a somewhat pitiful collection of silk pajamas, embroidered robes, and ties too bold to actually wear; dressed in this private splendor, he would strut before the mirror in his room or recline in satin on his window seat, gazing down at the courtyard and vaguely sensing this urgent, breathless excitement in which he felt he would never participate.

Strangely enough, he discovered during his senior year that he had earned a certain standing among his classmates. He realized that others saw him as something of a romantic character, an intellectual, a loner, a pillar of knowledge. This entertained him but also secretly delighted him—he started socializing, initially just a little and then quite extensively. He made the Pudding. He drank—discreetly and following established customs. People said about him that if he hadn't arrived at college so young, he could have "achieved remarkable success." In 1909, when he graduated, he was merely twenty years old.

Then he traveled abroad once more—this time to Rome, where he dabbled in architecture and painting, picked up the violin, and composed some terrible Italian sonnets that were supposedly the reflections of a thirteenth-century monk contemplating the pleasures of a life devoted to meditation. Word spread among his Harvard friends that he was living in Rome, and those who happened to be traveling in Europe that year sought him out and joined him on numerous moonlit adventures, exploring parts of the city that predated the Renaissance and even the ancient republic. Maury Noble from Philadelphia, for example, stayed for two months, and together they discovered the distinctive appeal of Latin women while enjoying the wonderful feeling of being young and free in a civilization that was ancient and liberated. Several of his grandfather's old acquaintances paid him visits, and if he had wanted, he could have become welcome in diplomatic circles—in fact, he found himself increasingly drawn to social gatherings, though the prolonged isolation of his teenage years and the resulting timidity continued to influence his behavior.

He came back to America in 1912 due to one of his grandfather's sudden health problems, and following an extremely exhausting conversation with the constantly ailing elderly man, he chose to postpone his plans of living overseas permanently until after his grandfather passed away. Following an extended search, he found an apartment on Fifty-second Street and seemed to establish himself there for the long term.

In 1913, Anthony Patch was in the process of finding his place in the world. Physically, he had gotten better since his college years—he was still too skinny, but his shoulders had broadened and his dark-haired face had lost the scared expression from his first year of college. He was privately neat and always perfectly groomed—his friends said they had never seen his hair messed up. His nose was too pointed; his mouth was one of those unlucky reflectors of emotion that tended to sag noticeably when he was upset, but his blue eyes were attractive, whether bright with intelligence or half-shut in an expression of sad amusement.

One of those men lacking the balanced facial features that define the Aryan ideal, he was nonetheless regarded as handsome by some people—furthermore, he maintained exceptional cleanliness, both in how he appeared and in actuality, possessing that particular kind of cleanliness that comes from true beauty.

The Reproachless Apartment

Fifth and Sixth Avenues appeared to Anthony like the vertical rails of an enormous ladder extending from Washington Square all the way to Central Park. Riding uptown on the top deck of a bus heading toward Fifty-second Street always made him feel as though he were pulling himself up one dangerous rung after another, and when the bus lurched to a halt at his destination, he experienced something close to relief as he climbed down the precarious metal steps onto the sidewalk.

After that, he only needed to walk half a block down Fifty-second Street, passing a stuffy row of brownstone family homes—and then in an instant he was beneath the tall ceilings of his spacious front room. This arrangement was completely satisfactory. Here, ultimately, his real life began. Here he slept, ate breakfast, read, and hosted guests.

The house was made of dark, dingy materials and had been constructed in the late 1890s; to meet the increasing demand for small living spaces, every floor had been completely renovated and leased out as separate units. Among the four apartments, Anthony's second-floor unit was the most appealing.

The front room featured beautiful high ceilings and three large windows that looked down pleasantly onto Fifty-second Street. In its furnishings, it managed to avoid belonging to any specific era by a comfortable margin; it avoided rigidity, staleness, emptiness, and deterioration. It carried neither the scent of smoke nor incense—it was spacious and had a subtle blue quality. A deep sofa made of the finest brown leather sat there with drowsiness floating around it like a mist. A tall Chinese lacquer screen dominated the space, decorated primarily with geometric fishermen and hunters rendered in black and gold; this created a corner nook for a large chair protected by an orange-colored floor lamp. Deep within the fireplace, a divided shield had been burned to a dark black.

Walking through the dining room, which was simply a magnificent space with unrealized potential since Anthony only ate breakfast at home, and continuing down a relatively long hallway, you would reach the heart and center of the apartment—Anthony's bedroom and bathroom.

Both rooms were enormous. Beneath the soaring ceilings of the bedroom, even the grand four-poster bed appeared merely ordinary in size. An luxurious crimson velvet carpet covered the floor, feeling as soft as wool beneath his bare feet. His bathroom presented a striking contrast to the somewhat imposing atmosphere of his bedroom—it was cheerful, luminous, remarkably comfortable, and even slightly playful. Mounted on the walls were framed photographs of four famous theatrical beauties of the era: Julia Sanderson in "The Sunshine Girl," Ina Claire in "The Quaker Girl," Billie Burke in "The Mind-the-Paint Girl," and Hazel Dawn in "The Pink Lady." Positioned between the photographs of Billie Burke and Hazel Dawn was a print depicting a vast expanse of snow dominated by a harsh and intimidating sun—this image, Anthony insisted, represented the cold shower.

The bathtub was low and spacious, fitted with a clever book holder. Next to it stood a wall wardrobe that bulged with enough linens for three men and contained a whole collection of neckties. There wasn't some thin, glorified towel masquerading as a carpet—instead, there was a luxurious rug, like the one in his bedroom, that was incredibly soft and seemed to almost massage wet feet stepping out of the tub.

All in all, it was a room that sparked the imagination—you could easily tell that Anthony got dressed there, styled his perfectly groomed hair there, and basically did everything except sleep and eat in that space. This bathroom was his pride and joy. He believed that if he had someone he loved, he would have hung her photograph directly across from the bathtub so that while relaxing in the comforting warmth of the hot water, he could lie back and gaze up at her image, thinking tenderly and passionately about her beauty.

Nor Does He Spin

The apartment was maintained spotlessly by an English servant who bore the remarkably, almost dramatically fitting name of Bounds, whose professional skills were compromised only by his choice to wear a soft collar. If he had served Anthony exclusively, this flaw would have been quickly corrected, but he also worked for two other gentlemen in the area. Between eight and eleven each morning, he belonged completely to Anthony. He would arrive carrying the mail and prepare breakfast. At half past nine, he would tug at the corner of Anthony's blanket and utter a few brief words—Anthony could never recall exactly what they were and had a suspicion they carried a tone of disapproval; then he would serve breakfast on a card table in the front room, make the bed, and after inquiring with a certain coldness whether anything else was needed, he would leave.

In the mornings, at least once a week, Anthony visited his broker. His income was just under seven thousand dollars annually, earned from interest on money he had inherited from his mother. His grandfather, who had never permitted his own son to move beyond a very generous allowance, believed this amount was adequate for young Anthony's requirements. Every Christmas he sent him a five-hundred-dollar bond, which Anthony typically sold when possible, since he was always somewhat short of money, though not desperately so.

The visits to his broker ranged from casual, friendly conversations to serious discussions about the security of eight percent investments, and Anthony always found them enjoyable. The massive trust company building appeared to connect him directly to the great fortunes whose strength he admired and to reassure him that he was properly protected by the financial establishment. From these busy men he gained the same feeling of security that he experienced when thinking about his grandfather's wealth—actually even more, because the latter seemed, in some unclear way, like a loan that the world had made based on Adam Patch's moral virtue, while this downtown money appeared to have been seized and maintained through pure unstoppable determination and extraordinary acts of willpower; furthermore, it seemed more clearly and unmistakably—money.

Anthony lived right up to his income, but he felt it was sufficient. Someday, naturally, he would be worth millions; for now, he had a purpose in writing theoretical essays about the Renaissance popes. This brings us back to the conversation he had with his grandfather right after he returned from Rome.

He had hoped to discover his grandfather dead, but when he called from the pier, he learned that Adam Patch was feeling relatively well again—the following day he hid his disappointment and traveled to Tarrytown. About five miles from the station, his taxi turned onto a meticulously maintained driveway that wound through what seemed like an endless maze of walls and wire fencing protecting the property—according to public opinion, this security existed because everyone knew that if the Socialists ever gained power, old Cross Patch would be among the first people they would kill.

Anthony was running late, and the respected philanthropist was waiting for him in a glass-walled sunroom, where he was looking through the morning newspapers for the second time. His secretary, Edward Shuttleworth—who before his transformation had been a gambler, bar owner, and all-around scoundrel—brought Anthony into the room, presenting his savior and patron as if he were showing off a priceless treasure.

They shook hands solemnly. "I'm really glad to hear you're feeling better," Anthony said.

The elder Patch, acting as though he had just seen his grandson the previous week, took out his watch.

"Is the train running late?" he asked gently.

It annoyed him to have to wait for Anthony. He was mistaken in believing not only that during his younger years he had managed his business matters with complete precision, including keeping every appointment exactly on time, but also that this was the main and most important reason for his success.

"It's been running late quite often this month," he said with a hint of gentle reproach in his voice—and then after a long sigh, "Sit down."

Anthony looked at his grandfather with the quiet astonishment that always came over him at the sight. The idea that this frail, dim-witted old man wielded so much power that, despite what the sensational newspapers claimed, the men in the country whose souls he couldn't have purchased either directly or through intermediaries would barely have been enough to fill White Plains, seemed as hard to believe as the thought that he had once been a rosy-cheeked baby.

The span of his seventy-five years had worked like a magical bellows—the first twenty-five years had filled him with life, and the final years had drawn it all away. Age had hollowed his cheeks and chest and diminished the fullness of his arms and legs. It had ruthlessly claimed his teeth, one after another, left his small eyes floating in dark-blue pouches, plucked away his hair, transformed him from gray to white in some areas, from pink to yellow in others—carelessly rearranging his colors like a child experimenting with a paint set. Then it had moved through his body and soul to assault his mind. It had brought him night sweats and tears and baseless fears. It had fractured his once-solid stability into gullibility and distrust. From the raw substance of his passion it had carved out countless humble yet irritable fixations; his vitality had shrunk to the bad mood of a spoiled child, and in place of his drive for power came a foolish childish longing for an earthly paradise of harps and hymns.

After the polite pleasantries had been carefully addressed, Anthony sensed that he was supposed to explain his plans—and at the same time, a gleam in the old man's eye cautioned him against mentioning, for now, his wish to live overseas. He hoped that Shuttleworth would be tactful enough to leave the room—he despised Shuttleworth—but the secretary had comfortably settled into a rocking chair and was splitting his tired glances between the two Patches.

"Now that you're here, you should do something," his grandfather said quietly, "achieve something."

Anthony waited for him to mention "leaving something accomplished when you die." Then he offered a suggestion:

"I thought—it seemed to me that perhaps I'm best qualified to write—"

Adam Patch cringed, imagining a family poet with long hair and three mistresses.

"—history," Anthony concluded.

"History? History of what? The Civil War? The Revolution?"

"Why—no, sir. A history of the Middle Ages." At the same time, an idea emerged for a history of the Renaissance popes, written from some fresh perspective. Nevertheless, he was pleased he had said "Middle Ages."

"Middle Ages? Why not your own country? Something you know about?"

"Well, you see I've lived so much abroad—"

"I don't understand why you'd want to write about the Middle Ages. We used to call them the Dark Ages. Nobody knows what actually happened back then, and nobody really cares either, except that we're glad they're behind us." He went on for several more minutes about how pointless that kind of information was, inevitably bringing up the Spanish Inquisition and the "corruption of the monasteries." Then:

"Do you think you'll be able to get any work done in New York—or do you actually plan to work at all?" This final question carried a gentle, barely noticeable hint of cynicism.

"Why, yes, I do, sir."

"When will you be done?"

"Well, there'll be an outline, you see—and a lot of preliminary reading."

"I would think you've already done enough of that."

The conversation lurched awkwardly toward a sudden end when Anthony stood up, checked his watch, and mentioned that he had an appointment with his broker that afternoon. He had planned to spend several days with his grandfather, but he felt exhausted and annoyed from a difficult ocean crossing, and he wasn't willing to endure any more subtle, self-righteous lecturing. He would return in a few days, he told him.

Nevertheless, this encounter had brought work into his life as a lasting concept. Throughout the year that had followed, he had created multiple lists of sources, had even tried out chapter headings and organized his work into different time periods, but not a single line of real writing existed at the moment, nor did it appear that any ever would. He accomplished nothing—and despite what conventional wisdom would suggest, he succeeded in entertaining himself with greater satisfaction than most people experience.

Afternoon

It was October 1913, in the middle of a week filled with beautiful days, where sunlight lingered in the intersecting streets and the air felt so heavy and drowsy it seemed thick with the invisible drift of autumn leaves. It felt wonderful to sit comfortably by the open window, completing a chapter of "Erewhon." It felt wonderful to stretch and yawn around five o'clock, throw the book onto a table, and walk leisurely down the hallway to his bath, humming as he went.

"To ... you ... beautiful lady,"

he was singing as he turned on the faucet.

"I raise ... my ... eyes;
To ... you ... beautiful lady
"My ... heart ... cries—"

He spoke louder to be heard over the rushing water filling the bathtub, and while gazing at the photograph of Hazel Dawn hanging on the wall, he lifted an invisible violin to his shoulder and gently drew an imaginary bow across it. He hummed through closed lips, creating a sound that he loosely thought might sound like a violin. After a few moments, his hands stopped their movements and moved to his shirt, which he started to unbutton. Once undressed, he struck a muscular pose similar to the tiger-skin man from the advertisement and admired himself in the mirror with some pleasure, pausing to dip an experimental toe into the water. He adjusted the faucet and let out a few preparatory grunts before lowering himself into the tub.

Once he got used to the water temperature, he settled into a sleepy, satisfied state. After finishing his bath, he would get dressed at a relaxed pace and stroll down Fifth Avenue to the Ritz, where he was meeting his two closest friends, Dick Caramel and Maury Noble, for dinner. Later, he and Maury planned to go to the theatre—Caramel would likely head home and continue working on his book, which should be completed fairly soon.

Anthony felt relieved that he wouldn't be working on his book today. The idea of sitting down and creating not just the words to express his thoughts, but thoughts that were actually worth expressing—the entire process seemed ridiculously far from what he wanted to do.

After stepping out of his bath, he dried and groomed himself with the careful precision of a shoe-shiner. He then made his way into the bedroom, humming a strange, wavering tune as he moved around, fastening buttons, making adjustments, and savoring the comfort of the plush carpet beneath his bare feet.

He lit a cigarette and flicked the match out through the open window, then suddenly stopped with the cigarette just two inches from his lips—his mouth dropping slightly open. His gaze fixed on a bright splash of color on the rooftop of a house further down the alley.

It was a young woman wearing a red silk negligee, drying her hair in the warm late afternoon sun. His whistle faded in the stale air of the room as he carefully took another step toward the window, suddenly struck by the impression that she was beautiful. A cushion matching the color of her outfit sat on the stone ledge beside her, and she rested both arms on it while gazing down into the bright courtyard below, where Anthony could hear the sounds of children at play.

He watched her for several minutes. Something stirred within him, something that couldn't be explained by the warm scent of the afternoon or the striking brilliance of red. He kept feeling that the girl was beautiful—then suddenly he realized what it was: her distance, not some rare and precious spiritual distance but distance nonetheless, even if only measured in physical yards. The autumn air lay between them, along with the rooftops and the muffled voices. Yet for one inexplicable moment, hanging strangely in time, his emotion had come closer to worship than in the most passionate kiss he had ever experienced.

He completed getting dressed, located a black bow tie, and carefully adjusted it using the three-way mirror in the bathroom. Then, giving in to a sudden urge, he walked briskly into the bedroom and looked out the window once more. The woman was now standing; she had thrown her hair back, giving him a complete view of her. She was overweight, clearly thirty-five years old, completely unremarkable. Making a clicking sound with his tongue, he went back to the bathroom and combed his hair again.

"To ... you ... beautiful lady,"

he sang softly,

"I raise ... my ... eyes—"

Then with a final gentle stroke that created a shimmering surface of pure shine, he left his bathroom and his apartment and walked down Fifth Avenue to the Ritz-Carlton.

Three Men

At seven o'clock, Anthony and his friend Maury Noble sit at a corner table on the cool rooftop. Maury Noble resembles nothing more than a large, slender, and commanding cat. His eyes are narrow and filled with constant, drawn-out blinks. His hair lies smooth and flat, as if it had been groomed by an enormous mother cat. During Anthony's years at Harvard, he had been regarded as the most distinctive person in his class, the most brilliant, the most creative—intelligent, reserved, and among the chosen.

This is the man whom Anthony considers his best friend. This is the only person among all his acquaintances whom he admires and, to a greater degree than he cares to acknowledge to himself, envies.

They're happy to see each other now—their eyes shine with warmth as both experience the complete impact of something fresh after being apart for a brief time. They're finding comfort in being together again, a renewed sense of calm; Maury Noble, with his refined and ridiculously feline features, is practically purring with contentment. And Anthony, usually jittery as a flickering light, always restless—he has found peace now.

They're having one of those casual, brief exchanges that only men under thirty or men experiencing intense pressure tend to engage in.

ANTHONY: Seven o'clock. Where's the Caramel? (Impatiently.) I wish he'd finish that endless novel. I've spent more time hungry——

MAURY: He's come up with a new title for it. "The Demon Lover"—not bad, right?

ANTHONY: (interested) "The Demon Lover"? Oh "woman wailing"—No—not a bit bad! Not bad at all—do you think?

MAURY: Pretty good. What time did you say?

ANTHONY: Seven.

MAURY: (His eyes narrowing—not unpleasantly, but to express a faint disapproval) Drove me crazy the other day.

ANTHONY: How?

MAURY: That habit of taking notes.

ANTHONY: Me, too. It seems I had said something the night before that he thought was important, but he had forgotten it—so he went after me. He would say "Can't you try to concentrate?" And I would say "You bore me to tears. How am I supposed to remember?"

(MAURY laughs silently, with a kind of gentle and appreciative broadening of his facial features.)

MAURY: Dick doesn't necessarily see more than anyone else. He simply manages to capture a larger portion of what he observes.

ANTHONY: That rather impressive talent——

MAURY: Oh, yes. Impressive!

ANTHONY: And energy—ambitious, well-directed energy. He's so entertaining—he's incredibly stimulating and exciting. There's often something breathless about being around him.

MAURY: Oh, yes.

(Silence, and then:)

ANTHONY: (With his thin, somewhat uncertain face at its most convinced) But not unstoppable energy. Someday, little by little, it'll fade away, and his rather impressive talent along with it, leaving behind only a shadow of a man, irritable and self-centered and talkative.

MAURY: (Laughing) Here we are, promising each other that little Dick doesn't see as deeply into things as we do. And I bet he feels somewhat superior on his end—the creative mind versus the merely critical mind and all that.

ANTHONY: Oh, absolutely. But he's mistaken. He tends to get swept up in countless foolish passions. If he weren't so caught up in realism and forced to wear the mask of a cynic, he would be as gullible as a campus chaplain. He's a dreamer at heart. Oh, definitely. He believes he isn't because he's turned his back on Christianity. Do you remember him back in college? He would devour every author completely, one right after the next—their ideas, their techniques, their characters—Chesterton, Shaw, Wells, absorbing each one just as readily as the previous.

MAURY: (Still thinking about what he just said) I remember.

ANTHONY: It's true. Natural born fetish-worshipper. Take art—

MAURY: Let's order. He'll be—

ANTHONY: Sure. Let's order. I told him—

MAURY: Here he comes. Look—he's going to bump into that waiter. (He raises his finger as a signal—raises it as if it were a gentle and friendly claw.) Here you are, Caramel.

A NEW VOICE: (Fiercely) Hello, Maury. Hello, Anthony Comstock Patch. How is old Adam's grandson doing? Are débutantes still chasing after you?

In person RICHARD CARAMEL is short and fair—he will be bald by thirty-five. He has yellowish eyes—one remarkably clear, the other cloudy like a murky pond—and a protruding forehead like a comic strip infant. He protrudes in other areas—his belly juts out ominously, his words seem to spill from his mouth, even his tuxedo pockets bulge, as if infected, with a worn collection of schedules, programs, and random pieces of paper—on these he jots down notes while squinting his mismatched yellow eyes and gesturing for quiet with his free left hand.

When he reaches the table he shakes hands with ANTHONY and MAURY. He is one of those men who always shake hands, even with people they saw just an hour earlier.

ANTHONY: Hello, Caramel. Glad you're here. We needed some comic relief.

MAURY: You're late. Have you been racing the mailman down the street? We've been picking apart your personality.

DICK: (Looking at ANTHONY intently with bright, eager eyes) What did you say? Tell me and I'll write it down. I cut three thousand words from Part One this afternoon.

MAURY: Noble aesthete. And I poured alcohol into my stomach.

DICK: I don't doubt it. I bet you two have been sitting here for an hour talking about liquor.

ANTHONY: We never faint, my clean-shaven young man.

MAURY: We never go home with women we meet when we're drunk.

ANTHONY: Everyone in our social circles is marked by a particular arrogant superiority.

DICK: The especially ridiculous type who brag about being "tanks"! The problem is you're both stuck in the eighteenth century. Following the School of the Old English Squire. Drink silently until you collapse under the table. Never enjoy yourselves. Oh, no, that simply isn't acceptable at all.

ANTHONY: This is from Chapter Six, I'll bet.

DICK: Are you going to the theater?

MAURY: Yes. We plan to spend the evening deeply contemplating life's problems. The subject is simply called "The Woman." I assume that she will "pay."

ANTHONY: My God! Is that what it is? Let's go to the Follies again.

MAURY: I'm sick of it. I've already seen it three times. (To DICK:) The first time we went, we left after the first act and discovered this incredible bar. When we returned, we walked into the wrong theater.

ANTHONY: We got into a long argument with a frightened young couple who we believed were sitting in our seats.

DICK: (As if speaking to himself) I believe—that after I finish another novel and a play, and perhaps a collection of short stories, I'll create a musical comedy.

MAURY: I know—with intellectual lyrics that no one will listen to. And all the critics will groan and complain about "Dear old Pinafore." And I shall continue shining as a brilliantly meaningless figure in a meaningless world.

DICK: (Pompously) Art isn't meaningless.

MAURY: It is in itself. It isn't in that it tries to make life less so.

ANTHONY: In other words, Dick, you're performing for an audience filled with ghosts.

MAURY: Put on a good show anyway.

ANTHONY:(To MAURY) Actually, I'd think that since it's a meaningless world, why bother writing? The very effort to give it purpose is pointless.

DICK: Well, even if I accept all of that, be a reasonable pragmatist and allow a poor man his basic instinct to survive. Would you really want everyone to buy into that philosophical nonsense?

ANTHONY: Yeah, I suppose so.

MAURY: No, sir! I believe that everyone in America except for a chosen thousand should be required to follow a very strict moral system—Roman Catholicism, for example. I don't object to traditional morality. Instead, I object to the average rebels who grab onto the discoveries of sophisticated thinking and pretend to have a moral freedom that their intelligence levels certainly don't qualify them for.

(Here the soup arrives and what MAURY might have gone on to say is lost for all time.)

Night

Afterward they visited a ticket speculator and, at a price, obtained seats for a new musical comedy called "High Jinks." In the theater lobby they waited a few moments to watch the opening night crowd arrive. There were opera cloaks made from countless multicolored silks and furs; there were jewels cascading from the arms, throats, and earlobes of women with pale and rosy skin; there were countless broad gleams running down the centers of countless silk top hats; there were shoes of gold and bronze and red and gleaming black; there were the elaborately styled, tightly arranged hairdos of many women and the sleek, pomaded hair of well-groomed men—above all there was the receding, surging, chattering, laughing, bubbling, slowly rolling wave-like effect of this joyful sea of people as tonight it poured its sparkling flood into the manufactured pool of entertainment....

After the play ended, they went their separate ways—Maury headed to a dance at Sherry's, while Anthony went home to bed.

He slowly made his way through the bustling evening crowds of Times Square, where the neon spectacle and its countless surrounding lights created a scene that was unexpectedly beautiful, brilliant, and filled with the intimate energy of a festival. Faces swirled around him in a kaleidoscope of women—some unattractive, even strikingly so, some too heavy, others too thin—yet all seemed to float on the autumn air as if carried by their own warm, passionate breath released into the night. Despite their coarseness, he thought, there was something faintly and mysteriously alluring about them. He breathed in deliberately, drawing into his lungs the mingled scents of perfume and the not unpleasant aroma of countless cigarettes. His eyes met those of a dark, beautiful young woman sitting alone in an enclosed taxi. In the dim light, her eyes evoked images of night and violets, and for a moment he felt that half-forgotten sense of distance from the afternoon stirring within him again.

Two young Jewish men walked past him, speaking loudly and stretching their necks to look around with foolish, arrogant glances. They wore suits that were extremely tight-fitting, which was somewhat fashionable at the time; their folded collars had notches at the throat; they had gray spats on their shoes and carried gray gloves draped over their walking stick handles.

A confused elderly woman passed by, carried along like a basket of eggs between two men who enthusiastically told her about the amazing sights of Times Square—they spoke so rapidly that the old woman, attempting to show equal interest in everything, turned her head back and forth like a piece of old orange peel being blown about by the wind. Anthony caught a fragment of their conversation:

"There's the Astor, mama!"

"Look! See the chariot race sign——"

"That's where we were today. No, there!"

"Good gracious! ..."

"You should worry and grow thin like a dime." He recognized the popular joke of the year as it rang out loudly from one of the couples standing beside him.

"And I said to him, I said——"

The gentle whoosh of taxis passing by him, and laughter, laughter rough as a crow's call, constant and booming, mixed with the rumbling of the subway trains below—and above everything, the spinning patterns of light, the brightening and dimming of light—light splitting like scattered pearls—creating and reshaping itself into sparkling strips and rings and enormous bizarre shapes carved spectacularly across the sky.

He gratefully turned into the quiet that swept like a dark wind from a side street, walking past a bakery-restaurant where a dozen roasted chickens rotated continuously on a mechanical spit in the windows. The doorway released an aroma that was warm, bread-like, and faintly rosy. Next came a pharmacy, breathing out the scents of medications, spilled soda water, and a pleasing hint from the makeup section; then a Chinese laundry, still operating, humid and suffocating, with the smell of pressed fabric and a subtle yellowish odor. All of these places made him feel downcast; when he reached Sixth Avenue, he stopped at a corner tobacco shop and came out feeling improved—the tobacco shop was welcoming, filled with people wrapped in a navy blue haze, purchasing something special.

Once he reached his apartment, he lit one final cigarette and sat in the darkness beside his open front window. For the first time in more than a year, he discovered himself genuinely appreciating New York. There was definitely a distinctive sharpness to it, an almost Southern character. Still, it was a lonely city. Though he had been raised in solitude, he had recently come to understand the importance of avoiding being alone. Over the past few months, he had made it a point, whenever he had no plans for the evening, to rush to one of his clubs and locate someone to spend time with. Yes, there was certainly a loneliness present here——

His cigarette glowed steadily, its smoke drifting along the delicate curtain folds and creating pale white wisps at their edges, until the clock at St. Anne's church down the street chimed one o'clock with its distinctive, elegant tone. The elevated train, running just half a block away on the quiet street, produced a thunderous rumbling sound—and if he were to lean out his window, he would catch sight of the train cutting through the darkness like a fierce eagle as it rounded the corner curve. This brought to mind a science fiction story he had recently read, where cities were attacked by bombs dropped from flying trains, and for a brief moment he imagined that Washington Square had gone to war against Central Park, with this northbound train serving as a threatening weapon carrying conflict and instant destruction. However, as the train continued past, this fantasy dissolved; the sound faded to barely audible drumbeats—then to the distant cry of a soaring eagle.

There were the bells and the ongoing muffled sound of car horns from Fifth Avenue, but his own street remained quiet and he felt protected here from all of life's dangers, for there was his door and the lengthy hallway and his sheltering bedroom—secure, secure! The streetlight glowing through his window appeared at this moment like the moon, except brighter and more lovely than the moon.

A Flashback in Paradise

Beauty, who was reborn every hundred years, sat in what seemed like an outdoor waiting area where gusts of white wind swept through and occasionally a breathless, hurried star rushed past. The stars gave her knowing winks as they traveled by, and the winds created a gentle, constant rustling in her hair. She was beyond understanding, because in her, soul and spirit existed as one— the beauty of her physical form was the very essence of her soul. She embodied that perfect unity that philosophers had searched for across many centuries. In this outdoor waiting area of winds and stars, she had been sitting for a hundred years, at peace while contemplating herself.

It eventually became clear to her that she would be reborn. With a sigh, she started an extended conversation with a voice that spoke through the white wind, a dialogue that lasted many hours and of which I can only share a small portion here.

BEAUTY: (Her lips barely moving, her eyes turned, as always, inward upon herself) Where shall I go now?

THE VOICE: To a new country—a land you have never seen before.

BEAUTY: (Petulantly) I hate having to break into these new civilizations. How long will we be staying this time?

THE VOICE: Fifteen years.

BEAUTY: And what's the name of the place?

THE VOICE: It is the most lavish, most magnificent land on earth—a land where the wisest are only slightly wiser than the most ignorant; a land where the rulers have minds like small children and the lawmakers believe in Santa Claus; where unattractive women control powerful men——

BEAUTY: (In astonishment) What?

31

THE VOICE: (Very much depressed) Yes, it really is a depressing sight. Women with weak chins and poorly shaped noses walk around in plain daylight commanding "Do this!" and "Do that!" and all the men, even the very wealthy ones, follow their women's orders without question, referring to them pompously as either "Mrs. So-and-so" or as "the wife."

BEAUTY: But this can't be true! I can understand, of course, their obedience to women of charm—but to fat women? to bony women? to women with scrawny cheeks?

THE VOICE: Even so.

BEAUTY: What about me? What chance will I have?

THE VOICE: It will be "more difficult," if I may borrow a phrase.

BEAUTY: (After a dissatisfied pause) Why not the ancient lands, the land of vineyards and eloquent men or the land of ships and oceans?

THE VOICE: They're expected to be very busy soon.

BEAUTY: Oh!

THE VOICE: Your life on earth will be, as it has always been, the time that passes between two meaningful looks in an ordinary mirror.

BEAUTY: What will I become? Tell me?

THE VOICE: Initially, it was believed that you would go this time as an actress in movies, but ultimately, that's not recommended. You will be disguised during your fifteen years as what is called a "society girl."

BEAUTY: What's that?

(A new sound emerges in the wind that we need to understand as THE VOICE scratching its head.)

THE VOICE: (At length) It's a kind of fake aristocrat.

BEAUTY: Bogus? What does bogus mean?

THE VOICE: You'll discover that in this land as well. You'll encounter many things that are fake. You'll also end up doing

32

many things that are fake.

BEAUTY: (Calmly) It all sounds so crude.

THE VOICE: Not nearly as crude as it actually is. During your fifteen years, people will label you as a ragtime kid, a flapper, a jazz-baby, and a baby vamp. You will dance the latest dances with neither more nor less grace than you showed when dancing the traditional ones.

BEAUTY: (In a whisper) Will I be paid?

THE VOICE: Yes, as usual—in love.

BEAUTY: (With a quiet laugh that barely moves her still lips) And will I enjoy being called a jazz-baby?

THE VOICE: (Soberly) You will love it....

The dialogue ends here, with Beauty still sitting quietly, the stars pausing in an ecstasy of appreciation, the wind, white and gusty, blowing through her hair.

All this happened seven years before Anthony sat by the front windows of his apartment and listened to the chimes of St. Anne's.

Chapter II: Portrait of a Siren

A crisp chill settled over New York a month later, ushering in November along with the three major football games and a magnificent display of fur coats flowing down fifth avenue. This change of season also brought a palpable tension to the city, along with barely contained excitement. Each morning, Anthony's mailbox overflowed with invitations. Three dozen well-bred women from the highest social circles were announcing their suitability, if not their outright eagerness, to bear children for three dozen millionaires. Five dozen respectable women from the second tier were declaring not only their capability in this regard, but also their fierce and unwavering ambitions toward those first three dozen young men, all of whom were naturally invited to each of the ninety-six social gatherings—along with the young women's circles of family friends, social connections, college men, and ambitious young newcomers. Beyond this, there existed a third social stratum extending from the city's outskirts, stretching from Newark and the new jersey suburbs up to the harsh reaches of Connecticut and the less desirable areas of long island—and undoubtedly additional layers extending all the way down to the city's foundation: Jewish women were making their debuts in Jewish society spanning from riverside to the Bronx, setting their sights on promising young stockbrokers or jewelers and anticipating kosher weddings; Irish young women were finally permitted to cast their gazes upon a world of emerging Tammany hall politicians, devout funeral directors, and former altar boys now grown to manhood.

And naturally, the city became infected with an atmosphere of anticipation—the working women, poor unfortunate souls, packaging soap in factories and displaying merchandise in department stores, fantasized that perhaps amid the dramatic excitement of this winter they might secure for themselves the desired man—just as in a chaotic carnival crowd an incompetent thief might believe his opportunities have improved. And the smokestacks began to emit smoke and the subway's stench was renewed. And the performers appeared in fresh productions and the publishing houses released new books and the Castles introduced new dances. And the railroad companies issued new timetables featuring new errors instead of the familiar ones that commuters had become accustomed to....

The City was emerging!

Anthony was walking down Forty-second Street one afternoon beneath a steel-gray sky when he unexpectedly bumped into Richard Caramel, who was coming out of the Manhattan Hotel barber shop. The weather was cold, the first truly cold day of the season, and Caramel wore one of those knee-length, sheep-

34

lined coats that had long been popular among working men in the Middle West and were just beginning to gain fashionable acceptance. His soft hat was a subtle dark brown, and beneath it his bright eyes blazed like topaz. He stopped Anthony with enthusiasm, slapping him on the arms more to keep himself warm than out of playfulness, and after their customary handshake, he burst into animated conversation.

"Cold as hell—Good Lord, I've been working like crazy all day until my room got so cold I thought I'd catch pneumonia. The damn landlady, trying to save money on coal, finally came up when I yelled down the stairs for her for half an hour. She started explaining why and everything. God! First she drove me insane, then I began to think she was quite a character, and took notes while she talked—so she couldn't see me, you know, just as though I were writing casually—"

He had grabbed Anthony's arm and was walking him quickly up Madison Avenue.

"Where to?"

"Nowhere in particular."

"Well, then what's the point?" Anthony demanded.

They came to a halt and looked at each other, and Anthony found himself wondering whether the freezing weather made his face look as unappealing as Dick Caramel's did, with his bright red nose, his protruding forehead turned blue from the cold, and his mismatched yellow eyes that were bloodshot and teary around the edges. After a brief pause, they resumed walking.

"I've made some good progress on my novel." Dick was staring intently at the sidewalk as he spoke with emphasis. "But I need to get out every now and then." He looked at Anthony with an apologetic expression, as if he was hoping for some encouragement.

"I need to talk things through. I think very few people actually sit down and really think—I mean truly contemplate and develop ideas in a logical order. I do my best thinking when I'm writing or having conversations with others. You need some kind of starting point—something to either defend or argue against—wouldn't you agree?"

Anthony grunted and carefully pulled his arm back.

"I don't mind carrying you, Dick, but with that coat—"

"I mean," Richard Caramel went on seriously, "that when you're writing, your opening paragraph holds the concept you plan to criticize or expand upon. When you're talking with someone, you have their previous comment to respond to—but when you're just thinking to yourself, well, your thoughts simply follow one another like slides in a magic lantern show, with each new idea pushing out the one before it."

They passed Forty-fifth Street and slowed their pace a bit. Both of them lit cigarettes and exhaled huge clouds of smoke mixed with their visible breath into the cold air.

"Let's walk up to the Plaza and have an eggnog," Anthony suggested. "It'll do you good. The fresh air will clear the awful nicotine from your lungs. Come on—I'll let you talk about your book the entire way there."

"I don't want to if it bores you. I mean you don't have to do it just to be nice." The words rushed out quickly, and although he tried to keep his expression relaxed, his face twisted with uncertainty. Anthony felt compelled to object: "Bore me? Absolutely not!"

"I have a cousin—" Dick started to say, but Anthony cut him off by extending his arms and letting out a quiet cry of triumph.

"Beautiful weather!" he called out, "don't you think? It makes me feel like I'm ten years old again. I mean it makes me feel the way I should have felt back when I was actually ten. It's maddening! Oh, God! One moment the world belongs to me, and the next moment I'm just the world's fool. Today the world is mine and everything feels effortless, so effortless. Even nothingness feels effortless!"

"I have a cousin who stays at the Plaza. She's quite well-known. We could go up and meet her. She's been living there during the winter months—at least recently—with her parents."

"I didn't know you had cousins in New York."

"Her name's Gloria. She's from home—Kansas City. Her mother's a practicing Bilphist, and her father's quite dull but a perfect gentleman."

"What are they? Literary material?"

"They try to be. All the old man does is tell me he just encountered the most amazing person who would make a perfect character for a novel. Then he describes some foolish friend of his and says: 'Now there's a character for you! Why don't you write about him? Everyone would find him fascinating.' Or he'll talk to me about Japan or Paris, or some other predictable location, and suggest: 'Why don't you write a story set in that place? It would make a fantastic backdrop for a story!'"

"What about the girl?" Anthony asked casually. "Gloria—Gloria what?"

"Gilbert. Oh, you've heard of her—Gloria Gilbert. She goes to college dances—all that kind of thing."

"I've heard her name."

"Good-looking—in fact damned attractive."

They arrived at Fiftieth Street and turned toward the Avenue.

"I don't usually like young girls," said Anthony, frowning.

This wasn't entirely accurate. Although he believed that most young women making their social debut spent every moment of their day thinking and discussing what high society had planned for them to do next, he found himself deeply fascinated by any woman who earned her living directly through her beauty.

"Gloria's really nice—she just doesn't have a brain in her head."

Anthony let out a short, sharp laugh.

"By that you mean she doesn't have any literary small talk."

"No, I don't."

"Dick, you know what you consider intelligence in a woman. Serious young women who sit with you in a corner and have deep conversations about life. The type who, when they were sixteen, debated with solemn expressions whether kissing was right or wrong—and whether it was immoral for college freshmen to drink beer."

Richard Caramel felt insulted. His frown wrinkled like crumpled paper.

"No—" he started to say, but Anthony cut him off without mercy.

"Oh, yes; the kind who right now sit in corners and discuss the newest Scandinavian Dante that's available in English translation."

Dick turned toward him, his entire expression suddenly dropping. His question sounded almost like a plea.

"What's wrong with you and Maury? Sometimes you talk like I'm some kind of lesser person."

Anthony felt confused, but he was also cold and somewhat uncomfortable, so he sought safety by going on the offensive.

"I don't think your intelligence matters, Dick."

"Of course they matter!" Dick shouted angrily. "What are you talking about? Why wouldn't they matter?"

"You might know too much for your pen."

"I couldn't possibly."

"I can picture," Anthony insisted, "someone who knows too much for their abilities to communicate effectively. Just like me. Let's say, for example, that I possess more wisdom than you do, but have less natural ability. This combination would make it difficult for me to express myself clearly. You, on the other hand, have sufficient knowledge to fill your capacity and a large enough capacity to contain all that knowledge."

"I don't understand you at all," Dick complained, his voice heavy with disappointment. He appeared utterly dismayed, seeming to swell with objection. He was gazing fixedly at Anthony while bumping into one pedestrian after another, each of whom shot him angry, indignant looks.

"I simply mean that someone with Wells's level of talent could handle the intellectual depth of a Spencer. However, a lesser talent can only achieve elegance when dealing with simpler ideas. The more limited your perspective on something, the more entertaining you can make it."

Dick thought it over, unable to determine exactly how critical Anthony meant to be with his comments. But Anthony, with that effortless ability that seemed to come so naturally to him, kept talking, his dark eyes shining in his lean face, his chin lifted, his voice elevated, his entire physical presence heightened:

"Suppose I am proud, rational, and wise—an Athenian among Greeks. Well, I might fail where a lesser person would succeed. That person could copy others, could embellish, could show enthusiasm, could be optimistically productive. But this imagined version of myself would be too proud to copy others, too rational to show enthusiasm, too refined to be idealistic, too Greek to embellish."

"Then you don't think the artist works from his intelligence?"

"No. He continues to refine, if possible, what he copies in terms of style, and selects from his own understanding of the world around him what serves as his material. But ultimately every writer writes because that's how he makes his living. Don't tell me you actually believe in this 'Divine Function of the Artist' nonsense?"

"I'm not even used to calling myself an artist."

"Dick," Anthony said, his tone shifting, "I need to ask for your forgiveness."

"Why?"

"I apologize for that outburst. I'm genuinely sorry. I was just speaking for dramatic effect."

Feeling somewhat appeased, Dick responded:

"I've often said you were a Philistine at heart."

It was a crisp evening when they walked beneath the white front of the Plaza and slowly savored the frothy, golden richness of their eggnog. Anthony glanced at his friend. Richard Caramel's nose and forehead were gradually returning to a similar color; the redness was fading from one, the blue disappearing from the other. Looking into a mirror, Anthony was pleased to see that his own complexion hadn't changed color. Instead, a subtle warmth had appeared in his cheeks—he thought he had never looked better.

"That's enough for me," Dick said, speaking with the tone of an athlete in training. "I want to go up and see the Gilberts. Won't you come?"

"Why—yes. If you don't introduce me to the parents and rush off to the corner with Dora."

"Not Dora—Gloria."

A clerk announced them over the phone, and after going up to the tenth floor, they walked down a winding hallway and knocked on door 1088. A middle-aged woman answered—Mrs. Gilbert herself.

"How do you do?" She spoke in the typical polite language that American ladies used with one another. "Well, I'm terribly pleased to see you—"

Hasty interjections by Dick, and then:

"Mr. Pats? Well, please come in, and you can leave your coat over there." She gestured toward a chair and shifted her tone to an apologetic laugh filled with tiny breaths. "This is absolutely wonderful—wonderful. Richard, you haven't visited in such a long time—no!—no!" Those final single words functioned partly as replies and partly as punctuation to Dick's uncertain attempts to speak. "Please, sit down and tell me what you've been up to."

One walked back and forth across the room; one stood and bowed with the utmost politeness; one smiled repeatedly with awkward foolishness; one wondered if she would ever take a seat, until finally one gratefully sank into a chair and prepared for an enjoyable visit.

"I guess it's because you've been busy—more than anything else," Mrs. Gilbert said with a smile that seemed to carry hidden meaning. She relied on the phrase "more than anything else" to prop up all her shakier statements. She had two other go-to expressions: "at least that's how I see it" and "plain and simple"—these three phrases, used in rotation, made each of her comments sound like profound observations about life, as if she had weighed every possible reason and finally identified the most important one.

Richard Caramel's face, Anthony noticed, had returned to its usual appearance. His forehead and cheeks showed their natural skin tone, and his nose appeared unremarkable. He had focused his bright-yellow gaze on his aunt, giving her the kind of intense and overly attentive look that young men typically reserve for women they consider to be of no remaining interest.

"Are you a writer too, Mr. Pats? ... Well, perhaps we can all bask in Richard's fame."—Gentle laughter led by Mrs. Gilbert.

"Gloria's not here," she said, speaking as if she was stating a fundamental truth that would lead to other conclusions. "She's off dancing somewhere. Gloria just goes and goes and goes. I keep telling her I don't understand how she can handle it. She dances all afternoon and all night long, until I think she's going to exhaust herself completely. Her father is really concerned about her."

She smiled at each of them in turn. Both of them smiled back.

She was made up, Anthony noticed, of a series of curves and arcs, like the decorative patterns that skilled people create on typewriters: her head, arms, chest, hips, thighs, and ankles formed a confusing arrangement of rounded shapes. She appeared neat and well-groomed, with hair dyed a deep gray; her broad face framed weathered blue eyes and was decorated with the slightest hint of white facial hair above her lip.

"I always say," she told Anthony, "that Richard has an old soul."

In the awkward silence that came next, Anthony thought about making a pun—something about how Dick had been stepped on quite a bit.

"We all have souls of different ages," Mrs. Gilbert continued with a radiant expression; "at least that's what I believe."

"Maybe you're right," Anthony agreed, his tone brightening as if a promising thought had just occurred to him. The voice continued chattering:

"Gloria has a very young soul—she's irresponsible more than anything else. She has no sense of responsibility."

"She's sparkling, Aunt Catherine," Richard said pleasantly. "A sense of responsibility would ruin her. She's too beautiful."

"Well," Mrs. Gilbert admitted, "all I know is that she just keeps going and going and going—"

The count of strikes against Gloria was forgotten in the rattling sound of the doorknob as it turned to let Mr. Gilbert enter.

He was a short man with a mustache that sat like a small white cloud beneath his unremarkable nose. He had reached the point where his worth as a member of society was a dark and immeasurable negative. His beliefs were the popular misconceptions of twenty years earlier; his thinking followed a shaky and weak path behind the daily newspaper editorials. After graduating from a small but intimidating Western university, he had entered the film business, and since this demanded only the tiny amount of intelligence he possessed, he succeeded for several years—actually until around 1911, when he started trading contracts for unclear agreements with the motion picture industry. The motion picture industry had decided around 1912 to swallow him up, and at this moment he was, so to speak, carefully balanced on its tongue. In the meantime he was supervising manager of the Associated Mid-western Film Materials Company, spending six months of each year in New York and the rest in Kansas City and St. Louis. He believed trustingly that something good was coming his way—and his wife believed so, and his daughter believed so too.

He didn't approve of Gloria: she came home late at night, she hardly ever ate her meals, she was constantly getting into trouble—he had annoyed her one time and she had said things to him that he never knew she was capable of saying. His wife was simpler to handle. After fifteen years of constant, low-level conflict he had worn her down—it was a battle between confused hopefulness and systematic boredom, and somehow the sheer number of times he could say "yes" to drain the life out of any conversation had given him the upper hand.

"Yes-yes-yes-yes," he would say, "yes-yes-yes-yes. Let me see. That was the summer of—let me see—ninety-one or ninety-two—Yes-yes-yes-yes——"

Fifteen years of constant agreement had worn down Mrs. Gilbert. Another fifteen years of that relentless, hollow "yes," paired with the endless flicking of ash from thirty-two thousand cigars, had completely broken her spirit. To this husband of hers, she made the final surrender that married life demands—one that is more total and permanent than any initial compromise—she actually listened to him. She convinced herself that the passing years had given her patience and understanding—in reality, they had destroyed whatever small amount of moral courage she had once possessed.

She introduced him to Anthony.

"This is Mr. Pats," she said.

The young man and the elderly gentleman shook hands; Mr. Gilbert's hand felt soft, worn down to the mushy texture of a squeezed grapefruit. Afterward, the husband and wife greeted each other—he mentioned that it had gotten colder outside; he explained that he had walked down to a newsstand on Forty-

43

fourth Street to buy a Kansas City newspaper. He had planned to take the bus back, but he discovered it was too cold, yes, yes, yes, yes, far too cold.

Mrs. Gilbert made his adventure more exciting by being impressed with his bravery in facing the harsh weather.

"Well, you've got guts!" she said with admiration. "You really have courage. I wouldn't have gone out there for anything."

Mr. Gilbert, displaying typical masculine indifference, completely ignored the intimidation he had caused his wife. He shifted his attention to the two young men and decisively defeated them in a discussion about the weather. Richard Caramel was asked to recall November weather in Kansas. But as soon as the topic was directed toward him, it was aggressively pulled back by its originator, who proceeded to dwell on it, handle it roughly, stretch it out, and thoroughly drain it of any life or interest.

The age-old idea that the days in that place were warm while the nights were quite enjoyable was convincingly presented, and they settled on the precise distance along an unknown railway line between two locations that Dick had accidentally brought up. Anthony locked eyes with Mr. Gilbert in an unwavering gaze and slipped into a daze, which Mrs. Gilbert's cheerful voice broke through after a moment:

"It feels like the cold here is more penetrating—it seems to seep right into my bones."

Since this comment, which Mr. Gilbert had been about to agree with completely, was right on the tip of his tongue, he couldn't be faulted for switching topics somewhat suddenly.

"Where's Gloria?"

"She should be here any minute."

"Have you met my daughter, Mr.——?"

"I haven't had the pleasure of meeting her. I've heard Dick mention her frequently."

"She and Richard are cousins."

"Yes?" Anthony smiled with some difficulty. He wasn't accustomed to being around older people, and his mouth felt tense from forcing unnecessary cheerfulness. The idea of Gloria and Dick being cousins was such a delightful thought. He managed to steal a pained look at his friend within the next minute.

Richard Caramel was worried they would have to leave.

Mrs. Gilbert felt deeply sorry.

Mr. Gilbert thought it was unfortunate.

Mrs. Gilbert had another thought—something about being happy they had visited, regardless, even if they had only encountered an elderly woman far too old to flirt with them. Anthony and Dick clearly found this to be a clever joke, as they laughed in a rhythm that sounded like three-four time.

Would they return again soon?

"Oh, yes."

Gloria would be terribly sorry!

"Good-by——"

"Good-by——"

Smiles!

Smiles!

Bang!

Two heartbroken young men walked down the tenth-floor hallway of the Plaza Hotel toward the elevator.

A Lady's Legs

Behind Maury Noble's appealing laziness, his lack of importance and his casual ridicule, there existed an unexpected and unwavering maturity of intention. His goal, as he had expressed it during college, was to spend three years traveling, three years in complete idleness—and then to become enormously wealthy as rapidly as he could.

His three years of traveling had come to an end. He had circled the globe with such thoroughness and fascination that in anyone else it would have appeared scholarly to the point of being dull, lacking any saving grace of spontaneity, almost like a human guidebook editing itself; but in his case, it took on the quality of some mysterious mission and meaningful plan—as if Maury Noble were some destined opponent of Christ, driven by fate to visit every place there was to visit on earth and to witness all the countless millions of people who lived and cried and killed one another across its surface.

Back in America, he threw himself into the pursuit of entertainment with the same unwavering intensity. He had never consumed more than a few cocktails or a pint of wine in one session, but now he trained himself to drink the way he might have learned Greek—like Greek, it would open the door to a treasure trove of new sensations, new mental states, new responses to happiness or despair.

His daily routines were the subject of mysterious guesswork. He maintained three rooms in a bachelor apartment on Forty-fourth Street, but he was rarely found there. The telephone operator had been given strict orders that no one should even speak with him without first providing a name for approval. She kept a list of about six people to whom he was never available, and the same number to whom he was always available. At the top of the latter list were Anthony Patch and Richard Caramel.

Maury's mother lived with her married son in Philadelphia, and Maury typically went there for weekends, so one Saturday night when Anthony was wandering the cold streets in complete boredom and stopped by the Molton Arms, he was delighted to discover that Mr. Noble was home.

His excitement rose faster than the speeding elevator. This felt wonderful, absolutely wonderful, knowing he was about to see Maury—who would be just as delighted to see him. They would gaze at each other with genuine warmth hidden just beneath the surface, both masking their feelings behind some lighthearted teasing. If it had been summer, they would have ventured out together to leisurely enjoy a couple of tall Tom Collinses, loosening their collars while watching the mildly entertaining atmosphere of some relaxed August nightclub. But the weather outside was harsh, with wind whipping around the corners of the towering buildings and December lurking just around the corner, so much better to spend an evening together beneath the gentle glow of lamplight with a drink or two of Bushmill's, or perhaps a small glass of Maury's Grand Marnier, surrounded by books that sparkled like decorations along the walls, while Maury emanated a blissful laziness as he settled, large and feline, into his beloved chair.

There he was! The room seemed to wrap around Anthony, filling him with warmth. The radiance of that powerful, compelling intellect, that disposition almost Eastern in its external calm, warmed Anthony's troubled spirit and gave him a tranquility that could only be compared to the peace that a simple woman provides. One must comprehend everything—otherwise one must accept everything without question. Maury dominated the space, like a tiger, like a god. The winds beyond the walls grew quiet; the brass candlesticks on the fireplace mantel shone like candles before a sacred altar.

"What's keeping you here today?" Anthony stretched out across a soft sofa and propped himself up on his elbow among the pillows.

"I've only been here for an hour. There was a tea dance, and I stayed so late that I missed my train to Philadelphia."

"It's strange that he's staying so long," Anthony remarked with curiosity.

"Exactly. What did you do?"

"Geraldine. Little usher at Keith's. I told you about her."

"Oh!"

"She visited me around three o'clock and stayed until five. What a strange little person—she understands me. She's completely foolish."

Maury remained quiet.

"As strange as it might sound," Anthony went on, "from my perspective, and as far as I can tell, Geraldine is a model of virtue."

He had known her for a month, a girl with unremarkable and wandering ways. Someone had casually introduced her to Anthony, who found her entertaining and quite enjoyed the innocent and delicate kisses she had given him on the third evening of their friendship, when they had ridden in a taxi through the Park. She had an unclear family situation—a mysterious aunt and uncle who lived with her in an apartment somewhere in the numbered streets of the upper hundreds. She provided companionship that was comfortable and somewhat intimate and soothing. Beyond that he didn't want to explore further—not because of any moral concerns, but because he feared letting any complicated relationship upset what he believed was the increasing peace in his life.

"She has two tricks," he told Maury; "one is to get her hair to fall over her eyes somehow and then blow it away, and the other is to say 'You're cra-a-azy!' whenever someone makes a comment that goes over her head. It captivates me. I sit there for hours on end, completely fascinated by the crazy things she thinks she sees in my imagination."

Maury shifted in his chair and began to speak.

"It's amazing that someone can understand so little while living in such a complicated society. A woman like this actually accepts the entire universe as completely ordinary. Everything from Rousseau's influence to how tariff rates affect the cost of her dinner is completely foreign to her. She's simply been transported from an era of spear points and dropped into this time with an archer's tools for fighting a gun battle. You could erase the whole layer of history and she would never notice the difference."

"I wish our Richard would write about her."

"Anthony, surely you don't think she's worth writing about."

"As much as anyone," he replied, yawning. "You know, I was thinking today that I have tremendous faith in Dick. As long as he focuses on people rather than abstract concepts, and as long as his inspiration comes from real life instead of from art, and assuming he develops normally, I believe he'll become a great man."

"I would think that the appearance of the black notebook would prove that he's going to live."

Anthony propped himself up on his elbow and responded with enthusiasm:

"He attempts to draw from real life. Every author does this except for the absolute worst ones, but most of them end up relying on secondhand material. The event or person might come from actual experience, but the writer typically understands it through the lens of whatever book they last read. For example, imagine he encounters a sea captain and believes he's discovered an original character. The reality is that he notices the similarities between this sea captain and the most recent sea captain that Dana portrayed, or whoever it is that writes about sea captains, and so he understands how to put this sea captain down on paper. Dick can certainly capture any deliberately colorful, stereotypical character, but would he be able to accurately portray his own sister?"

Then they spent the next half hour discussing literature.

"A classic," Anthony suggested, "is a successful book that has managed to survive the backlash of the following period or generation. Once it does that, it becomes safe, much like an architectural or furniture style. It gains a charming dignity that replaces its original trendiness...."

After some time, the topic temporarily lost its appeal. The interest of the two young men wasn't especially technical. They were fascinated by broad concepts. Anthony had recently discovered Samuel Butler, and the sharp aphorisms in the notebook struck him as the essence of criticism. Maury, his entire mind so completely softened by the very rigidity of his life philosophy, appeared naturally the more wise of the two, yet in the actual substance of their intellects they were not, it seemed, fundamentally different.

They moved from discussing letters to sharing the interesting details of each other's daily experiences.

"Whose tea was it?"

"People named Abercrombie."

"Why did you stay late? Did you meet a gorgeous young woman?"

"Yes."

"Did you really?" Anthony's voice rose with surprise.

"Not exactly a débutante. She said she came out two winters ago in Kansas City."

"Kind of left-over?"

"No," Maury replied with a hint of amusement, "I think that's the last thing I would say about her. She appeared—well, somehow like the youngest person there."

"Not too young to make you miss a train."

"Young enough. Beautiful child."

Anthony let out a short, sharp laugh.

"Oh, Maury, you're acting like a child again. What do you mean by beautiful?"

Maury stared helplessly into the distance.

"Well, I can't describe her exactly—except to say that she was beautiful. She was—tremendously alive. She was eating gum-drops."

"What!"

"It was a kind of weakened bad habit. She's the nervous type—she said she always ate gumdrops at tea parties because she had to stand in one spot for such a long time."

"What did you talk about—Bergson? Bilphism? Whether the one-step is immoral?"

Maury remained calm and composed; his fur appeared to be sticking out in every direction.

"Actually, we did discuss Bilphism. It turns out her mother is a Bilphist. But mostly, we talked about legs."

Anthony swayed back and forth with delight.

"My God! Whose legs?"

"Hers. She talked extensively about hers. As if they were some kind of carefully selected collectibles. She sparked an intense curiosity to see them."

"What is she—a dancer?"

"No, I discovered she was Dick's cousin."

Anthony bolted upright so abruptly that the pillow he let go of stood on end like something alive and plunged to the floor.

"Your name is Gloria Gilbert?" he exclaimed.

"Yes. Isn't she remarkable?"

"I'm sure I don't know—but for sheer dullness her father—"

"Well," Maury interrupted with unwavering certainty, "her family might be as gloomy as hired mourners, but I'm inclined to believe she's a genuinely authentic and original person. She has all the surface characteristics of a typical Yale prom date and everything that goes with that—but she's different, very distinctly different."

"Keep going, keep going!" Anthony encouraged him. "As soon as Dick told me she didn't have any brains, I knew she had to be pretty attractive."

"Did he say that?"

"Swore to it," said Anthony with another snorting laugh.

"Well, what he means by intelligence in a woman is—"

"I know," Anthony interrupted eagerly, "he's talking about a superficial collection of literary misinformation."

"That's it. The type who thinks the country's yearly moral decline is either a great thing or a deeply troubling sign. Either uptight intellectuals or people putting on an act. Well, this girl kept talking about legs. She also talked about skin—specifically her own skin. Always her own. She described the kind of tan she wanted to achieve during the summer and how close she typically came to getting it."

"You sat captivated by her deep, rich voice?"

"By her low alto! No, by tan! I started thinking about tan. I started to think about what color I turned when I last exposed myself to the sun about two years ago. I did used to get a pretty good tan. I used to get a sort of bronze color, if I remember correctly."

Anthony sank back into the cushions, trembling with laughter.

"She's got you hooked—oh, Maury! Maury the Connecticut lifeguard. The human nutmeg. Breaking news! Wealthy heiress runs away with coast guard because of his gorgeous skin tone! Later discovered there's Tasmanian heritage in his bloodline!"

Maury let out a sigh; getting up, he walked over to the window and pulled up the shade.

"Snowing hard."

Anthony, still chuckling softly to himself, didn't respond.

"Another winter." Maury's voice drifted from the window, barely above a whisper. "We're getting old, Anthony. I'm twenty-seven, for God's sake! Just three years until thirty, and then I'll be what college students call a middle-aged man."

Anthony remained quiet for a moment.

"You're getting old, Maury," he finally agreed. "The first signs of a really wild and shaky old age—you've spent the whole afternoon talking about tanning and a woman's legs."

Maury yanked the window shade down with a sharp, abrupt sound.

"Idiot!" he shouted, "that coming from you! Here I am, young Anthony, sitting as I'll sit for a generation or longer, watching vibrant souls like you and Dick and Gloria Gilbert pass by me, dancing and singing and loving and hating each other and feeling things, always feeling things. And the only thing that moves me is my complete lack of feeling. I'll sit here and the snow will fall—oh, if only I had a Caramel to take notes—and another winter will pass and I'll turn thirty while you and Dick and Gloria continue being eternally passionate and dancing past me and singing. But after you've all moved on, I'll be saying things for new Dicks to write down, and listening to the disappointments and bitter observations and feelings of new Anthonys—yes, and talking to new Glorias about the summer tans that are still to come."

The firelight danced and flickered on the hearth. Maury stepped away from the window, stirred the flames with a poker, and placed a log on the andirons. He then settled back into his chair as the last traces of his voice disappeared into the fresh fire that crackled with red and yellow sparks along the bark.

"After all, Anthony, you're the one who's very romantic and young. You're the one who's infinitely more susceptible and afraid of having your calm disrupted. I'm the one who tries over and over to be moved—I let myself go a thousand times and I'm always myself. Nothing—quite—stirs me."

"Yet," he whispered after another lengthy silence, "there was something about that young girl with her ridiculous tan that seemed timeless and ancient—just like me."

Turbulence

Anthony rolled over drowsily in his bed, encountering a cool patch of sunlight on his bedspread, marked with shadows from the diamond-paned window. Morning light filled the entire room. The ornate chest in the corner and the old, mysterious wardrobe stood around the space like dark reminders of how indifferent objects can be; only the carpet seemed welcoming and temporary beneath his mortal feet, and Bounds, strangely out of place in his casual collar, appeared as fleeting as the misty vapor of his frozen breath. He stood near the bed, his hand still positioned where he had been tugging at the top blanket, his deep brown eyes gazing steadily at his master.

"Bows!" mumbled the sleepy god. "Is that you, Bows?"

"It's me, sir."

Anthony turned his head, opened his eyes wide, and blinked with a sense of victory.

"Bounds."

"Yes, sir?"

"Can you get off—yeow-ow-oh-oh-oh God!—" Anthony yawned unbearably and his thoughts seemed to collapse into a thick jumble. He tried again.

"Could you come by around four o'clock and serve some tea and sandwiches or something like that?"

"Yes, sir."

Anthony thought about it with a disturbing absence of creativity. "Some sandwiches," he said again without much hope, "oh, some cheese sandwiches and jelly ones and chicken and olive, I suppose. Don't worry about breakfast."

The mental effort of creating was overwhelming. He closed his eyes tiredly, allowed his head to fall back limply, and quickly let go of whatever muscle control he had managed to recover. From a corner of his consciousness emerged the hazy yet unavoidable ghost of the previous evening—but it turned out to be nothing more than what seemed like an endless discussion with Richard Caramel, who had visited him at midnight; they had consumed four bottles of beer and chewed on stale pieces of bread while Anthony sat through a recitation of the opening section of "The

Demon Lover."

A voice came after many hours had passed. Anthony ignored it as sleep washed over him, settling down around him and creeping into the hidden corners of his mind.

Suddenly he was awake, saying: "What?"

"How many will be dining, sir?" It was still Bounds, standing patiently and perfectly still at the foot of the bed—Bounds who split his attention between three gentlemen.

"How many what?"

"I think, sir, I should know how many people are coming. I'll need to plan for the sandwiches, sir."

"Two," Anthony whispered hoarsely; "a lady and a gentleman."

Bounds said, "Thank you, sir," and walked away, carrying with him his humiliating and accusatory soft collar, which served as a rebuke to each of the three gentlemen, who had only asked him to pay a third of the cost.

After a considerable amount of time, Anthony got up and pulled on a shimmering dressing gown in shades of brown and blue over his slender, attractive frame. With one final yawn, he walked into the bathroom, and switching on the vanity light (since the bathroom had no windows to the outside) he examined himself in the mirror with mild curiosity. What a terrible sight, he reflected; this was typically his morning assessment—sleeping always left his complexion unnaturally pale. He lit up a cigarette and looked through various pieces of mail and the morning Tribune.

An hour later, freshly shaved and dressed, he sat at his desk examining a small piece of paper he had pulled from his wallet. It was covered with barely readable notes: "See Mr. Howland at five. Get haircut. Check on Rivers' bill. Go to bookstore."

—And under the last: "Cash in bank, $690 (crossed out), $612 (crossed out), $607."

Finally, at the bottom in hurried handwriting: "Dick and Gloria Gilbert for tea."

This final detail filled him with clear pleasure. His day, typically resembling a jellyfish-like being, a formless, boneless entity, had developed a prehistoric framework. It was moving forward confidently, even cheerfully, toward a peak moment, just as a theatrical performance should unfold, just as any day ought to progress. He feared the instant when the day's foundation would crumble, when he would finally encounter the young woman, engage in conversation with her, and then escort her cheerful departure through the doorway, left with nothing but the sorrowful remnants in the tea cups and the increasing staleness of the untouched sandwiches.

Anthony's days were becoming increasingly dull and colorless. This feeling weighed on him constantly, and he sometimes connected it to a conversation he'd had with Maury Noble a month earlier. It seemed ridiculous that something as naive and self-righteous as a sense of wasted time should trouble him so much, but he couldn't deny what had happened. Three weeks ago, some unwanted remnant of an old obsession had driven him to the public library, where he'd used Richard Caramel's library card to check out half a dozen books about the Italian Renaissance. The fact that these books still sat stacked on his desk exactly as he'd carried them home, accumulating twelve cents in late fees each day, didn't lessen what they represented. These cloth and leather-bound volumes served as evidence of his failure to follow through. Anthony had experienced several hours of sharp and overwhelming panic.

In defense of his way of life, there was first, naturally, The Meaninglessness of Life. Serving as assistants and advisors, attendants and companions, servants and footmen to this great ruler were a thousand books gleaming on his shelves, there was his apartment and all the wealth that would be his when the old man upriver should die choking on his final moral principle. From a world filled with the threat of young society women and the foolishness of many Geraldines he was gratefully freed—instead he should copy the cat-like stillness of Maury and display with pride the accumulated wisdom of countless generations.

Over and against these things was something that his mind constantly examined and wrestled with as a troublesome puzzle, but which, despite being logically resolved and courageously suppressed, had driven him out through the wet slush of late November to a library that didn't have any of the books he really needed. It's reasonable to examine Anthony as deeply as he could examine himself; beyond that point it would naturally be presumptuous. He discovered within himself a deepening sense of dread and isolation. The thought of eating by himself terrified him; instead he frequently had dinner with men he despised. Travel, which had once delighted him, now seemed unbearable, nothing more than superficial beauty without meaning, a ghostly pursuit of his own dream's reflection.

"If I'm fundamentally weak," he thought, "I need something to work on, something to keep me busy." It troubled him to consider that he might be nothing more than a shallow, average person—lacking both Maury's composure and Dick's passion. It felt tragic to desire nothing at all, yet he did want something, definitely something. In brief moments of clarity, he understood what it was: some direction filled with hope that would guide him away from what seemed like the approaching and threatening prospect of growing old.

After cocktails and lunch at the University Club, Anthony felt much better. He had bumped into two classmates from Harvard, and compared to the dull weight of their conversation, his own life seemed vibrant and colorful. Both men were married: one spent his time over coffee describing an extramarital affair while the other listened with bland, approving smiles. Anthony thought both of them were future versions of Mr. Gilbert; their tendency to say "yes" to everything would need to multiply four times over, their personalities would need to be soured by twenty more years—and then they would become nothing more than outdated and broken machines, pretending to be wise but utterly worthless, cared for in complete mental decline by the very women whose lives they had destroyed.

Ah, he was much more than that, as he walked back and forth across the long carpet in the living room after dinner, stopping at the window to gaze out at the busy street. He was Anthony Patch, brilliant, charismatic, the inheritor of many years and many generations. This was his world now—and that final powerful irony he longed for was just ahead.

With a lingering trace of boyish ambition, he envisioned himself as a force in the world; using his grandfather's fortune, he could construct his own platform and become a Talleyrand, a Lord Verulam. His sharp intellect, its refinement, its adaptable brilliance, all reaching their peak and guided by some purpose not yet conceived, would discover meaningful work for him. At this thought his fantasy began to dissolve—meaningful work: he attempted to picture himself in Congress, digging through the mess of that unbelievable cesspit alongside the narrow-minded and pig-like faces he occasionally saw featured in the newspaper photo sections on Sundays, those elevated working-class politicians mindlessly spouting to the country the thoughts of high school students! Small-minded men with textbook dreams who through their ordinariness had hoped to rise above ordinariness into the dull and unexciting paradise of a government run by the masses—and the finest among them, the handful of cunning leaders at the summit, self-centered and cynical, were satisfied to conduct this ensemble of formal dress and stiff collars in a jarring and remarkable anthem, made up of a hazy mix-up between riches as a prize for goodness and riches as evidence of corruption, along with endless applause for God, the Constitution, and the Rocky Mountains!

Lord Verulam! Talleyrand!

Back in his apartment, the grayness settled over him again. The effects of his cocktails had worn off, leaving him drowsy, somewhat foggy-minded and prone to irritability. Lord Verulam—him? The mere idea was painful. Anthony Patch with no accomplishments to his name, lacking courage, without the strength to accept truth when it was offered to him. Oh, he was a pompous fool, building a life around cocktails while quietly and shamefully mourning the downfall of his inadequate and pathetic idealism. He had refined his soul with the most sophisticated taste, and now he yearned for the old garbage. He felt hollow, it seemed, as empty as a discarded bottle—

The doorbell rang. Anthony jumped up and picked up the speaking tube, holding it to his ear. Richard Caramel's voice came through, stiff and mockingly playful:

"Announcing Miss Gloria Gilbert."

"How are you doing?" he said, smiling and holding the door slightly open.

Dick bowed.

"Gloria, this is Anthony."

"Well!" she exclaimed, extending a small gloved hand. Beneath her fur coat, her dress was Alice-blue, with white lace gathered stiffly around her throat.

"Let me carry your things for you."

Anthony stretched out his arms and the brown mass of fur tumbled into them.

"Thanks."

"What do you think of her, Anthony?" Richard Caramel asked bluntly. "Isn't she beautiful?"

"Well!" the girl cried defiantly, yet remaining completely unmoved.

She was absolutely stunning—radiant; it was painful to take in her beauty with just one look. Her hair, filled with an otherworldly allure, stood out brilliantly against the cold, wintry tones of the room.

Anthony moved around like a magician, transforming the mushroom lamp into a brilliant orange glow. The fire he had stirred polished the copper andirons on the fireplace—

"I'm completely frozen," Gloria said casually, looking around with eyes that had the most delicate and transparent bluish-white irises. "What an amazing fire! We discovered a spot where you could stand on some kind of iron-bar grating, and it blew warm air up at you—but Dick wouldn't stay there with me. I told him to go ahead by himself and let me enjoy it."

This was ordinary enough. She appeared to be speaking simply for her own enjoyment, without any strain. Anthony, seated at one end of the couch, studied her silhouette outlined against the lamp's light: the perfect symmetry of her nose and upper lip, her chin, subtly firm, gracefully poised on a somewhat short neck. In a photograph she would have looked entirely classical, almost austere—but the radiance of her hair and cheeks, simultaneously rosy and delicate, made her the most vibrant person he had ever encountered.

"... I think you've got the best name I've heard," she was saying, still apparently talking to herself; her eyes settled on him for a moment and then moved past him—to the Italian wall lamps hanging like glowing yellow turtles at regular intervals along the walls, to the books lined up row after row, then to her cousin on the other side. "Anthony Patch. Only you should look kind of like a horse, with a long thin face—and you should be wearing rags."

"That covers everything about Patch, though. What should Anthony look like?"

"You look like Anthony," she told him earnestly—he thought she had barely noticed him—"quite majestic," she went on, "and serious."

Anthony gave an uneasy smile.

"I just love names that start with the same sound," she continued, "all of them except my own. Mine's way too flashy. I used to know two girls with the last name Jinks, though, and just imagine if they'd been called anything other than what they were actually named—Judy Jinks and Jerry Jinks. Adorable, right? Don't you think so?" Her youthful lips were slightly open, waiting for a response.

"Everyone in the next generation," Dick suggested, "will be named Peter or Barbara—because right now all the intriguing literary characters are named Peter or Barbara."

Anthony continued the prophecy:

"Naturally, Gladys and Eleanor, having adorned the previous generation of heroines and currently being at the height of their social popularity, will be handed down to the next generation of working-class women—"

"Pushing out Ella and Stella," Dick interrupted.

"And Pearl and Jewel," Gloria added warmly, "and Earl and Elmer and Minnie."

"And then I'll step in," Dick said, "and by taking that outdated name, Jewel, I'll give it to some charming and appealing character, and it will begin its journey all over again."

Her voice picked up the conversation and continued with slightly rising, half-amused tones at the end of each sentence—as if challenging anyone to interrupt—punctuated by moments of quiet laughter. Dick had told her that Anthony's servant was called Bounds—she found that absolutely delightful! Dick had made some terrible joke about Bounds doing patchwork, but if there was anything worse than a pun, she declared, it was someone who responded to a pun by giving the joke-teller one of those fake disapproving looks.

"Where are you from?" Anthony asked. He already knew the answer, but her beauty had made him lose his ability to think clearly.

"Kansas City, Missouri."

"They removed her at the same time they banned cigarettes."

"Did they ban cigarettes? I can see my holy grandfather's influence in this."

"He's a reformer or something, isn't he?"

"I feel embarrassed for him."

"I feel the same way," she admitted. "I can't stand reformers, particularly the kind who want to change me."

"Are there many of those?"

"Dozens. It's 'Oh, Gloria, if you smoke so many cigarettes you'll lose your pretty complexion!' and 'Oh, Gloria, why don't you marry and settle down?'"

Anthony agreed wholeheartedly while he wondered who had dared to speak so boldly to someone of such importance.

"And then," she continued, "there are all the subtle reformers who tell you the wild stories they've heard about you and how they've been sticking up for you."

He eventually noticed that her eyes were gray, remarkably steady and composed, and when she looked at him he grasped what Maury had meant when he said she was both very young and very old. She constantly spoke about herself the way a delightful child might speak, and her remarks about what she liked and disliked were genuine and natural.

"I have to admit," Anthony said seriously, "that even I've heard something about you."

Alert immediately, she straightened up. Those eyes, carrying the grayness and timelessness of a soft granite cliff, met his.

"Tell me. I'll believe it. I always believe anything anyone tells me about myself—don't you?"

"Without exception!" the two men agreed in perfect harmony.

"Well, tell me."

"I'm not sure I should," Anthony said teasingly, smiling despite himself. She was clearly so fascinated, completely caught up in herself in an almost comical way.

"He's talking about your nickname," her cousin said.

"What name?" Anthony asked, courteously confused.

Immediately she became shy—then she laughed, leaned back against the cushions, and looked up as she spoke:

"Coast-to-Coast Gloria." Her voice overflowed with laughter, laughter as indefinable as the shifting shadows that danced between firelight and lamplight across her hair. "O Lord!"

Still Anthony was puzzled.

"What do you mean?"

"Me, I mean. That's what some foolish boys came up with for me."

"Can't you see, Anthony," Dick explained, "she's a traveler with nationwide fame and all that. Isn't that what you've heard? People have been calling her that for years—ever since she was seventeen."

Anthony's eyes grew sad and amused.

"Who's this ancient woman you've brought in here, Caramel?"

She ignored this, and perhaps even felt annoyed by it, because she returned to the main subject.

"What have you heard of me?"

"Something about your physique."

"Oh," she said, coolly disappointed, "that's all?"

"Your tan."

"My tan?" She looked confused. Her hand moved up to her throat, pausing there for a moment as if her fingers were sensing different shades of color.

"Do you remember Maury Noble? The man you met about a month ago. You made a great impression on him."

She paused to think for a moment.

"I remember—but he didn't call me up."

"He was afraid to, I don't doubt."

It was pitch black outside now, and Anthony was amazed that his apartment had ever appeared gray to him—the books and pictures on the walls seemed so warm and welcoming, with good old Bounds respectfully offering tea from the shadows, and the three pleasant people sharing waves of interest and laughter back and forth across the cheerful fire.

Unhappy

or

Not Satisfied

On Thursday afternoon, Gloria and Anthony shared tea in the grill room at the Plaza. She wore a gray suit trimmed with fur—"because when you wear gray, you need to use plenty of makeup," she explained—and a small hat perched stylishly on her head, letting golden waves of hair flow out with cheerful elegance. In the brighter lighting, Anthony noticed that her personality seemed infinitely gentler—she appeared so youthful, barely eighteen; her figure beneath the fitted dress, called a hobble-skirt back then, was remarkably graceful and slim, and her hands, neither overly "artistic" nor thick, were as small as a child's hands ought to be.

As they walked in, the orchestra was playing the opening notes of a maxixe, a melody filled with castanets and smooth, slightly dreamy violin harmonies that perfectly matched the packed winter restaurant buzzing with an enthusiastic college crowd, excited about the approaching holidays. Gloria carefully examined several spots, and much to Anthony's irritation, led him in a roundabout way to a table for two on the opposite side of the room. Once they arrived, she paused to think again. Should she sit on the right side or the left? Her lovely eyes and lips showed deep concentration as she made her decision, and Anthony once more reflected on how innocent her every movement seemed; she approached all of life's choices as if they were hers to select and distribute, as if she were constantly choosing gifts for herself from an endless display counter.

She watched the dancers absent-mindedly for a few moments, making quiet comments as a couple swirled close by.

"There's a pretty girl in blue"—and as Anthony looked obediently—"there! No. behind you—there!"

"Yes," he agreed helplessly.

"You didn't see her."

"I'd rather look at you."

"I know, but she was pretty. Except that she had big ankles."

"Was she?—I mean, did she?" he said with indifference.

A girl's greeting came from a couple dancing near them.

"Hello, Gloria! O Gloria!"

"Hello there."

"Who's that?" he demanded.

"I don't know. Someone." She spotted another face in the crowd. "Hello, Muriel!" Then she turned back to Anthony: "That's Muriel Kane over there. I think she's pretty attractive, except not really."

Anthony chuckled with appreciation.

"Attractive, except not very," he repeated.

She smiled and became interested right away.

"Why is that funny?" Her voice carried a desperately earnest quality.

"It just was."

"Do you want to dance?"

"Do you?"

"Sort of. But let's sit," she decided.

"And talk about you? You love to talk about you, don't you?"

"Yes." Caught up in her own vanity, she laughed.

"I imagine your autobiography would be a classic."

"Dick says I don't have one."

"Dick!" he exclaimed. "What does he know about you?"

"Nothing. But he says the biography of every woman begins with the first kiss that truly matters, and ends when her last child is placed in her arms."

"He's speaking from his book."

"He says unloved women have no biographies—they have histories."

Anthony laughed again.

"Surely you don't claim to be unloved!"

"Well, I suppose not."

"Then why don't you have a biography? Haven't you ever had a kiss that mattered?" The moment the words escaped his mouth, he inhaled sharply as if trying to pull them back. This child!

"I don't understand what you mean by 'counts,'" she protested.

"I wish you'd tell me how old you are."

"Twenty-two," she said, looking directly into his eyes with a serious expression. "What age did you think I was?"

"About eighteen."

"I'm going to start being that. I don't like being twenty-two. I hate it more than anything in the world."

"Being twenty-two?"

"No. Growing old and everything. Getting married."

"Don't you ever want to get married?"

"I don't want to have responsibility and a lot of children to take care of."

Clearly, she believed that everything she said was perfectly acceptable. He waited anxiously for her next comment, anticipating it would build on what she had just said. She was smiling—not with humor, but in a pleasant way—and after a pause, a few words dropped into the silence between them:

"I wish I had some gum-drops."

"You will!" He motioned to a waiter and sent him to the cigar counter.

"Do you mind? I love gum-drops. Everyone teases me about it because I'm always chewing on one—whenever my dad's not around."

"Not at all.—Who are all these children?" he asked suddenly. "Do you know them all?"

"Why—no, but they're from—oh, from everywhere, I suppose. Don't you ever come here?"

"Very seldom. I don't care particularly for 'nice girls.'"

Instantly, he captured her focus. She deliberately turned her back on the dancers, settled comfortably in her chair, and insisted:

"What do you do with yourself?"

Thanks to a cocktail, Anthony welcomed the question. In a talkative mood, he also wanted to impress this girl whose interest seemed so frustratingly hard to pin down—she would pause to explore unexpected topics, then rush past things that seemed obviously important. He wanted to show off. He wanted to suddenly appear before her in fresh and heroic ways. He wanted to shake her out of that indifferent attitude she displayed toward everything except herself.

"I don't do anything," he started, realizing at the same time that his words wouldn't have the smooth confidence he wanted them to have. "I don't do anything, because there's nothing I can do that's actually worth doing."

"Well?" He hadn't surprised her or even captured her attention, yet she had clearly understood him, assuming he had actually said anything worth understanding.

"Don't you approve of lazy men?"

She nodded.

"I suppose so, if they're gracefully lazy. Is that possible for an American?"

"Why not?" he asked, feeling unsettled.

But her thoughts had drifted away from the topic and traveled up ten floors.

"My dad is angry with me," she noted without emotion.

"Why? But I want to know exactly why it's impossible for an American to be gracefully idle"—his words grew more confident—"it amazes me. It—it—I don't understand why people believe that every young man should go downtown and work ten hours a day for the best twenty years of his life at boring, uninspiring work, certainly not selfless work."

He stopped speaking abruptly. She observed him with an unreadable expression. He waited for her to either agree or disagree, but she did neither.

"Don't you ever make judgments about things?" he asked with some frustration.

She shook her head and her gaze drifted back to the dancers as she replied:

"I don't know. I don't know anything about—what you should do, or what anybody should do."

She left him feeling bewildered and disrupted his train of thought. The ability to express himself had never felt both so appealing and so unattainable at the same time.

"Well," he admitted apologetically, "I don't either, of course, but—"

"I simply think about people," she went on, "whether they appear to belong exactly where they are and match their surroundings. I don't care if they don't accomplish anything. I don't understand why they should have to; actually, it always surprises me when anyone accomplishes anything at all."

"You don't want to do anything?"

"I want to sleep."

For a moment he was shocked, almost as if she had actually meant what she said word for word.

"Sleep?"

"Sort of. I just want to be lazy, and I want some of the people around me to be active and doing things, because that makes me feel comfortable and secure—and I want some of them to be doing absolutely nothing, because they can be graceful and good company for me. But I never want to change people or get worked up about them."

"You're a charming little determinist," Anthony laughed. "It's your world, isn't it?"

"Well—" she said with a quick upward glance, "isn't it? As long as I'm—young."

She hesitated just before saying the final word, and Anthony had a feeling she was about to say "beautiful." There was no doubt that's what she had meant to say.

Her eyes lit up and he waited for her to expand on the subject. He had gotten her to open up, at least—he leaned forward a little to hear what she would say.

But "Let's dance!" was all she said!

Admiration

That winter afternoon at the Plaza marked the beginning of a series of dates Anthony arranged with her during the hazy and exciting days leading up to Christmas. She was always busy. It took him quite a while to discover which particular circles of the city's social scene she moved in. It hardly seemed to matter. She went to the semi-public charity dances at the large hotels; he spotted her multiple times at dinner parties at Sherry's, and on one occasion while he waited for her to get dressed, Mrs. Gilbert, speaking about her daughter's tendency to be constantly "going out," rattled off an incredible holiday schedule that featured at least six dances for which Anthony had received invitations.

He arranged to meet her multiple times for lunch and tea—the lunch dates were rushed and, at least from his perspective, quite disappointing experiences, since she appeared drowsy and distracted, unable to focus on anything or pay sustained attention to what he was saying. After two of these lackluster meals, when he confronted her about giving him only the leftover scraps of her day, she laughed and offered him a tea date three days later. This turned out to be far more satisfying.

One Sunday afternoon just before Christmas, he called her and discovered she was in that calm period right after some significant but puzzling argument. She told him with a voice mixing anger and entertainment that she had thrown a man out of her apartment—at this point Anthony's mind raced with speculation—and that this same man had been planning to host a small dinner party for her that very evening, which she obviously wasn't going to attend now. So Anthony took her out for supper instead.

"Let's go do something!" she suggested as they rode down in the elevator. "I want to see a show, don't you?"

Asking at the hotel's ticket desk revealed just two Sunday night "concerts."

"They're always the same," she complained unhappily, "same old Yiddish comedians. Oh, let's go somewhere!"

To hide his guilty feeling that he should have organized some sort of entertainment for her enjoyment, Anthony put on a fake air of confident cheerfulness.

"We'll go to a good cabaret."

"I've seen everyone in town."

"Well, we'll find a new one."

She was in a terrible mood; that was obvious. Her gray eyes had turned hard as stone. When she wasn't talking, she stared straight ahead as if looking at something unpleasant in the lobby that only she could see.

"Well, come on, then."

He followed her, a graceful girl even in her thick fur coat, out to a taxi, and with the manner of someone who knew exactly where he was going, told the driver to head over to Broadway and then turn south. He tried several times to start a casual conversation, but since she put up an impenetrable wall of silence and responded to him with sentences as gloomy as the cold darkness inside the taxi, he gave up and, adopting a similar attitude, sank into a deep melancholy.

A dozen blocks down Broadway, Anthony's attention was drawn to a large and unfamiliar electric sign that spelled out "Marathon" in brilliant yellow script, decorated with electric leaves and flowers that flickered on and off, casting their glow on the wet and gleaming street. He leaned forward and tapped on the taxi window, and within moments he was getting information from a Black doorman: Yes, this was a cabaret. An excellent cabaret. The best show in the city!

"Should we give it a try?"

With a sigh, Gloria threw her cigarette out the open door and got ready to follow it; then they had moved beneath the loud, garish sign, under the broad entrance, and up in a cramped elevator into this overlooked temple of entertainment.

The glamorous worlds of both the extremely wealthy and the desperately poor, the incredibly stylish and the deeply criminal, along with the recently popularized bohemian lifestyle, become familiar to impressionable high school girls in places like Augusta, Georgia, and Redwing, Minnesota, not just through the illustrated and captivating features in Sunday entertainment sections but also through the scandalized and alarming perspectives of writers like Mr. Rupert Hughes and other documentarians of America's frenzied lifestyle. However, the adventures of Harlem venturing into Broadway, the mischief of the boring and the celebrations of the proper remain secret knowledge known only to those who actually take part in them.

A tip gets passed around—and at this well-known spot, the lower social classes gather on Saturday and Sunday evenings—

those small, anxious men who appear in comic strips as "the Consumer" or "the Public." They've ensured this place meets three criteria: it's affordable; it mimics the dazzling entertainment of the grand cafes in the theater district with a kind of cheap and artificial longing; and—most importantly—it's somewhere they can "bring a respectable girl," which naturally means that everyone has become equally safe, timid, and dull due to their lack of money and creativity.

There on Sunday nights gather the gullible, emotional, underpaid, overworked people with compound job titles: bookkeepers, ticket sellers, office managers, salespeople, and, above all, clerks—clerks from the express company, from the post office, from the grocery store, from the brokerage firm, from the bank. Alongside them are their giggling, overly dramatic, pitifully pretentious wives, who gain weight with their husbands, give birth to too many children, and drift helplessly and dissatisfied in a bland ocean of monotonous work and shattered dreams.

They call these cheap, flashy nightclubs after luxury train cars. The "Marathon"! They don't use the suggestive comparisons borrowed from Parisian cafés! This is where their obedient customers bring their "respectable women," whose deprived imaginations are all too eager to believe that the atmosphere is relatively lively and cheerful, and even slightly scandalous. This is living! Who worries about tomorrow?

Abandoned people!

Anthony and Gloria sat and observed their surroundings. At the nearby table, a group of four was being joined by three latecomers—two men and a woman—and the woman's behavior offered a fascinating glimpse into social dynamics. She was meeting new people and putting on a desperate act. Through her gestures, her words, and the barely noticeable movements of her eyelids, she was trying to convey that she belonged to a social class slightly above the one she was currently mingling with, suggesting that she had recently been—and would soon return to—a more elevated and exclusive social circle. Her refinement was almost painful to watch—she wore a hat from the previous season, decorated with violets that were no more artificially pretentious and obviously fake than she was herself.

Captivated, Anthony and Gloria observed the girl as she took her seat and projected the sense that she was only there as a favor. Her eyes seemed to communicate that for her, this was essentially a venture into the lower classes, something to be disguised with dismissive laughter and half-hearted apologies.

The other women passionately conveyed the feeling that while they were part of the crowd, they didn't truly belong to it. This wasn't the kind of establishment they were used to frequenting; they had simply stopped by because it was nearby and convenient—every group in the restaurant gave off this same impression... who could say for certain? They were all constantly shifting between social classes—the women frequently marrying into better circumstances than their backgrounds would suggest, the men suddenly striking it rich through some wildly successful advertising venture or a revolutionary ice cream cone concept. In the meantime, they gathered here to dine, turning a blind eye to the cost-cutting measures evident in the infrequent changing of tablecloths, in the casual attitude of the cabaret entertainers, and most notably in the informal, overly familiar manner of the waiters. It was clear that these servers weren't the least bit impressed by their customers. One had the sense that any moment now they might simply sit down at the tables themselves...

"Do you have a problem with this?" Anthony asked.

Gloria's face grew warm and for the first time that evening she smiled.

"I love it," she said honestly. It was impossible to question her sincerity. Her gray eyes wandered here and there, sometimes drowsy, sometimes idle or alert, moving from one group to the next with obvious pleasure, and Anthony could clearly see the different angles of her profile, the remarkably expressive movements of her mouth, and the genuine elegance of her face, figure, and bearing that made her stand out like a single beautiful flower among a collection of worthless trinkets. Seeing her happiness, a magnificent feeling rose in his eyes, overwhelmed him, made his nerves tingle, and filled his throat with rough and intense emotion. A silence fell over the room. The casual violins and saxophones, the sharp grating cry of a nearby child, the voice of the girl wearing the violet hat at the neighboring table, all seemed to slowly fade away, retreat, and disappear like dim reflections on the polished floor—and the two of them, it appeared to him, were alone and infinitely distant, peaceful. Certainly the bloom of her cheeks seemed like a delicate projection from a realm of subtle and unexplored colors; her hand shining on the stained tablecloth was like a shell from some distant and completely untouched sea....

Then the illusion shattered like a web of threads; the room formed itself around him, voices, faces, movement; the harsh glare of the overhead lights became real, became ominous; breathing began, the slow rhythm that she and he shared with this obedient crowd, the rising and falling of chests, the endless meaningless exchange and back-and-forth and throwing around and repeating of words and phrases—all of this forced his senses open to the stifling weight of life—and then her voice reached him, cool as the floating dream he had left behind.

"I belong here," she whispered, "I'm just like these people."

For a moment this felt like a cruel and pointless contradiction thrown at him from across the unbridgeable gap she had built around herself. Her fascination had grown stronger—her gaze was fixed on a Jewish violinist who moved his shoulders in time with the smoothest fox-trot of the year:

"Something—goes
Ring-a-ting-a-ling-a-ling

74

Right in your ear—"

Again she spoke from the heart of this all-encompassing delusion that belonged entirely to her. It astonished him. It felt like hearing blasphemy spoken by a child.

"I'm just like them—like Japanese lanterns and crepe paper, and the music of that orchestra."

"You're a young fool!" he declared frantically. She shook her blonde head.

"No, I'm not. I'm just like them.... You should see.... You don't really know me." She paused and her gaze returned to him, suddenly settling on his eyes, as if she was startled to find him still standing there. "I have this streak of what you'd probably call tackiness. I don't know where it comes from, but it's there—oh, things like this place and flashy colors and cheap showiness. I feel like I belong here. These people would value me and accept me as I am, and these men would fall for me and look up to me, while the intelligent men I usually meet would just pick me apart and tell me I'm one way because of this or another way because of that."

Anthony desperately wanted to paint her in that moment, to capture her exactly as she was right then, knowing that with each passing second she would never be quite the same again.

"What were you thinking?" she asked.

"I'm just not a realist," he said, and then added: "No, only the romantic preserves what's truly worth preserving."

From Anthony's deep sophistication came an understanding, nothing primitive or mysterious, hardly even physical at all—an understanding passed down through the romantic thoughts of countless generations. As she spoke and caught his gaze and turned her beautiful head, she stirred something in him that had never been stirred before. The body that housed her soul had taken on meaning—that was everything. She was like the sun, brilliant, expanding, collecting light and holding it within—then after what seemed like forever, releasing it through a look, a piece of a sentence, to that part of him that treasured all beauty and all dreams.

Chapter III: The Connoisseur Of Kisses

From his college years as editor of the Harvard crimson, Richard Caramel had wanted to become a writer. However, during his senior year, he had developed the grandiose belief that some men were chosen for "Service" and, upon entering the world, were meant to achieve some undefined, longing purpose that would result in either eternal reward or, at minimum, the personal fulfillment of having worked toward the greatest benefit for the greatest number of people.

This mindset has been stirring up American colleges for a long time. It typically starts during the naive and easily influenced freshman year—sometimes even earlier in preparatory school. Well-funded preachers famous for their dramatic performances make their way around universities and, by scaring the gentle followers and numbing the awakening of interest and intellectual curiosity that forms the foundation of all education, create a puzzling sense of guilt, reaching back to childhood wrongdoings and the constant threat of "women." These presentations attract rebellious students who come to mock and laugh, while the fearful ones swallow these appealing remedies, which might be harmless when given to farmers' wives and devout pharmacy clerks but prove to be quite risky treatment for these "future leaders of men."

This octopus possessed enough strength to wrap a winding tentacle around Richard Caramel. The year following his graduation, it drew him into New York's slums to work with confused Italians as secretary for an "Alien Young Men's Rescue Association." He worked there for over a year before the repetitive nature of the job started to tire him. The immigrants arrived endlessly—Italians, Poles, Scandinavians, Czechs, Armenians—bringing the same problems, the same remarkably unattractive faces, and largely the same odors, though he imagined these became more abundant and varied as the months went by. His final thoughts about the usefulness of service remained unclear, but regarding his own connection to it, they were sudden and firm. Any friendly young man, his mind buzzing with the newest cause, could achieve just as much as he could with Europe's refugees—and it was time for him to begin writing.

He had been living in a downtown YMCA, but when he gave up the impossible task of trying to make something worthwhile out of worthless material, he moved uptown and immediately started working as a reporter for The Sun. He continued this work for a year, doing occasional writing on the side with little success, and then one day an unfortunate incident abruptly ended his newspaper career. On a February afternoon he was assigned to cover a Squadron A parade. With snow threatening, he decided to take a nap in front of a warm fire instead, and when he woke up he wrote a polished column about the muffled sound of horses' hooves in the snow... This is what he turned in. The next morning a marked copy of the newspaper was sent to the City Editor with a hastily written note: "Fire the man who wrote this." It turned out that Squadron A had also noticed the threatening snow—they had postponed the parade to another day.

A week later he had started working on "The Demon Lover."

In January, during the Mondays of the month, Richard Caramel's nose remained constantly blue, a mocking blue that vaguely brought to mind flames dancing around a condemned soul. His book was almost finished, and as it became more complete, it also seemed to become more demanding, draining him and overwhelming him until he wandered around looking worn out and defeated, living in its shadow. He didn't just share his hopes, bragging, and uncertainty with Anthony and Maury, but with anyone he could convince to listen. He visited courteous but confused publishers, he talked about it with whoever happened to be sitting across from him at the Harvard Club; Anthony even insisted that one Sunday night, Richard had been found arguing about moving Chapter Two around with a well-read ticket-collector in the cold and gloomy depths of a Harlem subway station. The most recent addition to his list of confidants was Mrs. Gilbert, who would sit with him for hours, switching back and forth between Bilphism and literature in an passionate exchange of ideas.

"Shakespeare was a Bilphist," she told him with a forced smile. "Oh, absolutely! He was definitely a Bilphist. It's been proven."

At this point, Dick would appear somewhat confused.

"If you've read 'Hamlet' you can't help but see."

"Well, he lived in a more trusting time—a more religious era."

But she demanded the whole loaf:

"Oh, yes, but you see Bilphism isn't a religion. It's the science of all religions." She smiled defiantly at him. This was the clever phrase that captured her belief perfectly. There was something about how these words were arranged that gripped her mind so completely that the statement seemed to stand above any need to explain what it actually meant. She probably would have embraced any idea wrapped up in this brilliant phrase—though perhaps it wasn't really a formula at all; it was the ultimate reduction to absurdity of all formulas.

Then eventually, but magnificently, Dick's turn would come.

"You've heard about the new poetry movement, haven't you? You haven't? Well, it's made up of many young poets who are breaking away from traditional forms and creating excellent work. What I wanted to tell you is that my book is going to launch a new prose movement, something like a renaissance."

"I'm sure it will," Mrs. Gilbert said with a bright smile. "I'm absolutely certain it will. Last Tuesday, I visited Jenny Martin, the palm reader that everyone's been raving about. I mentioned that my nephew was working on a project, and she told me I'd be delighted to know that his success would be remarkable. But she had never met you or learned anything about you—she didn't even know your name."

Having expressed his amazement at this remarkable occurrence with the appropriate sounds, Dick dismissed her topic with a wave of his hand as if he were a traffic officer directing cars, and essentially signaled for his own conversation to move forward.

"I'm completely focused, Aunt Catherine," he reassured her, "I truly am. All my friends are teasing me—oh, I can see the humor in it and I don't mind. I believe a person should be able to handle teasing. But I have this kind of strong feeling," he finished with a gloomy tone.

"You're an old soul, I always say."

"Maybe I am." Dick had reached the point where he stopped resisting and simply gave in. He imagined, in a twisted way, that he must be an old soul—so ancient that he was completely decayed. Still, hearing those words repeated made him feel awkward and sent unpleasant chills down his spine. He switched to a different topic.

"Where is my distinguished cousin Gloria?"

"She's out somewhere with someone."

Dick stopped, thought for a moment, and then, twisting his face into what clearly started as a smile but turned into a frightening scowl, made a remark.

"I think my friend Anthony Patch is in love with her."

Mrs. Gilbert jumped slightly, smiled a half-second too late, and whispered her "Really?" in the tone of a detective's stage whisper.

"I think so," Dick corrected seriously. "She's the first girl I've ever seen him spend so much time with."

"Well, naturally," Mrs. Gilbert said with deliberate nonchalance, "Gloria never confides in me. She keeps everything to herself. Just between us"—she leaned in carefully, clearly intent on ensuring that only God and her nephew would hear what she was about to say—"just between us, I'd love to see her find someone and settle down."

Dick stood up and walked back and forth across the room with serious intent, a short, energetic, already round young man with his hands awkwardly shoved into his bulging pockets.

"I'm not saying I'm definitely right, you understand," he said to the endlessly proper hotel steel engraving that smiled respectably back at him. "I'm not saying anything I'd want Gloria to find out about. But I believe Mad Anthony is interested—extremely interested. He talks about her all the time. In anyone else, that would be a warning sign."

"Gloria has such a young spirit—" Mrs. Gilbert started to say enthusiastically, but her nephew cut her off with a rushed comment:

"Gloria would be completely foolish not to marry him." He stopped and turned to face her, his expression showing a complex mix of lines and dimples, tightened and stretched to display the utmost intensity—as if trying to compensate for any impropriety in his words through sheer earnestness. "Gloria's a wild one, Aunt Catherine. She's impossible to control. I don't understand how she's managed it, but recently she's gathered quite a collection of the most peculiar friends. She doesn't appear to care at all. And the men she used to date in New York were—" He paused to catch his breath.

"Yes-yes-yes," interrupted Mrs. Gilbert, making a weak attempt to conceal the enormous fascination with which she was listening.

"Well," Richard Caramel went on seriously, "that's how it is. What I'm saying is that the men she used to spend time with and the people she associated with were once top-notch. Now they're not."

Mrs. Gilbert blinked rapidly—her chest trembled, swelled, stayed that way for a moment, and as she breathed out, her words poured forth in a rush.

She knew, she whispered through her tears; oh yes, mothers notice these things. But what was she supposed to do? He was familiar with Gloria. He'd observed enough of Gloria to understand how pointless it would be to try reasoning with her. Gloria had been pampered—in a thoroughly extraordinary way. She had been nursed until she was three, for example, when she could have easily eaten solid food. Maybe—you never could tell—this was what had given her entire personality that vitality and resilience. And then from the time she turned twelve, she'd had boys surrounding her constantly—oh, so constantly you couldn't even move. At sixteen she started attending dances at boarding schools, and then came the universities; and wherever she went, boys, boys, boys. Initially, oh, until she reached eighteen there had been so many that none seemed more important than any of the others, but then she started choosing favorites.

She was aware that there had been a series of romantic relationships spanning approximately three years, possibly twelve in total. At times the men were college students, other times recent graduates—each relationship typically lasted several months, with brief flings occurring between the longer ones. On one or two occasions they had continued for extended periods and her mother had anticipated an engagement, but invariably someone new would appear—someone new—

The men? Oh, she made them absolutely miserable! There was only one who had managed to maintain any dignity, and he had been just a boy, young Carter Kirby, from Kansas City, who was so full of himself that he simply floated away on his own pride one afternoon and departed for Europe the following day with his father. The rest had been—utterly wretched. They never seemed to understand when she had grown tired of them, and Gloria had rarely been intentionally cruel. They would continue calling, sending her letters, attempting to see her, making lengthy journeys to follow her across the country. Some of them had opened up to Mrs. Gilbert, telling her with tears streaming down their faces that they would never recover from Gloria... though at least two of them had gotten married since then.... But Gloria, it appeared, struck with deadly precision—to this very day Mr. Carstairs telephoned once a week, and sent her flowers which she no longer even bothered to turn away.

Several times—at least twice—Mrs. Gilbert was certain things had progressed to a private engagement, once with Tudor Baird and another time with that Holcome boy from Pasadena. She felt confident this was true because—and this information must remain confidential—she had walked in unexpectedly and discovered Gloria behaving in a way that clearly indicated she was engaged. Naturally, she hadn't confronted her daughter about it. She possessed a certain sense of propriety and, furthermore, on each occasion she had anticipated a formal announcement within a few weeks. However, the announcement never materialized; instead, a different man would appear on the scene.

Dramatic scenes everywhere! Young men pacing back and forth through the library like trapped tigers! Young men shooting angry looks at each other in the hallway as one arrived and another departed! Young men making phone calls only to have the receiver slammed down on them in frustration! Young men making wild threats about fleeing to South America! Young men composing the most heartbreaking letters! (She never said anything along these lines, but Dick imagined that Mrs. Gilbert's eyes had witnessed some of these letters.)

And Gloria, caught between tears and laughter, feeling sorry yet glad, falling out of love while falling in love again, miserable yet nervous, trying to stay cool, surrounded by the endless returning of gifts, swapping out pictures in old frames, taking hot baths to wash it all away, and starting over—with the next one.

That situation continued and seemed like it would last forever. Nothing hurt Gloria, changed her, or affected her in any way. Then suddenly, without any warning, she told her mother that college students bored her. She was definitely not going to any more college dances.

This marked the beginning of her transformation—not necessarily in what she actually did, since she still went dancing and had just as many dates as before—but the spirit behind those dates had completely shifted. In the past, it had been a source of pride, a way to feed her own vanity. She had likely been the most famous and pursued young beauty in the entire country. Gloria Gilbert of Kansas City! She had consumed this attention without mercy—relishing the crowds that gathered around her, savoring how the most desirable men would pick her out from everyone else; delighting in the intense jealousy of other girls; taking pleasure in the incredible, even shocking, and as her mother was happy to point out, completely baseless stories that circulated about her—like the rumor that she had jumped into the Yale swimming pool one evening while wearing a chiffon gown.

And from loving it with a pride that was almost masculine—it had been like a triumphant and brilliant career—she suddenly became numb to it all. She withdrew. She who had ruled over countless parties, who had moved gracefully through many ballrooms to the admiring gazes of many eyes, no longer seemed to care. Anyone who fell in love with her now was rejected completely, almost with anger. She went halfheartedly with the most uninteresting men. She constantly canceled engagements, not as she had in the past from a calm confidence that she was beyond reproach, that the man she had offended would come back like a loyal pet—but carelessly, without scorn or arrogance. She seldom lost her temper with men anymore—she simply found them boring. She appeared—and it was so odd—she appeared to her mother to be becoming emotionally distant.

Richard Caramel listened carefully. Initially, he had stayed on his feet, but as his aunt's speech grew more detailed—what's recorded here has been cut in half, removing all the tangential comments about Gloria's youthful spirit and Mrs. Gilbert's personal emotional struggles—he pulled up a chair and paid close attention while she drifted, alternating between tears and pitiful helplessness, through the lengthy account of Gloria's life. When she reached the story of this past year, a story filled with cigarette butts scattered across New York in small ashtrays labeled "Midnight Frolic" and "Justine Johnson's Little Club," he started nodding his head slowly, then more and more rapidly, until, as she concluded with a sharp, abrupt tone, his head was bouncing energetically up and down, ridiculously resembling a doll's spring-loaded head, conveying—practically anything at all.

In a way, Gloria's history was already familiar territory to him. He had observed it with a journalist's eye, since he planned to write a book about her eventually. However, his current concerns were more personal in nature. He was particularly curious about Joseph Bloeckman, whom he had noticed with her on multiple occasions, as well as those two women who were always in her company—Rachael Jerryl and Miss Kane. Certainly Miss Kane didn't seem like the type of person one would expect to see associated with Gloria!

The moment had slipped away. Mrs. Gilbert, having struggled up the steep slope of explanation, was now ready to plummet down the steep descent of breakdown. Her eyes resembled a blue sky glimpsed through two circular, red window frames. The skin around her mouth was quivering.

And at that moment the door opened, allowing Gloria and the two young women just mentioned to enter the room.

Two Young Women

"Well!"

"How are you doing, Mrs. Gilbert!"

Miss Kane and Miss Jerryl are introduced to Mr. Richard Caramel. "This is Dick" (laughter).

"I've heard so much about you," Miss Kane says, her voice caught somewhere between a giggle and a shout.

"How do you do," says Miss Jerryl shyly.

Richard Caramel attempts to carry himself as though he has a better physique. He finds himself conflicted between his natural friendliness and his belief that these girls are quite ordinary—nothing like the Farmover type at all.

Gloria has disappeared into the bedroom.

"Please, have a seat," Mrs. Gilbert says warmly, having fully regained her composure. "Go ahead and take off your coat." Dick worries she might comment on how old his soul is, but he pushes aside his concerns as he focuses on conducting a thorough, writer's assessment of the two young women.

Muriel Kane came from a family that was climbing the social ladder in East Orange. She was short rather than petite, and walked the bold line between being plump and broad. Her black hair was styled in an elaborate fashion. This, combined with her attractive yet somewhat cow-like eyes and her overly red lips, made her look like Theda Bara, the famous movie star. People constantly told her she was a "vamp," and she took them at their word. She hoped they might actually fear her, and she did everything possible in every situation to project an aura of danger. A creative person might picture the red flag she perpetually carried, waving it frantically, pleadingly—and sadly, with little dramatic effect. She was also incredibly current with trends: she knew all the newest songs, every single latest hit—whenever one played on the record player she would jump up and sway her shoulders back and forth while snapping her fingers, and when there was no music playing she would hum her own accompaniment.

Her conversation was also perfectly timed for the era: "I don't care," she would say, "I should worry and lose my figure"—and again: "I can't make my feet behave when I hear that tune. Oh, baby!"

Her fingernails were too long and elaborate, polished to an unnatural pink shine. Her clothes were too tight, too fashionable, too bright, her eyes too mischievous, her smile too flirtatious. She was almost sadly overdone from head to toe.

The other girl clearly had a more complex personality. She was an elegantly dressed Jewish woman with dark hair and beautiful pale skin. She appeared timid and distant, and these characteristics enhanced a delicate appeal that surrounded her. Her family were Episcopalians, owned three fashionable women's boutiques on Fifth Avenue, and resided in a luxurious apartment on Riverside Drive. After a short while, it struck Dick that she was trying to copy Gloria—he found it curious that people always seemed to choose impossible-to-copy individuals as their models.

"We had such a crazy time!" Muriel exclaimed with excitement. "There was this completely insane woman sitting behind us on the bus. She was absolutely, positively out of her mind! She kept muttering to herself about something she wanted to do to someone or something. I was terrified, but Gloria just refused to get off the bus."

Mrs. Gilbert opened her mouth, clearly impressed and overwhelmed.

"Really?"

"Oh, she was completely insane. But we shouldn't worry about it since she didn't actually harm us. So ugly! Good heavens! The guy sitting across from us said her face would be perfect for a night nurse working at a home for the blind, and naturally we all burst out laughing, so then the man tried to hit on us."

Gloria soon came out of her bedroom, and immediately everyone's attention turned to her. The two girls faded into the background, unnoticed and forgotten.

"We've been talking about you," Dick said quickly, "—your mother and I."

"Well," said Gloria.

A pause—Muriel turned to Dick.

"You're a great writer, aren't you?"

"I'm a writer," he admitted with embarrassment.

"I always say," Muriel said with genuine conviction, "that if I ever found the time to write down all my experiences, it would make an amazing book."

Rachael giggled with understanding; Richard Caramel's bow was nearly dignified. Muriel went on:

"But I don't understand how you can just sit down and write it. And poetry! Good heavens, I can't even make two lines rhyme. Well, why should I worry about it!"

Richard Caramel barely managed to hold back a burst of laughter. Gloria was chewing on an enormous piece of candy and gazing gloomily through the window. Mrs. Gilbert cleared her throat and smiled brightly.

"But you see," she said as if explaining something obvious to everyone, "you're not an old soul—like Richard."

The Ancient Soul let out a sigh of relief—it was finally free.

Then, as if she had been thinking about it for five minutes, Gloria suddenly made an announcement:

"I'm going to throw a party."

"Oh, can I come?" Muriel exclaimed with playful boldness.

"A dinner party. Seven people in total: Muriel and Rachael and myself, plus you, Dick, and Anthony, and that fellow named Noble—I found him quite likeable—and Bloeckman."

Muriel and Rachael burst into gentle, delighted expressions of excitement. Mrs. Gilbert's eyes sparkled as she smiled warmly.

Acting as though it were nothing special, Dick interrupted with a question:

"Who is this guy Bloeckman, Gloria?"

Sensing a subtle hostility, Gloria turned toward him.

"Joseph Bloeckman? He's in the movie business. He's vice-president of 'Films Par Excellence.' He and father do a lot of business together."

"Oh!"

"Well, will you all come?"

They would all come. A date was set within the week. Dick stood up, straightened his hat, coat, and scarf, and flashed a broad smile at everyone.

"Bye-bye," said Muriel, waving her hand cheerfully, "give me a call sometime."

Richard Caramel felt embarrassed on her behalf.

Deplorable End of The Chevalier O'keefe

It was Monday and Anthony took Geraldine Burke to lunch at the Beaux Arts—afterward they went up to his apartment and he rolled out the little wheeled table that held his collection of alcohol, choosing vermouth, gin, and absinthe for an appropriate drink.

Geraldine Burke, who worked as an usher at Keith's, had provided him with entertainment for several months. He appreciated her because she expected so little from him, especially since a disastrous relationship with a young socialite the previous summer had left him cautious around women of his own social standing. During that affair, he had learned that after just a few kisses, the woman expected a marriage proposal, which made him wary of girls from his social circle. It was far too simple to focus critically on their flaws: perhaps some physical roughness or an overall absence of refined manners—but when it came to a girl who worked as an usher at Keith's, he approached the situation with an entirely different mindset. A person could accept certain traits in a close personal attendant that would be completely unacceptable in a casual acquaintance from one's own social class.

Geraldine, curled up at the foot of the couch, watched him with narrowed, slanted eyes.

"You're always drinking, aren't you?" she said suddenly.

"Well, I guess so," Anthony replied, somewhat surprised. "Don't you?"

"No. I go to parties sometimes—you know, about once a week, but I only have two or three drinks. You and your friends keep drinking all the time. I would think you'd ruin your health."

Anthony felt somewhat moved.

"Why, aren't you sweet to worry about me!"

"Well, I do."

"I don't drink that much," he said. "Last month I went three weeks without touching a single drop. And I only get really drunk about once a week."

"But you drink something every day and you're only twenty-five. Don't you have any ambition? Think about what you'll become at forty?"

"I honestly hope I don't live that long."

She clicked her tongue against her teeth.

"You're crazy!" she said as he mixed another cocktail—and then: "Are you related to Adam Patch in any way?"

"Yes, he's my grandfather."

"Really?" She was clearly excited.

"Absolutely."

"That's funny. My dad used to work for him."

"He's a strange old man."

"Is he nice?" she asked.

"Well, in his personal life he's rarely unpleasant without reason."

"Tell us about him."

"Why," Anthony thought, "he's all withered and shrunken, and he has what's left of some gray hair that always looks like the wind has been blowing through it. He's extremely moral."

"He's done a lot of good," said Geraldine with intense gravity.

"Nonsense!" Anthony sneered. "He's a self-righteous fool— an idiot."

Her thoughts drifted away from the topic and moved on to other things.

"Why don't you live with him?"

"Why don't I stay at a Methodist parsonage?"

"You're crazy!"

Again she made a small clicking sound to show her disapproval. Anthony reflected on how deeply moral this little lost soul was at her core—how thoroughly moral she would remain even after the inevitable tide arrived that would sweep her away from the shores of respectability.

"Do you hate him?"

"I wonder. I never liked him. You never like people who do things for you."

"Does he hate you?"

"My dear Geraldine," Anthony protested with an amused frown, "please have another cocktail. I get on his nerves. When I light up a cigarette, he walks into the room making a show of sniffing around. He's self-righteous, tedious, and somewhat two-faced. I probably wouldn't be sharing this with you if I hadn't had a few drinks, but I don't think it really matters."

Geraldine remained deeply curious. She held her untouched glass between her finger and thumb, watching him with eyes that showed a hint of wonder.

"What do you mean by calling someone a hypocrite?"

"Well," Anthony said impatiently, "maybe he isn't. But he doesn't enjoy the same things I do, so as far as I'm concerned, he's boring."

"Hm." Her curiosity finally seemed satisfied. She settled back into the sofa and sipped her cocktail.

"You're quite amusing," she said with a thoughtful tone. "Does everyone want to marry you simply because your grandfather has money?"

"They don't—but I wouldn't blame them if they did. Still, you see, I never plan to marry."

She rejected this with contempt.

"You'll fall in love someday. Oh, you will—I know." She nodded wisely.

"It would be foolish to be overconfident. That's what destroyed the Chevalier O'Keefe."

"Who was he?"

"A product of my brilliant imagination. He's my sole creation, the Chevalier."

"Crazy!" she murmured pleasantly, using the awkward rope ladder with which she bridged all gaps and climbed after her intellectual superiors. Deep down she felt that it eliminated distances and brought the person whose imagination had escaped her back within reach.

"Oh, no!" Anthony protested, "oh, no, Geraldine. You can't psychoanalyze the Chevalier. If you don't think you can understand him, I won't invite him over. Besides, I'd feel somewhat uncomfortable because of his unfortunate reputation."

"I suppose I can understand anything that makes sense," Geraldine replied with a touch of irritation.

"In that case, there are several episodes in the Chevalier's life that might prove entertaining."

"Well?"

"His unexpected death brought him to mind and made him relevant to our conversation. I dislike bringing him up by starting with his ending, but it appears unavoidable that the Chevalier must enter your life backwards."

"Well, what about him? Did he die?"

"He did! In this way. He was an Irishman, Geraldine, a semi-fictional Irishman—the wild type with a refined brogue and 'reddish hair.' He was banished from Ireland in the final days of chivalry and, naturally, made his way to France. Now the Chevalier O'Keefe, Geraldine, had, like myself, one weakness. He was tremendously vulnerable to all kinds and classes of women. Apart from being a sentimentalist he was a romantic, a conceited fellow, a man of fierce passions, a little blind in one eye and nearly stone-blind in the other. Now a male wandering the world in this state is as defenseless as a lion without teeth, and as a result the Chevalier was made completely wretched for twenty years by a succession of women who despised him, exploited him, tired him, irritated him, disgusted him, squandered his money, made a fool of him—in short, as the world puts it, loved him.

"This was terrible, Geraldine, and since the Chevalier was a man of keen insight—except for this single flaw, this overwhelming vulnerability—he decided he would free himself once and for all from these burdens weighing on him. With this goal in mind, he traveled to a renowned monastery in Champagne called—well, known somewhat ironically as St. Voltaire's. The rule at St. Voltaire's dictated that no monk could ever go down to the ground floor of the monastery for as long as he lived, but instead had to spend his existence devoted to prayer and meditation in one of the four towers, which were named after the four principles of the monastery's rule: Poverty, Chastity, Obedience, and Silence."

When the day arrived that would see the Chevalier's final goodbye to the world, he felt completely at peace. He gave all his Greek books to his landlady, sent his sword in a golden sheath to the King of France, and gave all his Irish keepsakes to the young Huguenot who sold fish on the street where he lived.

"Then he rode out to St. Voltaire's, killed his horse at the entrance, and gave the dead animal to the monastery's cook."

"At five o'clock that evening, he experienced freedom for the first time—eternal freedom from sexual desire. No woman was permitted to enter the monastery; no monk was allowed to go below the second floor. As he climbed the spiral staircase leading to his cell at the very top of the Tower of Chastity, he stopped briefly at an open window that overlooked a road fifty feet below. Everything was so magnificent, he reflected, this world he was abandoning—the golden cascade of sunlight pouring down on the expansive fields, the clusters of trees in the distance, the vineyards, peaceful and verdant, stretching for miles ahead of him. He rested his elbows on the window frame and stared at the curving road."

At that very moment, Thérèse, a sixteen-year-old peasant girl from a nearby village, happened to be walking along the same road that passed in front of the monastery. Just five minutes earlier, the small ribbon that held up the stocking on her lovely left leg had worn out and snapped. Being an exceptionally modest young woman, she had planned to wait until she reached home before fixing it, but the loose stocking had become so bothersome that she felt she couldn't bear it any longer. Therefore, as she walked past the Tower of Chastity, she paused and with a graceful movement lifted her skirt—as minimally as possible, it should be noted to her honor—to fix her garter.

High up in the tower, the most recent newcomer to the ancient monastery of St. Voltaire felt as if an enormous and unstoppable force was drawing him forward, compelling him to lean out from the window. He leaned further and further until suddenly one of the stones gave way beneath his weight, breaking free from its mortar with a quiet, dusty crack—and first diving headfirst, then tumbling end over end, finally spinning in a grand and dramatic spiral, Chevalier O'Keefe plummeted toward the unforgiving ground and everlasting condemnation.

Thérèse was so deeply disturbed by what happened that she ran home as fast as she could and spent an hour each day for ten years praying in private for the soul of the monk who had broken both his neck and his vows on that tragic Sunday afternoon.

"And the Chevalier O'Keefe, being suspected of suicide, was not buried in consecrated ground, but was instead thrown into a nearby field, where he undoubtedly enriched the soil for many years that followed. This was the premature end of a very courageous and noble gentleman. What do you think, Geraldine?"

But Geraldine, who had been lost long before this moment, could only respond with a mischievous smile, playfully wag her index finger at him, and repeat her universal explanation, her answer for everything:

"Crazy!" she said, "you cra-a-azy!"

His slender face seemed kind, she thought, and his eyes appeared quite gentle. She found herself drawn to him because he carried himself with confidence without being vain, and because, unlike the men she encountered around the theater, he genuinely disliked drawing attention to himself. What a strange, meaningless tale! Yet she had found pleasure in the section about the stocking!

After his fifth cocktail, he kissed her, and they spent an hour together filled with laughter, playful touches, and bursts of barely contained passion. At four-thirty, she said she had another commitment and went into the bathroom to fix her hair. She wouldn't let him call her a taxi and paused for a moment in the doorway.

"You're going to get married," she kept insisting, "just wait and see."

Anthony was playing with an old tennis ball, and he bounced it carefully on the floor several times before he answered with a hint of sharpness:

"You're a little idiot, Geraldine."

She smiled in a way that was meant to provoke.

"Oh, I am, am I? Want to bet?"

"That would be silly too."

"Oh, it would, would it? Well, I'll just bet you'll marry somebody within a year."

Anthony slammed the tennis ball down hard. This was one of those days when he looked particularly handsome, she thought; some kind of fierce energy had replaced the sadness that usually filled his dark eyes.

"Geraldine," he finally said, "first of all, there's no one I want to marry; second, I don't have enough money to support two people; third, I'm completely against marriage for people like me; and fourth, I have a strong aversion to even thinking about it in theory."

But Geraldine just squinted her eyes with a knowing look, made her clicking sound, and said she had to leave. It was getting late.

"Call me soon," she reminded him as he kissed her goodbye, "you haven't called in three weeks, you know."

"I will," he promised with deep conviction.

He closed the door and walked back into the room, standing there for a moment deep in thought while still holding the tennis ball in his hand. One of his periods of loneliness was approaching, one of those times when he would wander the streets or sit at his desk, feeling aimless and dejected, chewing on a pencil. It was a kind of self-absorption that brought no comfort, a need for expression that had no way out, a feeling that time was rushing past endlessly and pointlessly—only eased by the belief that there was nothing to waste anyway, since all efforts and achievements were equally meaningless.

He thought with deep feeling—speaking out loud, in bursts of emotion, because he was wounded and bewildered.

"No idea of getting married, by God!"

Suddenly he threw the tennis ball violently across the room, where it nearly missed the lamp, and after bouncing around for a moment, came to rest on the floor.

Signlight and Moonlight

For her dinner Gloria had reserved a table at the Cascades in the Biltmore, and when the men gathered in the hallway outside shortly after eight o'clock, "that person Bloeckman" became the focus of six male gazes. He was a somewhat heavy-set, ruddy-complexioned Jewish man of approximately thirty-five years, with an animated face beneath neat sandy-colored hair—and undoubtedly, in most business settings his personality would have been viewed as charming. He walked over to the three younger men, who stood together smoking while they waited for their hostess, and introduced himself with slightly too obvious confidence—yet it's questionable whether he picked up on the subtle cold reception they intended to convey: his demeanor showed no sign that he understood their attitude.

"Are you related to Adam J. Patch?" he asked Anthony, releasing two thin streams of smoke from his unusually wide nostrils.

Anthony acknowledged it with the faintest hint of a smile.

"He's a fine man," Bloeckman declared with deep conviction. "He's an excellent example of an American."

"Yes," Anthony agreed, "he certainly is."

"I can't stand these half-baked men," he thought with cold disdain. "They look like they've been boiled! Someone should shove them back in the oven; just one more minute would finish the job."

Bloeckman squinted at his watch.

"It's about time these girls showed up..."

Anthony waited breathlessly; it came—

"... but then," with a widening smile, "you know how women are."

The three young men nodded in agreement. Bloeckman glanced around the room with a casual air, his gaze settling critically on the ceiling before moving downward. His expression blended the look of a Midwestern farmer evaluating his wheat harvest with that of an actor checking to see if anyone was watching—the typical public demeanor of all respectable Americans. When he completed his examination of the surroundings, he turned back swiftly to the quiet threesome, resolved to get straight to the heart of the matter.

"You college men? ... Harvard, eh. I see the Princeton boys beat you fellows in hockey."

Unfortunate man. He had come up empty-handed once again. They had been away for three years and only paid attention to the major football games. Whether Mr. Bloeckman would have realized he was in a cynical environment after this failed attempt is uncertain, because—

Gloria arrived. Muriel arrived. Rachael arrived. After a quick "Hello, people!" called out by Gloria and repeated by the other two, all three rushed past into the dressing room.

A moment later Muriel appeared in an elaborate state of undress and crept toward them. She was completely in her element: her black hair was slicked straight back against her head; her eyes were artificially darkened; she was drenched in overpowering perfume. She had dressed herself up to the best of her ability as a seductress, more commonly known as a "vamp"—someone who picks up and discards men, an unscrupulous woman who toys with emotions without feeling anything herself. Something about how thoroughly she had committed to this act fascinated Maury immediately—a woman with wide hips trying to move with panther-like grace! As they waited the additional three minutes for Gloria, and by polite pretense, for Rachael, he couldn't look away from her. She would turn her head to the side, lowering her eyelashes and biting her lower lip in an incredible display of shyness. She would place her hands on her hips and sway back and forth in rhythm with the music, saying:

97

"Have you ever heard such perfect ragtime? I just can't keep my shoulders still when I hear that."

Mr. Bloeckman clapped his hands with gallant enthusiasm.

"You should be an actor."

"I'd love to!" Muriel exclaimed. "Will you support me?"

"I sure will."

With appropriate modesty, Muriel stopped her movements and turned to Maury, asking what he had "seen" this year. He understood this as referring to the world of theater, and they had a lively and exciting exchange of titles, in this way:

MURIEL: Have you seen "Peg o' My Heart"?

MAURY: No, I haven't.

MURIEL: (Eagerly) It's wonderful! You want to see it.

MAURY: Have you seen "Omar, the Tentmaker"?

MURIEL: No, but I hear it's wonderful. I'm very anxious to see it. Have you seen "Fair and Warmer"?

MAURY: (Hopefully) Yes.

MURIEL: I don't think it's very good. It's trashy.

MAURY: (Faintly) Yes, that's true.

MURIEL: But I went to "Within the Law" last night and I thought it was excellent. Have you seen "The Little Cafe"?...

This went on until they had no more plays left. In the meantime, Dick focused his attention on Mr. Bloeckman, determined to get whatever value he could from this unpromising situation.

"I hear that all the new novels are being sold to the movie industry as soon as they're published."

"That's true. Of course the main thing in a movie is a compelling story."

"Yes, I suppose so."

"So many novels are filled with dialogue and psychological analysis. Obviously, those aren't as useful to us. It's nearly impossible to make much of that compelling on screen."

"You want plots first," Richard said brilliantly.

"Of course. Plots first—" He stopped mid-sentence and looked away. His pause expanded, drawing in the others with all the commanding presence of a cautionary gesture. Gloria, followed by Rachael, was emerging from the dressing room.

Among other things, it became clear during dinner that Joseph Bloeckman never danced, but instead spent the time when music played watching the others with the bored tolerance of an adult among children. He was a man of dignity and pride. Born in Munich, he had started his American career as a peanut vendor with a traveling circus. At eighteen, he worked as a sideshow barker; later, he became the manager of the sideshow, and soon after that, the owner of a second-rate vaudeville theater. Just when movies had moved beyond being a mere novelty and become a promising industry, he was an ambitious young man of twenty-six with some money to invest, persistent financial ambitions, and a solid working knowledge of the popular entertainment business. That had been nine years earlier. The movie industry had carried him upward with it even as it cast aside dozens of men with greater financial ability, more imagination, and more practical ideas...and now he sat here and gazed at the timeless Gloria for whom young Stuart Holcome had traveled from New York to Pasadena—watched her, and knew that soon she would stop dancing and return to sit on his left side.

He hoped she would hurry. The oysters had been sitting there for several minutes.

Meanwhile Anthony, who had been seated to Gloria's left, was dancing with her, keeping to one particular section of the dance floor. If there had been other men watching, this would have been a subtle message to the girl, essentially saying "Don't let anyone else cut in!" The gesture was deliberately intimate.

"Well," he began, looking down at her, "you look really beautiful tonight."

She looked into his eyes across the six inches of space between them.

"Thank you—Anthony."

"Actually, you're disturbingly beautiful," he said. This time, there was no smile.

"And you're very charming."

"Isn't this nice?" he laughed. "We actually approve of each other."

"Don't you normally?" She had quickly seized on his comment, just as she always did whenever there was any unclear reference to herself, no matter how subtle.

He lowered his voice, and when he spoke, there was only the faintest trace of playful teasing in his tone.

"Does a priest approve the Pope?"

"I don't know—but that's probably the vaguest compliment I've ever gotten."

"Maybe I can come up with a few clichés."

"Well, I wouldn't want you to overexert yourself. Look at Muriel! She's right here beside us."

He looked back over his shoulder. Muriel was pressing her flushed cheek against the lapel of Maury Noble's dinner jacket, and her powdered left arm seemed to be wrapped around his head. It made you wonder why she didn't just grab the back of his neck with her hand. Her eyes, gazing upward toward the ceiling, rolled back and forth dramatically; her hips moved rhythmically, and as she danced she maintained a steady, quiet singing. At first this appeared to be a translation of the song into some foreign language, but it gradually became clear that she was trying to match the rhythm of the song using the only words she knew—the words from the title—

"He's a rag-picker,"

A person who collects rags;

A ragtime guitar player,

Rag-picking, picking, pick, pick,
"Rag-pick, pick, pick."

—and so on, into phrases that became even more strange and primitive. When she noticed the entertained looks from Anthony and Gloria, she responded only with a slight smile and a partial closing of her eyes, showing that the music flowing into her soul had placed her in a blissful and incredibly alluring trance.

The music came to an end and they walked back to their table, where the lone but distinguished guest stood up and gave each of them such a charming smile that it felt as though he was shaking their hands and praising them for an outstanding performance.

"That blockhead will never learn to dance! I think he has a wooden leg," Gloria announced to everyone at the table. The three young men were startled and the gentleman she was talking about visibly flinched.

This was the only difficult point in Bloeckman's relationship with Gloria. She constantly made puns with his name. At first it had been "Block-house," and more recently, the more insulting "Blockhead." He had asked her, with clear irritation in his voice, to call him by his first name instead, and she had complied dutifully several times—but then she would slip back, unable to help herself, feeling sorry but bursting into laughter, to calling him "Blockhead" again.

It was a very sad and thoughtless thing.

"I'm worried that Mr. Bloeckman sees us as a shallow group," Muriel sighed, gesturing toward him with an oyster balanced on her fork.

"He has that quality about him," Rachael whispered. Anthony tried to recall if she had spoken earlier. He didn't think so. This was her first comment.

Mr. Bloeckman suddenly cleared his throat and spoke in a loud, clear voice:

"On the contrary. When a man speaks, he's simply echoing tradition. At most, he has a few thousand years of history behind him. But a woman—she is the extraordinary voice of future generations."

In the shocked silence that came after this incredible statement, Anthony suddenly choked on an oyster and quickly brought his napkin to his face. Rachael and Muriel let out a gentle but somewhat startled laugh, which Dick and Maury joined in on, both of them flushed and clearly struggling to hold back their loud laughter.

"My God!" Anthony thought. "That's a subtitle from one of his films. The guy has memorized it!"

Gloria alone remained silent. She looked at Mr. Bloeckman with a gaze full of quiet disapproval.

"Well, for heaven's sake! Where in the world did you find that?"

Bloeckman glanced at her with uncertainty, unsure of what she meant. Within moments, though, he regained his composure and put on the smooth, deliberately patient smile of someone educated dealing with pampered and immature young people.

The soup arrived from the kitchen—but at the same time the orchestra leader emerged from the bar, where he had soaked up the atmosphere that comes with a large mug of beer. So the soup was left to grow cold while he performed a ballad called "Everything's at Home Except Your Wife."

Then the champagne arrived, and the party took on a more entertaining atmosphere. All the men drank generously, except for Richard Caramel; Gloria and Muriel each had just one glass; Rachael Jerryl didn't drink at all. They skipped the waltzes but danced to all the other songs—everyone except Gloria, who seemed to grow tired after some time and chose to remain at the table smoking, her eyes sometimes drowsy, sometimes alert, depending on whether she was listening to Bloeckman or watching an attractive woman on the dance floor. Anthony found himself wondering several times what Bloeckman was saying to her. He was rolling a cigar back and forth in his mouth, and had become more animated after dinner, making dramatic gestures with his hands.

Ten o'clock found Gloria and Anthony starting to dance. As soon as they moved beyond hearing distance from the table, she spoke quietly:

"Dance over by the door. I want to go down to the drug store."

Anthony obediently guided her through the crowd in the direction she indicated; in the hall she left him briefly, only to return with a cloak draped over her arm.

"I want some gum-drops," she said, with a playful, apologetic tone; "you can't possibly guess what I need them for this time. It's simply that I want to bite my fingernails, and I will if I don't get some gum-drops." She let out a sigh, and continued as they entered the vacant elevator: "I've been biting them all day. A little nervous, you understand. Pardon the pun. It wasn't deliberate— the words just fell into place like that. Gloria Gilbert, the comedic woman."

Reaching the ground floor, they innocently bypassed the hotel candy counter, went down the broad front staircase, and after walking through multiple hallways discovered a pharmacy in Grand Central Station. Following a thorough inspection of the perfume counter, she made her purchase. Then, acting on some shared unspoken impulse, they walked arm in arm, not back the way they had come, but out onto Forty-third Street.

The night pulsed with melting snow and ice; the air was so close to warm that a gentle breeze flowing along the sidewalk gave Anthony a glimpse of an unexpected spring filled with the sweet scent of hyacinths. Up in the rectangular patch of blue sky above them, and all around them in the touch of the drifting air, this feeling of a new season brought relief from the stuffy, stale atmosphere they had just escaped, and for a quiet moment the sounds of traffic and the soft murmur of water running in the gutters felt like a magical and pure extension of the music they had recently been dancing to. When Anthony finally spoke, he was certain that his words came from something breathless and yearning that the night had awakened in both their hearts.

"Let's grab a taxi and drive around for a while!" he suggested, without looking at her.

Oh, Gloria, Gloria!

A taxi waited at the curb with its door open. As it pulled away like a boat navigating a maze-like ocean and disappeared among the shapeless nighttime shadows of the towering buildings, among the sounds that were sometimes quiet, sometimes harsh—the shouts and metallic clanging—Anthony wrapped his arm around the girl, pulled her close to him and kissed her moist, youthful lips.

She remained quiet. She lifted her face toward him, pale beneath the scattered fragments of light that filtered through like moonbeams streaming through leaves. Her eyes shimmered like gentle waves across the white expanse of her face; the dark outline of her hair framed her forehead with an alluring yet distant twilight. Certainly no love existed there; nor any trace of love's touch. Her beauty felt as cool as the humid wind, as cool as the dewy tenderness of her lips.

"You look like a swan in this light," he whispered after a moment. The silences felt as rich and full as any sound. There were quiet moments that seemed ready to break apart, only saved from disappearing by his arms tightening around her and the feeling that she was resting there like a delicate feather that had drifted in from the darkness. Anthony laughed silently and joyfully, turning his face up and away from her, partly from an overwhelming rush of victory, partly so that her seeing him wouldn't ruin the perfect stillness of her expression. That kiss—it was like a flower pressed against his face, impossible to put into words, barely able to be remembered; as if her beauty was sending out waves of itself that settled briefly on his heart before already beginning to fade away.

The buildings faded into blurred shadows; they were in the Park now, and after some time the massive white specter of the Metropolitan Museum glided majestically by, resonating deeply with the sound of the rushing cab.

"Why, Gloria! Why, Gloria!"

Her eyes seemed to look at him from across thousands of years: any emotion she might have felt, any words she might have spoken, would have felt insufficient compared to the completeness of her silence, clumsy against the powerful expression of her beauty— and of her body, near him, slim and cool.

"Tell him to turn around," she whispered, "and drive pretty fast on the way back...."

Up in the dining room, the air was stifling. The table, cluttered with napkins and ashtrays, looked worn and neglected. They walked in during a break between dances, and Muriel Kane glanced up with remarkable mischief in her eyes.

"Well, where have you been?"

"To call my mother," Gloria replied calmly. "I promised her I would. Did we miss a dance?"

Then came an incident that, while minor at the time, would give Anthony reason to think about it for many years to come. Joseph Bloeckman, settling back comfortably in his chair, looked at him with an unusual expression that strangely combined several different emotions in a way that couldn't be separated. He didn't acknowledge Gloria beyond simply standing up, and he quickly returned to his discussion with Richard Caramel about how literature influences movies.

Magic

The best choice depends on your context and audience. "Amazing" or "Incredible" work well for most situations, while "Epic" or "Awesome" feel more casual and modern.

The harsh and surprising miracle of nighttime gradually disappears as the final stars slowly die out and the early newsboys begin their rounds. The fire withdraws to some distant and abstract flame; the white-hot heat has left the iron and the brightness has faded from the coal.

Along the shelves of Anthony's library, which filled an entire wall, a cold and arrogant beam of sunlight crept forward, touching with icy disapproval the books about Thérèse of France and Ann the Superwoman, Jenny of the Orient Ballet and Zuleika the Conjurer—and Hoosier Cora—then moving down a shelf and through the years, resting with pity on the overused shadows of Helen, Thaïs, Salome, and Cleopatra.

Anthony, freshly shaved and bathed, settled into his most comfortable, well-cushioned chair and observed it until the sun's steady ascent caused it to gleam briefly on the silken edges of the rug—then it disappeared.

It was ten o'clock. The Sunday Times lay scattered around his feet, announcing through its photographs and opinion pieces, through society news and sports pages, that the world had been deeply absorbed during the past week in the process of moving toward some magnificent yet rather unclear objective. As for Anthony, he had visited his grandfather once, gone to his broker twice, and made three trips to his tailor—and in the final hour of the week's final day he had kissed a very beautiful and charming girl.

When he arrived home, his mind was overflowing with intense, unfamiliar dreams. Suddenly, there were no questions troubling his thoughts, no eternal problems demanding solutions. He had felt an emotion that wasn't purely mental or physical, nor simply a combination of both, and his love of life completely consumed him, pushing everything else aside. He was satisfied to let this experience stand alone and unrepeatable. With an almost detached certainty, he was convinced that no woman he had ever encountered could compare to Gloria in any way. She was authentically herself; she was genuinely sincere—of this he was absolutely sure. Next to her, the two dozen schoolgirls and debutantes, young wives and lost souls he had known were merely females in the most dismissive sense of the word, creatures meant for breeding and childbearing, still carrying that faintly unpleasant atmosphere of primitive caves and nurseries.

As far as he could tell, she hadn't given in to any of his wishes or flattered his ego—except that her enjoyment of his company was itself a form of flattery. In fact, he had no reason to believe she had given him anything she wouldn't give to others. This was exactly how it should be. The thought of any romantic complications arising from the evening was as unlikely as it would have been unwelcome. And she had dismissed and put the incident to rest with a deliberate lie. Here were two young people with enough imagination to tell the difference between a game and reality—who by the very casual way they met and moved on would prove themselves unaffected.

Having made this decision, he walked over to the telephone and called the Plaza Hotel.

Gloria was out. Her mother didn't know where she had gone or when she would be back.

It was at this moment that the first thing went wrong in the situation. There was something heartless, almost inappropriate, about Gloria not being home. He had a feeling that by going out, she had somehow put him at a disadvantage. When she came back, she would see his name and smile. Very carefully! He should have waited several hours to show how completely unimportant he thought the whole thing was. What a stupid mistake! She would assume he felt specially chosen. She would believe he was responding with clumsy familiarity to something that was really quite minor.

He recalled that the previous month, his building superintendent, whom he had given a somewhat confused speech about "brotherhood of man," had shown up the next day and, based on their conversation from the night before, had settled into the window seat for a friendly and talkative thirty minutes. Anthony was horrified at the thought that Gloria might see him the same way he had viewed that man. Him—Anthony Patch! The horror of it!

He never realized that he was simply a passive object, influenced by forces far greater than Gloria herself, that he was nothing more than the sensitive film on which a photograph was being captured. Some enormous photographer had aimed the camera at Gloria and click!—the helpless film could only process what it received, limited like everything else by its own fundamental nature.

But Anthony lay on his couch, staring at the orange lamp, running his thin fingers constantly through his dark hair as he created new ways to mark the passing time. She was in a store now, he imagined, moving gracefully among the velvets and furs, her own dress creating an elegant rustling sound as she walked through that world of silky whispers, light soprano laughter, and the fragrances of many cut but still-vibrant flowers. The Minnies and Pearls and jewels and Jennies would surround her like attendants at court, carrying delicate wisps of Georgette crepe, fine chiffon that would softly reflect the color of her cheeks in gentle pastels, creamy lace that would lie in soft folds against her neck—damask was only used to cover priests and couches in those days, and cloth of Samarkand was recalled only by romantic poets.

She would eventually move on to other shops, turning her head in countless directions while trying on numerous bonnets, searching unsuccessfully for artificial cherries that would complement her lips or feathers that could match the elegance of her own flexible figure.

Noon would arrive—she would rush down Fifth Avenue, like a Nordic Ganymede, her fur coat swaying stylishly with each step, her cheeks flushed red from the wind's touch, her breath forming a charming cloud in the crisp air—and the Ritz's revolving doors would turn, the crowd would part, fifty men's eyes would snap to attention and gaze, as she reminded the husbands of numerous overweight and ridiculous women of dreams they had long forgotten.

One o'clock. She would tease the heart of a beloved artichoke with her fork, while her companion presented himself through the rich, flowing words of a man completely captivated.

Four o'clock: her small feet moving to the rhythm, her face clear among the crowd, her dance partner as happy as a spoiled puppy and as crazy as a mad hatter.... Then—then evening would drift down and perhaps bring another humid night. The neon signs would pour their light onto the street. Who could tell? No more knowledgeable than he was, they perhaps tried to recreate that image painted in cream and shadow they had witnessed on the quiet Avenue the previous night. And they just might, oh, they just might! A thousand taxi cabs would wait at a thousand street corners, and only for him was that kiss lost forever and finished. In a thousand different forms Thaïs would call a taxi and lift her face for love. And her pale complexion would be pure and beautiful, and her kiss innocent as the moon....

He jumped up excitedly. How wrong it was that she wasn't there! He had finally understood what he wanted—to kiss her once more, to find peace in her profound stillness. She represented the end of all his restlessness, all his dissatisfaction.

Anthony got dressed and left his room, something he should have done much earlier, and headed down to Richard Caramel's room to listen to the final revision of the last chapter of "The Demon Lover." He didn't call Gloria again until six o'clock. He couldn't reach her until eight, and—what a disappointing turn of events!—she couldn't meet with him until Tuesday afternoon. A broken piece of rubber fell to the floor with a clatter as he slammed down the phone.

Black Magic

Tuesday was bitterly cold. He arrived at a dreary two o'clock, and as they shook hands he found himself wondering in confusion whether he had ever kissed her; it seemed almost impossible to believe—he genuinely questioned whether she even remembered it.

"I called you four times on Sunday," he told her.

"Did you?"

There was surprise in her voice and curiosity in her expression. He silently berated himself for having revealed this to her. He should have realized that her pride wouldn't stoop to such trivial victories. Even at that moment, he hadn't understood the real truth—that since she'd never needed to worry about attracting men, she rarely employed the cautious schemes, the strategic advances and retreats, that were the standard tools of other women. When she found a man appealing, that alone was strategy enough. If she believed she loved him—that became her final and devastating weapon. Her allure remained perpetually intact.

"I was eager to see you," he said simply. "I want to talk to you—I mean really talk, somewhere where we can be alone. May I?"

"What do you mean?"

He gulped down a sudden surge of panic. He sensed that she understood what he was after.

"I mean, not at a tea table," he said.

"Well, all right, but not today. I want to get some exercise. Let's walk!"

The weather was harsh and biting. All the malicious fury from February's wild heart had been woven into the desolate and freezing wind that sliced mercilessly through Central Park and swept down Fifth Avenue. Conversation was nearly impossible, and the discomfort left him so distracted that when he turned at Sixty-first Street, he discovered she was no longer walking beside him. He glanced around. She stood forty feet behind him, completely still, her face partially concealed by her fur coat collar, displaying what appeared to be either anger or amusement—he couldn't tell which. He began walking back toward her.

"Don't let me interrupt your walk!" she called.

"I'm really sorry," he replied, looking confused. "Did I go too fast?"

"I'm cold," she said. "I want to go home. And you walk too fast."

"I'm very sorry."

Side by side they headed toward the Plaza. He wished he could see her face.

"Men don't usually become so self-absorbed when they're around me."

"I'm sorry."

"That's very interesting."

"It's a bit too cold for walking," he said briskly, trying to conceal his irritation.

She didn't respond, and he wondered if she would send him away at the hotel entrance. However, she walked inside without saying a word and headed to the elevator, tossing him just one comment as she stepped into it:

"You'd better come up."

He paused for just a split second.

"Maybe I should call back at a different time."

"Exactly as you say." She spoke these words quietly, almost to herself. What really mattered to her at that moment was fixing a few loose strands of hair in the elevator mirror. Her cheeks glowed with color, her eyes shone brightly—she had never appeared so beautiful, so perfectly desirable.

Filled with self-loathing, he discovered he was trailing behind her like a servant as they walked down the tenth-floor hallway; he stood in the living room while she vanished to remove her fur coats. Something had gone awry—he felt he had surrendered a piece of his self-respect; in an unexpected but meaningful confrontation, he had been utterly crushed.

However, by the time she returned to the living room, he had rationalized his actions to his own satisfaction through clever self-deception. After all, he had done the most decisive thing possible, he believed. He had wanted to come upstairs, and he had done it. Yet what occurred later that afternoon must be attributed to the humiliation he had endured in the elevator; the girl was troubling him unbearably, to such an extent that when she emerged he unconsciously began to find fault with her.

"Who is this Bloeckman, Gloria?"

"A business friend of father's."

"What a strange guy!"

"He doesn't like you either," she said with a sudden smile.

Anthony laughed.

"I'm flattered by his attention. He clearly thinks of me as a—" He stopped abruptly and asked, "Is he in love with you?"

"I don't know."

"Like hell you don't," he insisted. "Of course he is. I remember the look he gave me when we got back to the table. He probably would have had me quietly beaten up by a group of movie executives if you hadn't made up that phone call."

"He didn't mind. I told him afterward what really happened."

"You told him!"

"He asked me."

"I don't like that very much," he protested.

She laughed again.

"Oh, you don't?"

"What business is it of his?"

"None. That's why I told him."

Anthony, in a state of turmoil, bit savagely at his mouth.

"Why would I lie?" she asked bluntly. "I'm not embarrassed about anything I've done. He was curious to know whether I had kissed you, and since I was feeling cooperative at the time, I gave him a straightforward 'yes' to satisfy his curiosity. Being a reasonably intelligent man in his own way, he let the matter drop."

"Except to say that he hated me."

"Oh, it worries you? Well, if you must explore this incredible situation thoroughly, he didn't actually say he hated you. I just know that he does."

"It doesn't work——"

"Oh, let's drop it!" she exclaimed with energy. "It's completely uninteresting to me."

With enormous effort, Anthony managed to turn his agreement into a change of topic, and they slipped into a familiar back-and-forth game about their personal histories, slowly growing more comfortable as they found the timeless, eternal similarities in their preferences and thoughts. They shared things that revealed more than they meant to—but each acted as though they were taking the other at face value, or more accurately, at word value.

The development of close relationships follows a similar pattern. At first, we present our finest image—a polished and complete version of ourselves, patched up with bravado, lies, and wit. Then more information becomes necessary, so we create a second version of ourselves, then a third—eventually our best features start to contradict each other, and our true nature is finally revealed. The different layers of our personas have blended together and betrayed us, and no matter how much we try to reinvent ourselves, we can no longer convince anyone. We have to settle for hoping that the foolish stories we tell about ourselves to our spouses, children, and colleagues will be believed as truth.

"It seems to me," Anthony said with genuine conviction, "that a man who has neither pressing needs nor driving ambition finds himself in an unfortunate position. God knows it would be pathetic for me to feel sorry for myself—but sometimes I find myself envying Dick."

Her silence served as encouragement. It was the closest she ever came to deliberately enticing someone.

"—And there used to be respectable careers for a gentleman who had free time, activities that were somewhat more productive than polluting the scenery with smoke or manipulating someone else's finances. There's science, naturally: sometimes I wish I had gotten a solid education, perhaps at Boston Tech. But now, by God, I would have to spend two years working through the basic principles of physics and chemistry."

She yawned.

"I've told you I don't know what anyone should do," she said rudely, and her indifference sparked his resentment once more.

"Aren't you interested in anything except yourself?"

"Not much."

He glared; his increasing pleasure in their conversation was torn apart. She had been irritable and spiteful all day, and it felt to him that in this moment he despised her cruel selfishness. He gazed gloomily at the fire.

Then something strange happened. She turned toward him and smiled, and when he saw that smile, every trace of anger and wounded pride fell away from him—as if his emotions were merely the surface ripples of her own feelings, as if no emotion could arise in his heart unless she chose to pull some all-powerful controlling string.

He stepped closer and, taking her hand, drew her gently toward him until she was half-reclining against his shoulder. She looked up at him with a smile as he kissed her.

"Gloria," he whispered very quietly. Once again she had created a kind of magic, delicate and all-encompassing like spilled perfume, impossible to resist and utterly sweet.

Afterward, neither the next day nor after many years, could he remember the important things of that afternoon. Had she been moved? In his arms had she spoken a little—or at all? What measure of enjoyment had she taken in his kisses? And had she at any time lost herself ever so little?

Oh, he had no doubt whatsoever. He had gotten up and walked back and forth across the room in pure joy. That such a girl could exist; that she would sit curled up in the corner of the couch like a swallow that had just landed from a graceful, swift flight, watching him with mysterious eyes. He would stop walking and, feeling somewhat shy at first each time, put his arm around her and find her lips with his.

She was captivating, he told her. He had never encountered anyone like her before. He pleaded with her in a lighthearted yet sincere way to make him leave; he didn't want to fall in love. He wasn't going to visit her anymore—she had already invaded too many aspects of his life.

What wonderful romance! His genuine response wasn't fear or sadness—just this profound joy in being with her that transformed his ordinary words and made the sentimental seem melancholy and the pretentious seem insightful. He would return—forever. He should have realized!

"This is all. It's been very rare to have known you, very strange and wonderful. But this wouldn't work—and wouldn't last." As he spoke, there was a trembling in his heart that we mistake for sincerity in ourselves.

Afterward he remembered one of her responses to something he had asked her. He recalled it in this particular way—perhaps he had unconsciously organized and refined it:

115

"A woman should be able to kiss a man beautifully and romantically without any desire to be either his wife or his mistress."

As always when he was with her, she seemed to slowly age until eventually thoughts too profound for words would settle in her eyes like winter.

An hour went by, and the fire flared up in small bursts of joy as if its dying flames were delightful. It was now five o'clock, and the clock above the fireplace began to chime audibly. Then, as if some crude awareness within him was awakened by those sharp, metallic sounds reminding him that the beauty of the flowery afternoon was slipping away, Anthony swiftly pulled her to her feet and held her powerless, breathless, in a kiss that was neither playful nor respectful.

Her arms dropped to her sides. In that moment, she was free.

"Don't!" she said quietly. "I don't want that."

She settled into a seat on the opposite side of the living room and stared directly ahead. A worried expression had formed between her eyebrows. Anthony dropped down next to her and placed his hand over hers. Her hand felt cold and didn't respond to his touch.

"Why, Gloria!" He started to put his arm around her, but she pulled away.

"I don't want that," she repeated.

"I'm very sorry," he said, with a hint of impatience in his voice. "I—I had no idea you drew such precise distinctions."

She didn't respond.

"Won't you kiss me, Gloria?"

"I don't want to." It seemed to him she had not moved for hours.

"A sudden change, isn't it?" Irritation was building in his voice.

"Is it?" She seemed uninterested. It was almost as if she were looking at someone else.

"Maybe I should leave."

No response came. He stood up and looked at her with anger and uncertainty. He sat back down again.

"Gloria, Gloria, won't you kiss me?"

"No." Her lips, barely moving to form the word, had only slightly trembled.

Once again he stood up, this time with less determination and less certainty.

"Then I'll go."

Silence.

"All right—I'll go."

He recognized that his comments lacked any real originality, and there was nothing he could do to fix that. The entire atmosphere had become suffocating. He desperately wanted her to say something—to yell at him, to lash out, anything except this overwhelming and cold silence that filled the space between them. He called himself a pathetic fool; what he wanted most was to get a reaction from her, to cause her pain, to watch her flinch. Without meaning to and unable to stop himself, he made another mistake.

"If you're tired of kissing me I'd better go."

He noticed her lips curve into a slight smile, and whatever dignity he had left completely abandoned him. Finally, she spoke:

"I think you've said that several times already."

He glanced around right away, spotted his hat and coat on a chair, and fumbled into them during an unbearable moment. When he looked back at the couch, he noticed that she hadn't turned around or even shifted position. With a trembling "goodbye" that he instantly wished he could take back, he left the room quickly but without any grace.

For more than a moment, Gloria remained silent. Her lips were still curved; her gaze was direct, proud, and distant. Then her eyes became slightly unfocused, and she whispered three words quietly to the dying fire:

"Goodbye, you idiot!" she said.

Crisis

The man had experienced the most devastating blow of his life. He finally understood what he truly wanted, but in discovering this, it seemed he had placed it permanently out of reach. He arrived home in anguish, collapsed into an armchair without bothering to take off his overcoat, and remained there for more than an hour, his thoughts racing through endless cycles of pointless and miserable self-pity. She had dismissed him! This was the constant refrain of his despair. Rather than grabbing the woman and holding her through pure physical force until she surrendered to his wishes, rather than crushing her resistance with the power of his own determination, he had walked away from her doorstep, defeated and helpless, with his mouth turned downward and whatever strength might have existed in his pain and anger concealed behind the demeanor of a beaten child. One moment she had been tremendously fond of him—indeed, she had almost loved him. The next moment he had become meaningless to her, an arrogant and thoroughly humiliated man.

He felt little guilt about himself—some, naturally, but other feelings dominated him now, much more pressing. He wasn't simply in love with Gloria; he was obsessed with her. Unless he could be near her again, kiss her, hold her close and willing, he wanted nothing else from life. Through those three minutes of complete, unwavering coldness, the girl had elevated herself from an important but somewhat casual place in his thoughts to become his total obsession. No matter how wildly his thoughts swung between passionate longing for her kisses and an equally passionate urge to hurt and damage her, the deeper part of his mind yearned in a more refined way to possess the victorious spirit that had revealed itself during those three minutes. She was beautiful—but more than that, she was merciless. He had to own that power that could dismiss him so completely.

At this moment, Anthony couldn't perform any such analysis. His mental clarity and all those countless resources he believed his ironic perspective had given him were completely overwhelmed. Not just for that evening, but for the days and weeks ahead, his books would become nothing more than decorative objects and his friends merely individuals who existed and moved through a hazy, distant world he was attempting to flee from—that world felt cold and filled with harsh, bitter wind, and for a brief moment he had glimpsed inside a cozy home where warm fires glowed.

Around midnight, he started to feel hungry. He walked down to Fifty-second Street, where the cold was so intense he could barely see; moisture turned to ice on his eyelashes and at the corners of his mouth. A bleak chill had descended from the north, blanketing the narrow, joyless street where dark, bundled figures, even darker against the night, stumbled along the sidewalk through the howling wind, carefully sliding their feet forward as if they were skiing. Anthony headed toward Sixth Avenue, so lost in his thoughts that he didn't notice several people staring at him as they passed. His coat hung wide open, and the wind cut through him, sharp and filled with ruthless cold.

After some time, a waitress approached him—a heavy-set woman wearing black-rimmed glasses with a long black cord hanging from them.

"Order, please!"

Her voice, he thought, was louder than it needed to be. He glanced up with irritation.

"Do you want to order or not?"

"Of course," he protested.

"Well, I asked you three times. This isn't a restroom."

He looked at the large clock and realized with surprise that it was past two o'clock. He was somewhere down near Thirtieth Street, and after a moment he located and interpreted the

The illustration displays the word "CHILD's" reflected in a mirror.

in white semicircular lettering across the glass storefront. The establishment was occupied by only three or four grim and nearly frozen night owls.

"Give me some bacon and eggs and coffee, please."

The waitress gave him one final look of disgust and, appearing absurdly scholarly in her thick-rimmed glasses, quickly walked away.

God! Gloria's kisses had been like flowers. He remembered her voice's gentle freshness as if it were years ago, the graceful curves of her body visible through her clothing, her face pale as a lily beneath the streetlights—beneath those glowing lamps.

Misery hit him once more, adding a kind of terror to the pain and longing he already felt. He had lost her. That was the truth—there was no denying it, no making it easier to bear. But a fresh thought had burned across his mind—what about Bloeckman! What would happen now? Here was a wealthy man, old enough to be patient with a beautiful wife, to spoil her whims and put up with her unreasonable behavior, to display her as she might want to be displayed—a lovely flower in his lapel, protected and safe from the things that frightened her. He sensed that she had been toying with the thought of marrying Bloeckman, and it was entirely possible that this letdown with Anthony might push her suddenly into Bloeckman's waiting arms.

The thought made him lose control like a child having a tantrum. He desperately wanted to kill Bloeckman and make him pay for his disgusting arrogance. He kept repeating this to himself with his jaw clenched tight, his eyes filled with an overwhelming mixture of hatred and terror.

But beneath this shameful jealousy, Anthony had finally fallen in love—deeply and genuinely in love, in the truest sense of what love means between a man and a woman.

His coffee arrived beside him and released a thin trail of steam that slowly faded away. The night manager, sitting at his desk, looked over at the still figure sitting alone at the far table, then with a sigh got up and walked toward him just as the hour hand moved past three on the large clock.

Wisdom

After another day passed, the chaos settled down and Anthony started to think more clearly. He was in love—he declared this to himself with intense passion. The obstacles that just a week earlier would have seemed impossible to overcome, his modest income, his longing to remain carefree and independent, had within these forty hours turned into nothing more than dust in the wind of his obsession. If he didn't marry her, his life would become a weak imitation of his own youth. To be able to face other people and bear the constant reminders of Gloria that his entire existence had become, he needed to have hope. So he constructed hope desperately and stubbornly from the material of his dreams, a hope fragile enough, certainly, a hope that shattered and dissolved dozens of times each day, a hope born from ridicule, but still, a hope that would give strength and substance to his self-respect.

Out of this emerged a spark of wisdom, a genuine insight that arose from his effortless past.

"Memory is short," he thought.

So incredibly brief. At the critical moment, the Trust President stands trial, a potential criminal who needs only one final push to become a convict, despised by honest people for miles around. Should he be found not guilty—within a year, everything is erased from memory. "Yes, he did experience some difficulties once, merely a technicality, I think." Oh, how fleeting memory truly is!

Anthony had encountered Gloria roughly twelve times in total, perhaps twenty-four hours altogether. What if he stayed away from her for an entire month, making no effort to see her or talk to her, and steering clear of every location where she might appear? Wouldn't it be likely, even more likely since she had never been in love with him, that by the end of that period the whirlwind of daily life would erase his presence from her thoughts, and along with his presence, his wrongdoing and shame? She would move on, because there would be other men. He flinched. The reality hit him hard—other men. Two months—Dear God! Better make it three weeks, two weeks——

He had this thought on the second evening following the disaster as he was getting undressed, and at that moment he collapsed onto the bed and remained there, shaking just a little and staring up at the canopy above him.

Two weeks—that would be even worse than no time at all. In two weeks he would approach her in much the same way he would have to approach her now, lacking any sense of personality or confidence—still being the same man who had overstepped his bounds and then, for what lasted only a moment in time but felt like an eternity in reality, had whined pathetically. No, two weeks simply wasn't enough time. Whatever emotional impact that afternoon had created for her needed time to fade away. He had to allow her a period where the incident would gradually disappear from her mind, followed by another period when she would slowly start to think of him again, even if only faintly, with genuine perspective that would recall his pleasant qualities alongside his embarrassing behavior.

He decided, at last, that six weeks would be roughly the right amount of time for what he had in mind, and he used a desk calendar to count off the days, discovering that it would land on April ninth. Fine, on that date he would call and ask if he could come see her. Until that moment—complete silence.

After making his decision, a gradual improvement became apparent. He had taken at least one step in the direction that hope was pointing toward, and he understood that the less he dwelled on thoughts of her, the better he would be able to make the impression he wanted when they eventually met.

In another hour he fell into a deep sleep.

The Interval

Nevertheless, as the days went by, the radiance of her hair gradually faded in his mind, and during a year of being apart it might have vanished entirely, but those six weeks contained many terrible days. He feared encountering Dick and Maury, wildly imagining that they knew everything—but when the three got together it was Richard Caramel and not Anthony who became the focus of everyone's attention; "The Demon Lover" had been accepted for immediate publication. Anthony felt that from this point forward he existed separately from others. He no longer yearned for the comfort and safety of Maury's companionship which had lifted his spirits as recently as November. Only Gloria could provide that now and no one else would ever be able to again. So Dick's success brought him only mild happiness and caused him considerable worry. It meant that the world was moving forward—writing and reading and publishing—and living. And he wanted the world to remain still and hold its breath for six weeks—while Gloria forgot.

Two Encounters

His greatest joy came from spending time with Geraldine. He took her out to dinner and a show once, and had her over to his place several times. When he was around her, she completely captivated his attention, though not in the same way Gloria had, but rather by calming those passionate feelings that had troubled him when it came to Gloria. It didn't matter how he kissed Geraldine. A kiss was simply a kiss—something to be fully enjoyed for its brief moment. For Geraldine, everything had its proper place: a kiss was one thing, anything beyond that was something entirely different; a kiss was acceptable; those other things were "wrong."

When half the time period had passed, two events happened on back-to-back days that disturbed his growing peace of mind and led to a brief setback.

The first was—he saw Gloria. It was a brief encounter. Both nodded. Both said something, yet neither listened to what the other was saying. But when it ended, Anthony read through a column of The Sun three times in a row without comprehending a single sentence.

You'd think Sixth Avenue would be a safe street! After deciding not to use his regular barber at the Plaza, he walked around the corner one morning to get a shave, and while waiting for his turn he removed his coat and vest, standing near the front of the shop with his soft collar unbuttoned at the neck. The day felt like an oasis in the cold wasteland of March, and the sidewalk was lively with people strolling and soaking up the sun. A heavy woman dressed in velvet, her sagging cheeks clearly over-massaged, swept past with her poodle pulling on its leash—creating the impression of a tugboat hauling in a cruise ship. Right behind them, a man wearing a striped blue suit, walking awkwardly in white spats, smiled at the scene and caught Anthony's attention, winking at him through the window. Anthony burst out laughing, suddenly finding himself in that mood where men and women seemed like clumsy and ridiculous figures, strangely shaped and contorted in a geometric world of their own making. They triggered the same feelings in him as those bizarre and alien fish that live in the mysterious green depths of aquarium tanks.

Two more people walking by caught his attention casually, a man and a woman—then in a horrifying moment the woman turned out to be Gloria. He stood there helpless; they walked closer and Gloria, looking inside, spotted him. Her eyes grew wide and she gave him a polite smile. Her lips moved. She was less than five feet away.

"How are you doing?" he mumbled pointlessly.

Gloria, happy, beautiful, and young—with a man he had never seen before!

It was at that moment when the barber's chair became empty and he read through the newspaper column three times one after another.

The second incident happened the following day. When he walked into the Manhattan bar around seven o'clock, he came face to face with Bloeckman. As luck would have it, the room was almost empty, and before they recognized each other, he had positioned himself within a foot of the older man and placed his drink order, making conversation between them unavoidable.

"Hello, Mr. Patch," said Bloeckman in a friendly enough manner.

Anthony took the offered hand and exchanged a few brief remarks about the changes in temperature.

"Do you come here often?" Bloeckman asked.

"No, very seldom." He chose not to mention that the Plaza bar had been his preferred spot until recently.

"Nice bar. One of the best bars in town."

Anthony nodded. Bloeckman finished his drink and picked up his walking stick. He was wearing formal evening attire.

"Well, I'll be hurrying on. I'm going to dinner with Miss Gilbert."

Death suddenly stared out at him from two blue eyes. If he had announced himself as his companion's future killer, he couldn't have delivered a more devastating blow to Anthony. The younger man must have turned visibly red, as every nerve in his body immediately screamed in alarm. With enormous effort, he managed a stiff—incredibly stiff—smile and offered a polite farewell. But that night he stayed awake until after four o'clock, nearly mad with sorrow, terror, and horrible thoughts.

Challenges

And one day during the fifth week, he picked up the phone to call her. He had been sitting in his apartment attempting to read "Sentimental Education," when something in the book triggered his thoughts to race in the direction they always went when left unchecked, like horses galloping toward their home stable. With his breathing suddenly quickening, he walked over to the telephone. When he spoke the number, it seemed to him that his voice cracked and broke like a young boy's. The operator must have been able to hear his heart pounding. The sound of the receiver being picked up on the other end felt like a death knell, and Mrs. Gilbert's voice, smooth as maple syrup pouring into a glass container, carried a terrifying quality for him in her simple "Hello-o-ah?"

"Miss Gloria isn't feeling well. She's resting in bed, sleeping. Who should I tell her stopped by?"

"Nobody!" he shouted.

In a wild panic he slammed down the phone; he collapsed into his armchair in a cold sweat of breathless relief.

Serenade

"Why did you cut your hair so short?" was the first thing he said to her, and she replied: "Yes, doesn't it look amazing?"

It wasn't trendy back then. It would become trendy in five or six years. At that time, it was thought to be extremely bold.

"It's beautiful and sunny outside," he said seriously. "Don't you want to go for a walk?"

She put on a light coat and a charming Napoleon hat in Alice Blue, and they strolled down the avenue to the zoo, where they dutifully admired the magnificent elephant and marveled at the towering height of the giraffe's neck, but they skipped the monkey house because Gloria complained that monkeys had such a terrible smell.

Then they walked back toward the Plaza, chatting about trivial things, but happy about the spring music floating through the air and the warm, soothing atmosphere that had settled over the suddenly gleaming city. The Park stretched out to their right, while on their left a massive structure of granite and marble seemed to mumble quietly a wealthy person's confused declaration to anyone willing to hear: something along the lines of "I labored and I put money aside and I was cleverer than everyone else and here I am, by God, by God!"

All the latest and most stunning car designs were displayed along Fifth Avenue, and the Plaza Hotel rose before them, appearing unusually bright and appealing. The graceful, leisurely Gloria walked just a few steps ahead of him, offering relaxed, offhand remarks that drifted briefly through the brilliant air before reaching his ears.

"Oh!" she exclaimed, "I want to go south to Hot Springs! I want to get outside in the fresh air and just roll around on the new grass and forget that winter ever existed."

"Don't you, though!"

"I want to hear a million robins making a frightful racket. I sort of like birds."

"All women are birds," he suggested.

"What kind am I?"—quick and eager.

"I believe she's a swallow, and occasionally a bird of paradise. Most girls are sparrows, naturally—do you see that line of nursemaids over there? They're sparrows—or perhaps they're magpies? And surely you've encountered canary girls—and robin girls."

"And swan girls and parrot girls. All grown women are hawks, I think, or owls."

"What am I—a buzzard?"

She laughed and shook her head.

"Oh, no, you're not a bird at all, are you? You're a Russian wolfhound."

Anthony recalled that they appeared pale and consistently seemed unnaturally starved. However, since they were typically photographed alongside dukes and princesses, he felt appropriately flattered.

"Dick is a fox terrier, a performing fox terrier," she went on.

"And Maury's a cat." At the same time, it struck him how much Bloeckman resembled a sturdy and repulsive pig. But he kept his thoughts to himself and remained diplomatically quiet.

Later, when they said goodbye, Anthony asked when he could see her again.

"Don't you ever make plans that last a long time?" he asked hopefully, "even if it's a week from now, I think it would be fun to spend an entire day together, both morning and afternoon."

"It would be, wouldn't it?" She paused to think for a moment. "Let's do it next Sunday."

"All right. I'll create a schedule that will fill every minute."

He did exactly that. He even calculated precisely what would unfold during the two hours when she would visit his apartment for tea: how the reliable Bounds would open the windows wide to welcome the fresh breeze—while also keeping a fire burning in case there was any chill in the air—and how there would be arrangements of flowers displayed in large, cool bowls that he would purchase specially for the occasion. They would sit together on the sofa.

When the day arrived, they sat together on the couch. After some time, Anthony kissed her because it felt completely natural; he discovered sweetness still resting on her lips and felt as though he had never left. The fire burned brightly and the breeze whispering through the curtains carried a soft dampness that promised May and a world of summer ahead. His spirit responded to distant melodies; he could hear the strumming of guitars far away and waves gently washing against a warm Mediterranean coastline—for he was as young now as he would ever be, and more victorious than death itself.

Six o'clock arrived too quickly and chimed the complaining melody of St. Anne's bells on the corner. Through the deepening twilight they walked to the Avenue, where the crowds, like freed prisoners, were finally walking with bouncing steps after the long winter, and the tops of the buses were packed with cheerful companions and the stores full of beautiful soft items for the summer, the precious summer, the joyful promising summer that seemed for love what winter was for money. Life was performing for its dinner on the corner! Life was serving cocktails in the street! There were old women in that crowd who felt they could have sprinted and won a hundred-yard race!

That night in bed with the lights turned off and the cool room bathed in moonlight, Anthony stayed awake and savored every moment of the day like a child playing with each treasured Christmas gift from a long-awaited pile. He had whispered to her tenderly, almost while they were kissing, that he loved her, and she had smiled and pulled him closer and whispered back, "I'm glad," gazing into his eyes. There had been something different in her manner, a fresh surge of pure physical desire for him and an unusual emotional intensity, which was powerful enough to make him clench his fists and catch his breath when he remembered it. He had felt closer to her than he ever had before. Overwhelmed with joy, he called out to the empty room that he loved her.

He called the next morning—without any hesitation now, without any uncertainty—instead filled with an ecstatic excitement that doubled and tripled when he heard her voice:

"Good morning—Gloria."

"Good morning."

"That's all I called to tell you, dear."

"I'm glad you did."

"I wish I could see you."

"You will, tomorrow night."

"That's a long time, isn't it?"

"Yes—" Her voice sounded hesitant. He gripped the phone tighter.

"Couldn't I come tonight?" He was willing to risk everything in the glory and revelation of that almost whispered "yes."

"I have a date."

"Oh—"

"But I might—I might be able to break it."

"Oh!"—a pure cry, a rhapsody. "Gloria?"

"What?"

"I love you."

Another pause and then:

"I—I'm glad."

Happiness, Maury Noble once observed, is simply the first hour following relief from particularly severe suffering. But Anthony's expression as he made his way down the tenth-floor hallway of the Plaza that evening! His dark eyes sparkled—the lines around his mouth were a joy to witness. He looked more handsome in that moment than ever before, heading toward one of those timeless instances that arrive so brilliantly that their lingering glow provides illumination for years to come.

He knocked and, when invited in, stepped through the doorway. Gloria, wearing a simple pink dress that was crisp and fresh like a newly bloomed flower, stood motionless on the far side of the room, staring at him with wide, startled eyes.

As he shut the door behind him, she let out a soft cry and quickly crossed the space between them, her arms lifting in anticipation of an embrace as she approached. Together they pressed against the rigid creases of her dress in one victorious and lasting hug.

Book Two

Chapter I: The Radiant Hour

After two weeks, Anthony and gloria started having what they called "Practical Discussions" - those conversations where they pretended to be realistic while actually walking together in a romantic, dreamlike state.

"Not as much as I love you," the literary critic would insist. "If you truly loved me, you'd want everyone to know it."

"I do," she protested; "I want to stand on the street corner like someone wearing a sandwich board, telling everyone who walks by."

"Then tell me all the reasons why you're going to marry me in June."

"Well, it's because you're so clean. You have this fresh, natural kind of cleanliness, just like me. There are two different types, you see. One is like Dick: his cleanliness is like polished cookware. You and I are clean in the way that flowing streams and breezes are clean. I can always tell when I look at someone whether they're clean, and if they are, I can tell which type of cleanliness they have."

"We're twins."

Ecstatic thought!

"Mother says"—she paused with uncertainty—"mother says that two souls are sometimes formed together and—and fall in love before they're even born."

Bilphism gained its easiest convert.... After some time, he raised his head and laughed silently at the ceiling. When he looked back at her, he noticed she was angry.

"Why did you laugh?" she demanded. "You've done that twice before. There's nothing amusing about how we relate to each other. I don't mind acting foolish, and I don't mind when you do it, but I can't bear it when we're both doing it at the same time."

"I'm sorry."

"Oh, don't apologize! If you can't come up with anything better than that, just stay quiet!"

"I love you."

"I don't care."

There was a pause. Anthony felt dejected.... Eventually Gloria whispered:

"I'm sorry I was mean."

"You weren't. I was the one."

Peace returned—the moments that followed were incredibly sweet, intense, and deeply moving. They became performers on this stage, each acting for an audience of just two: the intensity of their performance made it real. Here, at last, was the purest form of self-expression—though it seemed likely that most of the time their love revealed more about Gloria than about Anthony. He frequently felt like an barely welcome guest at a party she was hosting.

Telling Mrs. Gilbert had been an awkward situation. She sat squeezed into a small chair and listened with an intense and very blinking kind of focus. She must have realized it—for three weeks Gloria had seen no one else—and she must have observed that this time there was a genuine change in her daughter's behavior. She had been asked to mail special deliveries; she had paid attention to, as all mothers seem to notice, the nearby end of phone conversations, concealed but still quite affectionate—

Yet she had gracefully expressed surprise and said she was tremendously delighted; she undoubtedly was; just as the geranium plants blooming in the window boxes were, and just as the cab drivers were when the lovers looked for romantic solitude in horse-drawn carriages—charming contraption—and the formal menus on which they wrote "you know I do," sliding it across for the other to read.

But Anthony and this golden girl argued constantly between their kisses.

"Now, Gloria," he would cry, "please let me explain!"

"Don't explain. Kiss me."

"I don't think that's right. If I hurt your feelings, we should talk about it. I don't like this kiss-and-forget approach."

"But I don't want to argue. I think it's wonderful that we can kiss and make up, and when we can't, it'll be time to argue."

At one point, some trivial disagreement grew so significant that Anthony got up and angrily shoved himself into his overcoat—for a moment it seemed like the scene from the previous February would happen all over again, but understanding how deeply upset she was, he maintained his composure along with his pride, and within moments Gloria was crying in his arms, her beautiful face as miserable as a scared little girl's.

Meanwhile they continued revealing themselves to each other, reluctantly, through strange responses and avoidance, through dislikes and biases and accidental glimpses of their past. The girl was too proud to feel jealous and, since he was intensely jealous himself, this quality irritated him. He deliberately shared obscure stories from his own past to try to provoke even a hint of jealousy in her, but it was useless. She had him now—she had no interest in the years that were gone.

"Oh, Anthony," she would say, "whenever I'm cruel to you, I always regret it later. I'd give anything to spare you even a moment's suffering."

And in that moment her eyes filled with tears, though she didn't realize she was expressing something that wasn't real. But Anthony understood that there were times when they deliberately hurt each other—almost enjoying the pain they inflicted. She constantly confused him: one moment so close and delightful, desperately trying to reach some unknown, perfect connection; the next, quiet and distant, seemingly unaffected by their love or anything he might say. Eventually he would often discover that these ominous silences stemmed from some physical discomfort—which she never mentioned until it passed—or from some thoughtlessness or arrogance on his part, or from an unsatisfying meal at dinner, but even then the ways in which she created the vast emotional distances that surrounded her remained a puzzle, hidden somewhere deep within those twenty-two years of constant pride.

"Why do you like Muriel?" he asked one day.

"I don't very much."

"Then why do you go with her?"

"Just to have someone to go with. Those girls aren't any trouble at all. They basically believe everything I tell them—but I actually like Rachael. I think she's attractive—and so neat and polished, don't you think? I used to have other friends—in Kansas City and at school—all of them casual acquaintances, girls who simply drifted into my life and out of it for no other reason than that boys would take us places together. They stopped interesting me once circumstances no longer brought us together. Now most of them are married. What difference does it make—they were all just ordinary people."

"You prefer men, don't you?"

"Oh, much better. I've got a man's mind."

"You have a mind similar to mine. It's not strongly influenced by gender in either direction."

Later she told him how her friendship with Bloeckman had started. One day at Delmonico's, Gloria and Rachael had run into Bloeckman and Mr. Gilbert having lunch, and curiosity had driven her to turn it into a group of four. She had found herself liking him—somewhat. He provided a welcome change from younger men, content as he was with so little. He indulged her whims and laughed along, whether he actually understood her or not. She met with him several times, ignoring her parents' obvious disapproval, and within a month he had proposed to her, offering her everything from an Italian villa to a promising career in films. She had laughed right in his face—and he had laughed as well.

But he hadn't given up. By the time Anthony arrived on the scene, he had been making consistent progress. She treated him fairly well—though she always called him by an unflattering nickname—while recognizing that he was metaphorically walking alongside her as she balanced on the fence, prepared to catch her if she stumbled.

The evening before they announced their engagement, she told Bloeckman the news. The revelation hit him hard. She didn't share all the specifics with Anthony, but she suggested that Bloeckman hadn't held back from trying to change her mind. Anthony understood that their conversation had ended badly, with Gloria remaining calm and detached in her spot on the sofa while Joseph Bloeckman from "Films Par Excellence" walked back and forth across the room, his eyes focused and his head lowered. Gloria had felt sympathy for him, but she had decided it was better not to let it show. In one last act of compassion, she had attempted to make him despise her during those final moments. However, Anthony knew that Gloria's emotional distance was actually what made her most attractive, so he realized how pointless her effort must have been. He thought about Bloeckman from time to time, though without much concern, until eventually he stopped thinking about him altogether.

Peak

One afternoon they discovered front seats on the sunny roof of a bus and traveled for hours from the dimming Square up along the polluted river, and then, as the scattered rays of light escaped the westward streets, glided down the murky Avenue, growing dark with threatening swarms from the department stores. The traffic was thick and stuck in a chaotic jam; the buses were stacked four deep like elevated platforms above the crowd as they waited for the wail of the traffic whistle.

"Isn't it good!" cried Gloria. "Look!"

A miller's wagon, completely white with flour and driven by a dusty figure covered in powder, rolled past them, pulled by a white horse paired with its black companion.

"What a shame!" she said; "they would look so lovely in the twilight, if only both horses were white. I'm incredibly happy right now, in this city."

Anthony shook his head in disagreement.

"I think the city's a fraud. Always struggling to achieve the grand and impressive urban sophistication people attribute to it. Trying to be romantically cosmopolitan."

"I don't. I think it is impressive."

"For a moment. But it's really a see-through, fake kind of show. It has its publicity-driven stars and its cheap, temporary stage sets and, I'll admit, the largest crowd of extras ever gathered—" He stopped, gave a brief laugh, and continued: "Technically excellent, maybe, but not believable."

"I bet police officers think people are idiots," Gloria said thoughtfully, watching a large but timid woman being helped across the street. "They always see people scared and helpless and old—which they are," she added. Then she said: "We should get going. I told my mother I'd eat dinner early and go to bed. She says I look tired, damn it."

"I wish we were married," he said quietly; "then there wouldn't be any need for good nights and we could do whatever we wanted."

"Won't it be wonderful! I think we should travel extensively. I want to visit the Mediterranean and Italy. And I'd like to try acting on stage sometime—perhaps for about a year."

"You bet. I'll write a play for you."

"Won't that be wonderful! And I'll perform in it. And then sometime when we have more money"—old Adam's death was always referred to so tactfully in this way—"we'll build a magnificent estate, won't we?"

"Oh, yes, with private swimming pools."

"Dozens of them. And private rivers. Oh, I wish it were now."

Odd coincidence—he had just been wishing for exactly that. They dove like swimmers into the dark swirling crowd and emerged into the cool fifties, strolling leisurely toward home, endlessly romantic to each other ... both were walking alone in an emotionless garden with a spirit discovered in a dream.

Peaceful days drifted by like boats floating down gentle rivers; spring evenings filled with a wistful sadness that transformed the past into something both beautiful and painful, urging them to look backward and realize that the loves from other long-forgotten summers had died along with the forgotten dance music of those years. The most heart-wrenching moments always came when some artificial obstacle forced them apart: in the theater their hands would secretly find each other, intertwine, and exchange tender squeezes throughout the long darkness; in packed rooms they would silently mouth words to each other across the space— unaware that they were simply walking the same path as countless forgotten generations before them, yet dimly understanding that if truth represents life's ultimate purpose, then happiness serves as one way to experience it, something to treasure during its brief and fragile existence. Then, on one magical night, May transformed into June. Sixteen days remaining now—fifteen—fourteen——

Three Digressions

Just before the engagement was announced, Anthony had traveled up to Tarrytown to visit his grandfather, who had grown a bit more withered and gray as time played its final mocking games, and who received the news with deep cynicism.

"Oh, you're planning to get married, are you?" He spoke with such questionable gentleness and nodded his head so repeatedly that Anthony felt quite disheartened. Since he didn't know what his grandfather had in mind, he assumed that a significant portion of the money would be left to him. A considerable amount would certainly go to charitable causes; a substantial sum would be used to continue the work of reform.

"Are you going to work?"

"Why—" Anthony stalled, feeling somewhat unsettled. "I am working. You know—"

"Oh, I mean work," said Adam Patch without emotion.

"I'm not quite sure yet what I'll do. I'm not exactly a beggar, grandpa," he declared with some defiance.

The elderly man thought about this with his eyes nearly shut. Then, almost as if he were sorry, he asked:

"How much do you save each year?"

"Nothing so far—"

"And so after barely managing to survive on your income, you've somehow convinced yourself that through some miracle, two people can live on the same amount."

"Gloria has some money of her own. Enough to buy clothes."

"How much?"

Without finding this question rude, Anthony answered it.

"About a hundred a month."

"That comes to roughly seventy-five hundred dollars a year." Then he said quietly: "That should be more than enough. If you're smart about it, that should be plenty. But the real question is whether you actually have any common sense or not."

"I suppose it is." It was humiliating to be forced to put up with this self-righteous lecture from the old man, and his following words were hardened with pride. "I can handle things just fine. You appear certain that I'm completely useless. Anyway, I came up here only to inform you that I'm getting married in June. Goodbye, sir." With that he turned around and walked toward the door, not realizing that at that moment his grandfather, for the first time, actually liked him.

"Wait!" called Adam Patch, "I want to talk to you."

Anthony turned around.

"Well, sir?"

"Sit down. Stay all night."

Feeling somewhat appeased, Anthony sat back down.

"I'm sorry, sir, but I'm going to see Gloria tonight."

"What's her name?"

"Gloria Gilbert."

"New York girl? Someone you know?"

"She's from the Midwest."

"What business is her father in?"

"In some kind of celluloid corporation or trust or something like that. They're from Kansas City."

"Are you planning to get married out there?"

"Why, no, sir. We thought we'd be married in New York— rather quietly."

"Would you like to have the wedding out here?"

Anthony paused. The idea didn't appeal to him at all, but it would definitely be wise to give the old man some sense of ownership in his married life, if he could manage it. Besides, Anthony felt somewhat moved by the gesture.

"That's really nice of you, grandpa, but wouldn't that be a lot of work for you?"

"Everything's a lot of trouble. Your father was married here— but in the old house."

"Why—I thought he was married in Boston."

Adam Patch thought it over.

"That's true. He was married in Boston."

Anthony felt a brief moment of embarrassment for having made the correction, and he concealed it with words.

"Well, I'll talk to Gloria about it. Personally, I'd like to, but naturally it's up to the Gilberts, you understand."

His grandfather let out a deep sigh, partially closed his eyes, and settled back into his chair.

"In a hurry?" he asked, his tone shifting.

"Not especially."

"I wonder," Adam Patch said, gazing out with a gentle, caring look at the lilac bushes that swayed against the windows, "I wonder if you ever think about what happens after we die."

"Why—sometimes."

"I think a lot about what happens after we die." His eyes were clouded but his voice remained steady and clear. "I was sitting here today thinking about what awaits us, and somehow I started remembering an afternoon from almost sixty-five years ago, when I was playing with my little sister Annie, down where that gazebo stands now." He pointed toward the long flower garden, his eyes filling with tears, his voice trembling.

"I started thinking—and it struck me that you should give more thought to what comes after this life. You should be—more stable"—he stopped and appeared to search for the right word—"more hardworking—well—"

Then his expression changed, his whole personality seemed to click into place like a trap snapping shut, and when he spoke again the gentleness had disappeared from his voice.

"When I was only two years older than you are now," he said with a harsh, sly laugh, "I forced three partners from the company Wrenn and Hunt into poverty."

Anthony felt a sudden wave of embarrassment wash over him.

"Well, goodbye," his grandfather said suddenly, "you'll miss your train."

Anthony left the house feeling unusually uplifted, yet strangely sympathetic toward the elderly man; not because his riches couldn't purchase "neither youth nor digestion" but because he had invited Anthony to get married there, and because he had overlooked something about his son's wedding that he should have recalled.

Richard Caramel, who served as one of the ushers, brought Anthony and Gloria considerable anxiety during those final weeks by constantly drawing attention away from them. "The Demon Lover" had come out in April, and it disrupted their romance just as it seemed to disrupt everything else its writer encountered. The book was a highly creative, somewhat elaborate work of continuous narrative focusing on a Don Juan from New York's poorest neighborhoods. As Maury and Anthony had mentioned earlier, and as the more welcoming reviewers were noting at the time, no American author possessed such ability to portray the primitive and straightforward responses of that segment of society.

The book was uncertain at first but then suddenly took off. Print runs, starting small and then growing larger, followed one after another week by week. A representative from the Salvation Army condemned it as a cynical distortion of all the positive work happening in society's lower depths. Skillful publicity spread the baseless rumor that "Gypsy" Smith was starting a defamation lawsuit because one of the main characters was a mockery of him. It was banned from the public library in Burlington, Iowa, and a Midwestern newspaper columnist suggested through hints that Richard Caramel was in a mental health facility suffering from alcohol withdrawal.

The author truly lived his days in a state of delightful obsession. The book dominated his conversations three-quarters of the time—he eagerly wanted to discover if someone had heard "the latest news"; he would enter a bookstore and loudly announce orders for books to be billed to his account, hoping to capture even a small hint of recognition from a clerk or fellow customer. He knew precisely which regions of the country were experiencing the strongest sales; he understood exactly his profit from each printing, and whenever he encountered someone who hadn't read his work, or as happened far too frequently, hadn't even heard of it, he would sink into melancholy despair.

So it was only natural that Anthony and Gloria, driven by jealousy, concluded that he had become so inflated with pride that he was insufferable. Much to Dick's irritation, Gloria openly bragged that she had never read "The Demon Lover" and had no intention of doing so until everyone stopped discussing it. In reality, she had no time for reading at that moment, as gifts were flooding in—starting as a trickle, then becoming a deluge, ranging from trinkets sent by long-forgotten family friends to photographs from long-forgotten impoverished relatives.

Maury presented them with an elaborate "drinking set," complete with silver goblets, a cocktail shaker, and bottle openers. Dick's contribution was more traditional—a tea set from Tiffany's. Joseph Bloeckman sent a simple yet exquisite traveling clock, accompanied by his card. There was even a cigarette holder from Bounds; this gesture moved Anthony deeply and nearly brought him to tears—in fact, any emotion short of complete breakdown seemed perfectly natural among the half-dozen people caught up in this enormous tribute to social convention. The room reserved at the Plaza overflowed with gifts sent by Harvard friends and associates of his grandfather, along with mementos from Gloria's Farmover days, and rather touching keepsakes from her former suitors, which arrived with cryptic, wistful messages written on cards carefully tucked inside, beginning "I never imagined when—" or "I truly wish you all the happiness—" or even "By the time you receive this I will be on my way to—"

The most generous gift was also the most disappointing. It was a gesture from Adam Patch—a check for five thousand dollars.

Anthony remained indifferent to most of the gifts. He felt they would require maintaining a detailed record of all their friends' marriages for the next fifty years. Gloria, however, delighted in every single present, ripping through the tissue paper and packing material with the fierce intensity of a dog hunting for a buried bone, eagerly grabbing at ribbons or glimpses of metal until she finally revealed the complete item and examined it with a critical eye, her expression showing nothing but intense fascination without a trace of a smile.

"Look, Anthony!"

"Darn nice, isn't it!"

No response came until an hour had passed, when she would provide him with a detailed description of exactly how she felt about the gift, whether it would have been better if it were smaller or larger, whether receiving it had surprised her, and if it had, precisely how surprised she was.

Mrs. Gilbert organized and reorganized an imaginary house, placing the gifts throughout various rooms, categorizing items as "second-best clock" or "silver for everyday use," and making Anthony and Gloria uncomfortable with her half-joking mentions of a room she referred to as the nursery. She was delighted with old Adam's gift and from then on maintained that he possessed a very ancient soul, "more than anything else." Since Adam Patch never quite figured out whether she was referring to his mind's growing senility or to some personal and spiritual theory of her own, it couldn't be said that this pleased him. In fact, he always referred to her when speaking with Anthony as "that old woman, the mother," as if she were a character in a play he had watched performed countless times before. Regarding Gloria, he couldn't make up his mind. She fascinated him but, as she herself informed Anthony, he had concluded that she was shallow and was hesitant to give his approval of her.

Five days to go! A dancing platform was being built on the lawn at Tarrytown. Four days remaining! A special train had been chartered to transport the guests to and from New York. Three days left!

The Diary

She wore blue silk pajamas and stood beside her bed with her hand on the light switch, ready to plunge the room into darkness, when she had a change of heart and opened a table drawer to retrieve a small black book—a "Line-a-day" diary. She had maintained this diary for seven years. Many of the pencil entries had become nearly impossible to read, and there were notes and references to evenings and afternoons that had long been forgotten, since it wasn't a personal diary, despite beginning with the timeless phrase "I am going to keep a diary for my children." Still, as she flipped through the pages, the faces of many men seemed to peer out at her from their half-erased names. With one of them she had traveled to New Haven for the first time—in 1908, when she was sixteen and padded shoulders were the style at Yale—she had felt flattered because "Touch down" Michaud had "rushed" her throughout the evening. She let out a sigh, recalling the sophisticated satin dress she had taken such pride in and the orchestra performing "Yama-yama, My Yama Man" and "Jungle-Town." Such a long time ago!—the names: Eltynge Reardon, Jim Parsons, "Curly" McGregor, Kenneth Cowan, "Fish-eye" Fry (whom she had found appealing precisely because he was so unattractive), Carter Kirby—he had given her a gift; Tudor Baird had done the same;—Marty Reffer, the first man she had fallen in love with for longer than a single day, and Stuart Holcome, who had eloped with her in his car and attempted to force her into marriage. And Larry Fenwick, whom she had always respected because he had told her one evening that if she refused to kiss him she could step out of his car and walk home. What a catalog of

144

names!

... And, after all, an outdated list. She was in love now, ready for the everlasting romance that would bring together all romances, yet she felt melancholy for these men and these moonlit nights and for the excitement she had experienced—and the kisses. The past—her past, oh, what happiness! She had been overwhelmingly joyful.

Flipping through the pages, her gaze wandered casually over the random entries from the past four months. She read the most recent ones with careful attention.

"April 1st.—I know Bill Carstairs hates me because I was so unpleasant, but I hate being treated with excessive sentiment sometimes. We drove out to the Rockyear Country Club and the most beautiful moon kept shining through the trees. My silver dress is getting tarnished. It's strange how one forgets the other nights at Rockyear—with Kenneth Cowan when I loved him so much!"

"April 3rd.—After spending two hours with Schroeder, who I'm told has millions, I've come to the conclusion that this business of persisting with things exhausts a person, especially when those things involve people. Nothing gets overdone quite so frequently, and starting today I promise myself to find entertainment instead. We discussed 'love'—how ordinary! How many men have I spoken with about love?"

"April 11th.—Patch actually called today! And when he swore off me about a month ago, he stormed right out the door. I'm slowly starting to doubt that any man can be dealt a fatal blow."

"April 20th.—I spent the day with Anthony. Maybe I'll marry him someday. I really like his ideas—he brings out all the creativity in me. Blockhead showed up around ten in his new car and took me out to Riverside Drive. I liked him tonight: he's so thoughtful. He could tell I didn't want to talk, so he stayed quiet throughout the entire ride."

"April 21st.—I woke up thinking about Anthony, and sure enough, he called and sounded wonderful on the phone—so I canceled a date for him. Today I feel like I'd break anything for him, including the ten commandments and my neck. He's coming at eight and I'm going to wear pink and look very fresh and crisp——"

She stopped for a moment, recalling how after he left that evening, she had undressed while the chilly April breeze flowed through the open windows. Even so, it appeared she hadn't noticed the cold, kept warm by the deep, ordinary feelings glowing within her heart.

The next entry happened a few days later:

"April 24th.—I want to marry Anthony, because husbands are so often just 'husbands' and I need to marry someone who will remain a lover."

There are four general types of husbands.

"The husband who always wants to stay home in the evening, has no vices and works for a salary. Totally undesirable!"

"(2) The primitive master whose mistress one becomes, waiting to serve his desires. This type always views every attractive woman as 'superficial,' like a peacock that never fully matured."

"(3) Next comes the worshipper, the person who idolizes his wife and everything that belongs to him, completely forgetting about everything else. This type of man needs a wife who can act out emotions dramatically. God! What an exhausting effort it must be to maintain the appearance of being righteous."

"(4) And Anthony—a lover who burns with temporary passion but possesses enough wisdom to recognize when that passion has departed and understand that it inevitably must fade. And I want to marry Anthony."

"What pathetic creatures women become when they crawl through dull, lifeless marriages! Marriage wasn't meant to fade into the background but to stand out boldly. Mine will be extraordinary.

It won't be just the backdrop—it's going to be the main event, the vibrant, beautiful, dazzling show, with the entire world serving as our stage. I won't sacrifice my life for future generations. Certainly, we owe just as much to the people living now as we do to children we don't even want. What a terrible destiny—to become fat and unattractive, to stop loving myself, to think only about milk, baby food, caregivers, and diapers.... Sweet imaginary children, how much more lovely you are, brilliant little beings who dance (all imaginary children must dance) on shining, shining wings——

"These children, however, poor little ones, have very little connection to married life."

"June 7th.—Moral question: Was it wrong to make Bloeckman fall in love with me? Because I really did make him fall for me. He seemed almost touchingly sad tonight. How convenient it was that my throat is completely swollen and tears came easily. But he's just part of the past now—already buried beneath all my lavender."

"June 8th.—And today I've promised not to chew my mouth. Well, I won't, I suppose—but if he'd only asked me not to eat!"

"Blowing bubbles—that's what Anthony and I are doing. We created such beautiful ones today, and they'll pop, and then we'll blow more and more, I suppose—bubbles just as big and just as beautiful, until all the soap and water runs out."

On this note the diary ended. Her eyes drifted up the page, scanning over the June 8th entries from 1912, 1910, 1907. The oldest entry was written in the round, childish handwriting of a sixteen-year-old girl—it contained the name Bob Lamar and a word she couldn't make out. Then she realized what it was—and with that realization, her eyes filled with tears. There in a fading blur was the record of her first kiss, as worn and distant as that private afternoon on a rain-soaked porch seven years ago. She felt like she almost remembered something one of them had said that day, but the words wouldn't come. Her tears flowed more freely now, making it nearly impossible to see the page. She was crying, she told herself, because all she could recall was the rain and the wet flowers in the garden and the scent of damp grass.

After a moment she found a pencil and with shaking hands drew three parallel lines beneath the final entry. Then she wrote THE END in large capital letters, placed the book back in the drawer, and quietly slipped into bed.

Breath of The Cave

Back in his apartment after the wedding dinner, Anthony turned off his lights and climbed into bed, feeling detached and delicate like a piece of China sitting on a serving table. The night was warm—a single sheet provided enough comfort—and through his wide-open windows drifted sounds that were fleeting and summery, filled with distant promise. He reflected on how the young years behind him, empty yet vibrant, had been spent in shallow and wavering cynicism based on the recorded feelings of men long dead. But there was something more than that; he understood now. There was the joining of his soul with Gloria's, whose brilliant fire and vitality was the living essence from which the lifeless beauty of books was created.

From the night into his room with its high walls came a persistent yet fleeting and fading sound—something the city was throwing up and calling back again, like a child playing with a ball. In Harlem, the Bronx, Gramercy Park, and along the waterfronts, in small living rooms or on pebble-covered, moonlit rooftops, a thousand lovers were creating this sound, calling out little pieces of it into the air. The entire city was playing with this sound out there in the blue summer darkness, tossing it up and calling it back, promising that soon life would be as beautiful as a story, promising happiness—and through that promise, delivering it. It gave love hope for its own survival. It could do nothing more.

At that moment, a new sound broke through the gentle weeping of the night in a harsh, jarring way. The noise came from a courtyard less than a hundred feet from his back window—the sound of a woman laughing. It started quietly, persistent and whimpering—probably some housemaid with her boyfriend, he figured—and then it grew louder and became frantic, until it reminded him of a girl he had witnessed being overtaken by nervous laughter at a variety show. Then it faded and retreated, only to rise up again with actual words—a crude joke, some kind of unclear rough play that he couldn't make out. It would stop for a moment and he would barely catch the low murmur of a man's voice, then start up again—endlessly; first irritating, then strangely frightening. He trembled, and getting out of bed walked to the window. The laughter had reached its peak, strained and muffled, almost like a scream—then it stopped and left behind a silence that felt empty and threatening like the vast quiet above. Anthony remained by the window a little longer before returning to his bed. He discovered he was disturbed and shaken. No matter how hard he tried to suppress his response, something primitive in that wild laughter had seized his imagination, and for the first time in four months awakened his old disgust and dread toward all the affairs of life. The room had become stifling. He longed to be outside in some fresh and sharp wind, miles above the cities, and to exist peacefully and removed in the depths of his thoughts. Life was that noise outside, that horrible repeated female sound.

"Oh, my God!" he cried, drawing in his breath sharply.

Burying his face in the pillows, he tried unsuccessfully to focus on the details of the following day.

Morning

In the dim morning light, he discovered it was only five o'clock. He felt anxious regret about waking up so early—he would look exhausted at the wedding. He envied Gloria, who could conceal her tiredness with skillful makeup.

In his bathroom, he looked at himself in the mirror and noticed he was unusually pale—several small blemishes stood out against his morning-white skin, and overnight he had developed light stubble on his face—the overall appearance, he thought, was unattractive, worn-out, and somewhat sickly.

On his dressing table lay several items that he counted through carefully with suddenly clumsy fingers—their tickets to California, the book of traveler's checks, his watch, set to the exact half minute, the key to his apartment, which he had to remember to give to Maury, and most crucial of all, the ring. It was made of platinum and surrounded by small emeralds; Gloria had insisted on this choice; she had always wanted an emerald wedding ring, she said.

It was the third gift he had given her; the first had been the engagement ring, followed by a small gold cigarette case. He would be giving her many things from now on—clothing and jewelry and friends and excitement. It seemed ridiculous that he would be paying for all her meals from this point forward. This was going to be expensive: he wondered whether he had underestimated the costs for this trip, and whether he should have cashed a larger check. The question troubled him.

Then the overwhelming urgency of what was about to happen cleared his mind of all the small details. This was the day— unexpected and unplanned six months earlier, but now arriving with golden sunlight streaming through his eastern window, playing across the carpet as if the sun itself was chuckling at some old, familiar joke of its own.

Anthony let out a nervous, short laugh that sounded more like a snort.

"My God!" he whispered to himself, "I'm practically married!"

The Ushers

Six young men in Cross Patch's library became increasingly cheerful under the influence of Mumm's Extra Dry champagne, which had been secretly placed in cold buckets beside the bookcases.

THE FIRST YOUNG MAN: Wow! Trust me, in my next book I'm going to write a wedding scene that will absolutely amaze them!

THE SECOND YOUNG MAN: I met a young woman making her social debut the other day who said she thought your book was powerful. Generally speaking, young women have a strong desire for this kind of raw, fundamental material.

THE THIRD YOUNG MAN: Where's Anthony?

THE FOURTH YOUNG MAN: Walking back and forth outside talking to himself.

SECOND YOUNG MAN: Lord! Did you see the minister? What peculiar looking teeth he had.

FIFTH YOUNG MAN: They think they're natural. It's funny how people have gold teeth.

SIXTH YOUNG MAN: They claim they love them. My dentist once told me about a woman who came to his office and demanded to have two of her teeth capped with gold. There was absolutely no medical reason for it. Her teeth were perfectly fine just as they were.

FOURTH YOUNG MAN: I heard you published a book, Dicky. Congratulations!

DICK: (Stiffly) Thanks.

FOURTH YOUNG MAN: (Innocently) What is it? College stories?

DICK: (More stiffly) No. Not college stories.

FOURTH YOUNG MAN: What a shame! There hasn't been a good book about Harvard in years.

DICK: (Irritably) Why don't you make up for what's missing?

THIRD YOUNG MAN: I think I just saw a group of guests pulling into the driveway in a Packard.

SIXTH YOUNG MAN: We might as well open a couple more bottles to celebrate that.

THIRD YOUNG MAN: I was completely stunned when I found out the old man was planning to serve alcohol at his wedding. He's always been a fierce opponent of drinking, you know.

FOURTH YOUNG MAN: (Snapping his fingers excitedly) My God! I knew I'd forgotten something. I kept thinking it was my vest.

DICK: What was it?

FOURTH YOUNG MAN: My God! My God!

SIXTH YOUNG MAN: Here! Here! Why the tragedy?

SECOND YOUNG MAN: What did you forget? The way home?

DICK: (Maliciously) He forgot the plot for his book of Harvard stories.

FOURTH YOUNG MAN: No, sir, I completely forgot the gift! I forgot to buy old Anthony a present. I kept postponing it and postponing it, and damn it, I've forgotten it! What will they think?

SIXTH YOUNG MAN: (Jokingly) That's probably what's been delaying the wedding.

(THE FOURTH YOUNG MAN glances anxiously at his watch. Laughter.)

FOURTH YOUNG MAN: Good God! What an idiot I am!

SECOND YOUNG MAN: What do you think of the bridesmaid who thinks she's Nora Bayes? She kept telling me she wished this was a ragtime wedding. Her name's Haines or Hampton.

DICK: (Quickly trying to think of an explanation) Kane, you mean, Muriel Kane. She's like a debt of honor, I think. She once saved Gloria from drowning, or something like that.

SECOND YOUNG MAN: I didn't think she could stop that constant swaying long enough to swim. Fill up my glass, would you? The old man and I just had a lengthy conversation about the weather.

MAURY: Who? Old Adam?

SECOND YOUNG MAN: No, the bride's father. He must work for a weather bureau.

DICK: He's my uncle, Otis.

OTIS: Well, it's an honorable profession. (Laughter.)

SIXTH YOUNG MAN: The bride is your cousin, isn't she?

DICK: Yes, Cable, she is.

CABLE: She's definitely beautiful. Not like you, Dicky. I bet she'll make old Anthony come around.

MAURY: Why do people always call grooms "old"? I believe marriage is a mistake young people make.

DICK: Maury, the professional cynic.

MAURY: Why, you intellectual fraud!

FIFTH YOUNG MAN: Battle of the intellectuals here, Otis. Pick up whatever insights you can.

DICK: You're the faker! What do you know?

MAURY: What do you know?

LICK: Ask me anything. Any area of knowledge.

MAURY: All right. What's the fundamental principle of biology?

DICK: You don't know yourself.

MAURY: Don't hedge!

DICK: Well, natural selection?

MAURY: Wrong.

DICK: I give up.

MAURY: Ontogeny recapitulates phylogeny.

FIFTH YOUNG MAN: Take your base!

MAURY: Let me ask you another question. What effect do mice have on clover crops? (Laughter.)

FOURTH YOUNG MAN: What influence do rats have on the Ten Commandments?

MAURY: Shut up, you idiot. There is a connection.

DICK: What is it then?

MAURY: (Stopping for a moment, becoming increasingly confused) Well, let me think. I appear to have forgotten the exact details. Something about bees eating the clover.

FOURTH YOUNG MAN: And the clover eating the mice! Ha! Ha!

MAURY: (Frowning) Let me just think for a minute.

DICK: (Sitting up suddenly) Listen!

(A burst of conversation erupts in the next room. The six young men stand up, adjusting their neckties.)

DICK: (With gravity) We should join the firing squad. They're going to take the photograph, I suppose. No, that comes later.

OTIS: Cable, you take the ragtime bridesmaid.

FOURTH YOUNG MAN: I wish to God I had sent that present.

MAURY: If you give me another minute, I'll remember that thing about the mice.

OTIS: I was an usher last month for old Charlie McIntyre and——

(They move slowly toward the door as the conversation becomes a confused jumble of voices and the practice session before the overture produces long, reverent moans from ADAM PATCH'S organ.)

Anthony

Five hundred pairs of eyes seemed to pierce through the back of his formal coat while sunlight reflected off the minister's surprisingly middle-class gold teeth. He struggled to hold back laughter. Gloria spoke with a clear, confident voice, and he attempted to convince himself that this moment was final, that every passing second mattered, that his existence was being divided into two distinct chapters, and that the world itself was transforming right before his eyes. He tried to reclaim that blissful feeling he had experienced ten weeks earlier. All of these feelings escaped him—he couldn't even summon the physical anxiety he had felt that very morning—everything seemed like one enormous anticlimax. And those golden teeth! He found himself wondering whether the minister was married; he wondered, with strange curiosity, whether a minister could officiate at his own wedding ceremony....

But as he pulled Gloria into his embrace, he felt a powerful shift within himself. His blood was flowing with new energy through his veins. A drowsy and satisfying sense of contentment descended upon him like a heavy blanket, bringing with it responsibility and ownership. He was a married man.

Glory

So many mixed emotions swirled together that she couldn't tell one from another! She could have cried for her mother, who was weeping softly ten feet behind her, and for the beautiful June sunlight streaming through the windows. She was past all conscious awareness. There was only a feeling, tinged with wild, delirious excitement, that something of ultimate importance was taking place—and a trust, fierce and passionate, blazing within her like a prayer, that in just a moment she would be forever and completely safe.

Late one night they reached Santa Barbara, where the night clerk at the Hotel Lafcadio turned them away, claiming they weren't married.

The clerk believed that Gloria was beautiful. He didn't think that anything as beautiful as Gloria could be moral.

"Con Amore"

That first six months—the journey west, the long leisurely weeks along the California coastline, and the gray house near Greenwich where they stayed until late autumn turned the countryside bleak—those days, those locations, witnessed their most enchanted moments. The exhilarating romance of their engagement transformed, initially, into the passionate intensity of their deeper connection. The exhilarating romance abandoned them, escaped to find other couples; they glanced around one day and discovered it had vanished, though they barely understood how. If either had lost the other during those romantic days, the love that was lost would have remained forever for the one left behind as that vague longing without satisfaction that lies beneath all existence. But enchantment must move forward, and the lovers stay behind....

The peaceful time passed, taking with it the demanding intensity of youth. A day arrived when Gloria realized that other men no longer left her feeling bored; a day came when Anthony found that he could once again sit late into the evening, discussing with Dick those profound abstract ideas that had previously filled his world. However, understanding they had experienced the finest aspects of love, they held onto what was left. Love remained—through extended nighttime conversations that stretched into those harsh hours when the mind becomes thin and sharp and the fragments borrowed from dreams transform into the essence of all existence, through the deep and personal acts of kindness they cultivated toward one another, through their shared laughter at the same ridiculous things and their agreement about what deserved respect and what deserved sorrow.

It was, above all, a period of discovery. The qualities they uncovered in one another were so varied, so intertwined and, furthermore, so sweetened by love that they appeared at the time not so much as discoveries but as isolated occurrences—to be acknowledged, and then forgotten. Anthony discovered that he was living with a woman of enormous nervous energy and the most imperious selfishness. Gloria realized within a month that her husband was a complete coward when faced with any one of countless fears conjured by his imagination. Her awareness came in waves, for this cowardice would emerge, become almost embarrassingly obvious, then disappear and vanish as if it had existed only in her own mind. Her responses to it were not what might be expected of her gender—it stirred in her neither revulsion nor an early sense of maternal protectiveness. Being herself almost entirely without physical fear, she couldn't comprehend it, and so she focused on what she considered his fear's saving grace, which was that although he was a coward when shocked and a coward under pressure—when his imagination ran wild—he possessed a kind of bold recklessness that moved her during its brief appearances almost to admiration, and a dignity that typically sustained him when he believed he was being watched.

The trait first revealed itself through a series of small incidents that seemed like nothing more than anxiety—his cautioning of a taxi driver about speeding too fast in Chicago; his unwillingness to take her to a rough café she had always wanted to see; these incidents, naturally, could be explained in the usual way—that he was thinking of her safety; however, when taken together, their combined effect troubled her. But an event that happened in a San Francisco hotel, after they had been married for a week, made the situation clear.

It was past midnight and completely dark in their room. Gloria was drifting off to sleep and Anthony's steady breathing next to her led her to believe he was asleep, when suddenly she noticed him prop himself up on his elbow and gaze at the window.

"What is it, dearest?" she whispered softly.

"Nothing"—he had settled back against his pillow and turned to face her—"nothing, my darling wife."

"Don't call me 'wife.' I'm your mistress. Wife is such an ugly word. Your 'permanent mistress' sounds so much more real and appealing.... Come into my arms," she added with a sudden wave of tenderness; "I can sleep so peacefully, so peacefully with you in my arms."

Coming into Gloria's arms carried a very specific meaning. It meant he had to slip one arm beneath her shoulder, wrap both arms around her, and position himself to form something like a three-sided cradle for her comfortable rest. Anthony, who moved restlessly in his sleep and whose arms would go numb and tingly after thirty minutes in that position, would wait until she fell asleep and then carefully roll her over to her own side of the bed— afterward, free to move as he pleased, he would twist himself into his customary tangled positions.

Gloria, having found emotional comfort, settled back into her drowsy state. Five minutes passed on Bloeckman's travel clock; quiet filled the entire room, covering the strange, impersonal furniture and the somewhat oppressive ceiling that gradually disappeared into unseen walls on either side. Then suddenly there was a sharp rattling sound at the window, quick and loud against the still, confined air.

With a sudden movement, Anthony jumped out of bed and stood rigidly beside it.

"Who's there?" he shouted in a terrifying voice.

Gloria remained completely motionless, now fully alert and focused not so much on the rattling sounds as on the tense, breathless figure whose voice had carried from beside the bed into that threatening darkness.

The sound stopped; the room became quiet just as it had been before—then Anthony began pouring words into the telephone.

"Someone just tried to get into the room! ...

"Someone's at the window!" His voice was forceful now, tinged with fear.

"All right! Hurry!" He hung up the phone and stood completely still.

There was a sudden rush and commotion at the door, followed by knocking—Anthony went to open it and found an agitated night clerk with three bell-boys clustered behind him, staring. The night clerk gripped a wet pen between his thumb and finger like it was a weapon; one of the bell-boys had grabbed a telephone directory and was holding it awkwardly. At the same moment, the hastily called house-detective joined the group, and together they all pushed into the room.

Lights suddenly turned on with a sharp click. Wrapping a piece of the bedsheet around herself, Gloria quickly moved out of view, closing her eyes tightly to block out the terrible shock of this unexpected intrusion. In her overwhelmed mind, there was only one clear thought: that her Anthony was terribly to blame.

The night clerk spoke from the window, his voice carrying both the tone of a servant and that of a teacher scolding a student.

"There's nobody out there," he stated with certainty; "good heavens, nobody could possibly be out there. This is a straight drop of fifty feet down to the street. What you heard was just the wind pulling at the blind."

"Oh."

Then she felt sorry for him. She only wanted to comfort him and gently pull him back into her arms, to tell them to leave because what their presence implied was disgusting. But she couldn't lift her head because of her shame. She heard a fragmented sentence, apologies, the formal politeness of the employee, and one uncontrolled snicker from a bellboy.

"I've been nervous as hell all evening," Anthony was saying; "somehow that noise just shook me—I was only about half awake."

"Of course, I get it," the night clerk said with reassuring diplomacy; "I've been in that situation myself."

The door shut; the lights went out; Anthony walked quietly across the room and slipped into bed. Gloria, pretending to be deep in sleep, let out a soft little sigh and moved into his arms.

"What was it, dear?"

"Nothing," he replied, his voice still trembling; "I thought someone was at the window, so I looked outside, but I couldn't see anyone and the noise continued, so I called downstairs. Sorry if I bothered you, but I'm extremely nervous tonight."

Catching the lie, she felt a sudden shock inside—he hadn't walked to the window or even gone near it. He had remained standing by the bed before letting out his frightened cry.

"Oh," she said—and then: "I'm so sleepy."

For an hour they remained awake lying next to each other, Gloria keeping her eyes squeezed so tightly closed that blue circles appeared and spun against backgrounds of deep purple, while Anthony gazed sightlessly into the blackness above them.

After several weeks, the truth slowly emerged into the open, becoming something they could laugh and joke about. They created a ritual to handle it—whenever that overwhelming nighttime terror struck Anthony, she would wrap her arms around him and hum softly, gentle as a lullaby:

"I'll protect my Anthony. Oh, nobody's ever going to harm my Anthony!"

He would laugh as if it were a joke they were playing for their shared entertainment, but for Gloria it was never really a joke. At first, it was a sharp disappointment; later, it became one of those moments when she had to keep her temper in check.

Managing Gloria's temper, whether it flared up because there wasn't enough hot water for her bath or because of an argument with her husband, became nearly the most important task of Anthony's entire day. It had to be handled in exactly the right way—with precisely this amount of silence, exactly that amount of pressure, this degree of giving in, and that level of firmness. It was during her fits of anger, along with the cruel behavior that came with them, that her excessive self-centeredness showed itself most clearly. Because she was fearless, because she had been "spoiled," because of her shocking yet admirable ability to think for herself, and ultimately because of her arrogant belief that she had never encountered a girl as beautiful as herself, Gloria had grown into a devoted, practicing follower of Nietzschean philosophy. This was, naturally, mixed with undertones of deep emotion.

There was, for example, her stomach. She had grown accustomed to specific meals, and she firmly believed that she simply couldn't eat anything different. She needed lemonade and a tomato sandwich late in the morning, followed by a light lunch featuring a stuffed tomato. She didn't just demand food chosen from about twelve different dishes, but this food also had to be prepared in exactly the right way. One of the most frustrating thirty minutes during the first two weeks happened in Los Angeles, when an unfortunate waiter served her a tomato filled with chicken salad rather than celery.

"We always serve it that way, ma'am," he said with a trembling voice to the gray eyes that looked at him angrily.

Gloria didn't respond, but once the waiter had tactfully turned away, she slammed both fists down on the table, making the dishes and silverware clatter.

"Poor Gloria!" Anthony laughed without thinking, "you never can get what you want, can you?"

"I can't eat this stuff!" she snapped.

"I'll call the waiter back."

"I don't want you to! He doesn't know anything, the damn fool!"

"Well, it's not the hotel's fault. Either send it back, forget about it, or be a good sport and eat it."

"Shut up!" she said briefly.

"Why take it out on me?"

"Oh, I'm not," she cried out, "but I just can't eat it."

Anthony collapsed helplessly.

"We'll go somewhere else," he suggested.

"I don't want to go anywhere else. I'm tired of being dragged around to a dozen cafés and not getting a single thing that's decent to eat."

"When did we go around to a dozen cafés?"

"You'd have to in this town," Gloria insisted with quick-witted reasoning.

Anthony, confused, tried a different approach.

"Why don't you try to eat it? It can't be as bad as you think."

"Just—because—I—don't—like—chicken!"

She picked up her fork and started jabbing at the tomato with obvious disdain, and Anthony expected her to start throwing the contents everywhere. He was certain that she was about as furious as she had ever been—for a moment he had caught a flash of hatred aimed as much at him as at anyone else—and when Gloria was angry, she was, for now, completely unreachable.

Then, to his surprise, he noticed that she had cautiously lifted the fork to her mouth and tried the chicken salad. Her frown remained unchanged and he watched her nervously, saying nothing and barely daring to breathe. She took another bite—within moments she was eating. Anthony struggled to hold back a laugh; when he finally spoke, his words had absolutely nothing to do with chicken salad.

This incident, with different variations, repeated itself like a mournful musical theme throughout their first year of marriage; it always left Anthony confused, frustrated, and dejected. But another harsh clash of personalities, this time over laundry bags, he found even more irritating since it always ended with him suffering a complete defeat.

One afternoon in Coronado, where they had stayed the longest during their trip—more than three weeks—Gloria was dressing herself elegantly for tea. Anthony, who had been downstairs listening to the most recent war rumors from Europe, came into the room, kissed the back of her powdered neck, and walked over to his dresser. After much pulling out and pushing in of drawers, clearly with unsatisfactory results, he turned toward the Unfinished Masterpiece.

"Do you have any handkerchiefs, Gloria?" he asked. Gloria shook her golden head.

"Not a single one. I'm using one of yours."

"The last one, I figure." He let out a dry laugh.

"Is it?" She carefully applied lipstick to her lips with emphatic yet very delicate strokes.

"Isn't the laundry back?"

"I don't know."

Anthony hesitated—then, with a sudden flash of understanding, opened the closet door. His suspicions proved correct. Hanging on the hook was the blue laundry bag provided by the hotel. It was packed with his clothes—he had placed them there himself. The floor below was scattered with an incredible collection of expensive clothing—underwear, stockings, dresses, nightgowns, and pajamas—most of it barely used but all of it clearly belonging to Gloria's wardrobe.

He stood there, keeping the closet door open.

"Why, Gloria!"

"What?"

The lip line was being erased and adjusted according to some hidden perspective; not a single finger shook as she handled the lipstick, not one look shifted in his direction. It was a masterpiece of focus.

"Haven't you ever sent out the laundry?"

"Is it there?"

"It most certainly is."

"Well, I guess I haven't, then."

"Gloria," Anthony said, settling onto the bed and attempting to meet her gaze in the mirror, "you're really something, aren't you! I've taken care of it every single time since we left New York, and more than a week ago you promised you'd handle it for once. All you'd need to do is stuff your things into that bag and call for the maid."

"Oh, why worry about the laundry?" Gloria snapped irritably, "I'll handle it."

"I haven't worried about it. I'd be happy to share the trouble with you, but when we run out of handkerchiefs it's pretty much time something gets done."

Anthony believed he was being remarkably logical. However, Gloria remained unimpressed, put away her makeup, and casually turned her back to him.

"Help me out," she suggested; "Anthony, darling, I completely forgot about it. I really meant to, honestly, and I will today. Don't be upset with your sweetheart."

What else could Anthony do but pull her down onto his knee and kiss some of the color from her lips.

"But I don't mind," she whispered with a smile, glowing and generous. "You can kiss all the lipstick off my mouth whenever you want."

They went downstairs for tea. They purchased some handkerchiefs at a small goods store nearby. Everything was forgotten.

But two days later Anthony checked the closet and noticed the bag still hanging empty on its hook, while the bright and colorful pile on the floor had grown remarkably taller.

"Gloria!" he shouted.

"Oh—" Her voice was filled with genuine anguish. In desperation, Anthony walked to the telephone and called the chambermaid.

"It seems to me," he said impatiently, "that you expect me to be some sort of French valet to you."

Gloria laughed with such contagious joy that Anthony foolishly found himself smiling in response. What a mistake! Somehow his smile handed her complete control of the moment—wearing an expression of wounded dignity, she marched decisively to the closet and started shoving her clothes aggressively into the bag. Anthony observed her, feeling ashamed of his reaction.

"There!" she said, suggesting that her fingers had been worn down to the bone by a merciless boss.

He believed, however, that he had taught her a lesson and that the issue was settled, but in reality it was just starting. One pile of dirty laundry came after another—with long gaps between them; one shortage of handkerchiefs followed another—with brief intervals; not to mention shortages of socks, shirts, and everything else. And Anthony eventually discovered that he would either have to take care of the laundry himself or endure the increasingly uncomfortable experience of arguing with Gloria.

Gloria And General Lee

On their journey east, they paused for two days in Washington, wandering around with a sense of antagonism toward its environment of stark, unwelcoming light, its sense of remoteness without liberty, its grandeur without true magnificence—the city appeared bland and overly self-aware. On the second day, they made a poorly planned visit to General Lee's former residence at Arlington.

The bus carrying them was packed with hot, struggling people, and Anthony, who knew Gloria well, sensed trouble building. The storm erupted at the Zoo, where their group paused for ten minutes. The Zoo, apparently, reeked of monkeys. Anthony chuckled; Gloria called down divine punishment upon monkeys, extending her anger to include all the bus passengers and their sweating children who had rushed toward the monkey exhibits.

Eventually the bus continued on to Arlington. There it joined other buses, and immediately a crowd of women and children began leaving a trail of peanut shells through the halls of General Lee's home, eventually crowding into the room where he had been married. On the wall of this room, a conspicuous sign displayed in large red letters "Ladies' Toilet." At this final insult, Gloria broke down completely.

"I think it's absolutely awful!" she said angrily, "the thought of allowing these people to come here! And encouraging them by turning these houses into tourist attractions."

"Well," Anthony argued, "if they weren't maintained, they'd fall apart."

"What if they did!" she exclaimed as they made their way to the broad columned porch. "Do you think they've left even a trace of 1860 here? This has become something entirely of 1914."

"Don't you want to preserve old things?"

"But you can't, Anthony. Beautiful things grow to a certain point and then they fail and fade away, releasing memories as they deteriorate. And just as any era decays in our minds, the things from that era should decay as well, and in that way they're preserved for a time in the few hearts like mine that respond to them. That cemetery at Tarrytown, for example. The fools who donate money to preserve things have ruined that too. Sleepy Hollow is gone; Washington Irving is dead and his books are rotting in our opinion year by year—then let the cemetery rot too, as it should, as all things should. Trying to preserve a century by keeping its artifacts current is like keeping a dying man alive with stimulants."

"So you believe that when an era falls apart, its buildings should crumble along with it?"

"Absolutely! Would you treasure your Keats letter if someone had traced over the signature to make it last longer? It's precisely because I cherish the past that I want this house to reflect on its glamorous moment of youth and beauty, and I want its stairs to creak as though responding to the footsteps of women in hoop skirts and men wearing boots and spurs. But they've transformed it into a bleached, made-up old woman of sixty. It has no right to appear so prosperous. It should care enough about Lee to let a brick fall occasionally. How many of these—these creatures"— she gestured around—"gain anything from this, despite all the histories and guidebooks and restorations that exist? How many of them who believe that, at most, appreciation means speaking in hushed tones and walking on tiptoes would even bother coming here if it required any effort? I want it to smell of magnolias rather than peanuts and I want my shoes to crunch on the same gravel that Lee's boots once crunched on. There's no beauty without poignancy and there's no poignancy without the sense that it's fleeting, men, names, books, houses—destined for dust— mortal—"

A young boy appeared next to them and, swinging a bunch of banana peels in his hand, threw them boldly toward the Potomac River.

Sentiment

At the same time that Liège fell, Anthony and Gloria reached New York. Looking back, those six weeks felt incredibly happy. They had discovered, to a large degree—as most young couples do to some extent—that they shared many firm beliefs, interests, and strange quirks of personality; they were naturally compatible companions.

But it had been difficult to keep many of their conversations as discussions rather than fights. Arguments were devastating to Gloria's temperament. Throughout her life, she had only been around people who were either less intelligent than her or men who were so intimidated by her stunning beauty that they never dared to disagree with her; so naturally, it annoyed her when Anthony stopped treating her opinions as the final, unquestionable word on everything.

He didn't understand at first that this was partly due to her "female" education and partly because of her beauty, and he tended to group her with all women as strangely and clearly limited. It drove him crazy to discover she had no sense of justice. But he found that when a topic actually interested her, her mind didn't get tired as quickly as his did. What he mainly found missing in her thinking was the scholarly sense of purpose—the feeling for order and precision, the understanding of life as a mysteriously connected patchwork, but he came to realize after some time that having such a quality would have been out of place in her.

Of all the things they shared together, the most powerful was their almost mysterious ability to touch each other's hearts deeply. On the day they checked out of the hotel in Coronado, she sat down on one of the beds while they were packing their belongings, and started crying intensely.

"Darling—" He wrapped his arms around her and gently pulled her head down to rest on his shoulder. "What's wrong, my sweet Gloria? Tell me what's happening."

"We're leaving," she cried. "Oh, Anthony, this is kind of the first place we've lived together. Our two little beds here—right next to each other—they'll always be waiting for us, and we're never coming back to them again."

She was breaking his heart the way she always managed to do. Emotion overwhelmed him, bringing tears to his eyes.

"Gloria, look, we're moving on to another room. And there are two other little beds. We're going to be together for our entire lives."

Words poured out of her in a low, raspy voice.

"But it won't be—like our two beds—ever again. Everywhere we go and move on and change, something's lost—something's left behind. You can't ever quite repeat anything, and I've been so yours, here—"

He held her close with intense passion, understanding far beyond any judgment of her feelings, a wise embrace of the present moment, even if it meant simply allowing her need to weep—Gloria the dreamer, one who cherished her own fantasies, drawing deep emotion from the unforgettable experiences of life and youth.

Later that afternoon, when he came back from the station with the tickets, he discovered her sleeping on one of the beds, her arm wrapped around a dark object he couldn't immediately recognize. Moving closer, he saw it was one of his shoes—not especially new or clean—but her tear-streaked face was pressed against it, and he grasped her timeless and deeply meaningful gesture. There was nearly pure joy in rousing her and watching her smile at him, bashful yet fully conscious of her own delicate thoughtfulness.

With no judgment about the value or worthlessness of these two things, it seemed to Anthony that they existed somewhere close to the essence of love.

The Gray House

It's during our twenties that life's actual energy starts to slow down, and only someone truly naive would find as many things important and meaningful at thirty as they did ten years earlier. At thirty, an organ-grinder becomes just a worn-out man who operates an organ—when once he was an organ-grinder! The unmistakable mark of human experience touches all those detached and beautiful things that only young people can appreciate in their pure, impersonal magnificence. A dazzling ball, filled with bright romantic laughter, wears through its own silk and satin to reveal the basic structure of something made by human hands—oh, that everlasting influence!—a play, deeply tragic and profoundly divine, becomes nothing more than a series of lines, labored over by the eternal copycat during uncomfortable hours and performed by actors prone to muscle spasms, fear, and sentimental masculinity.

And this time with Gloria and Anthony, during their first year of marriage, the gray house captured them at that point when the organ-grinder was slowly going through his unavoidable transformation. She was twenty-three; he was twenty-six.

The gray house was initially meant to be purely a countryside retreat. During the first two weeks after returning from California, they lived restlessly in Anthony's apartment, surrounded by the suffocating atmosphere of open suitcases, too many visitors, and endless piles of laundry bags. They talked with their friends about the enormous challenge of deciding their future. Dick and Maury would join them, nodding seriously and almost contemplatively, as Anthony went through his catalog of what they "should" do and where they "should" make their home.

"I'd like to take Gloria overseas," he complained, "except for this damn war—and besides that I'd kind of like to have a place in the countryside, somewhere near New York, naturally, where I could write—or whatever I end up deciding to do."

Gloria laughed.

"Isn't he adorable?" she asked Maury. "'Whatever he chooses to do!' But what will I do if he gets a job? Maury, will you escort me around if Anthony starts working?"

"Anyway, I'm not going to work yet," Anthony said quickly.

It was loosely understood between them that someday in the future he would join some kind of prestigious diplomatic career and would be the envy of princes and prime ministers because of his beautiful wife.

"Well," Gloria said helplessly, "I honestly have no idea. We keep talking endlessly without reaching any conclusions, and when we ask our friends for advice, they simply tell us what they think we want to hear. I wish someone would just take care of us."

"Why don't you go out to—out to Greenwich or something?" suggested Richard Caramel.

"I'd like that," said Gloria, her face lighting up. "Do you think we could get a house there?"

Dick shrugged his shoulders and Maury laughed.

"You two crack me up," he said. "You're both so impractical! The moment someone mentions a place, you expect us to magically produce huge stacks of photographs from our pockets showing all the different architectural styles you can get in bungalows."

"That's exactly what I don't want," Gloria cried out, "a sweltering, cramped bungalow, with a bunch of babies next door and their father mowing the lawn in his undershirt—"

"For Heaven's sake, Gloria," Maury cut in, "nobody's trying to trap you in some bungalow. Who on earth even mentioned bungalows? But you're never going to find a place to live unless you actually get out there and look for one."

"Go where? You say 'go out and hunt for it,' but where?"

With dignity, Maury gestured around the room with his hand in a paw-like motion.

"Anywhere outside. Out in the countryside. There are plenty of places."

"Thanks."

"Listen!" Richard Caramel fixed his yellow eye on them with a mischievous glint. "The problem with you two is that you're completely scattered. Do you know anything about New York State? Be quiet, Anthony, I'm speaking to Gloria."

"Well," she finally confessed, "I've attended a few house parties in Portchester and other places around Connecticut—but obviously, that's not in New York State, is it? And Morristown isn't either," she concluded with sleepy randomness.

There was a burst of laughter.

"Oh, Lord!" Dick exclaimed, "Morristown isn't either!" No, and Santa Barbara isn't either, Gloria. Now listen. First of all, unless you're wealthy, there's no point in considering places like Newport or Southampton or Tuxedo. They're completely out of reach.

They all agreed to this solemnly.

"And personally I hate New Jersey. Then, of course, there's upper New York, above Tuxedo."

"Too cold," Gloria said curtly. "I went there once in a car."

"Well, it seems to me there are a lot of towns like Rye between New York and Greenwich where you could buy a little gray house of some—"

Gloria jumped on those words with triumph. For the first time since they had come back East, she knew exactly what she wanted.

"Oh, yes!" she exclaimed. "Oh, yes! That's exactly it: a small gray house with white trim and plenty of swamp maples that are as brown and gold as an October painting in an art gallery. Where can we find one?"

"Unfortunately, I've lost my list of small gray houses surrounded by swamp maples—but I'll try to locate it. In the meantime, take a piece of paper and write down the names of seven potential towns. Each day this week, take a trip to visit one of those towns."

"Oh, gosh!" protested Gloria, feeling completely defeated, "why won't you do it for us? I hate trains."

"Well, rent a car, and—"

Gloria yawned.

"I'm exhausted from talking about it. It feels like all we ever do is discuss where we should live."

"My wonderful wife is getting tired of thinking," Anthony said with irony. "She needs a tomato sandwich to wake up her worn-out nerves. Let's go out for tea."

As the unfortunate result of this conversation, they followed Dick's advice exactly, and two days later traveled out to Rye, where they wandered around with an annoyed real estate agent, like confused children lost in the forest. They were shown houses at a hundred dollars a month that were right next to other houses at a hundred dollars a month; they were shown remote houses that they consistently disliked intensely, though they gave in weakly to the agent's insistence that they "look at that stove—what a stove!" and endured extensive shaking of door frames and knocking on walls, clearly meant to demonstrate that the house wouldn't fall down right away, regardless of how persuasively it seemed like it might. They peered through windows at interiors decorated either in a "business-like" style with flat, board-like chairs and uncomfortable sofas, or in a "homey" way with the sad leftover decorations from previous summers—crossed tennis rackets, exercise couches, and depressing Gibson girl illustrations. With a sense of shame they examined a few genuinely attractive houses, distant, elegant, and refreshing—at three hundred dollars a month. They left Rye expressing their sincere gratitude to the real estate agent.

On the packed train returning to New York, the seat behind them was taken by a heavily breathing Latino man whose recent meals had clearly consisted entirely of garlic. They arrived at their apartment with relief, almost frantically, and Gloria hurried to take a hot bath in the spotless bathroom. Regarding the matter of finding a future home, both of them were unable to function for a week.

The situation eventually resolved itself in an unexpectedly romantic way. One afternoon, Anthony burst into the living room, practically glowing with "the idea."

"I've got it," he exclaimed as if he had just caught a mouse. "We'll get a car."

"Good grief! Don't we have enough problems just taking care of ourselves?"

"Give me a moment to explain, okay? Let's just leave our belongings with Dick and pack a few suitcases in our car, the one we're planning to purchase—we'll need one in the countryside anyway—and simply head toward New Haven. You see, once we get beyond commuting distance from New York, the rent will become more affordable, and as soon as we find a house we like, we'll just settle down there."

Through his constant and calming use of the word "just," he awakened her dormant excitement. Pacing aggressively around the room, he projected an image of energetic and compelling competence. "We'll buy a car tomorrow."

Life, struggling to keep up with imagination's giant strides, found them leaving town a week later in an inexpensive but gleaming new convertible, carried them through the confusing maze of the Bronx, then across a broad, hazy area that shifted between dreary blue-green expanses and neighborhoods bustling with intense and gritty energy. They departed New York at eleven and it was well after a sweltering and blissful midday when they drove stylishly through Pelham.

"These aren't real towns," Gloria said with disdain, "they're just city blocks dropped carelessly onto empty land. I bet all the men around here have coffee stains on their mustaches from drinking too fast in the morning."

"And play pinochle on the commuting trains."

"What's pinochle?"

"Don't take everything so literally. How would I know? But it sounds like they should play it."

"I like it. It sounds like something where you'd crack your knuckles or something.... Let me drive."

Anthony looked at her with suspicion.

"You swear you're a good driver?"

"Since I was fourteen."

He carefully pulled the car over to the side of the road and stopped, and they switched seats. Then the car lurched into gear with a terrible grinding sound, while Gloria burst into laughter that struck Anthony as unsettling and completely inappropriate.

"Here we go!" she yelled. "Whoo-oop!"

Their heads jerked backward like puppets controlled by the same string as the car shot forward and swerved sickeningly around a stationary milk wagon, whose driver rose up on his seat and shouted after them. Following the age-old tradition of the road, Anthony fired back with a few sharp comments about the crudeness of the milk-delivery business. He cut his remarks short, though, and turned to Gloria with the growing realization that he had made a serious error in giving up control and that Gloria was a driver with many quirks and endless recklessness.

"Remember!" he warned her anxiously, "the man told us we shouldn't go over twenty miles an hour for the first five thousand miles."

She gave a quick nod, but clearly wanting to cover the forbidding distance as fast as she could, she picked up her pace a little. A moment later, he tried again.

"See that sign? Do you want to get us caught?"

"Oh, for heaven's sake," Gloria exclaimed in frustration, "you always blow everything out of proportion!"

"Well, I don't want to get arrested."

"Who's arresting you? You're so stubborn—just like you were about my cough medicine last night."

"It was for your own good."

"Ha! I might as well be living with my mother."

"What a thing to say to me!"

A police officer standing on duty came into sight and was quickly left behind.

"Do you see him?" Anthony demanded.

"Oh, you drive me crazy! He didn't arrest us, did he?"

"When he does, it'll be too late," Anthony shot back cleverly.

Her response was contemptuous, almost offended.

"Why, this old thing won't go over thirty-five."

"It isn't old."

"It is in spirit."

That afternoon the car became another source of conflict, joining the laundry bags and Gloria's eating habits as part of their ongoing disputes. He kept warning her about railroad crossings, alerting her to oncoming cars, and eventually demanded to drive himself, leaving Gloria fuming and offended as she sat in stony silence beside him during the stretch between Larchmont and Rye.

But it was because of her angry silence that the gray house became real rather than just an idea, since just past Rye he gave in to his gloomy feelings and handed the steering wheel back to her. Without speaking, he pleaded with her, and Gloria, immediately brightened, promised to drive more carefully. However, when a rude streetcar stubbornly stayed on its tracks, Gloria turned down a side street—and for the rest of that afternoon, she could never find her way back to the Post Road. The street they eventually confused for the main road lost its Post Road appearance after they had traveled five miles from Cos Cob. The paved surface turned to gravel, then to dirt—and the road also became narrower and grew lined with maple trees, through which the blazing sun filtered down, endlessly experimenting with shadow patterns on the tall grass.

"We're lost now," Anthony complained.

"Read that sign!"

"Marietta—Five Miles. What's Marietta?"

"I've never heard of it, but let's keep going. We can't turn around here and there's probably a detour that will take us back to the Post Road."

The road became marked with deepening grooves and treacherous edges of stone. Three farmhouses appeared before them briefly, then passed by. A town emerged in a collection of drab rooftops surrounding a tall white church spire.

Then Gloria, caught between two different approaches and making her decision too late, drove straight over a fire hydrant and violently tore the transmission right out of the car.

It was dark when the Marietta real estate agent showed them the gray house. They found it just west of the village, where it sat against a sky that looked like a warm blue cloak fastened with tiny stars. The gray house had stood there since the days when women who owned cats were likely considered witches, when Paul Revere was making false teeth in Boston before he would go on to rally the great commercial population, when our forefathers were magnificently abandoning Washington in large numbers. Since that time, the house had been reinforced in a weak corner, extensively divided into new rooms and freshly plastered on the inside, expanded with a kitchen and enhanced by a side porch—but except for where some cheerful fool had covered the new kitchen with red tin roofing, it stubbornly remained Colonial in style.

"How did you end up coming to Marietta?" the real estate agent asked in a tone that bordered on suspicion. He was taking them through four large and well-ventilated bedrooms.

"We broke down," Gloria explained. "I drove over a fire hydrant and we had ourselves towed to the garage and then we saw your sign."

The man nodded, unable to keep up with such a burst of spontaneous action. There was something vaguely wrong about doing anything without spending several months thinking it over first.

They signed a lease that night and, in the agent's car, returned joyfully to the sleepy and run-down Marietta Inn, which was too broken-down for even the casual affairs and resulting festivities of a country roadhouse. Half the night they lay awake planning the things they would do there. Anthony was going to work at an incredible pace on his history and thereby win favor with his cynical grandfather.... When the car was fixed they would explore the countryside and join the nearest "really nice" club, where Gloria would play golf "or something" while Anthony wrote. This, naturally, was Anthony's idea—Gloria was certain she wanted nothing more than to read and dream and be served tomato sandwiches and lemonades by some heavenly servant still existing in a vague background. Between paragraphs Anthony would come and kiss her as she lay lazily in the hammock.... The hammock! a multitude of new dreams in harmony with its imagined swaying, while the wind moved it and waves of sunlight rippled over the shadows of swaying wheat, or the dusty road became spotted and darkened with gentle summer rain....

And guests—here they engaged in a lengthy debate, both attempting to appear exceptionally mature and wise. Anthony argued that they would require visitors at least every other weekend "as a kind of variety." This sparked a complex and deeply emotional discussion about whether Anthony didn't find Gloria stimulating enough. Although he promised her that he did, she continued to question him.... Finally the conversation took on its familiar, repetitive tone: "What then? Oh, what will we do then?"

"Well, we'll get a dog," Anthony suggested.

"I don't want one. I want a kitty." She launched into a detailed and passionate account of the history, habits, and preferences of a cat she had once owned. Anthony thought it must have been a terrible creature with no charm or faithful nature.

Later they slept, waking an hour before dawn with the gray house shimmering like a ghostly vision before their amazed eyes.

The Soul of Gloria

For that autumn the old gray house welcomed them with an overwhelming wave of emotion that disguised its bitter, weathered years. Certainly, there were still the laundry bags to deal with, Gloria's constant hunger, and Anthony's habit of dwelling on dark thoughts along with his restless anxiety, but there were also moments of unexpected peace they had never dared to hope for. Sitting close together on the porch, they would watch and wait for the moon to pour its light across the shimmering silver fields of farmland, leap over the dense woods, and cascade waves of brilliant light at their feet. Under such moonlight, Gloria's face took on an all-encompassing, nostalgic whiteness, and with just a little effort they could cast aside the limitations of routine life and discover in each other nearly the perfect essence of romance from that long-lost June.

One night, as her head rested on his chest and their cigarettes created swirling points of light in the darkness above their bed, she spoke for the first time, though in fragments, about the men who had been briefly captivated by her beauty.

"Do you ever think of them?" he asked her.

"Only occasionally—when something happens that brings a particular man to mind."

"What do you remember—their kisses?"

"All kinds of things.... Men behave differently around women."

"Different in what way?"

"Oh, completely—and beyond words. Men who had the strongest, most established reputations for being a certain way would sometimes act surprisingly differently with me. Harsh men showed tenderness, insignificant men proved remarkably loyal and endearing, and frequently, respectable men adopted positions that were far from respectable."

"For example?"

"Well, there was a boy named Percy Wolcott from Cornell who was quite a hero in college, a great athlete, and saved a lot of people from a fire or something like that. But I soon discovered he was stupid in a rather dangerous way."

"What way?"

"It seems he had some naive idea of what kind of woman would be 'suitable as his wife,' a specific notion that I encountered frequently and that always infuriated me. He wanted a girl who had never been kissed and who enjoyed sewing and staying home while boosting his ego. And I'd bet anything that if he's found some fool to sit around and act dumb with him, he's sneaking around on the side with some much more exciting woman."

"I'd feel sorry for his wife."

"I wouldn't. Just imagine what a fool she'd be if she didn't figure that out before marrying him. He's the type of man who thinks honoring and respecting a woman means never giving her any thrills. Despite his good intentions, he was completely stuck in the past."

"What was his attitude toward you?"

"I'm getting to that. As I mentioned to you—or did I mention it?—he was incredibly handsome: large brown sincere eyes and one of those smiles that promised the heart beneath it was pure gold. Being young and naive, I believed he had some sense of judgment, so I kissed him passionately one evening when we were driving around after a dance at the Homestead at Hot Springs. It had been a marvelous week, I recall—with the most beautiful trees spread like green foam, in a way, all across the valley and a mist rising from them on October mornings like fires lit to turn them brown—"

"What about your friend with the ideals?" Anthony interrupted.

"It appears that when he kissed me, he started to believe he might be able to push things further, that I didn't need to be treated with the same respect he'd show to some idealized, wholesome girl from his fantasies."

"What did he do?"

"Not much. I shoved him off a sixteen-foot embankment before he could really get going."

"Hurt him?" Anthony asked with a laugh.

"He broke his arm and sprained his ankle. He spread the story throughout Hot Springs, and after his arm healed, a man named Barley who was fond of me got into a fight with him and broke his arm all over again. Oh, the whole thing was a terrible mess. He made threats to take Barley to court, and Barley—who was from Georgia—was spotted purchasing a gun in town. But before any of that could unfold, mama had pulled me North once more, completely against my wishes, so I never learned what actually happened in the end—although I did see Barley one time in the Vanderbilt lobby."

Anthony laughed long and loud.

"What a career! I suppose I ought to be furious because you've kissed so many men. I'm not, though."

At this, she sat up in bed.

"It's funny, but I'm completely certain that those kisses didn't leave any mark on me—no trace of being promiscuous, I mean— even though a man once told me with complete seriousness that he couldn't stand the thought that I'd been like a shared drinking glass that everyone had used."

"He had his nerve."

"I simply laughed and suggested he think of me more like a cherished cup that's passed from person to person, yet remains just as precious despite being shared."

"For some reason it doesn't upset me—though it certainly would if you had done anything more than just kiss them. But I think you're completely unable to feel jealous unless your pride gets wounded. Why aren't you concerned about what I've done? Wouldn't you rather I had been completely pure?"

"It all comes down to the impression it might have left on you. I kissed him because he was attractive, or because the moon looked beautiful, or simply because I was feeling somewhat sentimental and a bit moved. But that's all there is to it—it hasn't affected me at all. But you would remember it and let those memories haunt you and cause you worry."

"Haven't you ever kissed anyone the way you've kissed me?"

"No," she replied simply. "As I've mentioned, men have attempted—oh, all sorts of things. Any attractive girl goes through that.... You see," she continued, "it doesn't concern me how many women you've been with before, as long as it was just physical pleasure, but I don't think I could bear the thought of you ever having lived with another woman for an extended time or even having wanted to marry some other girl. It's different in some way. There would be all those small intimate moments to remember— and they would diminish that newness that is, after all, the most valuable aspect of love."

Filled with overwhelming joy, he drew her down next to him onto the pillow.

"Oh, my darling," he whispered, "as if I could remember anything except your sweet kisses."

Then Gloria, speaking in a very gentle voice:

"Anthony, did I hear someone say they were thirsty?"

Anthony suddenly burst into laughter and, with an embarrassed yet entertained smile, climbed out of bed.

"With just a small piece of ice in the water," she added. "Do you think I could have that?"

Gloria always used the word "little" whenever she asked for a favor—it made the request seem less demanding. But Anthony laughed again—whether she wanted a small piece of ice or a large chunk of it, he still had to go downstairs to the kitchen.... Her voice trailed after him through the hallway: "And just a little cracker with just a little marmalade on it...."

"Oh, wow!" Anthony exclaimed in enthusiastic slang, "she's amazing, that girl! She's got it!"

"When we have a baby," she said one day—this had already been decided would happen after three years—"I want it to look like you."

"Except its legs," he suggested with a sly grin.

"Oh, yes, except his legs. He needs to have my legs. But everything else about him can be you."

"My nose?"

Gloria hesitated.

"Well, maybe my nose. But definitely your eyes—and my mouth, and I suppose the shape of my face. I wonder; I think he'd be kind of cute if he had my hair."

"My dear Gloria, you've taken over the entire baby."

"Well, I didn't mean to," she apologized cheerfully.

"At least let him have my neck," he insisted, studying himself seriously in the mirror. "You've always said you liked my neck because you can't see the Adam's apple, and anyway, your neck is too short."

"No, it's not!" she exclaimed indignantly, turning toward the mirror. "It's perfect. I don't think I've ever seen a more beautiful neck."

"It's too short," he said again in a teasing way.

"Short?" Her voice conveyed frustrated amazement.

"Short? You're out of your mind!" She stretched and compressed it to reassure herself of its snake-like flexibility. "You think that's a short neck?"

"One of the shortest I've ever seen."

For the first time in weeks, tears began to flow from Gloria's eyes, and the expression she gave him carried genuine anguish.

"Oh, Anthony—"

"My Lord, Gloria!" He walked over to her, completely confused, and gently held her elbows. "Please don't cry! Didn't you realize I was just joking? Gloria, look at me! Really, sweetheart, you have the longest neck I've ever seen. I mean it."

Her tears melted into a distorted smile.

"Well—you shouldn't have said that, then. Let's talk about the baby."

Anthony walked back and forth across the room and spoke as if he was practicing for a debate.

"To put it simply, we could have two different babies, two completely separate and logical possibilities, entirely distinct from each other. There's the baby that would combine the best qualities from both of us. Your physique, my eyes, my intellect, your intelligence—and then there's the baby that would inherit our worst traits—my body, your temperament, and my indecisiveness."

"I like that second baby," she said.

"What I'd really like," Anthony went on, "would be to have two sets of triplets born a year apart and then conduct experiments with the six boys—"

"Poor me," she interrupted.

"I would educate each of them in a different country using a different educational system, and when they reached twenty-three years old, I would bring them all together to see how they had turned out."

"Let's have them all with my neck," suggested Gloria.

The End of a Chapter

The car was finally fixed and with deliberate spite resumed exactly where it had stopped in its mission of creating endless conflict.

Who would drive? How fast should Gloria go? These two questions and the constant blame and accusations that came with them filled their days. They drove to the Post-Road towns—Rye, Portchester, and Greenwich—and visited a dozen friends, mostly Gloria's, who all appeared to be at various stages of pregnancy, which bored her to the point of nervous breakdown, along with everything else about them. For an hour following each visit, she would bite her fingers angrily and tend to take out her frustration on Anthony.

"I can't stand women," she said with mild irritation. "What can you possibly say to them—except engage in meaningless small talk? I've gushed over dozens of babies that I really just wanted to strangle. And every single one of those women is either starting to become jealous and suspicious of her husband if he's attractive, or she's beginning to get bored with him if he's not."

"Don't you ever plan to see any women?"

"I don't know. They never look clean to me—never—never. Except for just a few. Constance Shaw—you know, Mrs. Merriam who visited us last Tuesday—is almost the only one. She's so tall and fresh-looking and dignified."

"I don't like them so tall."

Though they attended several dinner dances at different country clubs, they concluded that autumn was nearly finished for them to socialize on any significant level, even if they had wanted to. He despised golf; Gloria enjoyed it only somewhat, and while she relished the enthusiastic attention that some college students showered on her one evening and was pleased that Anthony took pride in her beauty, she also noticed that their hostess that night, a Mrs. Granby, was rather troubled by the fact that Anthony's former classmate, Alec Granby, eagerly participated in pursuing her. The Granbys never called again, and although Gloria found it amusing, it bothered her quite a bit.

"You see," she explained to Anthony, "if I wasn't married it wouldn't bother her—but she's been to the movies in her time and she thinks I might be a vampire. But the thing is that keeping such people happy requires an effort that I'm simply not willing to make.... And those adorable little freshmen flirting with me and giving me ridiculous compliments! I've matured, Anthony."

Marietta itself provided very little in terms of social opportunities. About six farm estates formed a rough circle around the town, but these properties belonged to elderly men who appeared only as motionless, gray-haired figures slumped in the back seats of limousines heading to the train station, where they were occasionally joined by equally old and considerably larger wives. The local residents were a notably dull group— mostly consisting of unmarried women—whose interests never extended beyond school events and whose spirits seemed as cold and unwelcoming as the stark white design of the town's three churches. The only local person they had regular contact with was the wide-hipped, broad-shouldered Swedish girl who came daily to handle their household tasks. She worked quietly and effectively, and after Gloria discovered her sobbing intensely with her head buried in her arms at the kitchen table, Gloria developed a strange fear of her and stopped making any complaints about the meals. The girl remained in their employment because of her mysterious and deeply personal sorrow.

Gloria's tendency toward premonitions and her sudden episodes of unclear supernatural beliefs came as a surprise to Anthony. Either some complicated issue that had been properly and scientifically suppressed during her early years with her Bilphistic mother, or some inherited oversensitivity, made her vulnerable to any hint of psychic phenomena, and while she wasn't easily fooled about people's motivations, she was willing to believe any unusual event blamed on the unpredictable wanderings of the dead. The urgent creaking sounds throughout the old house on windy nights that Anthony interpreted as burglars holding loaded guns represented to Gloria the spiritual presences, malevolent and restless, of past generations, atoning for unforgivable sins around the old and romantic fireplace. One night, due to two sharp banging sounds from downstairs, which Anthony nervously but unsuccessfully investigated, they stayed awake almost until sunrise asking each other test-like questions about world history.

In October, Muriel came out for a two-week visit. Gloria had called her long-distance, and Miss Kane ended the conversation in her typical way by saying "All-ll-ll right. I'll be there with bells on!" She arrived carrying a dozen popular songs with her.

"You should get a phonograph for out here in the countryside," she said, "just a small Victrola—they're not expensive. Then whenever you feel lonely, you can have Caruso or Al Jolson right there with you."

She drove Anthony to distraction by constantly telling him that "he was the first intelligent man she had ever met and she was so exhausted by superficial people." He couldn't understand how people fell in love with women like her. Still, he imagined that under a certain passionate gaze, even she might reveal some tenderness and potential.

But Gloria, passionately displaying her love for Anthony, was drawn into a state of contented bliss.

Finally Richard Caramel arrived for a talkative and, to Gloria's dismay, painfully literary weekend, during which he talked about himself with Anthony long after she had fallen into childlike sleep upstairs.

"This whole success thing has been pretty amusing," Dick said. "Right before my novel was published, I'd been attempting to sell some short stories without any luck. Then, once my book was released, I revised three of those stories and got them accepted by one of the same magazines that had turned them down earlier. I've written quite a few more since then; the publishers won't pay me for my book until this winter."

"Don't let the victor belong to the spoils."

"You mean write trash?" He thought about it. "If you're asking whether I'm deliberately putting a sentimental ending into each story, I'm not doing that. But I don't think I'm being as careful as before. I'm definitely writing more quickly and I don't seem to be thinking as deeply as I used to. Maybe it's because I don't have anyone to talk to anymore, now that you're married and Maury has moved to Philadelphia. I don't have that old drive and ambition anymore. Early success and everything that comes with it."

"Doesn't it worry you?"

"Frantically. I experience something I call sentence-fever that must be similar to buck-fever—it's a kind of intense literary self-consciousness that occurs when I try to push myself. But the truly terrible days aren't when I believe I can't write. They're when I question whether any writing has value at all—I mean whether I'm not just some kind of glorified buffoon."

"I enjoy hearing you speak like that," Anthony said with a hint of his familiar condescending arrogance. "I was worried you'd become somewhat foolish about your work. I read the most ridiculous interview you gave——"

Dick interrupted with a pained expression.

"Good Lord! Don't mention it. A young lady wrote it—a very admiring young lady. She kept telling me my work was 'powerful,' and I kind of got carried away and made a bunch of odd statements. Some of it was good, though, don't you think?"

"Oh, yes; that part about the wise writer writing for the youth of his generation, the critic of the next, and the schoolmaster of ever afterward."

"Oh, I believe most of it," Richard Caramel admitted with a slight smile. "It was simply a mistake to share it."

In November they moved into Anthony's apartment, and from there they ventured out triumphantly to the Yale-Harvard and Harvard-Princeton football games, to the St. Nicholas ice-skating rink, to a complete round of theater shows, and to a variety of entertainments—ranging from small, formal dances to the grand events that Gloria adored, held in those exclusive homes where servants with powdered wigs hurried about in magnificent displays of English aristocratic style under the supervision of imposing head butlers. They planned to travel abroad at the beginning of the year or, at the very least, when the war ended. Anthony had actually finished a Chestertonian essay about the twelfth century as an introduction to his planned book, and Gloria had conducted extensive research on Russian sable coats—in fact, the winter was progressing quite pleasantly when the cosmic force of fate suddenly decided in mid-December that Mrs. Gilbert's soul had matured enough in its current life. As a result, Anthony took a devastated and emotionally distraught Gloria to Kansas City, where, following human custom, they paid the awful and soul-crushing respect to the deceased.

Mr. Gilbert became, for the first and last time in his life, a truly pitiful figure. The woman he had broken down to serve his physical needs and act as his devoted audience had ironically abandoned him—precisely when he could no longer have sustained her much longer anyway. He would never again be able to so thoroughly torment and dominate another human being with such satisfaction.

Chapter II: Symposium

Gloria had put Anthony's mind into a peaceful slumber. She, who appeared to be the most intelligent and exceptional of all women, hung like a dazzling curtain across his doorways, blocking out the sunlight. During those early years, everything he believed consistently carried gloria's influence; he always viewed the sun through the design of that curtain.

A kind of weariness brought them back to Marietta for another summer. Throughout a golden, draining spring they had wandered aimlessly, restless and carelessly wasteful, along the California coast, occasionally joining other groups and drifting from Pasadena to Coronado, from Coronado to Santa Barbara, with no more obvious purpose than Gloria's wish to dance to different music or notice some tiny variation among the shifting colors of the ocean. From the Pacific rose wild rocky shores and equally untamed hotels built so that at teatime one could drift into a drowsy wicker marketplace made glamorous by the polo outfits of Southampton and Lake Forest and Newport and Palm Beach. And just as the waves came together and crashed and sparkled in the most peaceful of the bays, so they joined this circle and that one, and moved with them from place to place, always talking about those mysterious, fleeting pleasures waiting just beyond the next green and fertile valley.

It was a simple, healthy leisure class—the finest men among them had a pleasant undergraduate quality—they appeared to be permanently on the waiting list for some idealized version of exclusive clubs like "Porcellian" or "Skull and Bones" that stretched endlessly into the wider world; the women, more beautiful than average, delicately athletic, somewhat foolish as hostesses but charming and endlessly decorative as guests. With composure and grace, they danced their carefully chosen steps during the pleasant afternoon tea hours, performing with a certain dignity the same movements that clerks and chorus girls across the country made into horrible parodies. It seemed ironic that Americans should undoubtedly excel in this solitary and discredited child of the arts.

Having danced and splashed through an extravagant spring, Anthony and Gloria discovered they had spent too much money and would need to retreat into seclusion for a while. There was

Anthony's "work," they claimed. Almost before they realized it, they were back in the gray house, more conscious now that other lovers had slept there, other names had been shouted over the railings, other couples had sat on the porch steps gazing at the gray-green fields and the dark mass of woods in the distance.

It was the same Anthony, more restless, only becoming animated after several drinks, showing a faint, almost unnoticeable indifference toward Gloria. But Gloria—she would turn twenty-four in August and was experiencing an attractive yet genuine anxiety about it. Six years until thirty! If she hadn't been so deeply in love with Anthony, her awareness of time passing would have manifested itself in a renewed interest in other men, in a conscious effort to capture a brief spark of romance from every potential suitor who looked at her with intense eyes across a gleaming dinner table. She said to Anthony one day:

"The way I see it is that if I wanted something, I'd go after it and take it. That's been my philosophy my entire life. But it turns out that I want you, and because of that, there's simply no space left for any other desires."

They were traveling east through a dry and barren Indiana, and she had glanced up from one of her cherished movie magazines to discover that a lighthearted conversation had suddenly become serious.

Anthony scowled through the car window. When the railroad tracks intersected with a country road, a farmer briefly came into view in his wagon; he was chewing on a piece of straw and seemed to be the exact same farmer they had encountered a dozen times already, sitting there in quiet and ominous significance. When Anthony looked back at Gloria, his scowl deepened.

"You worry me," he protested; "I can picture desiring another woman in certain fleeting situations, but I can't picture actually being with her."

"But I don't feel that way, Anthony. I can't be bothered fighting against the things I desire. My approach is simply not to desire them—to want no one except you."

"But when I consider that if you simply decided you liked someone—"

"Oh, don't be an idiot!" she exclaimed. "There'd be nothing casual about it. And I can't even imagine the possibility."

This firmly ended the conversation. Anthony's constant appreciation made her feel happier when she was with him than with anyone else. She truly enjoyed his company—she loved him. So the summer started very much like the previous one had.

There was, however, one major change in the household. The cold-hearted Scandinavian, whose strict cooking and sarcastic way of serving at the table had so discouraged Gloria, was replaced by an extremely capable Japanese man whose name was Tanalahaka, but who admitted that he responded to any call that included the two syllables "Tana."

Tana was unusually small even for a Japanese person, and showed a somewhat innocent view of himself as a sophisticated man. On the day he arrived from "R. Gugimoniki, Japanese Reliable Employment Agency," he invited Anthony into his room to display the treasures from his trunk. These contained a large collection of Japanese postcards, which he was eager to explain to his employer immediately, one by one and in great detail. Among them were half a dozen with pornographic content that were clearly of American origin, though the creators had modestly left out both their names and the mailing format. He then brought out some of his own work—a pair of American pants that he had made himself, and two sets of solid silk underwear. He told Anthony privately about the purpose for which these latter items were intended. The next item was a rather good copy of an etching of Abraham Lincoln, whose face he had given an unmistakable Japanese appearance. Finally came a flute; he had crafted it himself but it was broken: he was planning to repair it soon.

After these polite formalities, which Anthony assumed must be customary in Japan, Tana launched into a lengthy speech in broken English about the relationship between master and servant. From this, Anthony understood that Tana had worked on large estates but had always gotten into conflicts with the other servants because they weren't honest. They struggled considerably with the word "honest," and actually became quite frustrated with each other, since Anthony stubbornly insisted that Tana was trying to say "hornets," and even went so far as to make buzzing sounds like a bee and flap his arms to mimic wings.

After forty-five minutes, Anthony was finally let go with the enthusiastic promise that they would have more pleasant conversations where Tana would explain "how we do in my countree."

Such was Tana's talkative debut in the gray house—and he lived up to expectations. Although he was diligent and honest, he was undoubtedly an incredible bore. He appeared incapable of controlling his speech, often rambling on and on with an expression resembling pain in his small brown eyes.

Sunday and Monday afternoons he would read the comic sections of the newspapers. One cartoon featuring a humorous Japanese butler entertained him greatly, although he insisted that the main character, who clearly looked Asian to Anthony, actually had an American face. The problem with the comic strip was that by the time he had worked through the final three panels with Anthony's help, carefully sounding out each word and understanding their meaning with the kind of intense focus that would be suitable for studying Kant's "Critique," he had completely forgotten what had happened in the opening panels.

In mid-June, Anthony and Gloria marked their first anniversary by going on a "date." Anthony knocked on the door and she rushed to open it for him. They then sat side by side on the couch, reciting the special names they had created for each other—fresh variations of timeless terms of endearment. However, this "date" didn't end with a drawn-out goodnight filled with bittersweet longing.

Later in June, horror stared out at Gloria, attacked her and scared her bright spirit back half a generation. Then slowly it disappeared, faded back into that impenetrable darkness where it had come from—ruthlessly taking its share of youth with it.

With perfect timing for maximum drama, it selected a small train station in a miserable village close to Portchester. The station platform remained empty all day like an open field, baking under the harsh yellow sunlight and subject to the stares of that particularly annoying kind of rural resident who lives near a big city and has picked up its shallow sophistication without any of its genuine refinement. About twelve of these country folk, with bloodshot eyes and as cheerless as scarecrows, witnessed what happened. The event drifted through their muddled and bewildered thoughts, understood at best as a crude prank, at worst as something "disgraceful." All the while, there on that platform, some of the world's light dimmed forever.

With Eric Merriam, Anthony had spent the entire hot summer afternoon sitting over a bottle of Scotch, while Gloria and Constance Merriam were swimming and sunbathing at the Beach Club, with Constance positioned under a striped umbrella-awning and Gloria lying sensually on the warm, soft sand, bronzing her stunning legs. Afterward, all four of them had eaten light sandwiches without much thought; then Gloria had stood up, gently tapping Anthony's knee with her parasol to catch his attention.

"We need to leave, dear."

"Now?" He glanced at her reluctantly. In that moment, nothing felt more important than lounging on that cool, shaded porch sipping smooth Scotch, while his host shared endless memories about the behind-the-scenes drama of some long-forgotten political campaign.

"We really need to leave," Gloria said again. "We can catch a taxi to the station.... Come on, Anthony!" she said with a bit more authority.

"Listen here—" Merriam, his story interrupted, raised the usual protests while provocatively refilling his guest's glass with a highball that should have been slowly enjoyed over ten minutes. But when Gloria said with clear irritation "We really must go!" Anthony downed the drink in one gulp, stood up, and gave his hostess an elaborate bow.

"It seems we 'must,'" he said, with little grace.

In a moment he was walking behind Gloria along a garden path lined with tall rose bushes, her parasol gently brushing against the June-blooming leaves. How thoughtless of her, he reflected as they reached the road. With wounded innocence, he felt that Gloria shouldn't have disrupted such pure and harmless pleasure. The whiskey had both calmed and cleared the restless thoughts in his mind. It struck him that she had adopted this same approach several times before. Was he always supposed to withdraw from enjoyable moments at the touch of her parasol or a glance from her eye? His reluctance transformed into resentment, which swelled within him like an unstoppable bubble. He remained quiet, stubbornly suppressing an urge to confront her about it. They located a taxi in front of the Inn and rode in silence to the small station.

Then Anthony understood what he truly desired—to impose his will against this composed and unshakeable young woman, to achieve through one powerful effort a control that appeared endlessly appealing.

"Let's go visit the Barneses," he said without looking at her. "I don't want to go home."

Mrs. Barnes, formerly Rachael Jerryl, owned a summer home located several miles away from Redgate.

"We went there the day before yesterday," she replied curtly.

"I'm sure they'd be happy to see us." He sensed that wasn't quite forceful enough, steeled himself with determination, and continued: "I want to see the Barneses. I have no interest in going home."

"Well, I don't have any desire to go to the Barneses."

Suddenly they stared at each other.

"Anthony," she said irritably, "it's Sunday night and they probably have dinner guests. I don't know why we should show up at this hour—"

"Then why couldn't we have stayed at the Merriams'?" he burst out. "Why go home when we were having a perfectly good time? They invited us to dinner."

"They had to. Give me the money and I'll get the railroad tickets."

"I definitely won't! I'm not in the mood for a ride on that damn hot train."

Gloria stamped her foot on the platform.

"Anthony, you're acting like you're broke!"

"On the contrary, I'm perfectly sober."

But his voice had dropped to a rough whisper and she knew without a doubt that he was lying.

"If you're sober, you'll give me the money for the tickets."

But it was too late to speak to him like that. Only one thought occupied his mind—Gloria was being selfish, she was always selfish and would keep being selfish unless he established himself as her master right here and now. This was the perfect moment, since she had denied him pleasure simply because of a whim. His resolve hardened, briefly turning into a dull and bitter hatred.

"I'm not getting on that train," he said, his voice shaking slightly with rage. "We're heading to the Barneses' place."

"I'm not!" she cried. "If you go I'm going home alone."

"Go on, then."

Without saying anything, she turned toward the ticket office; at the same time he remembered that she had some money with her and that this wasn't the kind of victory he wanted, the kind he had to have. He took a step after her and grabbed her arm.

"Look here!" he muttered, "you're not going by yourself!"

"I certainly am—why, Anthony!" She exclaimed this as she attempted to pull away from him, but he only tightened his grip.

He stared at her with narrowed, spiteful eyes.

"Let go!" Her cry carried a fierce intensity. "If you have any decency, you'll let go."

"Why?" He already knew the answer. But he felt a confused and somewhat uncertain pride in keeping her there.

"I'm going home, do you understand? And you're going to let me go!"

"No, I'm not."

Her eyes were burning now.

"Are you going to make a scene here?"

"I'm telling you that you're not going! I'm sick of your constant selfishness!"

"I just want to go home." Two angry tears began to fall from her eyes.

"This time you're going to do what I say."

Gradually her body straightened: her head tilted back in a gesture of boundless contempt.

"I hate you!" Her quiet words shot out like poison through her gritted teeth. "Oh, let me go! Oh, I hate you!" She attempted to pull herself free but he simply grabbed her other arm. "I hate you! I hate you!"

At Gloria's fury his uncertainty came back, but he felt that now he had gone too far to back down. It seemed that he had always backed down and that deep down she had looked down on him for it. Sure, she might hate him now, but later she would respect him for taking control.

The approaching train let out a warning siren that rolled dramatically toward them down the gleaming blue tracks. Gloria pulled and struggled to break free, and words older than the Book of Genesis came to her lips.

"Oh, you monster!" she sobbed. "Oh, you monster! Oh, I hate you! Oh, you monster! Oh—"

On the train platform, other waiting passengers started turning around to look and stare at them; the rumbling sound of the approaching train could be heard, growing louder and more intense. Gloria's struggles became even more frantic, then stopped completely, and she remained standing there, shaking and with tears burning in her eyes from this powerless embarrassment, as the locomotive roared and thundered as it pulled into the station.

Low, beneath the rush of steam and the screeching of the brakes, her voice emerged:

"Oh, if there was just one man here you couldn't do this! You couldn't do this! You coward! You coward, oh, you coward!"

Anthony stood silent and trembling, holding her tightly, conscious that numerous faces—strangely emotionless, like shadows from a dream—were watching him. The bells rang out with metallic crashes that felt like physical agony, the smokestacks fired their volleys skyward in gradual succession, and amid the chaos of noise and gray, gaseous confusion, the row of faces swept past, moved away, and grew unclear—until suddenly there remained only the sun casting its slanted rays eastward across the railroad tracks and a fading volume of sound in the distance, like a train composed of thunderous tin. He released her arms. He had emerged victorious.

Now, if he wanted to, he could laugh. The test was over and he had maintained his determination through force. Let mercy follow in the footsteps of triumph.

"We'll rent a car here and drive back to Marietta," he said with dignified restraint.

In response, Gloria grabbed his hand with both of hers and lifted it to her mouth, biting down hard on his thumb. He barely felt the pain; when he saw the blood flowing, he automatically pulled out his handkerchief and bandaged the wound. This was also part of his victory, he figured—it was only natural that losing would provoke such resentment—and therefore wasn't worth his attention.

She was sobbing deeply and bitterly, almost without any tears.

"I won't go! I won't go! You can't make me go! You've killed any love I ever had for you, and any respect. But all that's left in me would die before I'd move from this place. Oh, if I'd thought you'd lay your hands on me—"

"You're coming with me," he said harshly, "even if I have to carry you."

He turned around, signaled to a taxi, and told the driver to head to Marietta. The driver got out and opened the door. Anthony looked at his wife and spoke through gritted teeth:

"Will you get in?—or will I put you in?"

With a quiet cry filled with endless pain and despair, she gave in and climbed into the car.

Throughout the entire long drive, as twilight gradually deepened into darkness around them, she remained curled up on her side of the car, her silence punctuated only by the occasional harsh, isolated sob. Anthony gazed out the window, his thoughts moving sluggishly as he tried to process the slowly shifting meaning of what had just happened. Something felt off—Gloria's final scream had touched something deep inside him that continued to resonate with strange and troubling unease. He had to be in the right—and yet, she looked so pitiful now, shattered and defeated, humiliated far beyond what anyone should have to endure. The sleeves of her dress hung in tatters; her parasol had vanished, left behind and forgotten on the platform. It was a brand-new outfit, he recalled, and she had been so delighted with it just that morning when they had stepped out of the house.... He found himself wondering whether anyone they knew had witnessed what happened. And over and over again, her scream kept echoing in his mind:

"All that remains within me would perish—"

This filled him with a growing sense of confusion and anxiety. It matched perfectly with the Gloria lying in the corner—no longer the proud Gloria he once knew, nor any version of Gloria he recognized. He wondered if such a thing could be possible. While he couldn't imagine she would stop loving him—that was obviously impossible to consider—he questioned whether Gloria stripped of her arrogance, her independence, her pure confidence and bravery, could still be the woman of his dreams, the brilliant woman who had been precious and captivating precisely because she was indescribably and magnificently herself.

He was extremely intoxicated at that point, so drunk that he couldn't even recognize how drunk he was. When they arrived at the gray house, he went to his room and, with his mind still struggling helplessly and gloomily with his actions, collapsed into a deep stupor on his bed.

It was past one in the morning, and the hallway felt unusually silent as Gloria walked through it, her eyes wide open and unable to sleep, before pushing his bedroom door open. He had been too confused to open any windows, leaving the air stale and heavy with the smell of whiskey. She paused for a moment beside his bed, a slim and beautifully graceful figure wearing her masculine silk pajamas—then she threw herself onto him without restraint, partially rousing him with the desperate intensity of her embrace as her warm tears fell onto his neck.

"Oh, Anthony!" she cried with intense emotion, "oh, my darling, you have no idea what you've done!"

Yet in the morning, when he came into her room early, he knelt down beside her bed and wept like a small child, as if his own heart had been shattered.

"Last night," she said seriously, her fingers running through his hair, "it felt like everything about me that you had loved, everything that made me worth knowing—all my pride and passion—had disappeared. I understood that whatever remained of me would always love you, but it would never be exactly the same kind of love."

Nevertheless, she knew even then that she would eventually forget and that life rarely delivers sudden blows but instead gradually wears us down. After that morning, the incident was never brought up again, and its deep wound healed under Anthony's care—and if there was any victory to be claimed, some darker power beyond their control had seized it, claiming both the understanding and the triumph.

Nietzschean Incident

Gloria's independence, like all genuine and deep-rooted qualities, had started without her being aware of it, but once Anthony's captivated recognition brought it to her consciousness, it took on something closer to the dimensions of an established philosophy. Based on her way of speaking, one might think that all her strength and liveliness were channeled into a fierce declaration of the defiant motto "Never give a damn."

"Not for anything or anybody," she said, "except myself and, by extension, for Anthony. That's how all life works, and even if it weren't, I'd still be that way. Nobody would do anything for me unless it satisfied them somehow, and I'd do just as little for them."

She was standing on the front porch of the most respectable woman in Marietta when she spoke these words, and as soon as she finished speaking, she let out a strange little cry and collapsed unconscious onto the porch floor.

The woman helped her recover and drove her home in her car. It had dawned on the respectable Gloria that she was likely pregnant.

She lay on the long couch downstairs. The day was gently fading through the window, caressing the late-blooming roses on the porch columns.

"All I ever think about is how much I love you," she cried out. "I treasure my body because you find it beautiful. And this body of mine—yours—to watch it become ugly and lose its shape? It's absolutely unbearable. Oh, Anthony, I'm not scared of the pain."

He tried desperately to comfort her—but it was useless. She went on:

"And then later on, I might end up with wide hips and pale skin, with all my youthful vitality gone and no shine left in my hair."

He walked back and forth across the room with his hands in his pockets, asking:

"Is it certain?"

"I don't know anything. I've always hated obstetrics, or whatever you call it. I thought I'd have a child someday. But not now."

"Well, for God's sake don't just lie there and fall apart."

Her crying gradually stopped. She pulled a comforting quiet from the evening darkness that had settled throughout the room. "Please turn on the lights," she asked. "The days feel so brief now—June used to have much longer days when I was a child."

The lights clicked on, and it seemed as if delicate blue silk curtains had been drawn behind the windows and door. Her pale complexion and stillness, now devoid of both sorrow and happiness, stirred his compassion.

"Do you want me to have it?" she asked without energy.

"I don't really care either way. I mean, I'm neutral about it. If you have it, I'll probably be happy. If you don't—well, that's perfectly fine too."

"I wish you'd make up your mind one way or the other!"

"Suppose you make up your mind."

She looked at him with contempt, refusing to dignify his words with a response.

"You'd think you were the only woman in the entire world chosen to suffer this ultimate humiliation."

"So what if I do!" she shouted furiously. "It's not degrading for them. It's their only reason for existing. It's the only thing they're capable of doing well. It's degrading for me.

"Look, Gloria, I'm on your side no matter what you decide to do, but please try to be reasonable about this."

"Oh, don't fuss at me!" she wailed.

They shared a silent glance that carried no specific meaning but held considerable tension. Anthony then pulled a book from the shelf and settled into a chair.

Half an hour later, her voice emerged from the profound silence that filled the room and lingered in the air like incense.

"I'll drive over and see Constance Merriam tomorrow."

"All right. And I'll go to Tarrytown and see Grampa."

"—You see," she continued, "it's not that I'm scared—of this or anything else. I'm just being true to myself, you know."

"I know," he agreed.

The Practical Men

Adam Patch, consumed by righteous anger toward the Germans, lived entirely on war news. Pin-covered maps covered his walls, while atlases sat stacked high on nearby tables alongside "Photographic Histories of the World War," official explanatory publications, and "Personal Impressions" written by war correspondents and enlisted men. Throughout Anthony's stay, his grandfather's secretary, Edward Shuttleworth—once the skilled bartender at "Pat's Place" in Hoboken, now filled with moral outrage—would regularly arrive carrying breaking news updates.

The elderly man attacked every newspaper with relentless intensity, ripping out articles that seemed important enough to keep and stuffing them into his already overflowing filing system.

"So, what have you been up to?" he asked Anthony casually. "Nothing? Well, that's what I figured. I've been planning to drive over and visit you all summer long."

"I've been writing. Don't you remember the essay I sent you— the one I sold to The Florentine last winter?"

"Essay? You never sent me any essay."

"Oh, yes, I did. We talked about it."

Adam Patch gently shook his head.

"Oh, no. You never sent me any essay. You may have thought you sent it but it never reached me."

"Why, you read it, Grandpa," Anthony insisted, feeling somewhat frustrated, "you read it and disagreed with it."

The elderly man suddenly recalled, though this became evident only through his mouth partially dropping open, revealing lines of gray gums. Looking at Anthony with a green and weathered gaze, he wavered between admitting his mistake and concealing it.

"So you're writing," he said quickly. "Well, why don't you go over there and write about these Germans? Write something real, something about what's actually happening, something people can read."

"Not just anyone can become a war correspondent," Anthony protested. "You need a newspaper that's willing to purchase your articles. And I don't have the money to go over there as a freelancer."

"I'll send you over there," his grandfather suggested unexpectedly. "I'll arrange for you to go as an official correspondent for whatever newspaper you choose."

Anthony pulled back from the thought—at almost the same moment he rushed toward it.

"I—don't—know—"

He would need to leave Gloria, whose entire existence longed for him and embraced him. Gloria was facing difficulties. The whole idea simply wasn't practical—not yet—he pictured himself dressed in khaki, leaning on a sturdy walking stick like all war correspondents do, with a portfolio slung over his shoulder—attempting to appear British. "I'd appreciate some time to consider this," he admitted. "It's really very generous of you. I'll give it some thought and get back to you with my decision."

Thinking it over consumed his thoughts during the trip to New York. He had experienced one of those sudden moments of clarity that come to all men who are controlled by a powerful and cherished woman, revealing to them a realm of tougher men, more intensely disciplined and wrestling with the complexities of philosophy and conflict. In that realm, Gloria's embrace would exist only as the passionate touch of a casual lover, deliberately pursued and easily dismissed....

These strange, unfamiliar figures pressed in around him as he boarded his train to Marietta at Grand Central Station. The car was packed with passengers; he managed to get the last empty seat and only after several minutes did he take a quick look at the man sitting next to him. When he finally did, he noticed a heavy jawline and nose, a curved chin, and small, puffy eyes. In that moment, he recognized Joseph Bloeckman.

At the same time, they both partially stood up, feeling somewhat awkward, and shared what could only be described as a tentative handshake. Then, as if to finish what they had started, they both let out uncertain laughs.

"Well," Anthony said without much enthusiasm, "I haven't seen you in quite a while." Right away he wished he hadn't said that and began to add: "I didn't know you lived in this area." But Bloeckman cut him off by asking in a friendly tone:

"How's your wife? ..."

"She's doing very well. How have you been?"

"Excellent." His tone amplified the grandeur of the word.

Anthony noticed that over the past year, Bloeckman had gained considerable dignity. His previously unfinished appearance had disappeared, and he finally seemed polished and complete. He was no longer dressed too formally or flashily. The silly, inappropriate patterns he used to choose for his ties had been replaced by a solid, dark design, and his right hand, which had once worn two large rings, was now free of any jewelry and didn't even show the obvious shine of a fresh manicure.

This dignity was also evident in his character. The final traces of the successful salesman had disappeared from him, along with that calculated charm whose crudest expression is the vulgar joke told in the smoking car of a train. One could imagine that, having been courted for his money, he had developed a sense of detachment; having been rejected by society, he had learned to be reserved. But whatever had given him substance rather than mere size, Anthony no longer felt appropriately superior when around him.

"Do you remember Caramel, Richard Caramel? I believe you met him one night."

"I remember. He was writing a book."

"Well, he sold it to the movies. Then they brought in some screenwriter named Jordan to work on it. Well, Dick subscribes to a clipping service and he's furious because about half the movie critics talk about the 'power and strength of William Jordan's "Demon Lover."' They didn't mention old Dick at all. You'd think this guy Jordan had actually come up with and created the whole thing."

Bloeckman nodded with complete understanding.

"Most of the contracts specify that the original writer's name must appear in all paid advertising. Is Caramel still writing?"

"Oh, yes. Writing is tough. Short stories."

"Well, that's fine, that's fine.... Do you take this train often?"

"About once a week. We live in Marietta."

"Is that so? Well, well! I live near Cos Cob myself. Bought a place there only recently. We're only five miles apart."

"You'll have to come and see us." Anthony was surprised by his own politeness. "I'm sure Gloria would be thrilled to see an old friend. Anyone can tell you where the house is—this is our second season there."

"Thank you." Then, as if returning a polite gesture in kind: "How is your grandfather?"

"He's been doing well. I had lunch with him today."

"A great character," Bloeckman said sternly. "A fine example of an American."

The Triumph of Lethargy

Anthony discovered his wife lounging comfortably in the porch hammock, luxuriously enjoying a lemonade and tomato sandwich while having what seemed to be a pleasant conversation with Tana about one of Tana's complex topics.

"In my country," Anthony recognized his usual opening line, "all the time—people—eat rice—because they don't have anything else. You can't eat what you don't have." If his nationality hadn't been so obviously clear, you might have thought he had learned about his homeland from elementary school geography books in America.

When the Oriental had been silenced and sent away to the kitchen, Anthony turned to Gloria with a questioning look:

"It's all right," she declared, grinning widely. "And it caught me off guard more than it surprises you."

"There's no doubt?"

"None! Couldn't be!"

They celebrated joyfully, feeling carefree once more with their renewed sense of freedom from responsibility. Then he shared with her his chance to travel overseas, and that he felt almost embarrassed to turn it down.

"What do you think? Just tell me honestly."

"Why, Anthony!" Her eyes showed surprise. "Do you want to leave? Without me?"

His expression dropped—but he understood, hearing his wife's question, that the moment had passed. Her embrace, tender yet suffocating, encircled him, because he had already made all these decisions in that hotel room at the Plaza a year earlier. This was a relic from a time when such fantasies seemed possible.

"Gloria," he lied, suddenly understanding everything clearly, "of course I don't. I was thinking you might work as a nurse or something like that." He wondered without much interest whether his grandfather would think this was acceptable.

As she smiled, he was struck once again by her beauty—a stunning young woman with an incredible freshness about her and eyes that were purely honest. She seized upon his idea with passionate enthusiasm, lifting it up like a sun she had created herself and warming herself in its light. She wove together an incredible outline for an elaborate tale of military adventure.

After dinner, having had enough of the topic, she yawned. She didn't want to talk anymore but simply wanted to read "Penrod," lying stretched out on the couch until she fell asleep at midnight. But Anthony, after he had romantically carried her upstairs, remained awake to think about the day, feeling somewhat annoyed with her and somewhat unsatisfied.

"What am I going to do?" he said at breakfast. "We've been married for a year now and we've just been wandering around aimlessly without even managing to be productive people with free time."

"Yes, you should do something," she agreed, feeling chatty and in good spirits. This wasn't the first time they'd had this conversation, but since these discussions typically cast Anthony as the main advocate for action, she had learned to steer clear of them.

"It's not that I have any moral issues with working," he went on, "but grandpa might die tomorrow or he could live another ten years. In the meantime, we're spending more than we earn and all we have to show for it is a beat-up car and some clothes. We're paying for an apartment we've only lived in for three months and a small old house out in the middle of nowhere. We're often bored, yet we won't make any effort to meet anyone except the same group of people who drift around California all summer wearing casual clothes and waiting for their relatives to pass away."

"You've really changed!" Gloria observed. "You once told me you couldn't understand why an American wasn't able to relax with style."

"Well, damn it, I wasn't married. And my mind was working at full capacity, but now it's spinning endlessly like a gear wheel with nothing to engage it. Actually, I believe that if I hadn't met you, I would have taken action. But you make idleness so cleverly appealing—"

"Oh, it's all my fault—"

"I didn't mean that, and you know I didn't. But here I am, almost twenty-seven and—"

"Oh," she cut in with frustration, "you're exhausting me! You're talking like I'm the one standing in your way or trying to stop you!"

"I was just talking about it, Gloria. Can't I talk about—"

"I would think you'd be strong enough to settle—"

"—something with you without—"

"—your own problems without coming to me. You talk constantly about finding work. I could definitely use more money, but I'm not making a fuss about it. I love you whether you work or not." Her final words fell softly like delicate snow on frozen earth. But at that moment, neither was really listening to the other—each was busy refining and polishing their own position.

"I've done some work." Anthony's response was a reckless display of his untapped potential. Gloria laughed, caught between amusement and mockery; she felt annoyed by his clever reasoning while simultaneously appreciating his casual indifference. She would never criticize him for being an unproductive dreamer as long as he was genuine about it, maintaining the belief that nothing was really worth the effort.

"Work!" she mocked. "Oh, you pitiful creature! You fraud! Work—that involves elaborate arranging of the desk and lighting, extensive sharpening of pencils, and 'Gloria, stop singing!' and 'Please keep that damned Tana away from me,' and 'Let me read you my opening line,' and 'I'll be working late, Gloria, so don't wait up for me,' and enormous amounts of tea or coffee consumption. And that's it. Within about an hour I hear that old pencil stop moving and glance over. You've pulled out a book and you're 'researching' something. Then you're reading. Then yawning—then off to bed and lots of tossing around because you're completely wired on caffeine and unable to sleep. Two weeks later the entire routine starts all over again."

With great effort, Anthony managed to preserve just a small shred of his dignity.

"That's a bit of an exaggeration. You know perfectly well I sold an essay to The Florentine—and it got quite a bit of attention given The Florentine's readership. And furthermore, Gloria, you know I stayed up until five in the morning to finish it."

She fell silent, giving him enough rope to hang himself. And if he hadn't actually hanged himself, he had certainly reached the end of it.

"At least," he concluded weakly, "I'm completely willing to work as a war correspondent."

But Gloria felt the same way. Both of them were eager and ready—desperate, even; they kept reassuring each other about their feelings. The evening concluded with an overwhelming sense of emotion, the grandeur of having time to spare, Adam Patch's poor health, and love regardless of the price.

"Anthony!" she shouted down from the banister one afternoon a week later, "someone's at the door." Anthony, who had been lounging in the hammock on the sun-dappled south porch, walked around to the front of the house. A foreign car, large and imposing, sat like an enormous and gloomy insect at the bottom of the path. A man in a soft pongee suit, with a matching cap, called out to him.

"Hello there, Patch. I ran over to see you."

It was Bloeckman; as usual, he appeared slightly more polished, with a more refined way of speaking and a more persuasive sense of confidence.

"I'm really glad you did." Anthony called out loudly toward a window covered with vines: "Glor-i-a! We have a visitor!"

"I'm in the bathtub," Gloria called out politely with a hint of distress.

With a smile, both men acknowledged the success of her alibi.

"She'll be down in a minute. Come around here to the side porch. Would you like a drink? Gloria's always in the bathtub—spends a good third of every day in there."

"It's a shame she doesn't live on the Sound."

"Can't afford it."

As the grandson of Adam Patch, Bloeckman interpreted this as a kind of joke. After fifteen minutes of impressive wit and clever conversation, Gloria arrived, looking fresh in her crisp yellow dress, bringing with her a lively atmosphere and renewed energy.

"I want to become a successful movie star," she declared. "I've heard that Mary Pickford earns a million dollars every year."

"You could, you know," said Bloeckman. "I think you'd look great on camera."

"Would you let me, Anthony? If I only take on simple roles?"

As the conversation dragged on in awkward pauses, Anthony

found himself wondering how this girl had once been the most exciting and energizing person that both he and Bloeckman had ever encountered—and now the three of them sat there like over-lubricated machines, without struggle, without anxiety, without joy, like heavily painted little figurines safe beyond pleasure in a world where death and war, lifeless feelings and dignified brutality were blanketing a continent with the haze of fear.

In a moment he would call Tana and they would drink a cheerful and refined poison that would briefly bring back the thrilling excitement of childhood, when every face in a crowd suggested wonderful and meaningful events happening somewhere for some grand and limitless purpose.... Life was nothing more than this summer afternoon; a gentle breeze moving the lace collar of Gloria's dress; the slow, warm sleepiness of the porch.... They all seemed unbearably still, distant from any romantic possibility of action. Even Gloria's beauty required intense emotions, required sharp feeling, required death....

"... Any day next week," Bloeckman was telling Gloria. "Here—take this card. What they do is give you a test using about three hundred feet of film, and they can determine pretty accurately from that."

"How about Wednesday?"

"Wednesday works for me. Just give me a call and I'll come along with you—"

He stood up, shaking hands energetically—then his car became nothing more than a ghostly cloud of dust disappearing down the road. Anthony turned to his wife, completely bewildered.

"Why, Gloria!"

"You don't mind if I give it a try, Anthony. Just a trial run? I have to go into town on Wednesday anyway."

"But that's ridiculous! You don't want to get into the film industry—hanging around a studio all day with a bunch of low-class performers."

"Mary Pickford sure does a lot of daydreaming and moping around!"

"Not everyone can be a Mary Pickford."

"Well, I can't see how you'd object to my trying."

"I do, though. I hate actors."

"Oh, you're exhausting me. Do you think I'm having an exciting time napping on this awful porch?"

"You wouldn't mind if you loved me."

"Of course I love you," she said with irritation, quickly building her argument. "It's precisely because I love you that I can't stand watching you fall apart by just lounging around and talking about how you should be working. Maybe if I actually went through with this for a while, it would motivate you enough to finally take action."

"It's just your craving for excitement, that's all it is."

"Maybe it is! It's a perfectly natural craving, isn't it?"

"Well, I'll tell you one thing. If you go to the movies I'm going to Europe."

"Well, go on then! I'm not stopping you!"

To demonstrate that she wasn't trying to prevent him, she dissolved into sorrowful tears. Side by side, they assembled the forces of emotion—words, kisses, tender expressions, and self-blame. They accomplished nothing. It was inevitable that they would accomplish nothing. At last, in an explosion of overwhelming feeling, each of them sat down and composed a letter. Anthony's letter was addressed to his grandfather; Gloria's was written to Joseph Bloeckman. It was a victory of inaction.

One day in early July, Anthony returned from an afternoon in New York and called upstairs to Gloria. When he got no response, he figured she was sleeping, so he headed to the pantry to grab one of the small sandwiches that were always made for them. He discovered Tana sitting at the kitchen table in front of a random collection of various items—cigar boxes, knives, pencils, can lids, and some pieces of paper filled with detailed figures and diagrams.

"What the hell are you doing?" Anthony asked with curiosity.

Tana smiled politely.

"I'll show you," he exclaimed enthusiastically. "I'll tell—"

"Are you building a doghouse?"

"No, sir." Tana grinned again. "Make typewriter."

"Typewriter?"

"Yes, sir. I think about it all the time, lying in bed thinking about the typewriter."

"So you thought you'd make one, eh?"

"Wait. Let me tell you."

Anthony, eating a sandwich, leaned casually against the sink. Tana opened and closed his mouth repeatedly as if checking whether it was ready to work. Then suddenly he started speaking:

"I've been thinking—the typewriter—has, oh, so many, many, many, many things. Oh, so many, many, many, many." "Many keys. I see."

"No? Yes! Many, many, many, many letters. Like this: a-b-c."

"Yes, you're right."

"Wait. Let me explain." He scrunched up his face in an enormous effort to express himself: "I've been thinking—many words—end the same way. Like i-n-g."

"You bet. A whole bunch of them."

"So—I make—typewriter—quick. Not so many letters—"

"That's a great idea, Tana. It'll save time. You're going to make a fortune. Press one key and there's 'ing.' I hope you work it out."

Tana laughed with contempt. "Wait. I tell—" "Where's Mrs. Patch?"

"She's out. Wait, let me tell you—" Once again he scrunched up his face, getting ready to speak. "My typewriter——"

"Where is she?"

"Here—I make." He gestured toward the assortment of junk scattered across the table.

"I mean Mrs. Patch."

"She's out," Tana reassured him. "She'll be back at five o'clock, she said."

"Down in the village?"

"No. She left before lunch. She went with Mr. Bloeckman."

Anthony jumped.

"Went out with Mr. Bloeckman?"

"She'll be back at five."

Without saying a word, Anthony walked out of the kitchen while Tana's dejected "I tell" echoed behind him. So this was what Gloria considered exciting, for God's sake! His hands were balled into fists; within seconds he had built himself up into a furious rage. He walked to the door and peered outside; there wasn't a car anywhere in sight and his watch showed four minutes before five. With angry determination he ran down to the end of the walkway—looking as far as the curve in the road a mile away he couldn't see any car—except—but that was just a farmer's old jalopy. Then, in an embarrassing attempt to maintain his dignity, he hurried back to the safety of the house just as quickly as he had rushed out.

Pacing back and forth across the living room, he started angrily practicing the speech he would deliver to her when she walked in—

"So this is love!" he would start—or no, that sounded too much like the popular saying "So this is Paris!" He needed to be dignified, wounded, sorrowful. In any case—"So this is what you do when I have to go up and trudge all day around the sweltering city on business. No wonder I can't write! No wonder I don't dare let you out of my sight!" He was getting carried away now, becoming passionate about his topic. "I'll tell you," he went on, "I'll tell you—" He stopped, hearing a familiar sound in those words—then he understood—it was Tana's "I tell."

Yet Anthony neither laughed nor seemed ridiculous to himself. To his frenzied imagination it was already six—seven—eight o'clock, and she was never going to come! Bloeckman, finding her bored and miserable, had convinced her to go to California with him....

There was quite a commotion outside, with someone cheerfully calling out "Yoho, Anthony!" He stood up shakily, feeling a weak surge of happiness as he watched her hurrying up the walkway. Bloeckman was walking behind her, holding his hat in his hand.

"Dearest!" she cried.

"We've had the most wonderful trip—all across New York State."

"I'll have to be heading home," said Bloeckman, almost immediately. "I wish you'd both been here when I arrived."

"I'm sorry I wasn't," Anthony replied curtly. After he left, Anthony hesitated. The fear had vanished from his heart, yet he sensed that some objection would be morally appropriate. Gloria settled his indecision.

"I knew you wouldn't mind. He came just before lunch and said he had to go to Garrison on business and wouldn't I go with him. He looked so lonely, Anthony. And I drove his car all the way."

Anthony slumped into a chair without energy, his mind exhausted—worn out by nothing in particular, worn out by everything, by the burden of the world that he had never asked to carry. He felt useless and somewhat powerless here, just as he always had been. He was one of those people who, despite all their talking, couldn't truly express themselves, and he seemed to have received only humanity's long legacy of disappointment—that, along with an awareness of mortality.

"I suppose I don't care," he answered.

One must be understanding about these matters, and Gloria, being young and beautiful, deserves certain reasonable privileges. Still, it troubled him that he couldn't comprehend her behavior.

Winter

She turned onto her back and remained motionless for a moment in the large bed, watching the February sunlight undergo one final weakened transformation as it filtered through the leaded glass windows into the room. For a while she couldn't clearly recall where she was or what had happened the day before, or even the day before that; then, like a pendulum that had been held still and released, her memory started to tick out its tale, delivering with each beat a heavy portion of time until her entire life was restored to her.

She could hear Anthony's labored breathing next to her now; she could smell the whiskey and cigarette smoke on him. She realized she didn't have full control over her muscles; when she tried to move, it wasn't the smooth, flowing motion where the effort spread naturally throughout her body—instead, it required an enormous strain on her nervous system, as if she had to hypnotize herself each time just to accomplish something that should have been impossible....

She was in the bathroom, brushing her teeth to eliminate that unbearable taste; then she returned to the bedside, listening to the sound of Bounds's key rattling in the front door.

"Wake up, Anthony!" she said sharply.

She got into bed next to him and shut her eyes. One of the last things she could recall was talking with Mr. and Mrs. Lacy. Mrs. Lacy had asked, "Are you sure you don't want us to call you a taxi?" and Anthony had answered that he thought they could manage to walk over to Fifth Avenue just fine. Then both of them had foolishly tried to bow—and tumbled ridiculously into a group of empty milk bottles right outside the door. There must have been

217

at least twenty-four milk bottles standing with their mouths open in the darkness. She couldn't think of any reasonable explanation for those milk bottles being there. Maybe they had been drawn by the singing coming from the Lacy house and had rushed over with their mouths wide open in amazement to watch the entertainment. Well, they had gotten the worst of it—though it felt like she and Anthony would never manage to get back up, those stubborn things kept rolling around so much....

Still, they had managed to find a taxi. "My meter's not working and it's going to cost you a dollar and a half to get home," the taxi driver told them. "Well," Anthony replied, "I'm young Packy McFarland and if you come down here I'll beat you until you can't stand up." At that moment the driver had taken off without them. They must have located another taxi, because they ended up back at the apartment.

"What time is it?" Anthony was sitting up in bed, looking at her with sharp, focused attention.

This was clearly a rhetorical question. Gloria couldn't think of any reason why she would be expected to know the time.

"Wow, I feel absolutely terrible!" Anthony muttered without emotion. Letting himself go limp, he collapsed back onto his pillow. "Bring on death itself!"

"Anthony, how did we finally get home last night?"

"Taxi."

"Oh!" Then, after a pause: "Did you put me to bed?"

"I don't know. It seems to me that you put me to bed. What day is it?"

"Tuesday."

"Tuesday? I hope so. If it's Wednesday, I have to start work at that ridiculous place. I'm supposed to be there by nine or some other awful hour."

"Ask Bounds," Gloria suggested weakly.

"Bounds!" he shouted.

Energetic and serious—a voice from a world that seemed like they had abandoned forever in the past two days, Bounds bounded down the hallway in quick steps and emerged in the dim light of the doorway.

"What day, Bounds?"

"I believe it was February twenty-second, sir."

"I mean day of the week."

"Tuesday, sir." "Thanks." After a pause: "Are you ready for breakfast, sir?"

"Yes, and Bounds, before you bring it, would you make a pitcher of water and place it here next to the bed? I'm feeling a bit thirsty."

"Yes, sir."

Bounds withdrew with quiet dignity down the hallway.

"Lincoln's birthday," Anthony confirmed without any enthusiasm, "or St. Valentine's or somebody's. When did we begin this crazy party?"

"Sunday night."

"After prayers?" he suggested with sarcasm.

"We raced all over town in those horse-drawn carriages, and Maury sat up front with his driver—don't you remember? Then we came home and he tried to cook some bacon, emerging from the pantry with a few blackened remains, insisting it was 'fried to the proverbial crisp.'"

Both of them laughed, naturally but with some effort, and lying there next to each other, they went over the series of events that had led to this gritty and disorderly morning.

They had been living in New York for nearly four months, ever since the countryside had become too cold in late October. This year they had decided against California, partly due to limited finances and partly because they were considering traveling overseas if this endless war, now dragging on into its second year, came to an end during the winter months. Recently their income had become less flexible; it no longer stretched to accommodate spontaneous desires and enjoyable luxuries, and Anthony had spent countless frustrated and disappointing hours hunched over a page covered with dense calculations, creating elaborate budgets that somehow still left enormous allowances for "entertainment, travel, etc.," while attempting to account for, even roughly, how they had spent their money in the past.

He recalled a period when going out on the town with his two closest friends meant that he and Maury consistently ended up covering more than their fair share of the costs. They would purchase the theater tickets or argue with each other over who would pay the restaurant bill. This arrangement had felt appropriate; Dick, with his innocence and his remarkable collection of personal stories, had been an entertaining, almost childlike character—like a court jester serving their nobility. However, this dynamic had shifted completely. Now it was Dick who always seemed to have cash available; it was Anthony who hosted gatherings within strict budgets—except for the occasional wild, alcohol-fueled nights when he would cash checks recklessly—and it was Anthony who felt serious regret the following morning, telling his contemptuous and irritated wife Gloria that they would need to be "more cautious going forward."

In the two years since "The Demon Lover" was published, Dick had earned more than twenty-five thousand dollars, with most of that money coming recently as fiction writers began receiving unprecedented rewards due to the movie industry's insatiable appetite for storylines. He earned seven hundred dollars for each story, which was a substantial payment for someone so young—he wasn't even thirty yet—and for every story that had enough "action" (romance, violence, and drama) suitable for films, he received an extra thousand dollars. His stories showed variety; all of them possessed a certain energy and natural instinct, but none captured the distinctive character of "The Demon Lover," and Anthony thought several were genuinely inferior. Dick sternly justified these lesser works as necessary to broaden his readership. Wasn't it accurate that writers who had achieved lasting significance, from Shakespeare to Mark Twain, had attracted both popular audiences and sophisticated readers?

Though Anthony and Maury had different opinions, Gloria encouraged him to move forward and earn as much money as possible—that was the only thing that really mattered anyway....

Maury, who had grown a bit heavier, slightly more mellow, and more agreeable, had taken a job in Philadelphia. He visited New York once or twice each month, and during these visits the four friends would follow the well-known entertainment circuit from dinner to the theater, then to the Frolic or, sometimes, at the insistence of the perpetually inquisitive Gloria, to one of the basement venues in Greenwich Village that had become famous during the intense but brief popularity of the "new poetry movement."

In January, after delivering countless one-sided speeches to his silent wife, Anthony decided to "find some work," at least for the winter months. He hoped to make his grandfather happy and also wanted to discover whether he might actually enjoy working. Through several exploratory social visits, he learned that employers had no interest in hiring a young man who planned to "give it a shot for just a few months or something like that." As Adam Patch's grandson, he was welcomed everywhere with notable politeness, but the old man had become irrelevant now— his golden age of fame, first as an "oppressor" and later as a champion of the people, had occurred during the twenty years before his retirement. Anthony even encountered several younger men who believed that Adam Patch had been dead for years.

Eventually Anthony approached his grandfather seeking guidance, and the advice he received was to pursue a career in the bond business as a salesman—a suggestion that struck Anthony as tedious, though he ultimately decided to follow it. The skillful handling of money held appeal under any circumstances, while nearly every aspect of manufacturing seemed unbearably boring. He thought about working for a newspaper but concluded that the irregular hours wouldn't suit a married man. He also entertained pleasant daydreams of becoming either the editor of a brilliant weekly opinion magazine, an American equivalent of Mercure de France, or a sparkling creator of satirical comedies and Parisian-style musical revues. However, entry into these professions appeared to be protected by insider knowledge and connections. People found their way into these fields through the winding paths of writing and performing. It was clearly impossible to land a position at a magazine without having previous magazine experience.

So in the end, he entered that sacred American space through his grandfather's letter, where the president of Wilson, Hiemer and Hardy sat at his "cleared desk," and emerged from there with a job. He was to begin work on February twenty-third.

To celebrate this significant event, they had planned a two-day celebration, since, as he explained, once he started working he would need to go to bed early on weeknights. Maury Noble had come down from Philadelphia on business that involved meeting someone on Wall Street (who, as it turned out, he never actually met), and Richard Caramel had been partly convinced, partly manipulated into coming along. They had attended a lavish and trendy wedding on Monday afternoon, and that evening brought the climax: Gloria, drinking more than her usual limit of exactly four carefully timed cocktails, led them in the most spirited and joyful wild party they had ever experienced, revealing a surprising mastery of dance moves and performing songs that she admitted her cook had taught her when she was naive and seventeen. She performed these again whenever asked throughout the night with such open friendliness that Anthony, rather than feeling irritated, was pleased by this new form of amusement. The night was unforgettable for other reasons as well—an extended discussion between Maury and a dead crab, which he was pulling along on a piece of string, about whether the crab truly understood how to use the binomial theorem, and the previously mentioned race in two horse-drawn carriages with the dignified and stately silhouettes of Fifth Avenue watching, which ended in a maze-like getaway into the shadows of Central Park. Eventually Anthony and Gloria had visited some reckless young newlyweds—the Lacys—and ended up passed out among the empty milk bottles.

Morning arrives—time for them to tally up the checks cashed at various clubs, stores, and restaurants. Time for them to clear out the musty, stale air thick with wine and cigarette smoke from the tall blue front room, to gather up the shattered glass and scrub at the stained upholstery of chairs and couches; to hand Bounds the suits and dresses that need dry cleaning; and finally, to drag their suffocating, half-feverish bodies and worn-down, dejected spirits out into the bitter February air, so that life could continue and Wilson, Hiemer and Hardy could secure the services of an energetic employee by nine the following morning.

"Do you remember," Anthony called out from the bathroom, "when Maury got off at the corner of One Hundred and Tenth Street and started directing traffic like a cop, waving cars forward and signaling them to stop? They probably thought he was some kind of private investigator."

After each memory they shared, both of them laughed excessively, their overstressed nerves reacting as sharply and harshly to joy as they did to sadness.

Gloria stood at the mirror, marveling at the beautiful color and vitality of her complexion—it appeared she had never looked better, even though her stomach was bothering her and her head was pounding terribly.

The day dragged on. Anthony, traveling by taxi to his broker's office to borrow money against a bond, discovered he had only two dollars in his pocket. The fare would consume all of that, but he felt that on this specific afternoon he couldn't have tolerated the subway. When the taxi meter reached his limit he would have to get out and walk.

With this, his thoughts wandered into one of his typical daydreams.... In this fantasy, he realized that the meter was running too quickly—the driver had dishonestly tampered with it. He calmly arrived at his destination and then casually gave the man exactly what he rightfully owed him. The man became aggressive, but almost before he could raise his hands, Anthony had knocked him down with one powerful punch. And when the driver got back up, Anthony quickly moved aside and knocked him out for good with a strike to the temple.

He was in court now. The judge had fined him five dollars and he didn't have any money. Would the court accept his check? But the court didn't know who he was. Well, he could prove his identity by having them call his apartment.

They did exactly that. Yes, it was Mrs. Anthony Patch on the phone—but how could she be certain that this man was actually her husband? How was it possible for her to know? The police sergeant should ask her whether she recalled anything about the milk bottles...

He quickly leaned forward and tapped on the glass. The taxi had only reached Brooklyn Bridge, but the meter already displayed a dollar and eighty cents, and Anthony would never have forgotten the ten percent tip.

Later that afternoon, he came back to the apartment. Gloria had been out shopping as well and was now sleeping, curled up in a corner of the couch with her purchase held tightly in her arms. Her face looked as peaceful as a young girl's, and the package she clutched against her chest was a child's doll—a deep and endlessly comforting remedy for her troubled and innocent heart.

Destiny

It was with this party, particularly with Gloria's role in it, that a clear shift started to transform their lifestyle. The grand attitude of not caring about anything changed completely overnight; what had once been simply one of Gloria's beliefs now became their whole comfort and reason for whatever they decided to do and whatever results followed. They resolved not to feel sorry, not to let out a single sound of regret, to live by a clear set of principles in how they treated each other, and to chase after immediate happiness as passionately and relentlessly as they could.

"Nobody cares about us except ourselves, Anthony," she said one day. "It would be absurd for me to walk around pretending I have any responsibilities to the world, and when it comes to worrying about what people think of me, I just don't, that's all there is to it. Ever since I was a young girl in dance class, I've been criticized by the mothers of all the girls who weren't as well-liked as I was, and I've always viewed criticism as a kind of jealous compliment."

This happened because of a party on the Boulevard Saint-Michel one evening, where Constance Merriam had spotted her as part of a very intoxicated group of four people. Constance Merriam, claiming to act "as an old school friend," had made the effort to invite her to lunch the following day so she could tell her how awful it was.

"I told her I couldn't understand it," Gloria said to Anthony. "Eric Merriam is basically a refined version of Percy Wolcott— you remember that guy from Hot Springs I mentioned to you— his way of showing respect for Constance is to leave her at home with her needlework and her baby and her reading, along with other harmless pastimes, whenever he's heading out to a party that looks like it might actually be entertaining."

"Did you tell her that?"

"I absolutely did. And I explained to her that what truly bothered her was that I was enjoying myself more than she was."

Anthony applauded her. He felt incredibly proud of Gloria, proud that she consistently outshone any other women who might be at the party, proud that men were always happy to celebrate with her in large, boisterous groups, without ever trying to do anything more than appreciate her beauty and the energy of her spirit.

These gatherings slowly became their main form of entertainment. Though they were still in love and deeply fascinated by one another, they discovered as spring approached that spending evenings at home had lost its appeal; books felt disconnected from reality; the old enchantment of solitude had disappeared long ago—instead they chose to endure boredom at a mindless musical comedy, or to have dinner with the most tedious of their friends, as long as there were enough cocktails to prevent the conversation from becoming completely unbearable. A group of younger married couples who had been their friends from school or college, along with a diverse collection of single men, started automatically thinking of them whenever liveliness and excitement were required, so hardly a day passed without a phone call, without someone saying "We were wondering what you were doing tonight." Wives, generally speaking, were wary of Gloria—her effortless ability to command attention, her seemingly innocent yet troubling talent for becoming popular with husbands—these qualities naturally pushed them toward deep suspicion, made worse by the fact that Gloria showed little interest in forming close friendships with other women.

On the scheduled Wednesday in February, Anthony had visited the impressive offices of Wilson, Hiemer and Hardy, where he listened to numerous unclear instructions given by an enthusiastic young man around his own age, called Kahler, who sported a bold yellow pompadour and, when introducing himself as an assistant secretary, conveyed the sense that this position was recognition of his outstanding talent.

"You'll discover there are two types of men in this place," he explained. "There's the guy who becomes an assistant secretary or treasurer and gets his name printed on our company materials before he turns thirty, and then there's the guy who doesn't get his name there until he's forty-five. The man who finally gets his name on there at forty-five remains in that position for the rest of his career."

"What about the guy who makes it there by thirty?" Anthony asked politely.

"You see, he moves up to this level." He gestured toward a list of assistant vice-presidents on the folder. "Or perhaps he becomes president, secretary, or treasurer."

"And what about these over here?"

"Those? Oh, those are the trustees—the men with capital."

"I see."

"Now some people," Kahler went on, "believe that whether a person begins early or late in life depends on having a college education. But they're mistaken."

"I see."

"I had one; I was Buckleigh, class of nineteen-eleven, but when I came down to the Street I quickly discovered that the things that would help me here weren't the sophisticated concepts I learned in college. In fact, I had to get a lot of that sophisticated material out of my head."

Anthony couldn't stop wondering what kind of "fancy stuff" he could have possibly learned at Buckleigh back in 1911. A persistent thought that it might have been some type of needlework kept coming back to him for the remainder of their conversation.

"See that fellow over there?" Kahler pointed to a young-looking man with attractive gray hair, seated at a desk behind a mahogany railing. "That's Mr. Ellinger, the first vice-president. He's been everywhere, seen everything; has an excellent education."

Anthony tried unsuccessfully to appreciate the excitement of finance; he could only think of Mr. Ellinger as someone who purchased the beautiful leather-bound collections of Thackeray, Balzac, Hugo, and Gibbon that filled the shelves of large bookstores.

During the dreary and depressing month of March, he underwent training for a career in sales. Without any real passion for it, he could only see the chaos and frantic activity around him as pointless effort directed toward a goal that made no sense, with the only concrete proof being the competing grand houses of Mr. Frick and Mr. Carnegie on Fifth Avenue. It struck him as absurd that these intimidating vice-presidents and board members were actually the fathers of the "best men" he had met during his time at Harvard.

He ate in an employee cafeteria upstairs with an uncomfortable feeling that he was being influenced, wondering during that first week whether the dozens of young office workers, some of them sharp and well-groomed, fresh out of college, lived with extravagant dreams of squeezing onto that thin piece of success before the devastating thirties hit. The conversations that wove through the daily work routine were all very similar. People discussed how Mr. Wilson had earned his wealth, what strategy Mr. Hiemer had used, and the tactics Mr. Hardy had relied on. Someone would share ancient but eternally exciting stories about fortunes discovered suddenly on Wall Street by a "butcher" or a "bartender," or "a damn messenger boy, for crying out loud!" and then they would talk about current investments, debating whether it was better to aim for a hundred thousand dollars a year or settle for twenty thousand. During the previous year, one of the assistant secretaries had put all his savings into Bethlehem Steel. The story of his remarkable success, his proud resignation in January, and the magnificent mansion he was now constructing in California had become the office's favorite topic. The man's name itself had taken on almost magical meaning, representing as it did the dreams of all ambitious Americans. Stories were shared about him—how one of the vice-presidents had recommended he sell, for crying out loud, but he had held on, even purchased more on credit, "and just look at him now!"

Such, clearly, was what life was made of—a dizzying triumph that dazzled everyone's eyes, a wandering siren that satisfied them with small wages and the mathematical unlikelihood of ever achieving success.

To Anthony, the idea became horrifying. He realized that to make it here, the concept of success would have to take over and constrain his thinking. It appeared to him that what defined these men at the top was their belief that their business dealings were the absolute center of existence. When everything else was the same, confidence and opportunism triumphed over technical expertise; it was clear that the more skilled work happened at lower levels—so, with fitting efficiency, the technical specialists were kept in those positions.

His resolve to stay home on weeknights didn't last, and about half the time he showed up to work with a pounding, nauseating headache and the packed nightmare of the morning subway echoing in his ears like sounds from hell.

Then, suddenly, he quit. He had stayed in bed all Monday, and late that evening, overwhelmed by one of those bouts of gloomy despair that regularly overtook him, he wrote and sent a letter to Mr. Wilson, admitting that he felt unsuited for the job. Gloria, returning from the theater with Richard Caramel, discovered him on the couch, quietly gazing at the high ceiling, more dejected and disheartened than he had been at any point since their wedding.

She wanted him to complain. If he had complained, she would have criticized him harshly, because she was quite irritated, but he just lay there looking so completely wretched that she felt pity for him, and getting down on her knees she gently touched his head, telling him how unimportant it was, how nothing really mattered as long as they had each other's love. It reminded her of their first year together, and Anthony, responding to her cool touch and her voice that whispered as softly as a breath in his ear, became almost upbeat, and discussed his future plans with her. He even quietly wished, before going to sleep, that he hadn't been so quick to send in his resignation letter.

"Even when everything appears to be falling apart, you can't rely on that assessment," Gloria had said. "What matters is the total of all your evaluations combined."

In mid-April, a letter arrived from the real estate agent in Marietta, urging them to rent the gray house for another year at a somewhat higher price, and including a lease ready for their signatures. For a week, both the lease and letter sat carelessly ignored on Anthony's desk. They had no plans to return to Marietta. They were tired of the place and had been bored for most of the previous summer. Furthermore, their car had broken down into a noisy heap of unreliable metal, and purchasing a new one would be financially unwise.

But after another wild party that lasted four days and involved more than a dozen people at various times, they actually signed the lease. They signed it in complete horror and sent it off, and right away it felt as if they could hear the gray house, now openly sinister and drab, licking its white lips while waiting to consume them.

"Anthony, where's that lease?" she called out in panic one Sunday morning, feeling sick and suddenly confronted with reality. "Where did you put it? It was right here!"

Then she knew where it was. She remembered the house party they had planned at the peak of their excitement; she remembered a room filled with men who, in their calmer moments, considered her and Anthony unimportant, and Anthony's proud claims about the exceptional quality and privacy of the gray house—how it was so remote that it didn't matter how much noise they made there. Then Dick, who had come to see them, exclaimed enthusiastically that it was the most wonderful little house you could imagine, and that they were foolish not to rent it for another summer. It had been simple to convince themselves of how hot and empty the city was becoming, and how cool and delightful the attractions of Marietta were. Anthony had grabbed the lease and waved it around excitedly, found Gloria cheerfully agreeable, and with one final explosion of talkative decision-making during which all the men agreed with serious handshakes that they would come out for a visit...

"Anthony," she exclaimed, "we've signed it and sent it off!"

"What?"

"The lease!"

"What the devil!"

"Oh, Anthony!" Her voice was filled with complete despair. They had created a prison for themselves, one that would last through the summer and perhaps forever. This realization seemed to shake the very foundation of their security. Anthony considered whether they might be able to work something out with the real estate agent. They could no longer manage to pay rent on two places, and moving to Marietta would mean abandoning his apartment—his perfect apartment with the beautiful bathroom and the rooms he had carefully furnished with his own belongings and decorations. This apartment was the closest thing to a real home he had ever known, filled with memories from four vibrant years of his life.

But it wasn't planned with the real estate agent, and in fact, it wasn't planned at all. Feeling dejected, without even discussing how to make the situation work, without even Gloria's usual reassuring "I don't care," they returned to the house that they now understood welcomed neither youth nor love—only those stern and private memories that they could never share with each other.

The Sinister Summer

There was a terrible dread in the house that summer. It arrived with them and draped itself over the entire place like a dark shroud, seeping through the downstairs rooms, slowly expanding and creeping up the steep staircase until it weighed down even their dreams. Anthony and Gloria came to despise being there by themselves. Her bedroom, which had once appeared so rosy and fresh and feminine, perfectly suited to her soft-colored undergarments scattered across the chair and bed, now seemed to murmur through its whispering curtains:

"Oh, my lovely young woman, you're not the first one whose beauty and grace has withered away here under the hot summer sun... countless generations of women who were never truly loved have dressed themselves up in front of that mirror for country men who didn't care at all.... Young women have entered this room wearing the palest blue and left it wrapped in the gray shrouds of hopelessness, and through many long nights, girls have stayed awake in that very bed, sending waves of suffering into the darkness."

Gloria finally dumped all her clothes and cosmetics unceremoniously out of it, announcing that she had decided to live with Anthony, and using the excuse that one of her room dividers was deteriorating and letting in insects. So her room was left to inconsiderate guests, and they got dressed and slept in her husband's bedroom, which Gloria somehow thought was "right," as if Anthony's presence there had served to eliminate any troubling remnants of the past that might have lingered around its walls.

The difference between "good" and "bad," which had been quickly and decisively removed from both their lives, had returned in a different way. Gloria demanded that anyone invited to the gray house had to be "good," which, when it came to women, meant they had to be either innocent and beyond reproach or, if not, they needed to have a certain stability and character. Having always been deeply suspicious of other women, her opinions now focused on whether women were clean or not. When she spoke of uncleanliness, she was referring to several things: a lack of self-respect, weakness of character, and above all, the obvious signs of sleeping around.

"Women get corrupted easily," she said, "much more easily than men. Unless a girl is very young and courageous, it's nearly impossible for her to fall into ruin without developing a certain frenzied brutishness, the sly, filthy kind of brutishness. A man is different—and I suppose that's why one of the most common characters in romance is a man going nobly to his destruction."

She tended to like many men, especially those who offered her genuine admiration and constant amusement—but frequently with a sudden moment of clarity she would tell Anthony that one of his friends was simply taking advantage of him, and therefore should be avoided. Anthony usually disagreed, maintaining that the person in question was a "good guy," but he discovered that his judgment was less reliable than hers, particularly when, as occurred on multiple occasions, he ended up stuck with a series of restaurant bills that he had to pay alone.

More out of their fear of being alone than from any genuine desire to deal with the hassle and trouble of hosting, they packed the house with guests every weekend, and frequently throughout the week as well. The weekend gatherings followed a predictable pattern. Once the three or four invited men had shown up, drinking became the main activity, followed by a lively dinner and a trip to the Cradle Beach Country Club, which they had joined because it was affordable, entertaining if not stylish, and practically essential for exactly these kinds of occasions. Furthermore, it didn't really matter what anyone did there, and as long as the Patch group kept their noise to a reasonable level, it made little difference whether the social leaders of Cradle Beach noticed the cheerful Gloria drinking cocktails in the dining room at regular intervals throughout the evening.

Saturday typically ended in glamorous chaos—it was often necessary to help a confused guest get to bed. Sunday brought the New York newspapers and a peaceful morning of recovery on the porch—and Sunday afternoon meant saying goodbye to the guest or two who had to return to the city, along with a renewed surge of drinking among the one or two who stayed until the following day, wrapping up with a friendly if not wildly entertaining evening.

The loyal Tana, a natural teacher and professional jack-of-all-trades, had come back with them. A tradition had developed among their regular visitors concerning him. One afternoon, Maury Noble mentioned that his actual name was Tannenbaum, and that he was a German spy stationed in this country to spread German propaganda throughout Westchester County, and following that comment, strange letters started arriving from Philadelphia addressed to the confused Asian man as "Lt. Emile Tannenbaum," containing several mysterious messages signed "General Staff," and decorated with an elaborate double column of mock Japanese characters. Anthony would always pass them to Tana with a straight face; hours later the recipient would be discovered studying them in the kitchen and insisting seriously that the vertical symbols were not Japanese, nor anything that looked like Japanese.

Gloria had developed an intense dislike for the man from the moment she came home unexpectedly from the village and found him lying on Anthony's bed, struggling to read a newspaper. All servants naturally loved Anthony and despised Gloria, and Tana followed this pattern perfectly. However, he was completely terrified of her and only showed his hatred during his darker moods by cleverly directing comments to Anthony that were really meant for her to hear:

"What does Miss Pats want for dinner?" he would ask, looking at his master. Otherwise, he would make remarks about the bitter selfishness of "American people" in such a way that left no doubt about who these "people" were that he was referring to.

But they didn't dare fire him. Taking such action would have gone against their natural tendency to avoid change. They put up with Tana the same way they tolerated bad weather, physical illness, and what they considered God's will—the way they endured everything in life, including their own existence.

In Darkness

One sweltering afternoon in late July, Richard Caramel called from New York to say that he and Maury were heading out their way, bringing a friend along. They showed up around five o'clock, slightly intoxicated, with a short, solidly built man of thirty-five in tow, whom they presented as Mr. Joe Hull, describing him as one of the finest people Anthony and Gloria would ever have the pleasure of meeting.

Joe Hull had a yellow beard that constantly pushed through his skin and spoke in a deep voice that shifted between a rich bass and a rough whisper. Anthony carried Maury's suitcase upstairs, followed him into the room, and carefully shut the door.

"Who is this guy?" he asked.

Maury laughed with enthusiasm.

"Who, Hull? Oh, he's fine. He's a good guy."

"Yes, but who is he?"

"Hull? He's just a good guy. He's a prince." His laughter grew even louder, ending in a series of pleasant catlike grins. Anthony wavered between smiling and frowning.

235

"He looks kind of strange to me. Those odd-looking clothes"—he stopped for a moment—"I have a growing suspicion that you two found him somewhere last night."

"That's ridiculous," Maury declared. "I've known him my entire life." But as he followed this statement with another round of laughter, Anthony felt compelled to respond: "Like hell you have!"

Later, just before dinner, while Maury and Dick were having a loud, animated conversation, with Joe Hull listening quietly as he sipped his drink, Gloria pulled Anthony into the dining room:

"I don't like this man Hull," she said. "I wish he'd use Tana's bathtub."

"I can't very well ask him to."

"Well, I don't want him in ours."

"He appears to be a simple person."

"He's wearing white shoes that look like gloves. I can see his toes right through them. Ugh! Who is he, anyway?"

"You've got me."

"Well, I think they have some nerve bringing him out here. This isn't a Sailor's Rescue Home!"

"They were drunk when they called. Maury said they've been partying since yesterday afternoon."

Gloria shook her head in frustration and, without saying another word, walked back to the porch. Anthony could see that she was attempting to push aside her doubts and focus on enjoying the evening.

The day had been swelteringly hot, and even as evening approached, heat waves continued to rise from the parched road, shimmering faintly like rippling sheets of translucent glass. The sky remained clear, but from somewhere far beyond the forest toward the Sound, a low, steady rumbling had begun. When Tana called them for dinner, the men, following Gloria's suggestion, stayed in their shirtsleeves and headed indoors.

Maury started singing a song, and they performed it together in harmony while eating the first course. The song had two lines and was set to a well-known tune called Daisy Dear. The lyrics were:

"The panic has overwhelmed us,"

"So that's it—the moral decline!"

Each performance was met with explosive enthusiasm and extended applause.

"Cheer up, Gloria!" suggested Maury. "You seem a little depressed."

"I'm not," she lied.

"Here, Tannenbaum!" he called over his shoulder. "I've poured you a drink. Come on!"

Gloria tried to stop his arm.

"Please don't, Maury!"

"Why not? Maybe he'll play the flute for us after dinner. Here, Tana."

Tana smiled broadly as he carried the glass to the kitchen. Within a few minutes, Maury handed him another one.

"Cheer up, Gloria!" he shouted. "For Heaven's sake everyone, cheer up Gloria."

"Sweetheart, have another drink," Anthony suggested.

"Please, go ahead!"

"Cheer up, Gloria," Joe Hull said casually.

Gloria flinched at his inappropriate use of her first name and looked around to see if anyone else had heard it. The way the word rolled so easily off the tongue of a man she thoroughly despised disgusted her. A moment later, she saw that Joe Hull had given Tana another drink, and her fury grew, intensified partly by the effects of the alcohol.

"—and once," Maury was saying, "Peter Granby and I went into a Turkish bath in Boston, around two o'clock in the morning. Nobody was there except the owner, and we shoved him into a closet and locked the door. Then some guy came in wanting a Turkish bath. He thought we were the attendants, for crying out loud! Well, we just grabbed him and threw him into the pool with all his clothes on. Then we pulled him out and put him on a table and slapped him until he was black and blue. 'Not so hard, guys!' he'd say in this little squeaky voice, 'please! ...'"

Was this really Maury? Gloria wondered. If anyone else had told her this story, she would have found it entertaining, but coming from Maury—who was endlessly thoughtful, the perfect example of sensitivity and consideration....

"The panic has overwhelmed us,"

"So ha-a-as—"

A thunderclap from outside drowned out the remainder of the song; Gloria trembled and attempted to finish her drink, but the initial sip made her feel sick, so she put it down. Dinner had ended and everyone filed into the large room, carrying multiple bottles and decanters. Someone had shut the porch door to block the wind, and as a result, swirling wisps of cigar smoke were already curling through the thick air.

"Paging Lieutenant Tannenbaum!" Once again it was the shapeshifter Maury. "Bring us the flute!"

Anthony and Maury hurried into the kitchen; Richard Caramel started the record player and walked over to Gloria.

"Dance with your well-known cousin."

"I don't want to dance."

"Then I'm going to carry you around."

As if he were performing a task of tremendous significance, he lifted her up in his chubby little arms and began moving solemnly around the room.

"Put me down, Dick! I'm getting dizzy!" she demanded.

He dropped her in a tumbling heap on the couch and hurried off to the kitchen, calling out "Tana! Tana!"

Then, without warning, she felt other arms around her, felt herself being lifted from the lounge chair. Joe Hull had picked her up and was drunkenly trying to imitate Dick.

"Put me down!" she said sharply.

His sentimental laugh and the sight of that stubbled yellow jaw so close to her face filled her with unbearable disgust.

"Right away!"

"The—pan-ic—" he started to say, but couldn't finish because Gloria's hand quickly swung around and slapped him across the cheek. When this happened, he immediately released his grip on her, and she dropped to the floor, her shoulder striking the table with a glancing blow as she fell.

Then the room appeared crowded with men and thick with smoke. There was Tana in his white coat, swaying unsteadily while Maury held him up. He was blowing into his flute a strange mixture of sounds that Anthony announced was called the Japanese train-song. Joe Hull had discovered a box of candles and was tossing them in the air, shouting "One down!" each time he dropped one, while Dick danced alone in a mesmerized spinning motion around the room. To her, it seemed as though everything in the room was lurching in bizarre, otherworldly rotations through overlapping layers of misty blue.

Outside, the storm had risen with incredible force—the quiet moments inside were filled with the scraping sound of tall bushes against the house and the thunderous pounding of rain on the kitchen's tin roof. The lightning was endless, releasing heavy crashes of thunder like molten pig iron dropping from the center of a blazing furnace. Gloria could see that rain was spraying through three of the windows—but she couldn't move to close them....

She was in the hall. She had said good night but no one had heard or paid attention to her. For a moment it seemed as if something had peered down over the top of the banister, but she couldn't have returned to the living room—madness would be better than the madness of that noise. Upstairs she searched for the light switch and couldn't find it in the darkness; a flash of lightning lit up the room and showed her the button clearly on the wall. But when the complete darkness returned, it once again escaped her searching fingers, so she took off her dress and slip and collapsed weakly onto the dry side of the half-soaked bed.

She closed her eyes. From downstairs came the chaotic noise of the drinkers, suddenly interrupted by the sharp, ringing sound of shattering glass, then another crash, followed by a rising piece of wobbly, off-key singing....

She remained there for more than two hours—at least that's what she figured out later by putting together the fragments of time. She stayed alert, even noticing after a considerable period that the commotion downstairs had quieted, and that the storm was drifting westward, leaving behind trailing bursts of sound that dropped, as heavy and lifeless as her spirit, into the waterlogged fields. This gave way to a gradual, hesitant dispersal of the rain and wind, until nothing remained outside her windows except a soft dripping and the rustling movement of a bunch of damp vines against the windowsill. She existed in a condition somewhere between sleep and consciousness, with neither state taking control... and she felt tormented by an urge to free herself from a burden weighing down on her chest. She sensed that if she could weep the burden would lift, and squeezing her eyelids shut she attempted to create a knot in her throat... without success....

Drip! Drip! Drip! The sound wasn't unpleasant—it reminded her of spring, of the cool rain from her childhood that created delightful mud in her backyard and watered the small garden she had cultivated with her tiny rake, spade, and hoe. Drip—dri-ip! It brought back memories of days when rain fell from golden skies that dissolved just before dusk and sent a single brilliant beam of sunlight slanting down through the heavens into the wet green trees. So refreshing, so clear and pure—and her mother had been there at the heart of everything, at the center of the rain, protected and dry and strong. She longed for her mother now, but her mother was gone, lost to sight and touch for all time. And this heaviness was bearing down on her, crushing her—oh, how it weighed upon her!

She froze completely. Someone had arrived at the door and stood there watching her, perfectly still except for a gentle swaying movement. She could make out the silhouette of his form clearly outlined against some unclear light source. There was no noise at all, just an overwhelming, compelling silence—even the dripping sound had stopped... only this figure, swaying back and forth in the doorway, an unclear and quietly threatening presence, a character disgusting beneath its polished surface, like pockmarks hidden under a coat of makeup. But her exhausted heart, pounding so hard it made her chest tremble, assured her that life still remained within her, violently disturbed, under threat....

The moment or series of moments stretched on endlessly, and a dizzying haze started to cloud her vision as her eyes stubbornly tried to penetrate the darkness toward the door. In the next instant, it felt as though some inconceivable power would destroy her completely... and then the silhouette in the doorway—it was Hull, she realized, Hull—turned purposefully and, still gently rocking, stepped back and away, as though he was being absorbed into that mysterious light that had given him form.

Blood surged back into her arms and legs, bringing life flowing through her body once more. Suddenly energized, she bolted upright, moving her body until her feet found the floor beside the bed. She understood exactly what needed to be done—right now, this very moment, before the opportunity slipped away. She had to get outside into the cool, humid air, to escape, to feel the wet grass brushing against her feet and the fresh dampness against her skin. Moving automatically, she pulled on her clothes, fumbling through the darkness of the closet to find a hat. She needed to leave this house where something lurked that weighed heavily on her chest, or transformed itself into strange, shifting shadows in the darkness.

In a panic, she fumbled awkwardly with her coat, locating the sleeve just as Anthony's footsteps echoed on the stairs below. She couldn't risk waiting any longer; he might prevent her from leaving, and even Anthony had become part of this burden, part of this sinister house and the gloomy darkness that was spreading around it....

Through the hall then... and down the back stairs, hearing Anthony's voice in the bedroom she had just left—

"Glory! Glory!"

But she had reached the kitchen now and stepped out through the doorway into the night. A hundred droplets, shaken loose by a sudden gust of wind from a dripping tree, splashed onto her and she pressed them eagerly against her face with her warm hands.

"Glory! Glory!"

The voice sounded incredibly distant, muffled and made sorrowful by the walls she had just walked away from. She went around the house and began walking down the front path toward the road, feeling almost triumphant as she turned onto it, and followed the strip of short grass beside it, moving carefully in the complete darkness.

"Gloria!"

She started running, tripping over a piece of branch that the wind had torn off. The voice was now coming from outside the house. Anthony had discovered the empty bedroom and stepped out onto the porch. But something was pushing her forward; it was back there with Anthony, and she had to keep running under this dark and heavy sky, pushing herself through the silence in front of her as if it were a solid wall blocking her path.

She had traveled some distance along the faint road, likely about half a mile, passing a single abandoned barn that rose up, dark and ominous, the only structure of any kind between the gray house and Marietta; then she reached the fork, where the road entered the woods and ran between two towering walls of leaves and branches that almost met overhead. She suddenly noticed a thin, lengthwise streak of silver on the road ahead of her, like a gleaming sword partially buried in the mud. As she drew nearer she let out a small cry of delight—it was a wagon rut filled with water, and looking up at the sky she saw a narrow break in the clouds and realized that the moon had come out.

"Gloria!"

She jumped suddenly. Anthony was less than two hundred feet behind her.

"Gloria, wait for me!"

She pressed her lips together firmly to stop herself from crying out, and walked faster. Within another hundred yards, the woods vanished, rolling away like a dark sock being pulled down from the road's leg. Three minutes of walking ahead of her, hanging in the now vast and endless sky, she spotted a delicate web of faint beams and sparkles, all focused in a steady rhythm around some unseen center. Suddenly she realized where she needed to go. That was the enormous network of wires that stretched high above the river, resembling the legs of a massive spider with the small green light in the switch-house as its eye, running alongside the railroad bridge toward the station. The station! That's where the train would be waiting to carry her away.

"Gloria, it's me! It's Anthony! Gloria, I won't try to stop you! For God's sake, where are you?"

She didn't respond but started running, staying on the upper side of the road and jumping over the shining puddles—flat pools of delicate, ethereal gold. Making a sharp left turn, she took a narrow cart path, managing to avoid a dark form lying on the ground. She glanced up as an owl called sadly from a lone tree. Just in front of her, she could see the framework that led to the railway bridge and the stairs climbing up to it. The station was located on the other side of the river.

Another sound startled her—the melancholy wail of an approaching train—and almost at the same time, a repeated call, faint now and distant.

"Glory! Glory!"

Anthony must have taken the main road. She laughed with a kind of spiteful cleverness at having escaped him; she had enough time to wait until the train passed by.

The siren wailed again, much closer now, and then, without any warning rumble or noise, a dark and winding shape appeared against the shadows far down the elevated track. With nothing but the whoosh of displaced air and the rhythmic clicking of the rails, it moved toward the bridge—it was an electric train. Above the engine, two bright streaks of blue light continuously formed a glowing, crackling arc between them. Like a flickering flame in a lamp next to a dead body, it illuminated for a moment the successive rows of trees and made Gloria instinctively step back to the far side of the road. The light felt warm, like the temperature of heated blood. The clicking suddenly merged into a steady rush of sound, and then, stretching out with dark flexibility, the machine roared blindly past her and thundered onto the bridge, chasing the eerie beam of fire it cast into the quiet river below. Then it quickly shrank away, drawing in its sound until only a lingering echo remained, which faded on the opposite bank.

Silence settled over the damp countryside once more; the gentle dripping started again, and all at once a heavy cascade of water drops fell on Gloria, rousing her from the dreamlike stupor that the train's passing had caused. She hurried down the sloping ground toward the riverbank and started ascending the metal stairs leading to the bridge, recalling that crossing it was something she had always wished to do, and that she would experience the extra thrill of walking across the narrow wooden plank that stretched alongside the railroad tracks above the water.

There! This felt much better. She had reached the top and could now see the surrounding landscape spread out before her in rolling waves of open countryside, cold beneath the moonlight, roughly divided and marked by thin lines and thick clusters of trees. To her right, about half a mile down the river that wound away behind the light like the gleaming, slippery trail left by a snail, the scattered lights of Marietta twinkled in the distance. Less than two hundred yards away at the bridge's end sat the station, identified by a dim lantern. The heavy feeling had lifted now—the treetops beneath her were swaying the young starlight into a mystical slumber. She extended her arms in a gesture of liberation. This was exactly what she had longed for, to stand by herself in a place that was high and cool.

"Gloria!"

Like a frightened child, she hurried along the wooden plank, hopping, skipping, and jumping with a joyful awareness of how light her body felt. Let him come now—she was no longer afraid of that, but she had to reach the station first because that was part of the game. She felt happy. Her hat, which had been pulled off, was gripped tightly in her hand, and her short curly hair bounced up and down around her ears. She had believed she would never feel this young again, but this was her night, her world. She laughed with triumph as she stepped off the plank, and when she reached the wooden platform, she threw herself down joyfully next to an iron roof support.

"Here I am!" she called out, as joyful as the morning light in her excitement. "Here I am, Anthony, dear—old, anxious Anthony."

"Gloria!" He reached the platform and ran toward her. "Are you all right?" When he got there, he knelt down and took her in his arms.

"Yes."

"What was wrong? Why did you leave?" he asked anxiously.

"I had to—there was something"—she stopped speaking and a flash of anxiety struck her thoughts—"there was something pressing down on me—right here." She placed her hand on her chest. "I had to leave and escape from it."

"What do you mean by 'something'?"

"I don't know—that man Hull—"

"Did he bother you?"

"He showed up at my door, drunk. I think I had become somewhat crazy by that point."

"Gloria, dearest—"

Exhausted, she rested her head against his shoulder.

"Let's go back," he suggested.

She shivered.

"Uh! No, I couldn't. It would come and sit on me again." Her voice rose to a cry that hung plaintively in the darkness. "That thing—"

"There, there," he comforted her, drawing her close to him. "We won't do anything you don't want to do. What would you like to do? Just sit here?"

"I want—I want to go away."

"Where?"

"Oh—anywhere."

"Good grief, Gloria," he exclaimed, "you're still drunk!"

"No, I'm not. I haven't been all evening. I went upstairs about, oh, I don't know, maybe half an hour after dinner... Ouch!"

He had accidentally touched her right shoulder.

"It hurts me. I hurt it somehow. I don't know—someone picked me up and dropped me."

"Gloria, come home. It's late and damp."

"I can't," she cried out. "Oh, Anthony, don't ask me to! I will tomorrow. You go home and I'll wait here for a train. I'll go to a hotel—"

"I'll go with you."

"No, I don't want you with me. I want to be alone. I want to sleep—oh, I want to sleep. And then tomorrow, when you've gotten all the smell of whiskey and cigarettes out of the house, and everything straightened up, and Hull is gone, then I'll come home. If I went now, that thing—oh—!" She covered her eyes with her hand; Anthony saw how pointless it would be to try to persuade her.

"I was completely sober when you left," he said. "Dick was sleeping on the couch and Maury and I were having a conversation. That guy Hull had wandered off somewhere. Then I started to realize I hadn't seen you for several hours, so I went upstairs—"

He stopped speaking abruptly when a cheerful "Hello, there!" suddenly echoed from the darkness. Gloria jumped up, and he stood up as well.

"It's Maury's voice," she shouted with excitement. "If Hull is with him, keep them away, keep them away!"

"Who's there?" Anthony called.

"Just Dick and Maury," came the reassuring reply from two voices.

"Where's Hull?"

"He's in bed. Passed out."

Their silhouettes appeared faintly on the platform.

"What the hell are you and Gloria doing here?" Richard Caramel asked, confused and groggy.

"What are you two doing here?"

Maury laughed.

"I have no idea. We followed you, and it was incredibly difficult to do. I heard you out on the porch shouting for Gloria, so I woke up Caramel here and managed to get it through his head, with some trouble, that if there was a search party we should be part of it. He slowed me down by sitting down in the road every so often and asking me what was going on. We tracked you by the distinctive smell of Canadian Club."

There was a burst of anxious laughter echoing beneath the low railway station roof.

"How did you actually track us down?"

"Well, we followed the road and then suddenly lost sight of you. It looks like you turned off onto a wagon trail. After some time, someone called out to us and asked if we were searching for a young girl. We approached and discovered it was a small, trembling old man sitting on a fallen tree, like a character from a fairy tale. 'She went down this way,' he told us, 'and nearly stepped on me while rushing somewhere in a terrible hurry, and then a fellow wearing short golf pants came running along and chased after her. He threw me this.' The old man was waving around a dollar bill—"

"Oh, that poor old man!" Gloria exclaimed, deeply moved.

"I tossed him another one and we continued on our way, even though he begged us to remain and explain what was happening."

"Poor old man," Gloria repeated sadly.

Dick sat down sleepily on a box.

"And now what?" he asked with a tone of stoic resignation.

"Gloria's upset," Anthony explained. "She and I are taking the next train to the city."

Maury had pulled a timetable from his pocket in the darkness. "Strike a match."

A small flame suddenly burst from the dark backdrop, lighting up the four faces that looked strange and unrecognizable out here in the open night.

"Let me check. Two, two-thirty—no, that's in the evening. My goodness, you won't be able to catch a train until five-thirty."

Anthony hesitated.

"Well," he said hesitantly, "we've made up our minds to remain here and wait for it. You two should probably head back and get some sleep."

"You should go too, Anthony," Gloria encouraged him. "I want you to get some rest, sweetheart. You've looked as white as a sheet all day."

"Why, you little idiot!"

Dick yawned.

"Very well. You stay, we stay."

He stepped out from beneath the shelter and looked up at the sky.

"It's actually quite a lovely night. The stars are visible and everything looks beautiful. There's an exceptionally delightful variety of them scattered across the sky."

"Let's see." Gloria followed him and the other two came after her. "Let's sit out here," she said. "I like it much better."

Anthony and Dick turned a long box into a backrest and found a board that was dry enough for Gloria to sit on. Anthony settled down next to her, and with some effort, Dick pulled himself up onto an apple barrel nearby.

"Tana fell asleep in the porch hammock," he said. "We brought him inside and placed him beside the kitchen stove to dry off. He was soaked through to the skin."

"That horrible little man!" Gloria sighed.

"How do you do!" The voice, deep and mournful, came from overhead, and they glanced up in surprise to discover that somehow Maury had made his way onto the roof of the shed, where he sat with his legs hanging over the side, silhouetted like a dark and eerie gargoyle against the now bright sky.

"It must be for occasions like this," he started quietly, his words seeming to drift down from a great height and land gently on his listeners, "that the virtuous people of this country cover the railways with billboards declaring in red and yellow letters that

249

'Jesus Christ is God,' positioning them, fittingly enough, right beside advertisements proclaiming that 'Gunter's Whiskey is Good.'"

There was soft laughter and the three people below kept their heads tilted upward.

"I think I'll tell you the story of my education," Maury continued, "under these mocking stars."

"Do! Please!"

"Should I, really?"

They waited with anticipation while he turned a thoughtful yawn toward the white, smiling moon.

"Well," he began, "when I was a baby, I used to pray. I saved up prayers to protect myself from future sins. One year I accumulated nineteen hundred 'Now I lay me down to sleep' prayers."

"Toss down a cigarette," someone whispered.

A small package arrived at the platform at the same time as the booming command:

"Silence! I am about to unburden myself of many memorable remarks reserved for the darkness of such earths and the brilliance of such skies."

Below, a lit match was passed from one cigarette to another. The voice continued:

"I became skilled at deceiving God. I would pray right after committing any wrongdoing until prayer and sin eventually became the same thing to me. I thought that when someone shouted 'My God!' as a safe crashed down on them, this proved that faith was deeply embedded in human nature. Then I started my education. For fourteen years, about fifty dedicated teachers pointed to old muskets and shouted at me: 'That's the genuine article. These modern guns are just shallow, surface-level copies.' They condemned the books I read and my thoughts by labeling them immoral; later, when trends shifted, they condemned things

250

by calling them 'clever'."

"And so I turned, wise beyond my years, away from the professors and toward the poets, listening—to Swinburne's lyrical tenor voice and Shelley's powerful tenor robusto, to Shakespeare with his deep bass and impressive range, to Tennyson with his second bass and occasional high falsetto notes, to Milton and Marlowe, those profound basses. I listened to Browning conversing, Byron proclaiming, and Wordsworth monotonously droning on. This, at the very least, caused me no damage. I discovered something about beauty—just enough to understand that it had no connection to truth—and I realized, furthermore, that no great literary tradition existed; there was only the tradition of each literary tradition's inevitable demise...."

"As I matured, the beautiful and appealing illusions of youth gradually disappeared. My thinking became rougher and less refined, while my perception became painfully sharp and clear. Life surrounded my isolated existence like an ocean, and soon I found myself struggling to stay afloat."

"The change happened gradually—this thing had been waiting for me for quite some time. It sets its sneaky, apparently harmless trap for everyone. What about me? No—I didn't attempt to seduce the janitor's wife—and I didn't run naked through the streets, declaring my masculinity. It's never really passion itself that causes the downfall—it's the mask that passion puts on. I grew bored—that's all it was. Boredom, which is just another word and a common disguise for life force, became the hidden driving force behind everything I did. Beauty was in my past, do you see?—I had matured." He stopped speaking. "End of school and college period. Opening of Part Two."

Three softly glowing points of light revealed where his audience sat listening. Gloria had positioned herself half-sitting, half-reclining across Anthony's lap. He held her so close that she could feel his heartbeat against her. Richard Caramel, seated on the apple barrel, occasionally shifted his position and let out a quiet grunt.

I came of age in this era of jazz music and immediately found myself overwhelmed by confusion so intense it was almost tangible. Life loomed over me like an unethical teacher, constantly revising my well-organized thoughts. However, with a misguided belief in the power of intellect, I continued forward. I studied Smith, who mocked compassion and argued that contempt was the purest form of expressing oneself—yet Smith himself became another obstacle blocking my understanding. I studied Jones, who systematically dismantled the concept of individualism—and there was Jones, still standing in my path. I wasn't truly thinking for myself—I had become a battlefield where the ideas of countless thinkers clashed; I was more like one of those coveted yet powerless nations that great empires fight over repeatedly.

"I grew up believing that I was collecting life experiences that would help me organize my existence for happiness. In fact, I managed to achieve the fairly common accomplishment of figuring out answers to every problem in my head well before I actually encountered them in real life—only to find myself defeated and confused all the same."

"But after sampling this experience just a few times, I'd had enough. Listen! I told myself, Experience isn't worth pursuing. It's not something that happens pleasantly to someone who's just sitting back passively—it's a wall that you crash into when you're actively moving forward. So I wrapped myself in what I believed was my unbreakable skepticism and concluded that my education was finished. But it was too late. No matter how much I tried to protect myself by avoiding new connections with tragic and doomed humanity, I was lost along with everyone else. I had exchanged the struggle against love for the struggle against loneliness, the struggle against life for the struggle against death."

He stopped speaking to emphasize his final point—after a

moment he yawned and continued.

"I think the start of the second stage of my education was a terrible feeling of dissatisfaction at being manipulated against my will for some mysterious purpose whose final objective I didn't understand—assuming there even was a final objective. It was a tough decision to make. The schoolmistress appeared to be telling us, 'We're going to play football and only football. If you don't want to play football, then you can't participate at all—'

"What was I supposed to do—the playtime was so short!"

"You see, I felt that we were even denied whatever comfort there might have been in being just an imaginary creation of a business executive getting up from his knees. Do you think that I jumped at this negative outlook, grabbed onto it as something smugly superior and sweet, no more truly depressing than, let's say, a gray fall day in front of a fireplace?—I don't believe I did that. I was far too passionate for that, and too full of life."

"It seemed to me that humanity had no ultimate purpose or direction. People were starting a strange and confused battle against nature—the same nature that through divine and magnificent chance had brought us to the point where we could defy her. She had created methods to eliminate the weaker members of our species and thereby give the survivors the strength to fulfill her higher purposes—or perhaps we should say her more entertaining purposes—though these remained unconscious and accidental. And driven by the greatest achievements of human enlightenment, we were trying to outsmart her. In this country I witnessed black people beginning to mix with white people—while in Europe an economic disaster was unfolding to rescue three or four sick and poorly governed races from the one form of control that might have organized them for material success."

"We create a Christ who can heal the leper—and now the leper's kind has become the salt of the earth. If anyone can discover any meaning in that, let them step forward."

"There's only one lesson to be learned from life, anyway," Gloria interrupted, not to argue but with a kind of sad understanding.

"What's that?" Maury asked sharply.

"That there's no lesson to be learned from life."

After a brief pause, Maury said:

"Young Gloria, the beautiful and ruthless woman, first viewed the world with the essential wisdom I have fought to achieve, that Anthony will never achieve, that Dick will never completely grasp."

A disgusted groan came from the apple barrel. Anthony, who had gotten used to the darkness, could clearly see the flash of Richard Caramel's yellow eye and the resentful expression on his face as he shouted:

"You're crazy! According to what you just said, I should have gained some experience by attempting it."

"Trying what?" Maury shouted angrily. "Trying to cut through the confusion of political idealism with some desperate, hopeless drive toward truth? Sitting day after day motionless in a stiff chair, completely disconnected from life, staring at the top of a church spire through the trees, attempting to distinguish once and for all between what can be known and what cannot be known? Trying to take a fragment of reality and infuse it with magic from your own spirit to recreate that indescribable quality it had in life but lost when transferred to paper or canvas? Working in a laboratory through exhausting years for just a tiny bit of relative truth in a collection of gears or a test tube—"

"Have you?"

Maury stopped speaking, and when he finally responded, his voice carried a hint of exhaustion and a sharp, bitter edge that hung in the air between the three of them for a moment before drifting away like a soap bubble floating toward the moon.

"Not me," he said quietly. "I was born exhausted—but when it comes to that natural wisdom, that intuitive gift that women like Gloria possess—despite all my talking and listening, despite my futile waiting for that universal truth that always seems to hover just beyond every debate and every theory, I haven't contributed even the smallest bit to that understanding."

In the distance, a deep sound that had been audible for several moments revealed itself through a mournful mooing similar to that of an enormous cow and by the gleaming dot of a headlight visible about half a mile away. This time it was a steam-powered train, rumbling and groaning, and as it thundered past with a tremendous roar it scattered a spray of sparks and cinders across the platform.

"Not one bit!" Once again Maury's voice drifted down to them as if from a towering height. "What a weak thing intelligence really is, with its tiny steps, its hesitations, its constant back-and-forth movement, its catastrophic withdrawals! Intelligence is nothing more than a tool shaped by circumstances. There are people who claim that intelligence must have created the universe—but intelligence has never built a steam engine! Circumstances built a steam engine. Intelligence is little more than a short ruler we use to measure the limitless accomplishments of Circumstances.

"I could quote you the philosophy of the hour—but, for all we know, fifty years may see a complete reversal of this self-denial that's consuming today's intellectuals, the victory of Christ over Anatole France—" He paused, then continued: "But all I understand—the enormous significance of myself to me, and the need to recognize that significance within myself—these things the wise and beautiful Gloria was born understanding, along with the agonizing pointlessness of attempting to understand anything else.

"Well, I started telling you about my education, didn't I? But I learned nothing, you see, very little even about myself. And if I had, I would die with my lips sealed and the cap on my pen—just as the wisest people have done since—oh, since the failure of a certain situation—a strange situation, by the way. It involved some skeptics who thought they could see far into the future, just like you and me. Let me tell you about them as an evening prayer before you all fall asleep.

"Once upon a time, all the intellectuals and brilliant minds in the world came to share the same belief—which is to say, they shared no belief at all. However, it troubled them to realize that within just a few years after their deaths, many religious movements, philosophical systems, and predictions would be attributed to them that they had never contemplated or meant to create. So they spoke to one another:"

"'Let's come together and create a magnificent book that will endure forever to ridicule human gullibility. Let's convince our most passionate poets to write about physical pleasures, and persuade some of our boldest journalists to contribute tales of legendary love affairs. We'll incorporate all the most ridiculous folklore that's popular today. We'll select the sharpest satirist of our time to construct a god from all the gods that humanity worships, a deity who will be more splendid than any of them, yet so pathetically human that he'll become a source of worldwide mockery—and we'll attribute to him all kinds of jokes and vanities and fits of anger, which he'll supposedly engage in for his own entertainment, so that people will read our book and reflect on it, and there will be no more foolishness in the world."

"'Finally, let us make sure that the book has all the qualities of excellent writing, so that it will endure forever as proof of our deep skepticism and our complete irony.'"

"So the men did exactly that, and they died."

"But the book endured forever, written with such beauty and filled with such remarkable imagination by these brilliant and gifted minds. Though they had forgotten to give it a title, after their deaths it came to be known as the Bible."

When he finished speaking, no one said anything. A heavy, drowsy atmosphere in the night air seemed to have cast a spell over everyone.

"As I mentioned, I began telling the story of my education. But my drinks are finished and the night is nearly over, and soon there will be terrible chattering happening everywhere—in the trees and the houses, and the two small shops over there behind the station—and there will be a great deal of rushing around on the earth for a few hours. Well," he finished with a laugh, "thank God the four of us can all move on to our eternal rest knowing we've left the world a little better for having lived in it."

A gentle wind began to blow, carrying with it delicate traces of life that pressed themselves against the sky.

"Your comments are becoming scattered and pointless," Anthony said drowsily. "You were hoping for one of those moments of sudden insight where you deliver your most clever and meaningful observations in precisely the right circumstances to spark the perfect discussion. In the meantime, Gloria has demonstrated her wise detachment by falling asleep—I can tell because she's managed to shift her full weight onto my aching body."

"Have I bored you?" asked Maury, looking down with some concern.

"No, you have let us down. You've fired plenty of arrows, but did you actually hit any birds?"

"I'll let Dick handle the birds," Maury said quickly. "I speak in a scattered way, in disconnected pieces."

"You won't get a reaction out of me," Dick muttered. "My head is occupied with all sorts of practical concerns. I want a hot bath far too badly to be concerned about how significant my work is or what percentage of us are pitiful characters."

Dawn announced itself through a growing brightness spreading white across the eastern sky above the river and the occasional chirping sounds coming from the nearby trees.

"Quarter to five," Dick sighed; "nearly another hour left to wait. Look! Two are out." He pointed toward Anthony, whose eyelids had drooped closed over his eyes. "Sleep of the Patch family—"

But within another five minutes, despite the growing louder chirps and tweets, his own head had dropped forward, bobbing down twice, three times....

Only Maury Noble stayed awake, sitting on the station roof with his eyes wide open, staring with exhausted focus at the distant glow of dawn. He found himself questioning how unreal ideas seemed, how the brightness of life was fading away, and how small obsessions were eagerly creeping into his existence, like rats invading an abandoned house. He felt no pity for anyone now— Monday morning would bring his work, and later there would be a girl from a different social class for whom he meant everything; these were the things closest to his heart. In the strange light of the approaching day, it felt arrogant that he had ever attempted to think with this weak, damaged tool that was his mind.

There was the sun, pouring down enormous glowing waves of heat; there was life, bustling and aggressive, swirling around them like a cloud of flies—the dark puffs of smoke from the locomotive, a sharp "all aboard!" and a bell clanging. In a daze, Maury noticed eyes from the milk train gazing with curiosity up at him, overheard Gloria and Anthony arguing quickly about whether he should accompany her to the city, then came another burst of noise and she had vanished and the three men, white as sheets, stood alone on the platform while a grimy coal worker rode down the street on top of a delivery truck, singing roughly to the summer morning.

———

Chapter III: The Broken Lute

It's seven-thirty on an August evening. The living room windows of the gray house stand wide open, slowly trading the stale indoor air thick with alcohol and cigarette smoke for the fresh sleepiness of the late, sweltering twilight. Fading flower fragrances drift through the air, so delicate and fleeting that they already whisper of summer becoming a memory. Yet August still announces itself boldly through a thousand crickets chirping around the side porch, and through one that has snuck inside the house and hidden boldly behind a bookcase, occasionally calling out to boast of his cunning and his unstoppable determination.

The room is in complete disarray. A bowl of fruit sits on the table—real fruit that somehow looks fake. Surrounding it is a menacing collection of decanters, glasses, and overflowing ashtrays, the ashtrays still sending curling ribbons of smoke into the stagnant air, creating a scene that would only need a skull to mirror that classic old print that once hung in every man's study, depicting the accessories of a pleasure-seeking life with both charm and sobering warning.

After some time, the lively solo of the cricket is interrupted rather than accompanied by a new sound—the sad, mournful cry of a poorly played flute. It's clear that the musician is practicing rather than performing, because every now and then the twisted melody stops abruptly and, after a pause filled with unclear mumbling, starts up again.

Just before the seventh false start, a third sound adds to the quiet discord. It's a taxi outside. A minute of silence follows, then the taxi sounds again, its loud departure nearly drowning out the scraping of footsteps on the cinder walkway. The doorbell rings sharply through the house.

From the kitchen comes a small, tired Japanese man, quickly buttoning up a white servant's jacket. He opens the front screen door and lets in an attractive thirty-year-old man wearing the kind of earnest clothing typical of those dedicated to helping humanity. His entire presence radiates good intentions: his look around the room combines curiosity with unwavering optimism; when he gazes at Tana, his eyes carry the full weight of wanting to uplift the godless Oriental. His name is FREDERICK E. PARAMORE. He attended Harvard with ANTHONY, where the alphabetical order of their last names meant they were always seated beside each other in classes. A casual friendship formed—but they haven't seen each other since then.

Nevertheless, PARAMORE enters the room with a certain air of arriving for the evening.

Tana is responding to a question.

TANA: (Grinning with ingratiation) Gone to the inn for dinner. Will be back in half an hour. Has been gone since half past six.

PARAMORE: (Looking at the glasses on the table) Do they have company?

TANA: Yes. Company. Mr. Caramel, Mr. and Mrs. Barnes, Miss Kane, all staying here.

PARAMORE: I see. (Kindly) They've been having a party, I see.

TANA: I don't understand.

PARAMORE: They've been having an affair.

TANA: Yes, they have drinks. Oh, so many, many, many drinks.

PARAMORE: (Tactfully changing the subject) "Didn't I hear music playing as I came up to the house?"

TANA: (With a sudden, uncontrollable giggle) Yes, I play.

PARAMORE: One of the Japanese instruments.

(He clearly subscribes to National Geographic Magazine.)

TANA: I play flu-u-ute, Japanese flu-u-ute.

PARAMORE: What song were you playing? One of your

260

Japanese melodies?

TANA: (His brow furrowing dramatically) I play train song. What do you call it?—railroad song. That's what we call it in my country. Like a train. It goes so-o-o; that's the whistle; the train starts. Then it goes so-o-o; that means the train is moving. It goes like that. Very nice song in my country. Children's song.

PARAMORE: It sounded very nice.

(At this point, it's clear that only an enormous effort at self-control is keeping Tana from rushing upstairs to get his postcards, including the six that were made in America.)

TANA: Should I make a highball for the gentleman?

PARAMORE: "No, thanks. I don't use it." (He smiles.)

TANA retreats to the kitchen, leaving the connecting door partially open. Through the gap, the melody of the Japanese train song suddenly emerges once more—this time clearly not a rehearsal, but a full performance, vibrant and energetic.

The phone rings. TANA, absorbed in his harmonics, pays no attention, so PARAMORE picks up the receiver.

PARAMORE: Hello.... Yes.... No, he's not here right now, but he'll be back any minute.... Butterworth? Hello, I didn't quite hear the name.... Hello, hello, hello. Hello! ... Huh!

The phone stubbornly refuses to produce any more sound. Paramore puts the receiver back.

At this point the taxi theme returns, bringing with it a second young man; he's carrying a suitcase and opens the front door without ringing the bell.

MAURY: (In the hall) "Oh, Anthony! Yoho!" (He comes into the large room and sees PARAMORE) How do?

PARAMORE: (Looking at him with growing intensity) Is this—is this Maury Noble?

MAURY: "That's it." (He moves forward, smiling, and extending his hand) How are you, old friend? I haven't seen you in years.

(He has a vague sense that the face is connected to Harvard, but he's not even certain about that. If he ever knew the name, he forgot it long ago. However, with remarkable sensitivity and equally admirable kindness, PARAMORE recognizes this awkward situation and tactfully comes to the rescue.)

PARAMORE: You've forgotten Fred Paramore? We were both in old Uncle Robert's history class.

MAURY: No, I haven't, Uncle—I mean Fred. Fred was—I mean Uncle was a great old fellow, wasn't he?

PARAMORE: (Nodding his head with amusement several times) Wonderful old fellow. Wonderful old fellow.

MAURY: (After a brief pause) Yes—he was. Where's Anthony?

PARAMORE: The Japanese servant informed me that he was at some inn. Having dinner, I assume.

MAURY: (Checking his watch) Has he been gone long?

PARAMORE: I suppose so. The Japanese said they would return soon.

MAURY: How about we grab a drink?

PARAMORE: No, thanks. I don't use it. (He smiles.)

MAURY: Do you mind if I do? (Yawning as he pours himself a drink from a bottle) What have you been up to since you graduated from college?

PARAMORE: Oh, many things. I've lived a very active life. Been around here and there. (His tone suggests everything from lion-hunting to organized crime.)

MAURY: Oh, have you been to Europe?

PARAMORE: No, I haven't—unfortunately.

MAURY: I suppose we'll all head over there eventually.

PARAMORE: Do you really think so?

MAURY: Absolutely! The country has been fed a steady diet of sensationalism for more than two years. Everyone is getting restless. They want to have some fun.

PARAMORE: Then you don't believe any ideals are at stake?

262

MAURY: Nothing particularly significant. People crave excitement from time to time.

PARAMORE: (Intently) It's really fascinating to hear you say that. I was just speaking with someone who had been over there——

(During the following speech, meant to be filled in by the reader with phrases like "Saw with his own eyes," "Splendid spirit of France," and "Salvation of civilization," MAURY sits with his eyes downcast, completely bored and detached.)

MAURY: (At the first chance he gets) By the way, did you know there's a German spy right here in this house?

PARAMORE: (Smiling cautiously) Are you serious?

MAURY: Absolutely. I feel it's my duty to warn you.

PARAMORE: (Convinced) A governess?

MAURY: (Whispering, pointing toward the kitchen with his thumb) Tana! That's not his actual name. I've heard he regularly receives mail addressed to Lieutenant Emile Tannenbaum.

PARAMORE: (Laughing with genuine amusement) You were just pulling my leg.

MAURY: I might be wrongly accusing him. But you haven't told me what you've been up to.

PARAMORE: For one thing—writing.

MAURY: Fiction?

PARAMORE: No. Non-fiction.

MAURY: What's that? Some kind of writing that's part fiction and part fact?

PARAMORE: Oh, I've stuck to the facts. I've been doing quite a bit of social service work.

MAURY: Oh!

(A flash of suspicion immediately sparks in his eyes. It's as if PARAMORE had just introduced himself as a hobby pickpocket.)

PARAMORE: Right now I'm doing service work in Stamford. Just last week someone told me that Anthony Patch lived so close by.

(They are interrupted by a commotion outside, clearly the sound of men and women talking and laughing together. Then ANTHONY, GLORIA, RICHARD CARAMEL, MURIEL KANE, RACHAEL BARNES and RODMAN BARNES, her husband, all enter the room together. They crowd around MAURY, automatically responding "Fine!" to his general "Hello." ... ANTHONY, meanwhile, walks over to his other guest.)

ANTHONY: Well, I'll be damned. How are you? Really glad to see you.

PARAMORE: It's good to see you, Anthony. I'm stationed in Stamford, so I thought I'd drop by. (Roguishly) We have to work like crazy most of the time, so we deserve a few hours off.

In intense concentration, ANTHONY struggles to remember the name. After a difficult mental effort, his memory produces only the fragment "Fred," which he quickly uses to construct the sentence "Glad you did, Fred!" Meanwhile, a brief silence that typically precedes an introduction settles over the group. MAURY, who could offer assistance, chooses instead to watch with spiteful amusement.

ANTHONY: (In desperation) Ladies and gentlemen, this is—this is Fred.

MURIEL: (With helpful cheerfulness) Hello, Fred!

RICHARD CARAMEL and PARAMORE greet each other warmly using their first names, with PARAMORE remembering that DICK was one of his classmates who had never bothered to speak to him before. DICK foolishly assumes that PARAMORE is someone he has met previously at ANTHONY'S house.

The three young women go upstairs.

MAURY: (In an undertone to DICK) Haven't seen Muriel since Anthony's wedding.

DICK: She's at the peak of her career right now. Her most recent catchphrase is "I'll say so!"

(ANTHONY struggles for a while with PARAMORE and eventually tries to shift the conversation to include everyone by offering drinks all around.)

MAURY: I've made good progress with this bottle. I've worked my way down from "Proof" to "Distillery." (He points to the words on the label.)

ANTHONY: (To PARAMORE) You never know when these two will show up. I said goodbye to them one afternoon at five o'clock, and I'll be damned if they didn't appear around two in the morning. A big hired touring car from New York pulled up to the door and out they stepped, drunk as lords, of course.

(In a state of intense contemplation, PARAMORE stares at the cover of a book he's holding. MAURY and DICK share a quick look.)

DICK: (Innocently, to PARAMORE) Do you work here in town?

PARAMORE: No, I'm at the Laird Street Settlement in Stamford. (To ANTHONY) You have no clue about how much poverty exists in these small Connecticut towns. Italians and other immigrants. Mostly Catholics, you understand, so it's extremely difficult to connect with them.

ANTHONY: (Politely) A lot of crime?

PARAMORE: Not so much crime as ignorance and dirt.

MAURY: That's my theory: immediate electrocution of all ignorant and dirty people. I'm all for the criminals—they give color to life. The trouble is if you started to punish ignorance you'd have to begin with the first families, then you could take up the moving picture people, and finally Congress and the clergy.

PARAMORE: (Smiling uneasily) I was talking about a more basic kind of ignorance—even about our own language.

MAURY: (Thoughtfully) I guess it really is pretty difficult. Can't even stay current with the new poetry.

PARAMORE: You only realize how terrible the conditions really are after the settlement work has been going on for months. As our secretary told me, you never notice how dirty your fingernails are until you actually wash your hands. We're already drawing a lot of attention, of course.

MAURY: (Rudely) Like your secretary would probably tell you, if you cram paper into a fireplace, it's going to flame up bright for just a second.

(At this point GLORIA, freshly made up and eager for admiration and entertainment, returns to the party, with her two friends following behind her. For several moments the conversation becomes completely disjointed. GLORIA pulls ANTHONY aside.)

GLORIA: Please don't drink too much, Anthony.

ANTHONY: Why?

GLORIA: Because you're so simple when you're drunk.

ANTHONY: Good Lord! What's the matter now?

GLORIA: (After a pause during which her eyes gaze coolly into his) Several things. First of all, why do you insist on paying for everything? Both of those men have more money than you do!

ANTHONY: Why, Gloria! They're my guests!

GLORIA: That's no reason why you should pay for a bottle of champagne Rachael Barnes smashed. Dick tried to fix that second taxi bill, and you wouldn't let him.

ANTHONY: Why, Gloria—

GLORIA: When we're forced to keep selling bonds just to cover our basic expenses, it's time to reduce unnecessary spending on generous gestures. Furthermore, I wouldn't pay so much attention to Rachael Barnes. Her husband disapproves of it just as much as I do!

ANTHONY: Why, Gloria—

GLORIA: (Imitating him with a sharp tone) "Why, Gloria!" But that's been happening way too much this summer—with

266

every attractive woman you come across. It's become a pattern, and I won't put up with it anymore! If you can fool around, so can I. (Then, as if just remembering) By the way, this Fred guy isn't another Joe Hull, is he?

ANTHONY: Good heavens, no! He most likely came up here to get me to coax some money out of grandfather for his congregation.

(GLORIA turns away from a very depressed ANTHONY and returns to her guests.)

By nine o'clock these can be separated into two groups—those who have been drinking steadily and those who have had little or nothing to drink. The second group includes the BARNESES, MURIEL, and FREDERICK E. PARAMORE.

MURIEL: I wish I could write. I get these ideas but I never seem to be able to put them in words.

DICK: As Goliath said, he understood how David felt, but he couldn't put it into words. The comment was instantly taken up as a slogan by the Philistines.

MURIEL: I don't understand you. I must be getting stupid in my old age.

GLORIA: (Moving unsteadily through the group like an excited angel) If anyone's hungry there's some French pastry on the dining room table.

MAURY: I can't stand those Victorian designs it comes in.

MURIEL: (Laughing hysterically) I'll definitely say you're drunk, Maury.

Her heart remains like a stone pathway that she presents to the hooves of countless passing stallions, hoping that their metal horseshoes might create even the smallest spark of romance in the shadows...

Messrs. Barnes and Paramore have been engaged in conversation about some wholesome topic, a topic so wholesome that Mr. Barnes has been attempting for several minutes to slip away into the more corrupted atmosphere around the main lounge. Whether Paramore is staying in the gray house out of courtesy or inquisitiveness, or to eventually write a sociological analysis on the decline of American society, remains uncertain.

MAURY: Fred, I thought you were very open-minded.

PARAMORE: I am.

MURIEL: Me, too. I believe one religion's as good as another and everything.

PARAMORE: There's some good in all religions.

MURIEL: I'm a Catholic, but like I always say, I'm not really practicing it.

PARAMORE: (With a tremendous burst of tolerance) The Catholic religion is a very—a very powerful religion.

MAURY: Well, someone with such an open mind should think about the heightened level of feeling and the boosted sense of optimism that comes with this cocktail.

PARAMORE: (Taking the drink, somewhat defiantly) Thanks, I'll give it a shot—just one.

MAURY: One? That's outrageous! Here we have a class of 1910 reunion, and you refuse to get even a little drunk. Come on!

"Here's a health to King Charles,"

Here's a health to King Charles,

"Bring the bowl that you boast about——"

(PARAMORE joins in with a strong, enthusiastic voice.)

MAURY: Fill the cup, Frederick. You know that everything we do is controlled by nature's plans for us, and her plan for you is to turn you into a heavy drinker who loves to party.

PARAMORE: If a man can drink like a gentleman—

MAURY: What is a gentleman, anyway?

ANTHONY: A man who never wears pins on his coat lapel.

MAURY: Nonsense! A man's social status is determined by how much bread he eats in a sandwich.

DICK: He's someone who would rather have the first edition of a book than the latest edition of a newspaper.

RACHAEL: A man who never pretends to be a drug addict.

MAURY: An American who can trick an English butler into believing he's English too.

MURIEL: A man who comes from a good family and attended Yale or Harvard or Princeton, who has money and dances well, and all that.

MAURY: Finally—the perfect definition! Cardinal Newman's is now outdated.

PARAMORE: I believe we should approach this question with a more open perspective. Wasn't it Abraham Lincoln who said that a gentleman is someone who never causes pain to others?

MAURY: I believe it's credited to General Ludendorff.

PARAMORE: You've got to be kidding me.

MAURY: Have another drink.

PARAMORE: I shouldn't. (Lowering his voice so only MAURY can hear) What if I told you this is only the third drink I've ever had in my entire life?

(DICK starts the record player, which causes MURIEL to stand up and sway from side to side, with her elbows pressed against her ribs and her forearms sticking out perpendicular to her body like fins.)

MURIEL: Oh, let's roll up the rugs and dance!

(Anthony and Gloria receive this suggestion with internal groans and weak smiles of reluctant agreement.)

MURIEL: Come on, you lazy-bones. Get up and move the furniture back.

DICK: Wait until I finish my drink.

MAURY: (Focused on his plan involving PARAMORE) Here's what we'll do. Let's each fill a glass, drink it down, and then we'll dance.

(A wave of protest crashes against the solid rock of MAURY'S unwavering determination.)

MURIEL: My head is just spinning right now.

RACHAEL: (In an undertone to ANTHONY) Did Gloria tell you to stay away from me?

ANTHONY: (Confused) Why, certainly not. Of course not.

(RACHAEL smiles at him mysteriously. Two years have given her a kind of tough, polished beauty.)

MAURY: (Raising his glass) Here's to the downfall of democracy and the collapse of Christianity.

MURIEL: Now really!

(She gives MAURY a playfully scolding look and then takes a drink.)

They all drink, though some struggle more than others to do so.

MURIEL: Clear the floor!

(This process seems unavoidable, so ANTHONY and GLORIA participate in the massive rearrangement of tables, stacking of chairs, rolling up of rugs, and smashing of lamps. Once the furniture has been piled into unsightly heaps along the walls, an area of roughly eight feet square becomes visible.)

MURIEL: Oh, let's have music!

MAURY: Tana will perform the love song of an eye, ear, nose, and throat specialist.

(With some confusion because TANA has gone to bed for the night, they get ready for the performance. The Japanese man in pajamas, holding his flute, is wrapped in a blanket and positioned in a chair on top of one of the tables, where he creates a ridiculous and bizarre sight. PARAMORE is noticeably intoxicated and so delighted with the idea that he makes it even more dramatic by mimicking comic strip stumbles and even letting out the occasional hiccup.)

PARAMORE: (To GLORIA) Want to dance with me?

GLORIA: No, sir! I want to do the swan dance. Can you do it?

PARAMORE: Sure. Do them all.

GLORIA: All right. You start from that side of the room and I'll start from this.

MURIEL: Let's go!

Then chaos erupts screaming from the bottles: TANA dives into the mysterious complexities of the train song, the mournful "tootle toot-toot" mixing its sad rhythms with the phonograph's "Poor Butterfly (tink-atink), by the blossoms waiting." MURIEL is too overcome with laughter to do anything but hold on desperately to BARNES, who, dancing with the threatening stiffness of a military officer, stomps humorlessly around the cramped area. ANTHONY is attempting to listen to RACHAEL's whisper—while avoiding GLORIA's notice....

But the bizarre, the unthinkable, the theatrical incident is about to happen, one of those incidents where life appears determined to passionately copy the cheapest forms of literature. PARAMORE has been attempting to imitate GLORIA, and as the chaos reaches its peak he starts to spin around and around, more and more dizzyingly—he stumbles, regains his balance, stumbles again and then falls toward the hall ... nearly into the arms of old ADAM PATCH, whose arrival has been made silent by the uproar in the room.

ADAM PATCH is extremely pale. He supports himself with a walking stick. The man beside him is EDWARD SHUTTLEWORTH, and he's the one who grabs PARAMORE by the shoulder and redirects his fall away from the respected philanthropist.

The time it takes for silence to settle over the room like an enormous shroud can be estimated at about two minutes, although for a brief moment afterward the phonograph sputters and the melody of the Japanese train song trickles from the tip of TANA'S

271

flute. Among the nine people present, only BARNES, PARAMORE, and TANA remain unaware of who this latecomer is. Of these nine individuals, not a single one knows that ADAM PATCH made a fifty-thousand-dollar donation to the national prohibition movement that very morning.

It falls to PARAMORE to shatter the growing silence; the peak of his life's moral corruption is revealed in his unbelievable comment.

PARAMORE: (Crawling quickly toward the kitchen on his hands and knees) I'm not a visitor here—I work here.

(Once again, silence descends—so profound now, so heavy with unbearably infectious dread, that RACHAEL lets out a nervous little laugh, and DICK finds himself repeating over and over a line from Swinburne, strangely fitting for the moment:

"One gaunt bleak blossom of scentless breath."

Out of the silence comes ANTHONY's voice, sober and tense, saying something to ADAM PATCH; then this, too, fades away.)

SHUTTLEWORTH: (Passionately) Your grandfather thought he would drive over to see your house. I called from Rye and left a message.

A series of small gasps, coming from what seems like nowhere and no one in particular, fills the following silence. ANTHONY has turned as white as chalk. GLORIA'S mouth is slightly open and her steady stare at the elderly man shows tension and fear. There isn't a single smile anywhere in the room. Not one? Or is CROSS PATCH'S tight mouth trembling slightly apart, revealing the neat rows of his narrow teeth? He speaks—five gentle and straightforward words.

ADAM PATCH: We'll go back now, Shuttleworth——

(And that's it. He turns around, and with his cane helping him, he walks out through the hallway, through the front door, and with ominous foreboding his unsteady footsteps crunch on the gravel walkway beneath the August moon.)

Retrospect

In this desperate situation, they were like two goldfish in a bowl that had been completely drained of water; they couldn't even swim across to reach each other.

Gloria would turn twenty-six in May. She had said there was nothing she wanted except to stay young and beautiful for a long time, to be cheerful and happy, and to have money and love. She desired what most women desire, but she craved it much more intensely and desperately. She had been married for over two years. Initially there had been days of peaceful understanding, building to moments of overwhelming possession and pride. Mixed with these times had come occasional hatred, lasting only a brief hour, and periods of forgetting that went on no longer than an afternoon. That had continued for half a year.

Then the peace and happiness they once shared had lost its joy and turned gray—only rarely, when jealousy sparked or they were forced apart, did the old passionate feelings return, that sense of deep connection between their souls, the emotional intensity. She could hate Anthony for an entire day, stay carelessly furious with him for a whole week. Arguments had replaced love as something to indulge in, almost like entertainment, and there were nights when they went to bed trying to recall who was mad and who should act distant the next morning. As their second year together was ending, two new problems had emerged. Gloria came to understand that Anthony had developed the ability to feel completely indifferent toward her—a temporary coldness that was more than half due to emotional exhaustion, but one that she could no longer break through with a whispered word or a certain intimate smile. There were days when her affectionate touches felt like suffocation to him. She was aware of these things, though she never fully acknowledged them to herself.

It was only recently that she realized that despite her worship of him, her jealousy, her devotion, her pride, she fundamentally looked down on him—and her disdain merged seamlessly with her other feelings.... All of this was her love—the essential and feminine delusion that had focused itself on him one April night, many months earlier.

For Anthony, despite these reservations, she remained his only obsession. If he had lost her, he would have become a shattered man, miserably and emotionally consumed by her memory for the rest of his life. He rarely enjoyed spending an entire day alone with her—most of the time he preferred having someone else there with them. There were moments when he felt that without complete solitude he would lose his mind—and there were occasions when he genuinely despised her. When he was drunk, he found himself briefly drawn to other women, revealing glimpses of an adventurous nature that had been buried until then.

That spring and summer, they had dreamed about their future happiness—how they would travel from one warm paradise to another, eventually returning to a magnificent estate with perhaps some perfect children, then moving into diplomacy or politics to achieve beautiful and meaningful things for a time, until finally as an elderly couple with gorgeous, silky white hair, they would relax in peaceful splendor, admired by all the middle-class people around them. These wonderful times would begin "when we get our money"; their hope depended on such fantasies rather than any contentment with their increasingly chaotic and wild lifestyle. On dreary mornings when the previous night's jokes had turned into crude remarks lacking any cleverness or class, they could somehow pull out this collection of shared dreams and go through them one by one, then look at each other with a smile and repeat, as their final word on the subject, Gloria's bold and heartfelt Nietzschean declaration: "I don't care!"

Things had been gradually getting worse. The money problem was becoming more irritating and threatening by the day; they had come to realize that alcohol had become essential for their entertainment—a common enough occurrence among the British upper class a century earlier, but quite troubling in a society that was steadily growing more moderate and careful. Furthermore, both of them appeared somewhat weaker in character, not so much in their actions but in their subtle responses to the world around them. Something had developed within Gloria that she had never required before—the framework, incomplete yet clearly recognizable, of her long-buried disgust, a conscience. This acknowledgment came at the same time as the gradual weakening of her physical bravery.

Then, on the August morning following Adam Patch's surprise visit, they woke up feeling sick and exhausted, discouraged with life, able to feel only one overwhelming emotion—fear.

Crisis

"Well?" Anthony sat up in bed and looked down at her. The corners of his mouth were turned down with sadness, his voice sounded tight and empty.

Her response was to lift her hand to her mouth and start slowly, carefully gnawing at her finger.

"We've done it," he said after a pause; then, when she remained quiet, he grew frustrated. "Why won't you say anything?"

"What on earth do you want me to say?"

"What are you thinking?"

"Nothing."

"Then stop biting your finger!"

A brief, muddled conversation followed about whether she had actually been thinking at all. Anthony felt it was crucial that she voice her thoughts about the previous night's catastrophe. Her quiet seemed like a way of placing all the blame on his shoulders.

275

From her perspective, there was no need to talk—this moment called for her to bite her fingernail like an anxious child.

"I need to sort out this terrible situation with my grandfather," he said with uncertain determination. A slight, emerging respect showed in how he said "my grandfather" rather than "grampa."

"You can't," she stated firmly. "You can't—ever. He'll never forgive you for as long as he lives."

"Maybe not," Anthony agreed miserably. "Still—I might be able to redeem myself through some kind of reform and that sort of thing—"

"He looked sick," she interrupted, "pale as flour."

"He is sick. I told you that three months ago."

"I wish he had died last week!" she said irritably. "Thoughtless old fool!"

Neither of them laughed.

"But let me tell you something," she said quietly, "if I ever see you behaving with any woman the way you did with Rachael Barnes last night, I'll leave you just like that! I absolutely will not put up with it!"

Anthony shrank back in fear.

"Oh, don't be ridiculous," he objected. "You know there's no other woman in the world for me but you—no one else, my darling."

His effort to strike a gentle tone fell flat completely—the more pressing threat crept back to the forefront.

"If I approached him," Anthony suggested, "and told him with the right biblical quotes that I had wandered too long down the path of sin and had finally seen the light—" He stopped mid-sentence and looked at his wife with an amused expression. "I wonder what his reaction would be?"

"I don't know."

She was wondering whether their guests would be smart enough to leave right after breakfast.

Anthony couldn't bring himself to make the trip to Tarrytown for an entire week. The thought of going there disgusted him, and if left to his own devices, he would never have been able to force himself to make the journey—but while his willpower had weakened over the past three years, so had his ability to resist pressure from others. Gloria forced him to go. Waiting a week was perfectly reasonable, she argued, since that would allow his grandfather's fierce anger time to subside—but waiting any longer would be a mistake—it would give that anger time to become permanently entrenched.

He went, filled with anxiety... and for nothing. Adam Patch wasn't feeling well, Shuttleworth said with irritation. Clear orders had been given that no visitors were allowed to see him. Under the former "gin-physician's" spiteful gaze, Anthony's confidence crumbled. He walked back to his taxi almost skulking—regaining only a bit of his dignity as he got on the train; relieved to escape, like a child, to the magnificent palaces of comfort that still stood tall and sparkled in his imagination.

Gloria felt contemptuous when he came back to Marietta. Why hadn't he pushed his way inside? That's exactly what she would have done!

Between them they wrote a letter to the old man, and after making many changes sent it out. It was partly an apology, partly a made-up explanation. The letter received no response.

A September day arrived, marked by shifting patterns of sun and rain—sunlight that carried no warmth, rainfall that brought no relief. That was the day they departed from the gray house that had witnessed their love at its peak. Four trunks and three enormous crates sat stacked in the stripped-bare room where, just two years earlier, they had lounged carelessly, lost in dreamy thoughts, feeling distant, drowsy, and satisfied. The room rang with hollowness. Gloria, wearing a new brown dress trimmed with fur, sat quietly on one of the trunks, while Anthony paced back and forth anxiously, cigarette in hand, as they both waited for the truck that would transport their belongings to the city.

"What are those?" she asked, pointing to some books stacked on one of the crates.

"That's my old stamp collection," he admitted with embarrassment. "I forgot to pack it."

"Anthony, it's so silly to carry it around."

"Well, I was going through it the day we moved out of the apartment last spring, and I chose not to put it in storage."

"Can't you sell it? Don't we have enough junk already?"

"I'm sorry," he said humbly.

With a loud rumbling noise, the truck pulled up to the entrance. Gloria raised her fist in defiance at the four walls surrounding her.

"I'm so excited to leave!" she exclaimed, "so excited. Oh, my God, how I despise this house!"

So the brilliant and beautiful woman traveled with her husband to New York. Right there on the train carrying them away, they argued—her harsh words came as frequently, as regularly, and as inevitably as the stations they passed.

"Don't be angry," Anthony pleaded desperately. "We only have each other, after all."

"Most of the time, we don't even have that," Gloria exclaimed.

"When haven't we?"

"Many times—starting with one incident on the train platform at Redgate."

"You don't mean to say that—"

"No," she interrupted coolly, "I don't dwell on it. It came and went—and when it left, it took something with it."

She stopped talking suddenly. Anthony sat quietly, feeling confused and sad. The dreary views of train-side Mamaroneck, Larchmont, Rye, Pelham Manor passed by one after another, broken up by stretches of ugly, cheap-looking wasteland that failed miserably at looking like countryside. He found himself thinking back to how one summer morning the two of them had left New York looking for happiness. Maybe they had never really expected to find it, but even so, that search itself had been happier than anything he thought he would ever experience again. Life, it seemed, had to be about building supports around yourself—otherwise everything fell apart. There was no peace, no calm. He had been foolish to want to just drift along and dream; nobody drifted without ending up in whirlpools, nobody dreamed without those dreams turning into wild nightmares filled with uncertainty and regret.

Pelham! They had argued in Pelham because Gloria insisted on driving. And when she pressed her small foot down on the gas pedal, the car had shot forward energetically, and both their heads had snapped backward like puppets controlled by the same string.

The Bronx—the houses clustering together and shining in the sunlight, which was now streaming down through vast brilliant skies and cascading waves of light into the streets below. New York, he figured, was home—the city of wealth and enigma, of impossible dreams and strange fantasies. Here on the edges, ridiculous stucco mansions rose up in the cool evening light, suspended for a moment in cool fantasy, then gliding away into the distance, replaced by the bewildering maze of the Harlem River. The train rolled forward through the deepening dusk, above and beyond dozens of lively, humid streets of the upper East Side, each one flashing past the car window like the gap between spokes of an enormous wheel, each one offering its energetic, vibrant display of poor children swarming in frantic motion like bright ants in corridors of red sand. From the apartment windows hung plump, round-faced mothers, like stars in this grimy sky; women resembling dark flawed gems, women like produce, women like enormous bundles of disgustingly soiled clothes.

"I like these streets," Anthony said out loud. "I always feel like it's a show being put on just for me; like the moment I walk by, they'll all stop jumping around and laughing and instead become really sad, remembering how poor they are, and go back into their houses with their heads hanging down. You see that kind of thing a lot in other countries, but rarely here in America."

Down on a busy main street, he spotted a dozen Jewish names displayed across a row of shops; in each doorway stood a small, dark-complexioned man observing the pedestrians with focused eyes—eyes that sparkled with wariness, with dignity, with sharpness, with greed, with understanding. New York—he couldn't separate it anymore from the gradual, steady rise of these people—the small businesses, growing larger, spreading out, merging together, relocating, supervised with the keen vision of a hawk and a bee's meticulous attention to every detail—they spread outward in all directions. It was striking—when viewed from a broader perspective, it was extraordinary.

Gloria's voice suddenly interrupted his thoughts with an oddly fitting timing.

"I wonder where Bloeckman has been this summer."

The Apartment

After the certainties of youth, a period of intense and unbearable complexity begins. For the soda fountain worker, this period is so brief it's almost insignificant. Men positioned higher on the social ladder endure longer in their efforts to maintain the finest details of human connection, to hold onto "impractical" concepts of honor. However, by the late twenties, life has become too complicated, and what was once immediate and bewildering has slowly become distant and unclear. Daily routine descends like dusk over a rough terrain, smoothing it until it becomes bearable. The complexity is too delicate, too diverse; our values shift completely with each loss of energy; it starts to seem that we can gain nothing from the past to help us confront the future—so we stop being spontaneous, persuadable people, concerned with what is morally correct down to the smallest details, we replace principles of honor with behavioral guidelines, we prize security over passion, we become, without realizing it, practical. Only a select few continue to focus persistently on the subtleties of human relationships—and even these few only during certain moments specifically reserved for this purpose.

Anthony Patch was no longer someone who sought mental challenges or felt curious about the world around him. Instead, he had become a person driven by bias and prejudice, desperately wanting to avoid any emotional disturbance. This slow transformation had been happening over several years, made worse by a series of worries that constantly troubled his thoughts. Most importantly, there was the feeling of wasted potential that had always lurked in his heart, now brought to the surface by his current circumstances. During moments when he felt uncertain about himself, he was tormented by the idea that life might actually have meaning after all. In his early twenties, he had been convinced that making any effort was pointless and that giving up was the wisest choice—beliefs that were reinforced both by the philosophical ideas he had come to admire and by his relationships with Maury Noble and later with his wife. However, there had been times—such as just before he first met Gloria, and when his grandfather had proposed that he travel overseas to work as a war correspondent—when his dissatisfaction had nearly pushed him to take decisive action.

One day just before they left Marietta for the final time, while casually flipping through the pages of a Harvard Alumni Bulletin, he discovered a column that revealed what his classmates had been doing during the six years since graduation. Most of them had gone into business, that much was true, and several were busy converting the non-believers of China or America to a vague form of protestantism; but a few, he discovered, were working meaningfully at jobs that were neither easy positions nor mindless routines. There was Calvin Boyd, for example, who, despite having just finished medical school, had developed a new treatment for typhus, had traveled overseas and was helping to heal some of the damage that the Great Powers had inflicted upon Serbia; there was Eugene Bronson, whose articles in The New Democracy were establishing him as a man with ideas that went beyond both cheap sensationalism and mass panic; there was a man named Daly who had been kicked out from the faculty of a self-righteous university for teaching Marxist theories in his classroom: in art, science, politics, he witnessed the genuine voices of his generation coming forward—there was even Severance, the quarterback, who had ended his life quite elegantly and gracefully with the Foreign Legion on the Aisne.

He put down the magazine and spent some time thinking about these different men. Back when he had his principles intact, he would have defended his position to the very end—like an Epicurus in paradise, he would have declared that to fight was to have faith, and to have faith was to set boundaries. He would have been just as likely to start attending church because the idea of eternal life appealed to him as he would have been to consider going into the leather trade because the fierce competition would have protected him from misery. But right now he didn't have such refined moral concerns. This fall, as he entered his twenty-ninth year, he felt drawn to shut his mind off to many things, to stop digging too deeply into reasons and underlying causes, and mainly to yearn intensely for protection from the world and from himself. He couldn't stand being by himself, and as mentioned before, he often feared being alone with Gloria.

Because of the gap that his grandfather's visit had created in front of him, and the resulting rejection of his recent way of living, it was unavoidable that he would search around in this suddenly unfriendly city for the friends and surroundings that had once felt the most welcoming and safe. His first move was a frantic effort to reclaim his former apartment.

In the spring of 1912, he had signed a four-year lease for seventeen hundred dollars annually, which included an option to renew. This lease had run out the previous May. When he first rented the space, the rooms had been nothing more than possibilities, barely recognizable as such, but Anthony had recognized these possibilities and negotiated terms in the lease requiring both him and the landlord to invest a specific amount in improvements. Rental prices had increased over the past four years, and last spring when Anthony chose not to exercise his renewal option, the landlord, a Mr. Sohenberg, had come to understand that he could command a much higher price for what had become an attractive apartment. Therefore, when Anthony contacted him about the matter in September, he was presented with Sohenberg's proposal for a three-year lease at twenty-five hundred dollars per year. This struck Anthony as completely unreasonable. It would mean that more than a third of their income would go toward rent. He argued unsuccessfully that his own money and his own concepts for redesigning the space had transformed the rooms into something desirable.

He offered two thousand dollars in vain—then twenty-two hundred, even though they could barely afford it: Mr. Sohenberg remained unmoved. It appeared that two other men were interested in the apartment; exactly that type of place was popular right now, and it wouldn't make business sense to rent it to Mr. Patch. Furthermore, although he had never brought it up before, several other tenants had complained about noise during the past winter—late-night singing and dancing, things like that.

Anthony, seething with anger inside, rushed back to the Ritz to tell Gloria about his humiliating defeat.

"I can just picture you," she raged, "letting him intimidate you!"

"What could I say?"

"You could have told him exactly what he was. I wouldn't have put up with it. No other man in the world would have tolerated it! You just allow people to push you around and deceive you and intimidate you and exploit you as if you were some foolish little child. It's ridiculous!"

"Oh, for Heaven's sake, don't lose your temper."

"I know, Anthony, but you are such an ass!"

"Well, maybe. Anyway, we can't afford that apartment. But we can afford it better than living here at the Ritz."

"You were the one who insisted on coming here."

"Yes, because I knew you'd be miserable in a cheap hotel."

"Of course I would!"

"At any rate we've got to find a place to live."

"How much can we pay?" she demanded.

"Well, we can afford to pay even his price if we sell more bonds, but we agreed last night that until I had found something definite to do we-"

"Oh, I know all that. I asked you how much we can pay out of just our income."

"They say you shouldn't pay more than a quarter."

"How much is a quarter?"

"One hundred and fifty a month."

"Are you telling me that we're only bringing in six hundred dollars each month?" Her voice took on a quieter, more troubled tone.

"Of course!" he replied with anger. "Do you think we could have continued spending over twelve thousand a year without seriously depleting our savings?"

"I knew we had sold bonds, but have we really spent that much in a year? How did we manage that?" Her amazement grew.

"Oh, I'll check those detailed records we maintained," he said with sarcasm, then continued: "Two rental payments most of the time, clothing, trips—why, each of those spring seasons in

California ran us about four thousand dollars. That blasted car was nothing but an expense from beginning to end. And celebrations and entertainment and—oh, one expense after another."

They were both excited and deeply depressed at the same time. The situation seemed worse when Gloria actually heard about it than it had when he first discovered it himself.

"You need to start earning some money," she said suddenly.

"I know it."

"And you need to try once more to visit your grandfather."

"I will."

"When?"

"When we get settled."

This situation came to pass a week later. They leased a small apartment on Fifty-seventh Street for one hundred and fifty dollars a month. The unit contained a bedroom, living room, kitchenette, and bathroom in a narrow, white-stone apartment building, and while the rooms were too cramped to showcase Anthony's finest furniture, they were spotless, modern, and in a pale and sterile manner, reasonably appealing. Bounds had traveled overseas to join the British military, and in his absence they endured rather than appreciated the work of a lean, large-framed Irish woman, whom Gloria despised because she spoke about the triumphs of Sinn Fein while serving breakfast. However, they had sworn they would employ no more Japanese staff, and English domestic workers were currently difficult to find. Like Bounds, the woman only prepared breakfast. They ate their remaining meals at restaurants and hotels.

What ultimately prompted Anthony to rush hastily to Tarrytown was a notice published in multiple New York newspapers stating that Adam Patch, the multimillionaire, the philanthropist, the respected reformer, was gravely ill and unlikely to survive.

The Kitten

Anthony wasn't allowed to see him. The doctors had given strict orders that he shouldn't speak with anyone, Mr. Shuttleworth explained—though he graciously offered to carry any message Anthony wanted to send and deliver it to Adam Patch when his health improved enough to receive it. However, through clear hints, he validated Anthony's grim suspicion that the wayward grandson would be especially unwanted at his grandfather's bedside. At one moment during their conversation, Anthony, remembering Gloria's firm instructions, started to move as if he might push past the secretary, but Shuttleworth smiled and set his muscular shoulders in a blocking position, making Anthony realize how pointless such an effort would be.

Feeling utterly intimidated and miserable, he went back to New York, where he and his wife spent a week filled with restlessness. A small event that happened one evening showed just how much strain their nerves were under.

Walking home down a side street after dinner, Anthony spotted a cat prowling near a fence in the darkness.

"I always have an instinct to kick a cat," he said casually.

"I like them."

"I gave in to it once."

"When?"

"Oh, that happened years ago, before I met you. It was one night during the intermission of a show. It was a cold night, just like this one, and I was a bit drunk—one of the first times I'd ever been drunk," he added. "The poor little thing was probably looking for somewhere to sleep, I suppose, and I was in a nasty mood, so I got the urge to kick it—"

"Oh, the poor kitty!" Gloria exclaimed, genuinely touched. Motivated by his storytelling instincts, Anthony expanded on the subject.

"It was really awful," he confessed. "The poor little creature turned around and gazed at me with such a pitiful expression, as if he was hoping I would scoop him up and show him some kindness—he was nothing more than a tiny kitten—and before he could react, a large foot kicked out at him and struck his small back"

"Oh!" Gloria's cry was filled with anguish.

"It was such a cold night," he went on, stubbornly maintaining the sad tone in his voice. "I suppose it was hoping for some kindness from someone, but all it received was pain—"

He stopped speaking abruptly—Gloria was crying. They had arrived home, and when they walked into the apartment she collapsed onto the couch, weeping as if he had wounded her deepest being.

"Oh, the poor little kitten!" she said again with deep sympathy, "the poor little kitten. So cold—"

"Gloria"

"Don't come near me! Please, don't come near me. You killed the gentle little kitten."

Moved, Anthony knelt down next to her.

"Dear," he said. "Oh, Gloria, darling. It isn't true. I made it all up—every single word of it."

But she wouldn't believe him. Something about the specific details he had decided to share made her cry herself to sleep that night—crying for the kitten, for Anthony, for herself, and for all the pain, bitterness, and cruelty that existed in the world.

The Death of An American Moralist

Old Adam passed away on a late November midnight with a devout prayer to his God upon his pale lips. This man, who had received so much praise throughout his life, departed while offering flattery to the Almighty Being that he imagined he might have offended during the more lustful periods of his younger years.

It was reported that he had negotiated some kind of peace agreement with the divine, though the specific conditions remained confidential, although people believed they involved a substantial monetary contribution. Every newspaper published his life story, and two of them featured brief editorials about his excellent character and his role in the industrial revolution that had shaped his era. They carefully mentioned the social reforms he had supported and funded. The legacies of Comstock and Cato the Censor were brought back to life and displayed like skeletal spirits throughout the newspaper columns.

Every newspaper noted that he left behind only one grandson, Anthony Comstock Patch, of New York.

The burial took place in the family plot at Tarrytown. Anthony and Gloria rode in the first carriage, too anxious to feel awkward, both desperately trying to read signs of their financial future in the faces of the servants who had been with him when he died.

They waited an anxious week out of respect, and then, having received no word whatsoever, Anthony phoned his grandfather's attorney. Mr. Brett was out but was expected to return within an hour. Anthony gave his phone number.

It was the last day of November, cold and crisp outside, with a dull sun casting pale light through the windows. While they waited for the phone call, pretending to read, the mood both inside and outside seemed deliberately designed to mirror their emotions. After what felt like forever, the phone rang, and Anthony, jumping suddenly, picked up the receiver.

"Hello..." His voice sounded strained and empty. "Yes—I did leave a message. Who am I speaking with, please?... Yes.... Well, it was about the estate. Of course I'm interested, and I haven't received any information about the will reading—I thought you might not have my current address.... What?... Yes..."

Gloria dropped to her knees. The pauses between Anthony's words felt like tourniquets tightening around her heart. She discovered herself frantically twisting the large buttons on a velvet pillow. Then:

"That's—that's extremely strange—that's really strange—that's very strange. Not even any—uh—mention or any—uh—explanation?"

His voice sounded weak and distant. She made a small noise, part gasp, part cry.

"Yes, I'll see.... All right, thanks ... thanks...."

The phone clicked. Her eyes, scanning the floor, caught sight of his feet breaking through a patch of sunlight that fell across the carpet. She stood up and met his gaze with a steady, gray look just as his arms wrapped around her.

"My dearest," he whispered in a rough voice. "He did it, damn him!"

Next Day

"Who are the heirs?" Mr. Haight asked. "You see, when you can tell me so little about it—"

Mr. Haight was tall and stooped with heavy, protruding eyebrows. He had been recommended to Anthony as a sharp and persistent lawyer.

"I only have a rough idea," Anthony replied. "There's a man called Shuttleworth, who was kind of his favorite, and he's handling everything as the administrator or trustee or whatever—everything except the direct donations to charity and the money set aside for the servants and those two cousins in Idaho."

"How distant are the cousins?"

"Oh, third or fourth place, whatever. I had never even heard of them."

Mr. Haight nodded with complete understanding.

"And you want to challenge a clause in the will?"

"I suppose so," Anthony admitted helplessly. "I want to do whatever seems most promising—that's what I need you to tell

289

me."

"You want them to refuse probate to the will?"

Anthony shook his head.

"You've got me. I have no idea what 'probate' means. I want a share of the estate."

"Let's say you give me some additional details. For example, do you know why the person who made the will cut you out of the inheritance?"

"Why—yes," Anthony started. "You see, he was always a pushover for moral reform, and all that—"

"I know," Mr. Haight interrupted without any humor.

"—and I don't think he ever believed I amounted to much. I never went into business, you understand. But I'm sure that until last summer I was one of the people who would inherit from him. We owned a house in Marietta, and one evening grandfather decided he wanted to visit us. It so happened that we were throwing quite a lively party, and he showed up completely unannounced. Well, he took one look around, along with this man Shuttleworth, then turned right around and rushed straight back to Tarrytown. From that point on, he never replied to my letters or even allowed me to visit him."

"He was a prohibitionist, wasn't he?"

"He was everything—a complete religious fanatic."

"How much time passed between when the will that cut you out of the inheritance was written and his death?"

"Recently—I mean since August."

"And you believe that the main reason he didn't leave you most of the estate was because he was upset with what you've been doing lately?"

"Yes."

Mr. Haight thought it over. What reasons did Anthony have for wanting to challenge the will?

"Why, isn't there something about evil influence?"

"Undue influence is one legal basis—but it's the most challenging to prove. You would need to demonstrate that such pressure was applied so that the deceased was in a state where he gave away his property against his true wishes—"

"Well, what if this guy Shuttleworth dragged him over to Marietta right when he figured some kind of celebration was likely happening?"

"That wouldn't affect the case at all. There's a clear distinction between giving advice and exerting influence. You would need to demonstrate that the secretary had malicious intent. I would recommend pursuing different grounds. A will is automatically denied probate if there's evidence of insanity, intoxication"—at this point Anthony smiled—"or mental weakness due to premature aging."

"But," Anthony protested, "his personal doctor, who was one of the people receiving money from the will, would swear that he was mentally sound. And he was right. The truth is, he probably did exactly what he meant to do with his money—it was completely in line with everything he had done throughout his entire life—"

"Well, you see, mental incapacity is very similar to undue influence—it suggests that the property wasn't distributed according to the original intentions. The most frequent basis for challenge is duress—physical coercion."

Anthony shook his head.

"I don't think there's much chance of that happening, I'm afraid. Undue influence seems like the best option to me."

After further discussion that was so technical Anthony could barely understand it, he hired Mr. Haight as his attorney. The lawyer suggested arranging a meeting with Shuttleworth, who served as executor of the will alongside Wilson, Hiemer and Hardy. Anthony was told to return later that week.

It turned out that the estate was worth about forty million dollars. The largest individual inheritance was one million dollars, which went to Edward Shuttleworth, who also received a thirty thousand dollar annual salary as administrator of the thirty-million-dollar trust fund that was left to be distributed to various charities and reform organizations essentially at his own judgment. The remaining nine million dollars were divided among the two cousins in Idaho and approximately twenty-five other beneficiaries: friends, secretaries, servants, and employees who had, at various times, gained Adam Patch's approval.

At the end of another two weeks, Mr. Haight, with a retainer fee of fifteen thousand dollars, had started preparing to contest the will.

The Winter of Discontent

Before they had lived in the small apartment on Fifty-seventh Street for even two months, it had taken on the same vague yet almost physical contamination that had saturated the gray house in Marietta. The smell of tobacco was everywhere—they both smoked constantly; it clung to their clothing, their bedding, the window treatments, and the ash-covered rugs. Combined with this was the miserable atmosphere of stale alcohol, carrying with it the unavoidable hint of beauty turned rotten and celebrations now remembered with revulsion. Around a specific collection of wine glasses on the dining room cabinet, the smell was especially strong, and in the living room the wooden table was marked with white rings where drinks had been placed on its surface. There had been countless gatherings—guests damaged belongings; guests became ill in Gloria's restroom; guests spilled alcohol; guests created unimaginable chaos in the small kitchen area.

These activities had become a routine part of their daily lives. Even though they made promises every Monday to change their ways, there was an unspoken agreement that as the weekend drew near, they should celebrate it with some kind of wild excitement. When Saturday arrived, they wouldn't talk about their plans directly, but instead would phone various people from their group of equally reckless friends and propose getting together. Only after their friends had arrived and Anthony had brought out the bottles of liquor would he casually mention "I think I'll just have one cocktail myself—"

Then they would disappear for two days—waking up on a cold, gray morning to realize they had been the loudest and most attention-grabbing people in what was already the loudest and most attention-grabbing group at the Boul' Mich', or the Club Ramée, or at other establishments that were far less concerned about how rowdy their customers got. They would discover that they had somehow blown through eighty or ninety dollars, though they could never figure out how; they usually blamed it on the fact that all the "friends" who had tagged along with them were broke.

It became common for their more genuine friends to confront them right in the middle of a party, warning them that they were heading toward a dark future where Gloria would lose her beauty and Anthony would destroy his health.

The story of the abruptly ended party in Marietta had naturally spread with all the details intact—"Muriel doesn't intend to tell everyone she knows," Gloria explained to Anthony, "but she believes each person she confides in will be the only one she'll ever tell"—and the gossip, thinly disguised, had been featured prominently in Town Tattle. When Adam Patch's will became public knowledge and newspapers ran stories about Anthony's lawsuit, the tale was perfectly completed—much to Anthony's endless humiliation. They started hearing gossip about themselves from every direction, stories that were typically based on a hint of truth but covered with ridiculous and ominous details.

On the surface, they showed no signs of decline. At twenty-six, Gloria remained the same Gloria she had been at twenty; her skin still fresh and dewy, providing a perfect backdrop for her honest eyes; her hair continued to be her crowning glory, gradually shifting from golden blonde to a rich auburn; her graceful figure still evoking images of a woodland sprite dancing through mystical forests. Male gazes, countless of them, tracked her with captivated attention whenever she moved through a hotel foyer or walked down a theater aisle. Men sought introductions to her, fell into extended periods of genuine infatuation, and pursued her romantically—for she remained a vision of extraordinary and breathtaking beauty. As for Anthony, he had actually improved rather than declined in his looks; his features had acquired a subtle hint of melancholy that created a striking contrast with his polished and impeccable appearance.

Early that winter, when everyone was talking about whether America would enter the war, and while Anthony was making a desperate and genuine effort to write, Muriel Kane showed up in New York and immediately came to visit them. Just like Gloria, she appeared never to age or change. She knew all the newest slang, danced the most current dances, and discussed the latest songs and shows with all the enthusiasm of her first season as a New York socialite. Her flirtatiousness remained forever fresh yet forever ineffective; her clothing was cutting-edge; her black hair was now cut short in a bob, just like Gloria's.

"I've come up for the midwinter prom at New Haven," she revealed, sharing her delightful secret. Although she was probably older than any of the college boys, she always managed to get some kind of invitation, vaguely imagining that the next party would bring the romance that would lead to a wedding at the altar.

"Where have you been?" asked Anthony, consistently entertained.

"I've been at Hot Springs. It's been exciting and lively this fall—more men!"

"Are you in love, Muriel?"

"What do you mean 'love'?" This was the rhetorical question of the year. "I'm going to tell you something," she said, changing the topic suddenly. "I guess it's not really my place to say, but I think it's time for you two to settle down."

"Well, we've settled down."

"Yes, you are!" she said mockingly. "Everywhere I go, I hear stories about your wild adventures. Let me tell you, I have a terrible time defending you."

"You don't need to bother," said Gloria coldly.

"Now, Gloria," she objected, "you know I'm one of your closest friends."

Gloria remained quiet. Muriel went on:

"It's not so much the idea of a woman drinking, but Gloria's so beautiful, and so many people recognize her everywhere around town, that it naturally draws attention—"

"What have you heard lately?" Gloria demanded, her dignity crumbling in the face of her curiosity.

"Well, for example, that the group in Marietta killed Anthony's grandfather."

Immediately, both husband and wife became filled with irritation.

"Why, I think that's outrageous."

"That's what they say," Muriel insisted stubbornly.

Anthony walked back and forth across the room. "This is absolutely ridiculous!" he exclaimed. "The same people we invite to our parties are spreading this story around like it's some hilarious joke—and sooner or later it comes back to us looking something like this."

Gloria started running her finger through a loose reddish curl. Muriel moistened her lips as she thought about what to say next.

"You should have a baby."

Gloria looked up with exhaustion.

"We can't afford it."

"Everyone in the slums has them," Muriel said triumphantly.

Anthony and Gloria shared a knowing look. They had arrived at a point where their fierce arguments were never truly resolved—fights that continued to simmer beneath the surface and erupted again periodically or simply faded away due to complete apathy. But Muriel's visit brought them together for the moment. When an outsider noticed the tension they were living with, it motivated them to stand united against this unfriendly world. These days, the desire to reconnect rarely came from their own hearts anymore.

Anthony began to see similarities between his own life and that of the apartment building's night elevator operator, a pale man around sixty with a scraggly beard who carried himself as if he deserved better than his current job. This sense of being above his position was likely what had gotten him hired in the first place; it made him a pitiful and unforgettable symbol of disappointment. Anthony remembered, without finding it amusing, an old joke about how an elevator operator's career was all about ups and downs—regardless, it was a confined existence filled with endless monotony. Every time Anthony got into the elevator, he held his breath waiting for the old man's predictable comment: "Well, I guess we're going to have some sunshine today." Anthony couldn't help but think about how little actual rain or sunshine this man would ever experience, trapped inside that cramped little box in the gray, windowless hallway.

A shadowy figure, he achieved a tragic end by departing from a life that had treated him so poorly. Three young armed men entered one evening, bound him with ropes, and abandoned him on a heap of coal in the basement while they ransacked the storage room. When the building superintendent discovered him the following morning, he had succumbed to the cold. He passed away from pneumonia four days afterward.

He was replaced by a smooth-talking Black man from Martinique who spoke with an oddly out-of-place British accent and had a habit of being rude, and Anthony couldn't stand him. The old man's death affected him in much the same way that the kitten story had affected Gloria. It reminded him of how cruel life could be and, as a result, made him more aware of the growing bitterness in his own life.

He was finally writing—and this time he was serious about it. He had gone to Dick and spent an intense hour listening to detailed explanations of those procedural technicalities that he had previously dismissed with contempt. He needed money right away—he was selling bonds every month just to cover their expenses. Dick was straightforward and clear:

"When it comes to writing articles about literature for these little-known magazines, you wouldn't earn enough to cover your rent. Naturally, if someone has a talent for humor, or gets the opportunity to write a major biography, or possesses some expert knowledge, they might hit it big. But in your case, fiction is your only option. You mentioned you need money immediately?"

"I certainly do."

"Well, it would take a year and a half before you'd earn any money from a novel. Try writing some popular short stories instead. And by the way, unless they're exceptionally brilliant, they need to be upbeat and support the winning side to make you any money."

Anthony reflected on Dick's latest work, which had been published in a popular monthly magazine. The stories primarily focused on the ridiculous behavior of a group of wooden, lifeless characters who were supposedly members of New York's high society, and they typically revolved around issues concerning the female protagonist's moral virtue, accompanied by pretentious social commentary about the "wild escapades of the elite four hundred."

"But your stories—" Anthony burst out, the words escaping him almost without thinking.

"Oh, that's different," Dick declared with surprising confidence. "I have a reputation, you see, so people expect me to tackle serious subjects."

Anthony felt a jolt of surprise inside, suddenly understanding from this comment just how far Richard Caramel had declined. Did he really believe that these incredible recent works were as good as his first novel?

Anthony returned to the apartment and got to work. He discovered that the business of optimism was quite a challenge. After several unsuccessful attempts, he went to the public library and spent a week studying the files of a popular magazine. Then, better prepared, he completed his first story, "The Dictaphone of Fate." It was based on one of his few remaining memories from those six weeks on Wall Street the previous year. It claimed to be the cheerful story of an office boy who, completely by chance, hummed a beautiful melody into the dictaphone. The cylinder was found by the boss's brother, a well-known producer of musical comedy—and then immediately lost. The main part of the story dealt with the search for the missing cylinder and the eventual marriage of the honorable office boy (now a successful composer) to Miss Rooney, the virtuous stenographer, who was part Joan of Arc and part Florence Nightingale.

He had figured out that this was exactly what the magazines were looking for. In his main characters, he presented the typical inhabitants of the sentimental literary world, placing them in a sweet, syrupy storyline that wouldn't upset a single reader in Marietta. He had the manuscript typed with double spacing—this final touch came from advice in a guidebook called "Success as a Writer Made Easy," written by R. Meggs Widdlestien, which promised aspiring writers that hard work was pointless, claiming that after completing a six-lesson course, anyone could earn at least a thousand dollars every month.

After reading it to a bored Gloria and getting from her the timeless comment that it was "better than a lot of stuff that gets published," he mockingly attached the pen name "Gilles de Sade," included the required return envelope, and mailed it off.

After completing the enormous task of creating his story, he chose to wait until he received word about the first one before starting another. Dick had mentioned that he could potentially earn as much as two hundred dollars. If it turned out to be unsuitable for some reason, the editor's response would likely provide him with guidance on what modifications needed to be made.

"It is, without question, the most terrible piece of writing that exists," said Anthony.

The editor most likely shared his opinion. He sent back the manuscript along with a rejection letter. Anthony mailed it to another publisher and started working on a new story. The second story was titled "The Little Open Doors"; he completed it in three days. It dealt with supernatural themes: a separated couple was reunited through a psychic performer in a variety show.

There were six in total, six miserable and pathetic attempts to "put words on paper" by someone who had never previously made any serious effort to write whatsoever. None of them held even a hint of life, and their combined output of elegance and charm was inferior to that of a typical newspaper article. While making their rounds, they accumulated, in sum, thirty-one rejection letters, tombstones for the manuscripts that he would discover lying like corpses at his doorstep.

In mid-January Gloria's father passed away, and they traveled once more to Kansas City—a terrible journey, as Gloria dwelled endlessly, not on her father's death, but on her mother's. After Russel Gilbert's estate was settled, they inherited approximately three thousand dollars and a considerable amount of furniture. The furniture was in storage, since he had spent his final days in a small hotel. It was because of his death that Anthony made a new discovery about Gloria. During the trip East she revealed herself, surprisingly, as a Bilphist.

"Why, Gloria," he exclaimed, "you don't mean to tell me you believe that nonsense."

"Well," she said defiantly, "why not?"

"Because it's—it's fantastic. You know that in every sense of the word you're an agnostic. You'd laugh at any orthodox form of Christianity—and then you come out with the statement that you believe in some silly rule of reincarnation."

"What if I do? I've heard you and Maury, along with everyone else whose intelligence I have any respect for, agree that life as we see it is completely meaningless. But it's always seemed to me that if I were unconsciously learning something here, it might not be so meaningless after all."

"You're not learning anything—you're just wearing yourself out. And if you need to have faith to make things easier, choose one that makes sense to reasonable people, not just a bunch of emotional women. Someone like you shouldn't accept anything unless it can be properly proven."

"I don't care about truth. I want some happiness."

"Well, if you have a good mind, the second point must be tempered by the first. Any naive person can fool themselves with worthless thoughts."

"I don't care," she declared firmly, "and furthermore, I'm not promoting any particular belief or theory."

The argument died down, but it came back to Anthony's mind several times after that. It was unsettling to discover this old belief, clearly absorbed from her mother, creeping back in under its ancient disguise as a natural instinct.

They arrived in New York in March following a costly and poorly planned week in Hot Springs, and Anthony returned to his unsuccessful attempts at writing fiction. As it became increasingly clear to both of them that salvation would not come through popular writing, their shared confidence and determination continued to deteriorate. An intricate battle raged constantly between them. All attempts to reduce their spending collapsed from pure apathy, and by March they were once more using any excuse as justification for throwing a "party." With a pretense of abandon, Gloria threw out the idea that they should take all their remaining money and embark on a genuine binge while it lasted—anything appeared preferable to watching it disappear in unsatisfying trickles.

"Gloria, you want parties as much as I do."

"It doesn't matter about me. Everything I do aligns with my beliefs: to make the most of every minute during these years while I'm young, having the best time I possibly can."

"What happens after that?"

"After that I won't care."

"Yes, you will."

"Well, I might—but I won't be able to do anything about it. And I'll have had my good time."

"You'll remain the same person then. In a way, we've had our fun, caused trouble, and now we're facing the consequences."

Nevertheless, the money continued to disappear. There would be two days of happiness, two days of gloom—an endless, almost unchanging cycle. The sudden wake-up calls, when they happened, usually resulted in a burst of work for Anthony, while Gloria, anxious and restless, stayed in bed or chewed mindlessly on her fingernails. After a day or two of this, they would make plans to go out, and then—Oh, what was the point? This evening, this warmth, the end of worry and the feeling that if life wasn't meaningful it was, at least, fundamentally romantic! Wine gave a kind of courage to their own defeat.

Meanwhile, the lawsuit moved forward at a slow pace, involving endless questioning of witnesses and organizing of evidence. The initial procedures for settling the estate had been completed. Mr. Haight couldn't see any reason why the case shouldn't go to trial before summer arrived.

Bloeckman showed up in New York in late March; he had spent nearly a year in England working on business related to "Films Par Excellence." His ongoing process of self-improvement continued—he always dressed slightly better, his speech had become smoother, and his demeanor showed noticeably more confidence that life's finer things belonged to him by natural and undeniable right. He stopped by the apartment and stayed for just an hour, during which he mostly discussed the war, and left saying he would visit again. During his second visit Anthony wasn't home, but a captivated and enthusiastic Gloria met with her husband later that afternoon.

"Anthony," she said, "would you still have a problem with it if I went into the movies?"

His entire heart turned against the thought. As she appeared to pull away from him, even if it was just a possibility, her presence became not just valuable but absolutely essential once more.

"Oh, Gloria—!"

"Blockhead said he'd get me in—but only if I'm going to do something, I'll have to start now. They only want young women. Think of the money, Anthony!"

"For you—yes. But what about me?"

"Don't you know that anything I have is yours too?"

"What a terrible career this is!" he exploded, the moral, the endlessly cautious Anthony, "and what a terrible group of people. And I'm completely sick of that guy Bloeckman showing up here and meddling. I can't stand anything to do with theater."

"It isn't theatrical! It's utterly different."

"What am I supposed to do? Chase you all over the country? Live on your money?"

"Then make some yourself."

The conversation escalated into one of the most heated arguments they had ever experienced. Following the reconciliation that came afterward and the unavoidable phase of emotional numbness, she came to understand that he had drained all the energy from the project. Neither of them ever brought up the likelihood that Bloeckman was far from having purely selfless motives, but they both understood that this was the real reason behind Anthony's opposition.

In April, war was declared against Germany. Wilson and his cabinet—a cabinet whose lack of distinction strangely echoed that of the twelve apostles—unleashed the deliberately restrained forces of war, and the press started howling frantically against the dark morals, dark philosophy, and dark music created by the German character. Those who considered themselves especially open-minded drew the refined distinction that only the German Government stirred them to frenzy; the others were whipped into a state of nauseating impropriety. Any song that included the word "mother" and the word "kaiser" was guaranteed enormous success. Finally everyone had something to discuss—and nearly everyone thoroughly relished it, as if they had been given roles in a dark and dramatic performance.

Anthony, Maury, and Dick submitted their applications for officer training camps, and the latter two walked around feeling strangely uplifted and without guilt; they talked to each other like college students about how war was the only excuse for and justification of the aristocrat, and they imagined an unrealistic class of officers that would apparently consist mainly of the most appealing graduates from three or four Eastern colleges. It seemed to Gloria that in this enormous red glow spreading across the country, even Anthony gained a new sense of allure.

The Tenth Infantry, returning to New York from Panama, found themselves being led from bar to bar by enthusiastic citizens, much to their confusion. West Point graduates started receiving

303

attention for the first time in years, and there was a widespread feeling that everything was wonderful, though not nearly as wonderful as it would soon become, and that everyone was a great person, and every nationality was exceptional—except for the Germans—and throughout all levels of society, those who had been rejected and blamed needed only to show up in military uniform to be pardoned, celebrated, and mourned over by family members, former friends, and complete strangers.

Unfortunately, a small and precise doctor determined that something was wrong with Anthony's blood pressure. He could not in good conscience approve him for officers' training camp.

The Broken Lute

Their third anniversary came and went without any celebration or acknowledgment. The season grew warmer as winter thawed, then melted into the heat of summer, which simmered and eventually burned away. In July, the will was submitted for probate, and when it was contested, the surrogate assigned it to trial term for court proceedings. The case dragged on into September—there was trouble finding an impartial jury because of the moral issues at stake. To Anthony's disappointment, a verdict was eventually delivered in favor of the person who had written the will, after which Mr. Haight had a notice of appeal served on Edward Shuttleworth.

As summer came to an end, Anthony and Gloria discussed what they would do once the money became theirs, and where they would travel after the war ended, when they would "see eye to eye on things again." Both of them anticipated a future when love would rise like a phoenix from its own ashes, reborn in its mysterious and incomprehensible depths.

He was drafted early in the fall, and the examining doctor didn't say anything about low blood pressure. It felt completely meaningless and heartbreaking when Anthony told Gloria one night that more than anything, he wanted to die. But, as usual, they felt sorry for each other for the wrong reasons at the wrong times....

They decided that for now she wouldn't accompany him to the Southern camp where his unit had been assigned. She would stay in New York to "make use of the apartment," to save money, and to monitor how the case was developing—it was currently waiting in the Appellate Division, whose schedule, Mr. Haight informed them, was significantly backlogged.

Almost their last conversation was a pointless argument about how to divide their income—with just one word, either of them would have gladly given it all to the other. It perfectly captured the chaos and disorder of their lives that on that October night when Anthony checked in at Grand Central Station for his trip to camp, she only managed to arrive in time to catch his eye above the worried heads of the assembled crowd. Through the dim light of the covered train platforms, their eyes met across a frantic space, thick with yellow weeping and the odors of impoverished women. They must have reflected on what they had inflicted upon each other, and each must have blamed themselves for creating this dark design through which they were moving both tragically and mysteriously. In the end, they were too distant for either to see the other's tears.

Book Three

Chapter I: A Matter of Civilization

At an urgent order from some unseen authority, Anthony fumbled his way inside. He realized that for the first time in over three years, he would be away from gloria for more than just one night. The permanence of this separation struck him with a grim sense of finality. It was his pure and beautiful girl that he was leaving behind.

They had reached what he believed was the most sensible financial arrangement: she would receive three hundred and seventy-five dollars each month—which wasn't excessive given that more than half would go toward rent—while he would take fifty dollars to add to his military pay. He didn't see any reason to need more than that: meals, clothing, and housing would all be supplied—a private soldier had no social responsibilities to worry about.

The car was packed and already heavy with the smell of people's breath. It was one of those cars called "tourist" cars, a kind of cheap imitation Pullman, with a bare floor and straw seats that desperately needed cleaning. Even so, Anthony welcomed it with relief. He had vaguely imagined that the journey South would happen in a freight car, with eight horses standing at one end and forty men crammed into the other. He had heard the "Hommes 40, Chevaux 8" story so many times that it had become both confusing and threatening in his mind.

As he swayed down the aisle with his military duffel bag hanging from his shoulder like an enormous blue sausage, he couldn't spot any empty seats, but then he noticed a single space currently taken up by the feet of a short, dark-skinned Sicilian man who had pulled his hat down over his eyes and sat hunched defiantly in the corner. When Anthony paused next to him, the man looked up with a menacing glare, clearly meant to intimidate; he must have developed this expression as protection against this whole overwhelming situation. When Anthony curtly asked "Is that seat taken?" the man very slowly raised his feet as if they were fragile cargo and carefully set them down on the floor. His gaze stayed fixed on Anthony, who settled into the seat and unbuttoned the military jacket he'd been given at Camp Upton the previous day. The coat rubbed uncomfortably against his underarms.

Before Anthony could examine the other passengers in their section, a young second lieutenant burst through the door at the far end of the car and glided smoothly down the aisle, declaring in a voice of shocking harshness:

"There will be no smoking in this car! No smoking! Don't smoke, men, in this car!"

As he sailed out at the other end, a dozen small bursts of protest erupted from all directions.

"Oh, cripe!"

"Jeese!"

"No smoking?"

"Hey, come back here, fella!"

"What's the idea?"

Two or three cigarettes were tossed out through the open windows. Others stayed inside, though they were carelessly hidden from sight. Here and there, with tones of defiance, ridicule, or resigned humor, a few comments were made that quickly dissolved into the apathetic and overwhelming silence.

The fourth person in Anthony's section suddenly spoke up.

"Goodbye, freedom," he said glumly. "Goodbye, everything except being an officer's dog."

Anthony looked at him. He was a tall Irishman whose face showed complete indifference and total contempt. His gaze

307

landed on Anthony, as if he was waiting for a response, and then shifted to the others. When he got nothing but a defiant glare from the Italian, he groaned and loudly spat on the floor as a way to return with dignity to his silence.

A few minutes later the door opened again and the second lieutenant swept in on his usual official breeze, this time announcing different news:

"All right, men, smoke if you want to! My mistake, men! It's all right, men! Go on and smoke—my mistake!"

This time Anthony took a careful look at him. The man was young and thin, already worn down by life; he resembled his own mustache in a way; he looked like a large piece of gleaming straw. His chin pulled back slightly, though this weakness was balanced by an impressive yet fake-looking frown—a frown that Anthony would come to recognize on the faces of many young officers in the year that followed.

Immediately everyone lit up cigarettes—whether they had wanted to smoke before or not. Anthony's cigarette added to the murky haze that seemed to drift back and forth in shimmering clouds with each movement of the train. The conversation, which had died down between the two striking visits from the young officer, now picked up again halfheartedly; the men sitting across the aisle started making awkward attempts to find the most comfortable position in their straw seats; two card games that had begun without much enthusiasm soon attracted several onlookers who perched on the armrests of nearby seats. Within a few minutes Anthony noticed a consistently annoying sound—the small, stubborn Sicilian had fallen into loud, audible sleep. It was exhausting to think about that living mass of flesh, rational only out of politeness, trapped in a train car by a bewildering civilization, being transported somewhere to perform some unclear task without purpose or meaning or importance. Anthony let out a sigh, opened a newspaper that he couldn't remember purchasing, and started reading under the dim yellow light.

Ten o'clock dragged stuffily into eleven; the hours became thick and sluggish, grinding to a crawl. The train kept stopping unexpectedly in the dark countryside, occasionally making brief, misleading movements either backward or forward, while blowing harsh celebratory whistles into the crisp October night. After finishing his newspaper completely—editorials, cartoons, and war poems—his gaze landed on a short column titled Shakespeareville, Kansas. Apparently, the Shakespeareville Chamber of Commerce had recently conducted a spirited discussion about whether American soldiers should be called "Sammies" or "Battling Christians." The idea disgusted him. He set the newspaper aside, yawned, and allowed his thoughts to wander elsewhere. He questioned why Gloria had arrived late. It already felt like such a distant memory—a wave of fleeting loneliness washed over him. He attempted to picture how she might view her new situation, what role he would continue to play in her thoughts. This reflection only deepened his gloom—he picked up his paper once more and started reading again.

The members of the Chamber of Commerce in Shakespeareville had chosen "Liberty Lads."

For two nights and two days they traveled south by train, making mysterious and unexplainable stops in what appeared to be barren wastelands, then rushing through major cities with an exaggerated sense of urgency. The unpredictable nature of this train journey gave Anthony a preview of the unpredictable nature of all military administration.

In the dry, barren landscape they received beans and bacon from the baggage car, food that initially he couldn't bring himself to eat—instead he made do with a meager meal of milk chocolate handed out by a local canteen. However, by the second day the food from the baggage car started to seem remarkably appetizing. On the third morning word spread through the group that they would reach their destination, Camp Hooker, within the hour.

It had become unbearably hot inside the car, and all the men had rolled up their sleeves. Sunlight streamed through the windows—a weary, ancient sun that appeared yellow as old parchment and distorted from its journey across the sky. The light attempted to enter in neat, triumphant rectangles but managed only to create twisted, uneven patches—yet it remained relentlessly constant. This steadiness troubled Anthony because he felt he should be the center around which all the meaningless sawmills, trees, and telephone poles spun so rapidly past him. Beyond the train, the sun cast its heavy, shimmering waves across dusty olive-colored roads and barren cotton fields, behind which stretched an irregular line of forest interrupted by jutting formations of gray stone. The immediate landscape was scattered thinly with miserable, poorly maintained shacks, among which would occasionally flash past a representative of South Carolina's lazy rural folk, or perhaps a wandering Black person with sullen and confused eyes.

Then the woods disappeared behind them and they rolled into a vast open area that looked like the baked surface of an enormous cake, dusted with countless tents arranged in precise geometric patterns across the ground. The train came to a hesitant halt, and the sun and the tent poles and the trees began to fade, and his world slowly settled back into its familiar routine, with Anthony Patch at its center. As the soldiers, tired and sweating, pushed their way out of the railroad car, he caught that unmistakable smell that fills every established military camp—the stench of rotting waste.

Camp Hooker was an amazing and impressive development that brought to mind "A Mining Town in 1870—The Second Week." It consisted of wooden shacks and pale gray tents, linked together by a network of roads, featuring hard tan training grounds bordered by trees. Scattered throughout were green Y.M.C.A. buildings, uninviting refuges that carried the stuffy smell of damp flannel and enclosed phone booths—and opposite each one there was typically a canteen, bustling with activity, lazily overseen by an officer who, with the help of a sidecar, generally turned his assignment into an enjoyable and sociable easy job.

Up and down the dusty roads raced the soldiers of the quartermaster corps, also riding in side-cars. Up and down drove the generals in their government automobiles, stopping occasionally to snap inattentive units to attention, to scowl disapprovingly at captains leading their companies, to establish the grandiose rhythm in that magnificent spectacle of displaying power that was unfolding triumphantly across the entire region.

The first week after Anthony's draft notice arrived was packed with endless rounds of vaccinations and medical checkups, along with basic military training. Each day left him utterly exhausted. A friendly, laid-back supply sergeant had given him boots in the wrong size, which caused his feet to swell so badly that the final hours of each afternoon became unbearable agony. For the first time in his life, he could collapse onto his narrow bed between dinner and the afternoon drill call, and as he seemed to sink deeper and deeper into the endless mattress with each passing moment, he would fall asleep instantly while the chatter and laughter surrounding him faded into a soothing hum of sleepy summer sounds. When morning came, he woke up stiff and sore, feeling hollow like a spirit, and rushed out to join the other ghostly figures who crowded the pale company streets as a sharp bugle wailed and sputtered toward the gray sky.

He served in an understaffed infantry company with roughly a hundred soldiers. Following the same daily breakfast of greasy bacon, cold toast, and cereal, all hundred men would race to the latrines, which no matter how well-maintained, always felt unbearable, resembling the restrooms in run-down hotels. Then they would head out to the field in disorganized formation—the limping soldier to his left awkwardly disrupting Anthony's

311

halfhearted attempts to maintain proper marching rhythm, while the platoon sergeants either performed dramatically to make an impression on the officers and new recruits, or quietly stayed close to the marching line, dodging both work and unwanted attention.

When they arrived at the field, work started right away—they stripped off their shirts for exercise drills. This was the only part of the day that Anthony actually liked. Lieutenant Kretching, who led the routines, was lean and strong, and Anthony followed his movements carefully, feeling like he was doing something genuinely beneficial for himself. The other officers and sergeants wandered around among the men with the cruelty of schoolchildren, gathering here and there around some poor soldier who struggled with physical coordination, shouting confusing directions and orders at him. When they found an especially pitiful, undernourished recruit, they would spend the entire half-hour making harsh comments and laughing quietly among themselves.

One small officer named Hopkins, who had previously served as a sergeant in the regular army, was especially irritating. He viewed the war as a personal gift of vengeance from the gods above, and he constantly lectured that these new recruits failed to understand the complete seriousness and duty of "the service." He believed that through careful planning and fearless competence, he had elevated himself to his present position of importance. He copied the specific harsh behaviors of every officer he had worked under in the past. His scowl was permanently etched on his face— before granting a soldier permission to visit town, he would carefully consider how such an absence might affect the company, the army, and the well-being of the military profession worldwide.

Lieutenant Kretching, a blonde, slow-witted, and unemotional man, methodically taught Anthony the basics of military drill: standing at attention, turning right, turning around, and standing at ease. His main weakness was his poor memory. He frequently left the entire company standing rigidly at attention for five minutes at a time while he positioned himself in front of them to demonstrate a new drill movement—consequently, only the soldiers in the middle could understand what was happening, since those on the left and right sides had been so strongly trained to keep their eyes focused straight ahead.

The training went on until noon. It involved focusing on an endless series of incredibly minor details, and while Anthony understood that this approach made sense within the framework of military thinking, it still frustrated him deeply. The fact that the same poor health condition that would have been considered inappropriate for an officer didn't prevent someone from serving as a regular soldier struck him as completely ridiculous. Sometimes, after enduring lengthy lectures about the supposedly important but seemingly pointless concept of military "courtesy," he began to suspect that the real purpose of the war was simply to give career army officers—men who thought and acted like overgrown schoolchildren—a chance to indulge in actual killing. He was being absurdly sacrificed to satisfy Hopkins's twenty years of waiting!

Of his three tent-mates—a flat-faced conscientious objector from Tennessee, a big, frightened Pole, and the scornful Celt who had sat next to him on the train—the first two spent their evenings writing endless letters home, while the Irishman sat in the tent entrance whistling the same half-dozen sharp and repetitive bird calls over and over. It was more to escape an hour of their company than from any expectation of entertainment that, when the quarantine ended at the week's close, he headed into town. He caught one of the many small buses that flooded the camp every evening, and within thirty minutes found himself dropped off in front of the Stonewall Hotel on the sweltering and sleepy main street.

Under the gathering twilight, the town was unexpectedly appealing. The sidewalks were filled with brightly dressed, heavily

313

made-up young women who chatted animatedly in soft, drawling voices, alongside dozens of taxi drivers who approached passing officers with calls of "Take you anywhere, Lieutenant," and a steady stream of poorly dressed, shuffling, deferential Black men. Anthony, wandering through the warm evening air, experienced for the first time in years the slow, sensual atmosphere of the South, present in the humid warmth of the air and the all-encompassing quieting of thought and time.

He had walked about a block when he was suddenly stopped by a sharp command right beside him.

"Haven't you been taught to salute officers?"

He stared blankly at the man speaking to him, a heavy-set, dark-haired captain who glared at him threateningly with bulging brown eyes.

"Come to attention!" The words thundered through the air. Several passersby nearby stopped in their tracks and stared. A gentle-eyed girl wearing a lilac dress giggled softly to her friend.

Anthony snapped to attention.

"What's your regiment and company?"

Anthony told him.

"From now on, whenever you see an officer walking down the street, you need to stand up straight and salute!"

"All right!"

"Say 'Yes, sir!'"

"Yes, sir."

The heavy-set officer grunted, spun around abruptly, and walked briskly down the street. After a brief pause, Anthony continued forward; the town had lost its lazy, mysterious charm; the enchantment had vanished from the twilight in an instant. His attention turned sharply inward to focus on the humiliation of his circumstances. He despised that officer, all officers—existence had become unbearable.

After walking half a block, he noticed that the girl in the lilac dress who had laughed at his embarrassment was strolling with her friend roughly ten steps in front of him. She had turned around multiple times to look at Anthony, her large eyes sparkling with amused laughter and appearing to match the same shade as her dress.

At the corner, she and her companion clearly slowed their pace—he had to decide whether to join them or walk past without acknowledging them. He walked by, paused, then reduced his speed. Within moments the two were beside him once more, now laughing together—not the harsh, loud laughter he would have anticipated from northern actresses performing this well-known routine, but a gentle, quiet sound that flowed like water, as if he had accidentally stumbled into some private joke.

"How are you?" he said.

Her eyes were gentle like shadows. Were they violet, or was it their deep blue mixing with the gray tones of twilight?

"Pleasant evening," Anthony said hesitantly.

"It really is," said the second girl.

"It hasn't been a very pleasant evening for you," the girl in lilac sighed. Her voice seemed as much a part of the night as the sleepy breeze that stirred the wide brim of her hat.

"He had to have a chance to show off," Anthony said with a scornful laugh.

"I think so," she agreed.

They rounded the corner and strolled leisurely up a side street, as though following a floating cable that held them connected. In this town it felt completely normal to turn corners in such a way, it felt normal to be heading nowhere specific, to be thinking about nothing at all.... The side street was dim, an unexpected branch leading into a neighborhood of wild rose hedges and small peaceful houses positioned well back from the road.

"Where are you going?" he asked politely.

"Just going." The response served as an apology, a question, and an explanation all at once.

"Can I walk along with you?"

"I think so."

It was helpful that she had a different accent. He wouldn't have been able to figure out what social class a Southern woman belonged to just from how she spoke—in New York, a girl from a lower social class would have been loud and unbearable—unless he was seeing her through the rose-colored glasses of being drunk.

Darkness was slowly falling. Speaking very little—Anthony asking careless, casual questions while the other two responded with the economical phrases and weight typical of people from smaller towns—they strolled past one corner, then another. Halfway down a block, they came to a stop under a streetlight.

"I live nearby," the other girl explained.

"I live around the block," said the girl in lilac.

"Can I walk you home?"

"To the corner, if you want to."

The other girl stepped back a few paces. Anthony took off his hat.

"You're supposed to salute," said the girl in lilac with a laugh. "All the soldiers salute."

"I'll learn," he replied seriously.

The other girl said, "Well—" paused, then added, "give me a call tomorrow, Dot," and stepped back from the yellow glow of the streetlight. Then, quietly, Anthony and the girl in lilac walked the three blocks to the small run-down house where she lived. At the wooden gate she paused.

"Well—thanks."

"Do you have to go in so soon?"

"I ought to."

"Can't you walk around a bit more?" She looked at him without emotion.

"I don't even know you."

Anthony laughed.

"It's not too late."

"I think I should go inside."

"I thought we might walk down and see a movie."

"I'd like to."

"Then I could take you home. I'd have just enough time. I need to be back at camp by eleven."

It was so dark that he could barely see her now. She was a dress that swayed almost imperceptibly in the wind, two clear, fearless eyes...

"Why don't you come, Dot? Don't you like movies? You should come."

She shook her head.

"I shouldn't."

He was drawn to her, understanding that she was deliberately stalling to see how it would affect him. He moved closer and grasped her hand.

"If we get back by ten, can't you? just to the movies?"

"Well—I suppose so—"

Hand in hand, they walked back toward downtown along a hazy, dusky street where a Black newsboy was calling out an extra edition in the rhythmic cadence of the local vendors' tradition, a cadence that was as musical as a song.

Dot

Anthony's relationship with Dorothy Raycroft was bound to happen because he had become increasingly reckless with his own life. He wasn't drawn to her because he wanted something he found attractive, and he didn't surrender to someone with a stronger, more captivating personality than his own, the way he had with Gloria four years earlier. Instead, he simply drifted into the situation because he couldn't make clear decisions. He was unable to say "No!" to anyone, whether man or woman; people asking for money and women trying to seduce him both discovered he was soft-hearted and easily influenced. In fact, he rarely made any decisions at all, and when he did, they were only frantic, emotional promises made in moments of shocked and devastating realization.

The specific weakness he gave in to this time was his craving for excitement and stimulation from outside sources. He sensed that for the first time in four years he could express and understand himself in a new way. The girl offered him peace; the hours spent with her each evening eased the unhealthy and inevitably pointless hammering of his mind. He had truly become a coward—entirely enslaved by countless chaotic and restless thoughts that had been set free when his genuine devotion to Gloria collapsed, which had been the main guard keeping his inadequacy locked away.

On that first night, as they stood by the gate, he kissed Dorothy and arranged to meet her the following Saturday. Then he returned to camp, and with the light burning against regulations in his tent, he wrote a lengthy letter to Gloria, a passionate letter, filled with sentimental darkness, filled with the remembered fragrance of flowers, filled with genuine and overwhelming tenderness—these feelings he had rediscovered for a moment in a kiss shared under the rich, warm moonlight just an hour earlier.

When Saturday night arrived, he found Dot waiting at the entrance of the Bijou Moving Picture Theatre. She wore the same lilac gown made of the most delicate organdy that she had worn the previous Wednesday, but it had clearly been washed and starched since then, as it looked fresh and unwrinkled. The daylight reinforced the impression he had formed that she was beautiful in an incomplete, imperfect way. She was neat and clean, her features were small and uneven, but they were expressive and suited each other well. She was a dark, fragile little flower—yet he believed he sensed in her some quality of spiritual reserve, of inner strength that came from her quiet acceptance of everything life brought her. In this belief, he was wrong.

Dorothy Raycroft was nineteen years old. Her father had run a small, struggling corner store, and she had graduated from high school in the bottom quarter of her class just two days before his death. During high school, she had developed a rather questionable reputation. In reality, her conduct at the class picnic, where the gossip began, had simply been unwise—she had maintained her virginity until more than a year afterward. The young man had worked as a clerk at a store on Jackson Street, and the day following their encounter, he left suddenly for New York. He had been planning to leave for quite some time, but had stayed to complete his romantic pursuit.

After some time, she shared the story with a female friend, and later, as she watched her friend walk away down the quiet street filled with dusty sunlight, she suddenly realized that her tale would spread to others. However, once she had told it, she felt considerably better, though somewhat resentful, and came as close to showing real character as she could manage by heading in a different direction and encountering another man with the genuine desire to please herself once more. Generally speaking, things simply occurred to Dot. She wasn't weak, since she had nothing within her that would indicate she was being weak. She wasn't strong either, since she never recognized that some of her actions required courage. She neither rebelled against expectations nor followed them blindly nor sought middle ground.

She lacked any sense of humor, but instead possessed a cheerful nature that prompted her to laugh at appropriate moments when she was around men. She had no clear goals— occasionally she felt a vague regret that her reputation had destroyed whatever opportunity she might have once had for stability. There had been no public scandal: her mother was concerned only with getting her out the door on time each morning for the jewelry store where she made fourteen dollars a week. But some of the boys she had known in high school now turned away when they were walking with "nice girls," and these moments wounded her feelings. When they happened she went home and wept.

Besides the Jackson Street clerk, there had been two other men. The first was a naval officer who passed through town during the early days of the war. He had stayed overnight to catch a connecting train and was casually leaning against one of the pillars of the Stonewall Hotel when she walked by. He ended up remaining in town for four days. She believed she was in love with him—she poured out all that initial passionate intensity that would have otherwise gone to the cowardly clerk. The naval officer's uniform—which was a rare sight in those days—had created the enchantment. He departed with empty promises on his lips, and once he was on the train, he felt relieved that he hadn't revealed his true name to her.

Her resulting depression had driven her into the arms of Cyrus Fielding, the son of a local clothing store owner, who had called out to her from his convertible one day as she walked along the sidewalk. She had always known him by name. If she had been born into a higher social class, he would have known her earlier. She had fallen a bit lower in status—so he finally met her after all. After a month, he had left for military training camp, somewhat fearful of their closeness, somewhat relieved to realize that she hadn't cared deeply for him, and that she wasn't the type who would ever cause problems. Dot romanticized this relationship and indulged her pride by telling herself that the war had taken these men away from her. She convinced herself that she could have married the navy officer. Still, it troubled her that within eight months there had been three men in her life. She thought with more anxiety than amazement in her heart that she would soon become like those "loose women" on Jackson Street at whom she and her gum-chewing, giggling friends had stared with captivated looks three years earlier.

For a time, she tried to be more cautious. She allowed men to approach her; she let them kiss her and even permitted certain other freedoms to be taken with her, but she didn't expand her group of three. After several months, her willpower—or more accurately, the urgent necessity driven by her fears—began to weaken. She became restless, drifting there outside of life and time as the summer months slipped away. The soldiers she encountered were either clearly beneath her social standing or, less obviously, above it—in which case they only wanted to exploit her; they were Yankees, rough and rude; they moved in large groups.... And then she encountered Anthony.

On that first evening, he had been nothing more than a pleasantly melancholy face, a voice, and a way to spend an hour, but when she met him as planned on Saturday, she looked at him with genuine interest. She found herself drawn to him. Without realizing it, she recognized her own sorrows reflected in his expression.

Again they went to the movies, and once more they strolled along the dim, fragrant streets, this time holding hands and speaking quietly in soft voices. They walked through the gate and headed up toward the small porch.

"I can stay for a while, can't I?"

"Shh!" she whispered, "we need to be extremely quiet. Mother is sitting up reading Snappy Stories." To confirm this, he could hear the soft rustling sound from inside as she turned a page. The open shutters created narrow slits that sent out horizontal beams of light, casting thin parallel lines across Dorothy's skirt. The street remained quiet except for a small group sitting on the steps of a house across the street, who occasionally lifted their voices in a gentle, playful song.

"—When you wake up
You shall have
All the pretty little houses—

Then, as if it had been waiting on a nearby rooftop for them to arrive, the moon suddenly slanted through the vines and transformed the girl's face to the color of white roses.

Anthony suddenly remembered something so clearly that behind his closed eyelids he could see it like a movie scene playing back—a spring night when the snow was melting, pulled from a winter he'd almost forgotten five years ago—another face, glowing and beautiful like a flower, turned up toward lights that seemed as magical as the stars—

Ah, the beautiful woman without mercy who lived in his heart, revealed to him in fleeting, fading magnificence through dark eyes at the Ritz-Carlton, through a mysterious look from a passing carriage in the Bois de Boulogne! But those nights were merely fragments of a song, a cherished memory of glory—here once more were the gentle breezes, the illusions, the everlasting present moment with its promise of romance.

"Oh," she whispered, "do you love me? Do you love me?"

The magic was shattered—the scattered pieces of starlight became nothing more than ordinary light, and the singing from down the street faded to a dull drone, then to the quiet chirping of insects in the grass. With something close to a sigh, he kissed her passionate lips as her arms slowly wrapped around his shoulders.

The Soldier

As the weeks passed by and disappeared, Anthony's journeys around the area expanded until he came to understand the camp and its surroundings. For the first time in his life, he found himself in continuous personal contact with the waiters he had once tipped, the drivers who had respectfully touched their caps to him, the carpenters, plumbers, barbers, and farmers who had previously stood out only because of how submissively they bowed in their professional roles. During his first two months at camp, he didn't have a single conversation lasting more than ten minutes with any one person.

On his service record, his occupation was listed as "student"; on the original questionnaire, he had hastily written down "author"; but when fellow soldiers in his unit asked about his job, he usually told them he was a bank clerk—if he had been honest and said he didn't work at all, they would have viewed him with suspicion as someone from the privileged class.

His platoon sergeant, Pop Donnelly, was a scrawny "old soldier," worn down by alcohol. He had previously spent countless weeks locked up in the guardhouse, but lately, due to a shortage of drill instructors, he had been promoted to his current position. His face was covered with pockmarks—it looked remarkably similar to those aerial photographs of "the battlefield at Blank." Once a week he would get drunk in town on cheap liquor, return quietly to camp and collapse on his bunk, appearing at reveille looking more than ever like a pale mask of death.

He held onto the incredible belief that he was cleverly "putting one over" on the government—he had worked eighteen years in government service for tiny pay, and he would soon retire (at this point he typically winked) on the substantial income of fifty-five dollars monthly. He viewed it as a magnificent prank that he had pulled on all those who had intimidated and looked down on him ever since he was a nineteen-year-old farm boy from Georgia.

Currently there were only two lieutenants—Hopkins and the well-liked Kretching. The latter was regarded as a decent man and an excellent leader, until a year later, when he vanished with a mess fund of eleven hundred dollars and, like so many leaders, turned out to be extremely difficult to follow.

Eventually there was Captain Dunning, the commanding figure of this small but complete world. He served as a reserve officer, displaying nervous energy and passionate enthusiasm. This enthusiasm, in fact, often manifested physically and could be seen as white foam gathering at the corners of his mouth. Like many leaders, he viewed his soldiers only from an official perspective, and through his optimistic vision, his unit appeared to be exactly the kind of outstanding force that such a noble war merited. Despite all his worry and intense focus, he was experiencing the most exciting period of his entire life.

Baptiste, the small Sicilian from the train, got into trouble with him during the second week of training. The captain had repeatedly ordered the men to be clean-shaven when they lined up each morning. One day an alarming violation of this rule was discovered, certainly a case of German scheming—overnight four men had grown hair on their faces. The fact that three of the four barely understood English made a practical demonstration all the more essential, so Captain Dunning firmly sent a volunteer barber back to the company area for a razor. Therefore, for the protection of democracy, half an ounce of hair was scraped dry from the cheeks of three Italians and one Pole.

Outside the company's world, a colonel would occasionally appear—a heavy-set man with menacing teeth who rode around the battalion drill field on a beautiful black horse. He was a West Point graduate and, by imitation, considered himself a gentleman. He had a plain wife and an unimaginative mind, spending much of his time in town exploiting the army's recently elevated social status. Finally, there was the general, who traveled the camp roads with his flag leading the way—a figure so stern, so distant, so impressive that he was almost impossible to understand.

December. Cool winds blew at night now, and damp, chilly mornings settled over the drill-grounds. As the heat disappeared, Anthony discovered himself increasingly grateful to be alive.

Strangely refreshed throughout his body, he worried little and lived in the present with a kind of animal satisfaction. It wasn't that Gloria or the life that Gloria represented occupied his thoughts less often—it was simply that she became, day by day, less real, less vivid. For a week they had written to each other passionately, almost frantically—then by an unspoken agreement they had stopped writing more than twice, and then once, a week. She was bored, she said; if his brigade was going to be stationed there for a long time she was coming down to join him. Mr. Haight was going to be able to present a stronger brief than he had anticipated, but doubted that the appealed case would come up until late spring. Muriel was in the city doing Red Cross work, and they went out together quite often. What would Anthony think if she joined the Red Cross? The problem was she had heard that she might have to bathe negroes in alcohol, and after that she hadn't felt so patriotic. The city was filled with soldiers and she'd seen many boys she hadn't laid eyes on for years....

Anthony didn't want her to come South. He convinced himself this was for several reasons—he needed some time away from her, and she needed the same from him. She would be incredibly bored in town, and she'd only be able to see Anthony for a few hours each day. But deep down, he was afraid it was because he felt drawn to Dorothy. The truth was, he lived in constant fear that Gloria might somehow discover the relationship he had developed. After two weeks, this complicated situation started causing him moments of anguish over his own unfaithfulness. Still, as each day came to an end, he couldn't resist the pull that would inevitably draw him out of his tent and over to the telephone at the Y.M.C.A.

"Dot."

"Yes?"

"I might be able to get in tonight."

"I'm so glad."

"Would you like to listen to my magnificent eloquence for a few magical hours?"

"Oh, you funny—" For a moment he remembered something from five years ago—Geraldine. Then—

"I'll arrive around eight."

At seven he would board a small bus heading to the city, where hundreds of young Southern women waited on moonlit porches for their boyfriends. He was already getting excited thinking about her warm, hesitant kisses and the amazed calmness in the way she looked at him—looks that came closer to worship than anything he had ever inspired before. He and Gloria had been equals, giving to each other without expecting gratitude or feeling obligated. To this girl, even his touches were an incredible gift. Crying softly, she had admitted to him that he wasn't the first man in her life; there had been one other—he understood that the relationship had ended almost as soon as it began.

Indeed, as far as she was concerned, she was telling the truth. She had forgotten about the clerk, the naval officer, and the clothier's son, forgotten the intensity of her emotions, which represents genuine forgetting. She understood that in some unclear and dim existence someone had taken her—it felt as though it had happened in a dream.

Almost every night Anthony would come into town. The weather had grown too cold for sitting on the porch, so her mother gave up the small living room to them, complete with its countless inexpensive framed prints, endless yards of ornamental trim, and the heavy air that came from being so close to the kitchen for several decades. They would start a fire—and then, joyfully and tirelessly, she would engage in the rituals of romance. Every evening at ten o'clock she would accompany him to the door, her dark hair disheveled, her face without makeup looking pale, appearing even paler beneath the white glow of the moon. Usually it would be bright and silvery outside; occasionally there would be a gentle, warm drizzle, so lazy it seemed barely able to make its way to the earth.

"Tell me you love me," she would whisper.

"Why, of course, you sweet baby."

"Am I a baby?" This almost wistfully.

"Just a little baby."

She had a vague awareness of Gloria's existence. The thought caused her pain, so she pictured Gloria as arrogant, proud, and emotionally distant. She had convinced herself that Gloria must be older than Anthony, and that no love existed between the married couple. Occasionally she allowed herself to fantasize that Anthony would divorce his wife after the war ended and then marry her—but she never spoke of this possibility to Anthony, though she couldn't quite explain why. She believed the same thing his company believed: that he was essentially a glorified office worker—she viewed him as respectable but financially struggling. She would often say:

"If I had some money, darling, I'd give every bit of it to you.... I'd like to have about fifty thousand dollars."

"I suppose that would be enough," Anthony agreed.

"In her letter that day, Gloria had written: 'I suppose if we could settle for a million, it would be better to tell Mr. Haight to go ahead and settle. But it would seem like a pity....'"

"We could have an automobile," Dot exclaimed in a final burst of triumph.

An Impressive Occasion

Captain Dunning took great pride in his ability to judge people's character. Within thirty minutes of meeting someone, he would typically categorize them into one of several remarkable classifications—fine man, good man, smart fellow, theorizer, poet, and "worthless." One day in early February, he had Anthony called to meet with him in the orderly tent.

"Patch," he said in a preachy tone, "I've been watching you for several weeks."

Anthony stood upright and completely still.

"And I think you've got the makings of a good soldier."

He waited for the warm feeling that this would naturally stir up to fade away—and then he went on:

"This is no child's play," he said, narrowing his brows.

Anthony agreed with a melancholy "No, sir."

"It's a man's game—and we need leaders." Then came the climax, quick, confident, and electrifying: "Patch, I'm going to promote you to corporal."

At this moment, Anthony should have stumbled back a bit, completely overwhelmed. He had been chosen as one of the quarter million selected for that ultimate responsibility. He was going to have the authority to call out the military command, "Follow me!" to seven other terrified men.

"You appear to be an educated man," said Captain Dunning.

"Yes, Sir."

"That's good, that's good. Education's a great thing, but don't let it go to your head. Keep on the way you're doing and you'll be a good soldier."

With those final words still echoing in his ears, Corporal Patch saluted, performed a sharp right turn, and exited the tent.

Though the conversation entertained Anthony, it sparked the thought that life might be more enjoyable as a sergeant or, if he could find a more lenient medical examiner, as an officer. He had little interest in the work, which appeared to contradict the army's celebrated bravery. During inspections, one didn't dress up to look good, one dressed up to avoid looking bad.

But as winter faded away—the brief, snowless winter characterized by humid nights and cool, rainy days—he was amazed at how rapidly the system had taken hold of him. He was a soldier—everyone who wasn't a soldier was a civilian. The world was split mainly into these two categories.

It struck him that all sharply defined groups, like the military, separated people into two categories: their own type—and everyone else. For the clergyman there were clergy and laypeople, for the Catholic there were Catholics and non-Catholics, for the black person there were blacks and whites, for the prisoner there were the imprisoned and the free, and for the sick person there were the sick and the healthy.... So, without ever considering it once in his entire life, he had been a civilian, a layperson, a non-Catholic, a Gentile, white, free, and healthy....

As American troops flooded into the French and British trenches, he started discovering the names of numerous Harvard graduates among the casualties listed in the Army and Navy Journal. Despite all the sweat and bloodshed, the situation seemed unchanged, and he could see no sign of the war ending anytime soon. In the ancient chronicles, one army's right wing would always defeat the other's left wing, while the left wing was simultaneously conquered by the enemy's right. Following this, the mercenaries would retreat. Everything had been so straightforward back then, almost as though it were planned in advance....

Gloria wrote that she was reading extensively. What a disaster they had made of their situation, she said. She had so little to occupy her time now that she spent her days imagining how things could have gone differently. Her entire world seemed unstable—and just a few years earlier she had appeared to have complete control over her own small domain.

In June her letters became rushed and arrived less often. She abruptly stopped writing about coming South.

Defeat

March in the countryside was beautiful with jasmine and daffodils and clusters of violets growing in the grass that was beginning to warm. Later he particularly remembered one afternoon that had such a fresh and magical charm that while he stood in the rifle pit marking targets, he recited "Atalanta in Calydon" to a confused Polish soldier, his voice blending with the tearing, whistling, and splattering sounds of bullets flying overhead.

"When the hounds of spring ..."

Spang!

"Are on winter's traces ..."

Whirr-r-r-r! ...

"The mother of months ..."

"Hey! Wake up! Mark three-e-e! ..."

In town the streets had returned to their sleepy, dreamlike state, and Anthony and Dot wandered together along the same paths they had taken the previous autumn until he started to develop a drowsy fondness for this South—a South that seemed more reminiscent of Algiers than Italy, with worn-down dreams that reached back through countless generations toward some warm, ancient paradise, free from hope or worry. Here every voice carried a tone of warmth and understanding. "Life plays the same beautiful and painful trick on all of us," they appeared to say through their melancholy yet pleasant rhythm, in the rising tone that ended on an unfinished, sorrowful note.

He enjoyed his barber shop where the pale, thin young man greeted him with "Hi, corporal!" and shaved him while running a cool vibrating machine continuously over his eager head. He loved "Johnston's Gardens" where they danced, where a melancholy Black musician created longing, haunting music on a saxophone until the bright hall transformed into a magical jungle of wild rhythms and hazy laughter, where losing himself in Dorothy's gentle sighs and soft whispers represented the fulfillment of every dream and desire.

There was an underlying sadness in her personality, a deliberate avoidance of everything except life's pleasant details.

Her violet eyes would stay seemingly unaware for hours as she lay thoughtlessly and carelessly in the sun like a cat. He wondered what the exhausted, lifeless mother thought about them, and whether during her most cynical moments she ever suspected their relationship.

On Sunday afternoons they strolled through the countryside, stopping occasionally to rest on the dry moss at the edge of a forest. Birds had congregated in this spot along with clusters of violets and white dogwood; the frost-covered trees gleamed like crystal in the cool air, untouched by the overwhelming heat that lingered beyond this sanctuary; it was here that he would speak from time to time in a drowsy, rambling way, carrying on conversations that meant nothing and required no responses.

July arrived with scorching heat. Captain Dunning received orders to assign one of his soldiers to learn blacksmithing. The regiment was expanding to full war capacity, and he required most of his experienced men to serve as drill instructors, so he chose the small Italian soldier, Baptiste, whom he could most readily spare. Little Baptiste had never worked with horses before. His terror only made the situation worse. He returned to the orderly room one afternoon and informed Captain Dunning that he wished to die if he couldn't be transferred from this duty. The horses were kicking at him, he explained; he was incompetent at the job. Eventually he dropped to his knees and pleaded with Captain Dunning, speaking in a combination of fractured English and biblical Italian, to remove him from this assignment. He hadn't slept in three nights; enormous stallions rose up and pranced wildly through his nightmares.

Captain Dunning scolded the company clerk, who had erupted in laughter, and assured Baptiste that he would try his best to help. However, after considering the situation, he concluded that he couldn't afford to assign a more capable person to the task. Little Baptiste's performance continued to deteriorate. The horses appeared to sense his terror and exploited it at every opportunity. Two weeks afterward, a massive black mare trampled his head with her hooves as he attempted to guide her out of her stall.

In mid-July, rumors began circulating, followed by official orders about relocating the camp. The brigade would move to an unoccupied military base a hundred miles further south, where it would be expanded into a division. Initially, the soldiers believed they were heading to the front lines, and throughout the evening small clusters gathered in the company street, calling out to one another with boastful declarations: "Su-u-ure we are!" When the actual truth emerged, they angrily dismissed it as a cover story designed to hide their true destination. They basked in their sense of self-importance. That evening they told their girlfriends in town that they were "going to fight the Germans." Anthony wandered among the groups for a while—then, flagging down a jitney, he rode into town to inform Dot that he was leaving.

She was waiting on the dark porch in an inexpensive white dress that highlighted the youthfulness and gentle features of her face.

"Oh," she whispered, "I've wanted you so much, honey. All day long."

"I have something to tell you."

She pulled him down next to her on the swinging seat, not picking up on his threatening tone.

"Tell me."

"We're leaving next week."

Her arms reached toward his shoulders but stayed suspended in the dark air, her chin lifted upward. When she spoke, the gentleness had disappeared from her voice.

"Leaving for France?"

"No. Less luck than that. Leaving for some damn camp in Mississippi."

She closed her eyes and he could see that her eyelids were shaking.

"Dear little Dot, life is so damn hard."

She was crying on his shoulder.

"So incredibly difficult, so incredibly difficult," he said again without purpose; "it simply causes pain to people and causes pain to people, until eventually it causes them so much pain that they can never be hurt again. That's the final and most terrible thing it accomplishes."

Frantic and wild with anguish, she pressed him tightly against her chest.

"Oh, God!" she whispered with a broken voice, "you can't leave me. I would die."

He couldn't manage to treat his leaving as just another ordinary, impersonal setback. He was too close to her to do anything more than keep saying "Poor little Dot. Poor little Dot."

"And then what?" she asked tiredly.

"What do you mean?"

"You're everything to me, that's all there is to it. I'd die for you right now if you asked me to. I'd grab a knife and end my life. You can't abandon me here."

Her tone frightened him.

"These things happen," he said calmly.

"Then I'm coming with you." Tears streamed down her cheeks. Her mouth quivered with overwhelming grief and terror.

"Sweet," he whispered with emotion, "sweet little girl. Can't you see we'd just be delaying what's inevitable? I'll be leaving for France in a few months—"

She pulled back from him and, clenching her fists, raised her face toward the sky.

"I want to die," she said, as if shaping each word carefully in her heart.

"Dot," he whispered with discomfort, "you're going to forget.

Things become more precious when they're gone. I understand this—because there was once something I desperately wanted and I actually got it. It was the only thing I ever truly desired with all my heart, Dot. And when I finally obtained it, it crumbled to nothing in my hands."

"All right."

Completely focused on his own thoughts, he went on:

"I've often thought that if I hadn't gotten what I wanted, things might have turned out differently for me. I might have discovered something within myself and taken pleasure in sharing it with the world. I might have been satisfied with that kind of work and felt some sweet pride from achieving success. I suppose there was a time when I could have had anything I desired, within reasonable limits, but that was the only thing I ever truly wanted with real passion. God! And that experience taught me that you can't have anything—you can't have anything at all. Because desire simply deceives you. It's like a ray of sunlight dancing here and there around a room. It pauses and illuminates some meaningless object, and we foolish people try to catch it—but when we reach for it, the sunbeam moves on to something else, and you're left holding the worthless part while the sparkle that made you want it has disappeared—" He stopped speaking abruptly, feeling uncomfortable. She had gotten up and was standing there, her eyes dry, plucking small leaves from a dark vine.

"Dot—"

"Go away," she said coldly. "What? Why?"

"I don't want just words. If that's all you have for me you'd better go."

"Why, Dot—"

"What death means to me is just a bunch of words to you. You arrange them so beautifully."

"I'm sorry. I was talking about you, Dot."

"Go away from here."

He walked toward her with his arms open wide, but she kept him at a distance.

"You don't want me to come with you," she said calmly; "perhaps you're planning to meet that—that woman—" She couldn't make herself say wife. "How would I know? Well, then, I suppose you're not my man anymore. So go away."

For a moment, as conflicting warnings and desires pulled at Anthony, it felt like one of those uncommon instances when he might act on an impulse from deep within himself. He paused. Then exhaustion washed over him like a crashing wave. It was too late—everything had become too late. For years he had let the world slip away in dreams, making choices based on emotions as unstable as flowing water. The young girl in the white dress held power over him as she moved closer to beauty through the rigid patterns of her longing. The fire burning in her wounded and darkened heart appeared to radiate around her like a glowing flame. Through some deep and mysterious pride, she had distanced herself and accomplished what she set out to do.

"I didn't mean to come across as so heartless, Dot."

"It doesn't matter."

The flames swept over Anthony. Something twisted violently in his gut, and he remained there powerless and defeated.

"Come with me, Dot—little loving Dot. Oh, come with me. I couldn't leave you now—"

With a sob, she wrapped her arms around him and allowed him to bear her weight as the moon, engaged in its endless task of concealing the world's flawed appearance, poured its forbidden sweetness over the sleepy street.

The Catastrophe

Early September at Camp Boone, Mississippi. The darkness, teeming with insects, pressed against the mosquito netting under which Anthony was attempting to write a letter. Sporadic conversation from a poker game drifted over from the neighboring tent, while outside a man wandered down the company street singing a popular piece of nonsense verse about "K-K-K-Katy."

With considerable effort, Anthony pushed himself up onto his elbow and, gripping his pencil, stared down at the empty sheet of paper before him. Then, skipping any sort of title or heading, he started writing:

I can't figure out what's wrong, Gloria. I haven't received a single letter from you in two weeks and it's completely natural for me to be worried—

He tossed it aside with an irritated grunt and started over:

I'm not sure what to think, Gloria. Your last letter arrived two weeks ago—brief, distant, without any expression of love or even a proper update about what you've been up to. It's only natural that I would start to wonder. If your feelings for me haven't completely died, it seems like you would at least try to keep me from worrying—

Once more, he crushed the paper into a ball and hurled it furiously through a rip in the canvas wall, instantly recognizing that he'd need to retrieve it come morning. He had no desire to make another attempt. He couldn't inject any warmth into his words—just an unrelenting jealousy and distrust. Ever since midsummer, these inconsistencies in Gloria's letters had become increasingly obvious. Initially, he had barely noticed them. He had grown so accustomed to the routine "dearest" and "darlings" sprinkled throughout her correspondence that he paid no attention to whether they appeared or not. But over these past two weeks, he had grown more and more conscious that something was wrong.

He had sent her a telegram that night telling her he had passed his examinations for officer training camp and expected to leave for Georgia soon. She hadn't responded. He had sent another wire—when he still heard nothing back, he thought she might be away from home. But the idea kept coming back to him that she wasn't out of town, and a flood of anxious thoughts started to torment him. What if Gloria, feeling bored and restless, had found someone else, just as he had. The possibility of this terrified him— it was mainly because he had been so confident in her faithfulness that he had thought about her so little during the past year. And now, as uncertainty crept in, the old fury and jealous rage came rushing back a thousand times stronger. What could be more natural than for her to fall in love again?

He recalled the Gloria who had promised that if she ever desired anything, she would simply take it, maintaining that since she would be acting purely for her own pleasure, she could emerge from such an encounter completely untainted—after all, she argued, only the impact on one's mind truly mattered, and her response would be the masculine reaction of satisfaction followed by mild distaste.

But that had been when they were first married. Later, when she discovered she could feel jealous about Anthony, she had changed her mind, at least on the surface. For her, no other men existed in the world. He had known this all too well. Realizing that a certain sense of refinement would hold her back, he had become careless about maintaining the fullness of her love—which, after all, was the foundation of their entire relationship.

Meanwhile all through the summer he had been supporting Dot in a boarding house downtown. To do this it had been necessary to contact his broker for money. Dot had concealed her trip south by leaving her house a day before the brigade broke camp, telling her mother in a note that she had gone to New York. On the evening that followed Anthony had visited as if to see her. Mrs. Raycroft was in a state of breakdown and there was a police officer in the living room. An interrogation had followed, from which Anthony had freed himself with considerable difficulty.

In September, as his doubts about Gloria grew stronger, spending time with Dot had become boring and then nearly unbearable. He felt on edge and easily annoyed from not getting enough sleep; his heart was heavy with worry and fear. Three days earlier, he had approached Captain Dunning to request leave, but was met with kind delays and excuses. The division was preparing to ship overseas, while Anthony was headed to an officers' training camp; any leave that could be granted had to go to the soldiers who were departing for foreign duty.

After Anthony refused, he headed toward the telegraph office planning to send Gloria a wire asking her to come South—but he reached the door and backed away in despair, realizing how completely impractical such a plan would be. He then spent the evening having an irritating argument with Dot before returning to camp feeling gloomy and furious with the world. There had been an unpleasant confrontation, during which he had abruptly left. What he should do about her didn't seem to matter much to him right now—he was entirely consumed by his wife's disheartening silence....

The tent flap suddenly folded back on itself, forming a triangle, and a dark head emerged against the darkness of the night.

"Sergeant Patch?" The accent was Italian, and Anthony could tell from the belt that the man was a headquarters orderly.

"Want me?"

"A lady called headquarters ten minutes ago. She said she needed to speak with you. Very important."

Anthony pushed away the mosquito netting and got to his feet. It could be a telegram from Gloria that had been called in.

"She said to get you. She'll call again at ten o'clock."

"All right, thanks." He grabbed his hat and within moments was walking alongside the orderly through the sweltering, nearly stifling darkness. At the headquarters building, he saluted a drowsy night-duty officer.

"Sit down and wait," the lieutenant suggested casually. "The girl seemed really eager to talk with you."

Anthony's hopes crumbled.

"Thank you very much, sir." And as the phone rang on the wall beside him, he knew who was calling.

"This is Dot," came a shaky voice, "I need to see you."

"Dot, I told you I couldn't come down for several days."

"I need to see you tonight. It's important."

"It's too late," he said coldly; "it's ten o'clock, and I have to be in camp at eleven."

"All right." Those two simple words carried so much misery that Anthony couldn't help but feel a pang of guilt.

"What's the matter?"

"I want to say goodbye to you."

"Oh, don't be such a fool!" he burst out. But his mood lifted immediately. How fortunate it would be if she left the city tonight! What a weight that would lift from his conscience. However, he said: "There's no way you can leave before tomorrow."

Out of the corner of his eye, he noticed the night-service officer looking at him with a puzzled expression. Then, surprisingly, Dot spoke her next words:

"I don't mean 'leave' that way."

Anthony gripped the phone tightly in his hand. He could feel his nerves going cold, as though all the warmth was draining from his body.

"What?"

Then suddenly he heard a wild, broken voice cry out:

"Goodbye—oh, goodbye!"

Click! She had hung up the phone. With a sound that was part gasp, part cry, Anthony rushed from the headquarters building. Outside, beneath the stars that hung like silver ornaments through the trees of the small grove, he stood still, uncertain. Had she intended to kill herself?—oh, what a fool! He was consumed with bitter hatred toward her. In this final outcome he found it impossible to believe that he had ever started such a complicated relationship, such a disaster, a disgusting mixture of anxiety and suffering.

He found himself walking slowly away, telling himself again and again that worrying was pointless. It would be better to return to his tent and get some rest. He desperately needed sleep. Dear God! Would he ever be able to sleep again? His thoughts were a chaotic storm of noise and disorder; when he reached the road he spun around in terror and started running, not back toward his unit but in the opposite direction. Soldiers were coming back now—he could catch a taxi. After a moment two yellow headlights came into view around the curve. In desperation he ran toward them.

"Jitney! Jitney!" ... It was an empty Ford.... "I want to go to town."

"Cost you a dollar."

"All right. If you'll just hurry—"

After what felt like an endless amount of time, he rushed up the steps of a dark, run-down little house and burst through the door, nearly colliding with a large Black woman who was walking down the hallway carrying a candle.

"Where's my wife?" he cried wildly.

"She has gone to bed."

Up the stairs three steps at a time, down the groaning hallway. The room was dark and quiet, and with shaking hands he lit a match. Two wide eyes stared up at him from a miserable bundle of clothing on the bed.

"Ah, I knew you'd come," she whispered with a broken voice.

Anthony's anger turned ice-cold.

"So it was just a scheme to get me down here and get me in trouble!" he said. "Damn it, you've cried 'wolf' one too many times!"

She looked at him with pity.

"I had to see you. I couldn't have lived. Oh, I had to see you—"

He sat down on the edge of the bed and slowly shook his head.

"You're worthless," he said with finality, speaking without thinking in the same way Gloria might have spoken to him. "This kind of behavior isn't fair to me, you know."

"Come closer." No matter what he might say, Dot felt happy now. He cared about her. She had managed to bring him to her side.

"Oh, God," Anthony said without hope. As exhaustion swept over him in its unstoppable tide, his rage diminished, pulled back, and disappeared completely. He suddenly crumpled, collapsing beside her on the bed in tears.

"Oh, my darling," she pleaded with him, "don't cry! Oh, don't cry!"

She cradled his head against her chest and comforted him, mixing her joyful tears with his bitter ones. Her fingers moved softly through his dark hair.

"I'm such a little fool," she whispered with a broken voice, "but I love you, and when you treat me coldly it feels like life isn't worth living anymore."

After all, this was peace—the quiet room filled with the mixed scent of women's powder and perfume, Dot's hand gentle as a warm breeze on his hair, the rhythm of her chest rising and falling with each breath—for a moment it felt as if Gloria were there, as if he had found rest in a home sweeter and safer than any he had ever experienced.

An hour went by. A clock started chiming in the hallway. He sprang to his feet and glanced at the glowing hands of his wristwatch. It was midnight.

He struggled to find a taxi willing to make the trip at that late hour. As he pressed the driver to go faster down the road, he considered the best way to get back into camp. He had been late multiple times lately, and he realized that if he got caught again, his name would likely be removed from the officer candidate list. He thought about whether he should pay off the taxi and try sneaking past the guard in the darkness. Then again, officers frequently drove past the sentries after midnight....

"Stop!" The single word emerged from the yellow beam that the headlights cast onto the shifting road. The taxi driver disengaged his clutch and a guard approached, holding his rifle at the ready. Unfortunately, the officer of the guard accompanied him.

"Out late, sergeant."

"Yes, sir. I was held up."

"Too bad. I have to take your name."

As the officer stood waiting with his notebook and pencil ready, something unplanned rushed to Anthony's lips— something driven by panic, confusion, and despair.

"Sergeant R.A. Foley," he replied, breathing heavily.

"And the outfit?"

"Company Q, Eighty-third Infantry."

"All right. You'll have to walk from here, sergeant."

Anthony saluted, quickly paid his taxi driver, and started running toward the regiment he had mentioned. Once he was out of sight, he changed direction, and with his heart pounding frantically, rushed to his company, sensing that he had made a terrible mistake in judgment.

Two days later, the officer who had commanded the guard spotted him in a downtown barbershop. Under the escort of a military policeman, he was brought back to the camp, where he was stripped of his rank without a trial and restricted to his company street for a month.

With this setback, a wave of complete despair washed over him, and within a week he was caught downtown again, stumbling around in an intoxicated stupor with a pint of illegal whiskey tucked in his back pocket. Due to his somewhat erratic behavior during the trial, his sentence to the guardhouse was reduced to just three weeks.

Bad Dream

Early in his imprisonment, he became convinced that he was losing his sanity. It felt as if his mind contained a collection of dark yet intense personalities, some familiar to him, others strange and frightening, all restrained by a small guardian who sat high above, watching over everything. What troubled him most was that this guardian was ill and struggling to maintain control. If this protector should surrender, if he should weaken even for an instant, these unbearable forces would break free—only Anthony understood what complete darkness would engulf him if the worst aspects of himself were allowed to roam through his consciousness without restraint.

The heat of the day had transformed somehow, becoming a polished darkness that pressed down mercilessly on a ruined landscape. Above him, the blue circles of threatening unknown suns, countless centers of flame, spun endlessly before his vision as if he lay perpetually exposed to the scorching light in a state of delirious unconsciousness. At seven each morning, something ghostly, something almost ridiculously unreal that he recognized as his dying body, went out with seven other inmates and two guards to labor on the camp roads. One day they hauled and unloaded tons of gravel, scattered it, smoothed it—the following day they worked with enormous barrels of blazing tar, covering the gravel with black, gleaming pools of liquid fire. At night, confined in the guardhouse, he would lie without thinking, without the strength to attempt thought, gazing at the uneven ceiling beams above until around three o'clock, when he would fall into a restless, disturbed sleep.

During work hours, he labored with restless urgency, trying, as the day moved toward the sweltering Mississippi sunset, to exhaust himself physically so that he could sleep deeply from complete fatigue in the evening. Then one afternoon during his second week, he sensed that two eyes were watching him from a spot just a few feet beyond one of the guards. This filled him with a kind of terror. He turned his back to the eyes and shoveled frantically, until he had to turn around and fetch more gravel. Then the eyes came into his view again, and his already strained nerves stretched to the breaking point. The eyes were staring at him menacingly. Out of the oppressive silence, he heard his name called in a desperate voice, and the ground swayed wildly back and forth amid a chaos of yelling and confusion.

When he regained consciousness, he found himself back in the guardhouse, with the other prisoners casting curious looks his way. The eyes never returned. It took him many days to understand that the voice must have belonged to Dot, that she had shouted to him and caused some kind of commotion. He came to this realization just before his sentence was about to end, when the dark cloud weighing on him had finally lifted, leaving him in a profound, dejected exhaustion. As the conscious mediator, the watchful presence that controlled that terrifying household of horrors, grew stronger, Anthony's physical strength diminished. He could barely manage to complete the two days of hard labor, and when he was finally released on a rainy afternoon and returned to his company, he made it to his tent only to collapse into a deep sleep, from which he woke before sunrise, sore and unrested. Next to his cot lay two letters that had been waiting for him in the orderly tent for quite some time. The first letter was from Gloria; it was brief and distant:

The case is going to trial in late November. Is there any chance you can get time off?

I've attempted to write to you repeatedly, but it only appears to make the situation worse. I want to meet with you regarding several issues, but you're aware that you once stopped me from visiting, and I'm reluctant to attempt it again. Given a number of circumstances, it appears essential that we have a meeting. I'm very pleased about your appointment.

Gloria.

He was too exhausted to try to make sense of it—or even to care. Her words, her motives, all seemed incredibly distant in an incomprehensible past. He barely looked at the second letter; it was from Dot—a rambling, tear-stained mess, overflowing with protest, affection, and sorrow. After reading one page, he let it fall from his lifeless hand and drifted back into his own vague, distant world. When drill call sounded, he woke up with a high fever and collapsed when he attempted to get out of his tent—by noon he was taken to the base hospital with influenza.

He knew this illness was meant to be. It protected him from falling back into hysteria, and he got better just in time to board the train on a wet November day heading for New York, and toward the endless slaughter that lay ahead.

When the regiment arrived at Camp Mills, Long Island, Anthony had only one thought: to get into the city and see Gloria as quickly as he could. It was clear now that an armistice would be signed within the week, but rumors suggested that troops would keep being sent to France right up until the final moment anyway. Anthony was horrified by the idea of the lengthy ocean crossing, the boring process of unloading at some French port, and potentially being stuck overseas for a year to take the place of soldiers who had actually seen combat.

His plan had been to get a two-day leave, but Camp Mills turned out to be under a strict influenza quarantine—it was impossible for even an officer to leave except on official business.

For a private it was completely out of the question.

The camp was a dismal mess—cold, battered by wind, and filthy, covered with the grime left behind by the many divisions that had passed through. Their train arrived at seven that evening, and they stood in line until one in the morning while some military confusion got sorted out up ahead. Officers rushed back and forth constantly, shouting orders and creating a tremendous commotion. It became clear that the problem stemmed from the colonel, who was furious because he was a West Point graduate, and the war was going to end before he could get sent overseas. If the warring governments had understood how many heartbroken older West Point officers there were during that week, they surely would have extended the carnage for another month. The situation was truly pitiful!

Looking out at the dreary stretch of tents that spread for miles across a trampled mess of slush and snow, Anthony realized how impossible it would be to walk to a telephone that night. He would call her as soon as he got the chance in the morning.

Awakened in the cold and harsh early morning, he stood at roll call and listened to an intense speech from Captain Dunning:

"You men might think the war is finished. Well, let me tell you something—it's not! Those guys aren't going to sign any armistice. This is just another trick, and we'd be foolish to let our guard down here in the company, because I'm telling you, we're shipping out from here within a week, and when we do, we're going to see some real combat." He stopped speaking so they could fully absorb what he had just announced. Then he continued: "If you believe the war's over, just go talk to anyone who's been fighting in it and ask them if they think the Germans are finished. They don't. Nobody does. I've spoken with people who know what they're talking about, and they say there's going to be at least another year of war ahead. They don't believe it's over. So you men better not get any foolish notions that it is."

Emphasizing this final warning twice, he commanded the troops to be dismissed.

At noon Anthony took off running toward the closest canteen telephone. As he got closer to what served as the downtown area of the camp, he saw that many other soldiers were running too, and that a man nearby had suddenly jumped into the air and clicked his heels together. The urge to run spread everywhere, and from small excited groups scattered around came the sounds of cheering. He stopped and listened—across the cold countryside whistles were blowing and the bells of the Garden City churches suddenly burst into echoing sound.

Anthony started running again. The shouts were now clear and sharp as they drifted upward with puffs of frozen breath into the cold air:

"Germany has surrendered! Germany has surrendered!"

The False Armistice

That evening in the thick darkness of six o'clock, Anthony squeezed between two freight cars, and after crossing the railroad tracks, he walked along the rails to Garden City, where he boarded an electric train bound for New York. He faced a real risk of getting caught—he was aware that military police frequently moved through the train cars checking for passes, but he figured that tonight their watchfulness might be less intense. However, regardless of the danger, he would have attempted to get through anyway, since he hadn't been able to reach Gloria by phone, and enduring another day of uncertainty would have been unbearable.

After unexplained stops and delays that brought back memories of the night he had departed New York more than a year earlier, they pulled into Pennsylvania Station, and he took the well-known route to the taxi stand, discovering it both absurd and strangely exciting to provide his own home address.

Broadway blazed with light, packed with crowds unlike anything he had ever witnessed—a carnival atmosphere that swept its sparkling path through scraps of paper piled ankle-deep along the sidewalks. Scattered throughout the scene, soldiers stood elevated on benches and boxes, addressing the oblivious masses, each face sharply defined and vivid under the harsh white glare from above. Anthony spotted several distinct figures—a drunk sailor, leaning backward and held upright by two fellow sailors, waved his hat while letting out a series of wild shouts; a wounded soldier, clutch in hand, was carried along in a swirling current on the shoulders of screaming civilians; a dark-haired girl sat cross-legged in quiet contemplation on top of a parked taxi. Here, without doubt, victory had arrived at the perfect moment, the climax timed with the greatest divine planning. The great wealthy nation had waged a triumphant war, endured enough suffering for emotional impact but not enough to breed resentment—thus the carnival, the celebration, the victory parade. Beneath these brilliant lights shone the faces of people whose glory had long since faded, whose very civilizations had crumbled—people whose ancestors had received news of victory in Babylon, in Nineveh, in Baghdad, in Tyre, a hundred generations earlier; people whose ancestors had witnessed flower-adorned, slave-decorated processions drift with their trail of captives down the streets of Imperial Rome....

Past the Rialto, the glittering facade of the Astor, the sparkling grandeur of Times Square... a stunning corridor of brilliant lights stretching ahead.... Then—was it years later?—he found himself paying the taxi driver in front of a white building on Fifty-seventh Street. He stood in the lobby—ah, there was the Black young man from Martinique, relaxed, unhurried, exactly the same.

"Is Mrs. Patch in?"

"I have just arrived, sir," the man announced with his incongruous British accent.

"Take me up—"

Then came the slow hum of the elevator, followed by three steps to the door, which swung open from the force of his knock.

"Gloria!" His voice was shaking. No response. A thin wisp of smoke drifted up from an ashtray—a copy of Vanity Fair lay open on the table.

"Gloria!"

He rushed into the bedroom and bathroom. She wasn't there. A robin's-egg blue nightgown spread across the bed gave off a subtle fragrance that was both elusive and recognizable. A pair of stockings and a street dress lay on a chair, while an open powder compact sat gaping on the dresser. She must have just left.

The phone rang suddenly and he jumped—he answered it feeling like a fraud.

"Hello. Is Mrs. Patch there?"

"No, I'm looking for her myself. Who is this?"

"This is Mr. Crawford."

"This is Mr. Patch speaking. I've just arrived unexpectedly, and I don't know where to find her."

"Oh." Mr. Crawford seemed somewhat surprised. "Well, I suppose she's at the Armistice Ball. I know she planned to attend, but I didn't expect she would leave this early."

"Where's the Armistice Ball?"

"At the Astor."

"Thanks."

Anthony slammed down the phone and stood up abruptly. Who was this Mr. Crawford? And who was the person taking her to the dance? How long had this situation been developing? These questions raced through his mind repeatedly, each time with different possible answers. Just being so close to her was driving him nearly insane with frustration.

Consumed by suspicion, he frantically darted around the apartment, searching for any evidence of another man's presence, throwing open the bathroom cabinet, desperately rummaging through the dresser drawers. Then he discovered something that caused him to halt abruptly and collapse onto one of the matching beds, his mouth turning downward as if he might cry. There in the corner of her drawer, bound with a delicate blue ribbon, lay every letter and telegram he had sent her over the past year. He was overwhelmed with joyful and tender embarrassment.

"I'm not worthy enough to touch her," he shouted to the empty room. "I'm not worthy enough to touch her delicate hand."

Nevertheless, he went out to look for her.

In the Astor lobby, he was immediately surrounded by such a thick crowd that moving forward became nearly impossible. He had to ask half a dozen people for directions to the ballroom before he could get a clear and coherent response from someone who was sober. Finally, after one last lengthy wait, he checked his military overcoat at the coat check.

It was only nine o'clock, but the dance was already in full swing. The scene was incredible. Women were everywhere—girls made cheerful by wine, singing in high-pitched voices above the noise of the dazzling crowd covered in confetti; girls highlighted by the uniforms of soldiers from a dozen different countries; heavy women falling ungracefully to the floor while maintaining their dignity by shouting "Hurray for the Allies!"; three women with white hair dancing hand in hand around a sailor, who spun in a dizzying circle on the floor, clutching an empty champagne bottle to his chest.

Anthony frantically searched through the dancers, his eyes sweeping over the chaotic lines of people weaving single file between the tables, taking in the horn-blowing, kissing, coughing, laughing, drinking crowds beneath the massive, full-bodied flags that hung in brilliant colors above the spectacle and noise.

Then he spotted Gloria. She was seated at a table for two directly across the room. Her dress was black, and above it her lively face, touched with the most enchanting rose color, created what he believed to be a moment of striking beauty in the room. His heart jumped as if responding to a new melody. He pushed his way through the crowd toward her and called out her name just as her gray eyes looked up and met his. For that moment as their bodies came together and merged, the world, the celebration, the cascading murmur of the music dissolved into a blissful single tone, quiet as the hum of bees.

"Oh, my Gloria!" he cried.

Her kiss was like a cool stream flowing from her heart.

Chapter II: A Matter of Aesthetics

On the night when Anthony had departed for camp hooker a year earlier, all that remained of the beautiful gloria gilbert—her exterior, her youthful and lovely body—walked up the wide marble steps of grand central station with the rhythm of the train engine pounding in her ears like a dream, and emerged onto Vanderbilt avenue, where the massive structure of the Biltmore loomed over the street and, down at its low, shining entrance, drew in the multicolored opera cloaks of magnificently dressed young women. For a moment she stopped by the taxi stand and observed them—wondering that just a few years earlier she had been among them, always heading out for a brilliant somewhere, perpetually on the verge of having that ultimate passionate adventure for which the girls' cloaks were delicate and beautifully lined with fur, for which their cheeks were painted and their hearts soared higher than the temporary dome of pleasure that would consume them, hairstyle, cloak, and everything.

The air was getting colder, and the men walking by had turned up the collars of their coats. This shift in weather felt like a small mercy to her. It would have been an even greater kindness if everything had transformed—the weather, the streets, the people—and if she could have been swept away to awaken in some elevated, sweet-smelling room, by herself, feeling both inwardly and outwardly like a statue, just as she had in her pure and vibrant youth.

Inside the taxi she cried helpless tears. The fact that she hadn't been happy with Anthony for more than a year didn't matter much. Lately his presence had meant nothing more than what it stirred in her from that unforgettable June. The recent Anthony, irritable, weak, and broke, could only make her irritable as well—and bored with everything except the memory that in their highly imaginative and passionate youth they had come together in a joyful celebration of emotion. Because of this shared vivid memory she would have done more for Anthony than for any other person— so when she climbed into the taxi she wept intensely, and wanted to shout his name out loud.

Miserable and lonely like a forgotten child, she sat in the silent apartment and wrote him a letter filled with jumbled emotions:

I can almost look down the railroad tracks and see you leaving, but without you, my dearest, I can't see or hear or feel or think. Being separated—no matter what has happened or will happen between us—is like pleading for compassion from a hurricane, Anthony; it's like aging. I want to kiss you so badly—on the back of your neck where your dark hair begins. Because I love you, and whatever we do or say to each other, or have done, or have said, you must understand how deeply I do, how lifeless I become when you're away. I can't even despise the awful presence of PEOPLE, those people in the train station who have no right to exist—I can't even resent them even though they're contaminating our world, because I'm consumed with wanting you so much.

If you despised me, if your body was covered with sores like someone with leprosy, if you left me for another woman or let me go hungry or struck me—how ridiculous this sounds—I would still desire you, I would still love you. I KNOW, my darling.

It's late—I have all the windows open and the air outside is just as gentle as spring, yet somehow much more youthful and delicate than spring. Why do people portray spring as a young woman, why does that fantasy dance and sing its way for three months through the world's absurd emptiness. Spring is a skinny old workhorse with its ribs visible—it's a heap of garbage in a field, dried by the sun and rain to a threatening purity.

In a few hours you'll wake up, my darling—and you'll feel miserable and disgusted with life. You'll find yourself in Delaware or Carolina or somewhere else, feeling so insignificant. I don't think there's anyone alive who can see themselves as something temporary, as a luxury or an unnecessary burden. Very few people who emphasize how pointless life is actually notice how pointless they themselves are. Maybe they believe that by declaring how terrible living is, they somehow rescue their own value from the wreckage—but they don't, not even you and I....

... I can still see you. There's a blue mist hanging around the trees where you'll be traveling, too lovely to take over the landscape. No, the empty patches of farmland will be what you see most often—they'll stretch alongside the railroad tracks like grimy, rough brown fabric hanging out to dry in the sunlight, vibrant, machine-like, disgusting. Nature, that careless old woman, has been lying down in those fields with every old farmer or Black person or immigrant who wanted to possess her....

So you can see that now that you're gone, I've written a letter completely filled with contempt and despair. And that simply means that I love you, Anthony, with everything there is to love with in your

Gloria.

After addressing the letter, she walked to her twin bed and lay down, clutching Anthony's pillow tightly against her as if the sheer intensity of her feelings could transform it into his warm, living

353

body. At two o'clock, she remained awake with dry eyes, gazing into the darkness with relentless, unwavering sorrow, remembering everything without mercy, condemning herself for countless imagined cruelties, and creating an image of Anthony that resembled a martyred and glorified Christ. For a while, she saw him the way he likely viewed himself during his more emotional moments.

At five in the morning, she was still wide awake. A strange grinding sound that occurred every morning from across the courtyard let her know what time it was. She heard an alarm clock go off and watched a light create a yellow rectangle on what appeared to be a blank wall across from her. With the half-formed decision to follow him South right away, her sadness became distant and dreamlike, drifting away from her just as the darkness moved toward the west. She finally fell asleep.

When she woke up, seeing the empty bed next to her brought back a wave of sadness, though this feeling was soon pushed away by the natural indifference that comes with a bright morning. While she didn't realize it at the time, there was actually some relief in eating breakfast without having to look at Anthony's exhausted and anxious face across from her. Now that she was by herself, she completely lost any urge to complain about the food. She decided she would change what she ate for breakfast—she would have lemonade and a tomato sandwich instead of the endless routine of bacon and eggs and toast.

Nevertheless, at noon when she had called several of her friends, including the fierce Muriel, and discovered that each one was busy for lunch, she surrendered to a gentle self-pity about her isolation and loneliness. Curled up on the bed with a pencil and paper, she wrote Anthony another letter.

Late that afternoon, a special delivery package arrived, sent from a small town in New Jersey, and the familiar way it was written, along with the almost audible tone of worry and dissatisfaction, felt so recognizable that it brought her comfort. Who could say? Maybe military discipline would toughen Anthony up and get him used to the concept of working. She held unwavering belief that the war would end before he would be required to fight, and in the meantime the lawsuit would be won, and they could start over, this time on different terms. The first change would be that she would have a baby. It was intolerable that she should be so completely alone.

It was a week before she could stay in the apartment without the likelihood of crying. The city seemed to offer little entertainment. Muriel had been moved to a hospital in New Jersey, and she only took breaks to visit the city every other week. With Muriel's absence, Gloria began to understand how few real friends she had actually made during all her years living in New York. The men she was acquainted with had joined the military. "Men she was acquainted with"?—she had vaguely admitted to herself that every man who had ever fallen in love with her counted as her friends. Each of them had once claimed, for a significant period, that her affection meant more to them than anything else in the world. But now—where had they all gone? At least two had died, six or more had gotten married, and the others were spread out everywhere from France to the Philippines. She found herself wondering if any of them still thought about her, and if so, how frequently, and in what way. Most of them probably still imagined the young girl of about seventeen, the teenage temptress from nine years earlier.

The girls had also scattered far and wide. She had never been well-liked at school. She had been too stunning, too indolent, not adequately aware of her role as a Farmover girl and a "Future Wife and Mother" written in eternal capital letters. And girls who had never experienced a kiss would suggest, with scandalized looks on their unremarkable but hardly virtuous faces, that Gloria had. Then these girls had traveled east or west or south, gotten married and become "people," predicting, if they made predictions about Gloria, that she would meet a terrible fate—not realizing that no conclusions were terrible, and that they, like her, were certainly not the controllers of their own destinies.

Gloria mentally reviewed all the people who had come to visit them at the gray house in Marietta. Back then, it had felt like they constantly had guests staying with them—she had quietly believed that each visitor left owing her something. In her mind, they each owed her a kind of moral debt, like ten dollars, and if she ever found herself in trouble, she could theoretically call in these imaginary favors. But now they had all disappeared, blown away like grain husks, mysteriously and completely vanished whether in spirit or in reality.

By Christmas, Gloria felt certain once again that she should be with Anthony, but this time it wasn't a sudden feeling—it had become a persistent longing. She made up her mind to write and tell him she was coming, but she delayed sending the message because Mr. Haight advised her to wait, since he anticipated the case would go to trial almost any week.

One day in early January, while walking along Fifth Avenue, which was now bright with military uniforms and decorated with flags from the allied nations, she encountered Rachael Barnes, someone she hadn't seen in almost a year. Even Rachael, whom she had come to dislike, provided a welcome break from her boredom, so they went together to the Ritz for tea.

After their second cocktail, they grew enthusiastic. They genuinely enjoyed each other's company. They discussed their husbands, with Rachael speaking in that characteristic tone of public pride mixed with private doubts that wives typically use.

"Rodman is overseas serving in the Quartermaster Corps. He holds the rank of captain. He was determined to enlist, and he didn't believe he could qualify for any other military branch."

"Anthony's in the Infantry." These words, combined with the cocktail, filled Gloria with a kind of warmth. With every sip, she felt herself drawing closer to a cozy and reassuring sense of patriotism.

"By the way," Rachael said half an hour later as they were leaving, "can't you come to dinner tomorrow night? I'm having two really wonderful officers over who are about to be deployed overseas. I think we should do everything we can to make their evening special."

Gloria accepted gladly. She wrote down the address, recognizing from the number that it was a fashionable apartment building on Park Avenue.

"It's been really wonderful to see you, Rachael."

"It's been wonderful. I've wanted to."

With these three sentences, a particular evening in Marietta from two summers earlier was forgiven—that night when Anthony and Rachael had paid each other more attention than necessary. Gloria forgave Rachael, and Rachael forgave Gloria. They also forgave the fact that Rachael had witnessed the most devastating catastrophe in the lives of Mr. and Mrs. Anthony Patch—

Time moves forward as we make compromises with the events that unfold.

The Wiles of Captain Collins

The two officers were captains specializing in the popular military skill of machine gunnery. During dinner, they described themselves with deliberate tedium as members of the "Suicide Club"—during that era, every obscure division of the military called itself the Suicide Club. One of the captains—Rachael's captain, Gloria noticed—was a tall, horse-faced man of thirty with an attractive mustache and unattractive teeth. The other, Captain Collins, was plump, rosy-cheeked, and prone to bursting into unrestrained laughter whenever he made eye contact with Gloria. He was instantly drawn to her, and during the entire meal he bombarded her with foolish flattery. After her second glass of champagne, Gloria realized that for the first time in months she was completely enjoying herself.

After dinner, someone suggested they all go out dancing somewhere. The two officers grabbed bottles of alcohol from Rachael's sideboard—military personnel weren't allowed to be served at bars—and with their supplies in hand, they danced countless fox trots at several sparkling nightclubs along Broadway, dutifully switching partners throughout the evening—while Gloria grew increasingly wild and entertaining to the rosy-cheeked captain, who rarely let his cheerful grin fade from his face.

At eleven o'clock, to her great surprise, she found herself in the minority for wanting to stay out. The others wanted to go back to Rachael's apartment—to get more liquor, they said. Gloria argued persistently that Captain Collins's flask was half full—she had just seen it—then catching Rachael's eye, she received an unmistakable wink. She deduced, somewhat confusedly, that her hostess wanted to get rid of the officers and agreed to being bundled into a taxi outside.

Captain Wolf sat on the left with Rachael on his lap. Captain Collins took the middle seat, and as he got comfortable, he slid his arm around Gloria's shoulder. His arm lay there motionless for a moment before clamping down like a steel trap. He leaned toward her.

"You're incredibly beautiful," he whispered.

"Thank you kindly, sir." She felt neither pleased nor annoyed. Before Anthony arrived, so many other men had done the same thing that it had become nothing more than a gesture, sentimental but meaningless.

In Rachael's spacious front room, a small fire and two lamps with orange silk shades provided the only illumination, filling the corners with deep, drowsy shadows. The hostess moved gracefully in a dark-patterned gown of flowing chiffon, enhancing the room's already sensual ambiance. Initially, all four of them gathered together, sampling the sandwiches arranged on the tea table—but soon Gloria found herself sitting alone with Captain Collins on the fireside sofa; Rachael and Captain Wolf had moved to the opposite side of the room, where they spoke in hushed tones.

"I wish you weren't married," Collins said, his face a ridiculous mockery of genuine seriousness.

"Why?" She extended her glass to be filled with a highball.

"Don't drink any more," he urged her, frowning.

"Why not?"

"You'd be nicer—if you didn't."

Gloria suddenly understood the hidden meaning behind his comment and the mood he was trying to establish. She felt like laughing—but then she recognized there wasn't really anything funny about it. She had been having a good time that evening and didn't want to leave—yet it wounded her pride to be flirted with in such a shallow way.

"Pour me another drink," she insisted.

"Please—"

"Oh, don't be ridiculous!" she cried in exasperation.

"Very well." He gave in reluctantly.

Then his arm wrapped around her once more, and once again she offered no resistance. However, when his flushed cheek moved closer to hers, she pulled back.

"You're really sweet," he said in a distracted way.

She started singing quietly, hoping he would move his arm away. All at once, she noticed an intimate moment happening across the room—Rachael and Captain Wolf were locked in a passionate kiss. Gloria trembled a little, though she couldn't understand why.... The pink face came closer again.

"You shouldn't look at them," he whispered. Almost immediately his other arm wrapped around her... his breath warmed her cheek. Once again absurdity won out over disgust, and her laughter became a weapon that required no sharpened words.

"Oh, I thought you were a good sport," he was saying.

"What's a sport?"

"Why, a person who likes to—to enjoy life."

"Is kissing you generally considered a joyful affair?"

They were interrupted when Rachael and Captain Wolf suddenly appeared in front of them.

"It's late, Gloria," Rachael said—her face was flushed and her hair was messy. "You should stay here for the night."

For a moment Gloria thought the officers were being dismissed. Then she realized what was happening, and once she understood, she stood up as casually as she could manage.

Rachael continued without understanding:

"You can have the room right next to this one. I can lend you everything you need."

Collins's eyes pleaded with her like a dog's; Captain Wolf's arm had wrapped comfortably around Rachael's waist; they were waiting.

But the appeal of casual relationships, vibrant, diverse, complex, and always carrying a hint of something unpleasant and worn-out, held no attraction or possibility for Gloria. If she had wanted that lifestyle, she would have stayed without any doubt or second thoughts; instead, she could calmly confront the six unfriendly and insulted gazes that watched her leave into the hallway with fake courtesy and empty phrases.

"He wasn't even decent enough to offer to take me home," she thought in the taxi, and then with a sudden wave of resentment: "How completely vulgar!"

Bravery

In February she had a completely different kind of experience. Tudor Baird, an old boyfriend, a young man she had once been completely set on marrying, came to New York through the Aviation Corps and visited her. They went to the theater several times, and within a week, much to her delight, he was as deeply in love with her as he had ever been. She made this happen quite intentionally, realizing too late that she had caused harm. He got to the point where he would sit with her in wretched silence whenever they went out together.

A member of Yale's Scroll and Key society, he had the proper restraint of a "good egg," the right ideas about chivalry and noble duty—and, naturally but regrettably, the right prejudices and the right absence of original thinking—all those characteristics that Anthony had taught her to look down on, but which she nonetheless found herself respecting. Unlike most men of his background, she discovered he wasn't tedious. He was attractive, clever in an effortless way, and when she spent time with him she sensed that due to some trait he had—whether you called it simple-mindedness, devotion, emotional softness, or something less precise than any of those three—he would have done everything within his ability to make her happy.

He shared this with her along with other thoughts, speaking with proper composure and a weighty masculine dignity that concealed genuine pain. Though she felt no love for him, she began to feel pity and kissed him tenderly one evening because he was so appealing, a remnant of a disappearing era that embraced a self-righteous yet elegant fantasy and was being succeeded by less noble idiots. Later she felt grateful she had kissed him, because the following day when his aircraft plummeted fifteen hundred feet at Mineola a fragment of a gasoline engine tore through his heart.

Gloria Alone

When Mr. Haight informed her that the trial wouldn't happen until fall, she made up her mind to enter the film industry without telling Anthony. Once he witnessed her success, both as an actress and financially, once he realized she could get whatever she wanted from Joseph Bloeckman while giving nothing back, he would abandon his foolish prejudices. She stayed awake until the early hours one night mapping out her career and savoring her anticipated triumphs, and the following morning she telephoned "Films Par Excellence." Mr. Bloeckman was in Europe.

But this time the idea had taken such a strong hold on her that she made up her mind to visit the movie studio employment agencies. As had happened so many times before, her keen sense of smell sabotaged her good intentions. The employment agency reeked as if something had been decomposing there for ages. She spent five minutes looking over her unappealing competition— then she walked quickly out to the most remote areas of Central Park and stayed there so long that she ended up catching a cold. She was attempting to get the stench of the employment agency out of her clothes.

In the spring she started to sense from Anthony's letters—not from any single one but from their combined impact—that he didn't want her to come South. Strangely repetitive excuses that seemed to trouble him precisely because they were so inadequate appeared with psychological predictability. He included them in every letter as if he worried he had left them out the previous time, as if it were urgently important to convince her of their validity. And the sprinkling of his letters with loving pet names became routine and forced—almost as if, after finishing the letter, he had reviewed it and deliberately inserted them, like witticisms in an Oscar Wilde play. She leaped to the obvious conclusion, dismissed it, felt angry and sad alternately—eventually she closed her mind to it with dignity, and let a growing distance slip into her side of their correspondence.

Recently, she had discovered plenty to keep her busy. A number of pilots she had met through Tudor Baird visited her in New York, and two other former admirers appeared, stationed at Camp Dix. When these men received orders to go overseas, they essentially passed her along to their friends. However, after another quite unpleasant encounter with a would-be Captain Collins, she made it clear that whenever someone was introduced to her, they should have no confusion about her situation and personal goals.

When summer arrived, she learned to do what Anthony did—watch the officers' casualty lists. She found a kind of sad satisfaction in reading about the death of someone she had once danced a German with, and in recognizing the names of younger brothers of men who had once courted her. As the military advance toward Paris continued, she thought that the world was finally heading toward its inevitable and well-deserved destruction.

She was twenty-seven. Her birthday passed by almost unnoticed. Years earlier, turning twenty had scared her, and reaching twenty-six had bothered her somewhat—but now she gazed into the mirror with quiet satisfaction, seeing her distinctly British fresh complexion and her figure still boyish and slender as it had always been.

She tried not to think of Anthony. It was as if she were writing to a complete stranger. She told her friends that he had been promoted to corporal and felt frustrated when they responded with polite indifference. One evening she cried because she felt sorry for him—if he had shown even the slightest warmth, she would have rushed to him on the first available train without a second thought—whatever he was going through, he needed someone to care for his emotional well-being, and she believed she could now provide even that kind of support. Lately, without his constant emotional demands draining her inner strength, she discovered herself remarkably refreshed. Before his departure, she had found herself dwelling on missed chances simply because of their close connection—now she had returned to her usual mindset, confident, proud, living each day for what it offered. She purchased a doll and made clothes for it; one week she cried while reading "Ethan Frome"; the following week she immersed herself in several of Galsworthy's novels, appreciating his ability to recreate, through hope emerging from despair, that fantasy of passionate young love that women eternally anticipate and eternally remember.

In October Anthony's letters became more frequent, growing almost desperate—then abruptly stopped. For an anxious month she had to use all her self-control to keep from leaving right away for Mississippi. Then a telegram informed her that he had been hospitalized and that she could expect him in New York within ten days. Like a character from a dream he returned to her life across the ballroom that November evening—and throughout the long hours filled with familiar joy she held him close to her heart, cherishing an illusion of happiness and safety she had never expected to experience again.

Discomfiture of The Generals

After a week, Anthony's regiment returned to the Mississippi camp to be discharged. The officers locked themselves in their compartments on the Pullman cars and drank the whiskey they had purchased in New York, while in the coaches the soldiers also got as drunk as they could manage—and whenever the train stopped at a village, they pretended they were just coming back from France, where they had essentially defeated the German army. Since they all wore overseas caps and claimed they hadn't had time to get their gold service stripes sewn on, the rural folks along the coast were quite impressed and asked them what the trenches were like—to which they responded "Oh, boy!" with lots of tongue clicking and head shaking. Someone took a piece of chalk and wrote on the side of the train, "We won the war—now we're going home," and the officers laughed and left it there. They were all trying to get whatever pride they could from this shameful return.

As they traveled toward camp, Anthony felt anxious that he might find Dot waiting for him patiently at the station. To his relief, he neither saw nor heard anything of her, and thinking that if she were still in town she would certainly try to communicate with him, he concluded that she had left—where, he neither knew nor cared. He wanted only to return to Gloria—Gloria reborn and wonderfully alive. When he was finally discharged, he left his company on the back of a large truck with a group who had given tolerant, almost sentimental cheers for their officers, especially for Captain Dunning. The captain, for his part, had addressed them with tears in his eyes about the pleasure, and so forth, and the work, and so forth, and time not wasted, and so forth, and duty, and so forth. It was very dull and human; having listened to it, Anthony, whose mind was refreshed by his week in New York, renewed his deep hatred for the military profession and everything it represented. In their childish hearts, two out of every three professional officers believed that wars were made for armies and not armies for wars. He was pleased to see general and field officers riding sadly about the barren camp, stripped of their commands. He was pleased to hear the men in his company laugh mockingly at the incentives offered to them to remain in the army. They were to attend "schools." He knew what these "schools" were.

Two days later, he was with Gloria in New York.

Another Winter

Late one February afternoon, Anthony entered the apartment and felt his way through the small hallway, completely dark in the winter twilight, where he discovered Gloria sitting by the window. She turned around when he walked in.

"What did Mr. Haight have to say?" she asked without interest.

"Nothing," he replied, "just the usual. Maybe next month."

She studied him carefully; her ear, finely tuned to his voice, detected the faintest slur in the two-syllable word.

"You've been drinking," she said without emotion.

"A couple of glasses."

"Oh."

He yawned in the armchair and there was a moment's silence between them. Then she suddenly demanded:

"Did you go to Mr. Haight? Tell me the truth."

"No." He smiled weakly. "Actually, I didn't have time."

"I thought you didn't go.... He sent for you."

"I don't care anymore. I'm tired of sitting around in his office waiting. You'd think he was the one doing me a favor." He looked over at Gloria, hoping she might agree with him, but she had already gone back to staring out at the gloomy and uninviting view outside.

"I feel pretty tired of life today," he said hesitantly. She remained quiet. "I ran into a guy and we had a conversation at the Biltmore bar."

The evening darkness had suddenly grown deeper, but neither of them moved to switch on the lights. Absorbed in whatever thoughts occupied their minds, they remained seated until a sudden swirl of snow prompted a weary sigh from Gloria.

"What have you been doing?" he asked, finding the silence oppressive.

"Reading a magazine—filled with ridiculous articles by wealthy writers about how awful it is for poor people to purchase silk shirts. And as I read it, I couldn't think of anything except how much I wanted a gray squirrel coat—and how we can't afford one."

"Yes, we can."

"Oh, no."

"Oh, yes! If you want a fur coat you can have one."

Her voice cutting through the darkness carried a hint of contempt.

"You mean we can sell another bond?"

"If I have to. I don't want to do without things. We've spent quite a bit, though, since I got back."

"Oh, shut up!" she said in irritation.

"Why?"

"Because I'm fed up with listening to you go on about how much we've spent or what we've been doing. You returned two months ago and we've been partying practically every single night since then. We've both wanted to go out, and that's exactly what we've done. Well, you haven't heard me grumbling about it, have you? But all you ever do is complain, complain, complain. I don't give a damn anymore about what we do or what happens to us, and at least I'm being honest about it. But I absolutely will not put up with your griping and doom-and-gloom predictions——"

"You're not very pleasant yourself sometimes, you know."

"I don't have to be. You're not even trying to change anything."

"But I am—"

"Huh! Seems to me I've heard that before. This morning you weren't going to touch another drink until you'd found a job. And you didn't even have the courage to go see Mr. Haight when he asked you to come about the lawsuit."

Anthony stood up and turned on the lights.

"Look here!" he shouted, squinting, "I'm getting tired of your cutting remarks."

"Well, what are you going to do about it?"

"Do you think I'm especially happy?" he went on, disregarding her question. "Do you think I don't realize we're not living the way we should?"

In an instant Gloria stood trembling beside him.

"I won't stand for this!" she exploded. "I refuse to be preached at. You and your pain! You're nothing but a pathetic weakling and you always have been!"

They stood facing each other foolishly, neither able to make an impression on the other, both feeling tremendously and painfully bored. Then she walked into the bedroom and closed the door behind her.

His return had brought all their pre-war frustrations back to the surface. Prices had risen dramatically while their income had shrunk to just over half of what it used to be. There had been the substantial retainer fee for Mr. Haight; there were stocks purchased at one hundred dollars that were now worth only thirty or forty, along with other investments that weren't generating any returns. The previous spring, Gloria had been given a choice: either leave the apartment or sign a year-long lease at two hundred and twenty-five dollars per month. She had signed the lease. As their need to economize grew more urgent, they discovered they were completely incapable of saving money as a couple. They fell back on their old habit of making excuses and putting things off. Exhausted by their own incompetence, they would talk about what they were going to do—oh—tomorrow, about how they would "stop going to parties" and how Anthony would find a job. But when evening arrived, Gloria, who was used to having plans every night, would feel that familiar restlessness washing over her. She would stand in the bedroom doorway, nervously biting her fingers and occasionally catching Anthony's eye when he looked up from his book. Then the phone would ring, and her tension would ease as she answered it with barely hidden excitement. Someone was coming over "for just a few minutes"—and then came the exhausting charade, the appearance of the wine table, the temporary revival of their worn-out spirits—and the harsh awakening, like reaching the middle of a sleepless night through which they drifted.

As winter passed and the returning troops marched along Fifth Avenue, they grew increasingly aware that their relationship had completely transformed since Anthony came back. Following that brief revival of tenderness and passion, each had retreated into their own private dreams that the other couldn't share, and whatever affectionate gestures they exchanged seemed to flow from one empty heart to another, creating hollow echoes of what they finally understood had disappeared forever.

Anthony had once again visited all the major city newspapers and had once again been turned away without any hope by a mix of office assistants, receptionists, and city editors. The message was always the same: "We're holding any open positions for our own staff members who are still serving in France." Then, toward the end of March, he spotted an advertisement in the morning newspaper and as a result finally discovered what appeared to be a job opportunity.

You Can Sell!!!

Why not earn money while you're learning?

Our sales representatives make $50-$200 each week.

There was an address on Madison Avenue listed below, along with instructions to show up at one o'clock that afternoon. Gloria, looking over his shoulder after one of their typical late breakfasts, noticed him staring at it casually.

"Why don't you try it?" she suggested.

"Oh—it's one of these crazy schemes."

"It might not be. At least it would be experience."

At her urging, he arrived at one o'clock at the designated address, where he discovered himself among a crowded mix of men gathered in front of the entrance. The group included everyone from a messenger boy who was clearly wasting his employer's time to an ancient man with a twisted body leaning on a gnarled walking stick. Some of the men looked worn down, with hollow cheeks and swollen pink eyes—others appeared young, perhaps still attending high school. After a chaotic fifteen minutes where they all observed each other with indifferent distrust, a well-dressed young man appeared, wearing a fitted suit and carrying himself like an assistant minister, who guided them upstairs into a spacious room that looked like a classroom filled with countless desks. The potential salesmen took their seats here—and waited once more. After some time, a platform at the far end of the hall filled with half a dozen serious yet energetic men who, except for one, arranged themselves in a semicircle facing the gathered audience.

The exception was the man who appeared most sober, most energetic, and youngest among them all, and who stepped forward to the front of the platform. The audience examined him with hope. He was fairly small and quite attractive, with the kind of good looks you'd find in business rather than on the stage. He had straight blond thick eyebrows and eyes that were almost ridiculously sincere, and as he reached the edge of his speaking platform he seemed to cast these eyes out toward the audience, at the same time extending his arm with two fingers stretched out. Then as he swayed himself into a balanced position, an anticipatory quiet fell over the hall. With complete confidence the young man had taken control of his audience and his words when they finally came were firm and assured and belonged to the style of speaking that was direct and honest.

"Men!" he started, then stopped. The word faded away with a drawn-out echo at the far end of the hall, and the faces looking at him—some hopeful, others cynical, many tired—all became suddenly focused and absorbed. Six hundred eyes tilted slightly upward toward him. With a smooth but awkward delivery that made Anthony think of bowling balls rolling down a lane, he plunged into his lengthy explanation.

"This bright and sunny morning you picked up your favorite newspaper and discovered an advertisement that made a simple, straightforward statement: you could sell. That was all it said—it didn't specify 'what,' it didn't explain 'how,' it didn't mention 'why.' It simply made one single declaration that you and you and you"— pointing at individuals—"could sell. Now my job isn't to make you successful, because every person is born successful and only makes themselves a failure; it's not to teach you how to speak, because each person is a natural speaker and only makes themselves tongue-tied; my purpose is to tell you one thing in a way that will help you understand it—it's to tell you that you and you and you have an inheritance of wealth and prosperity waiting for you to come and claim it."

At this point, an Irishman with a gloomy expression stood up from his desk near the back of the hall and left.

"That man believes he'll go search for it in the bar around the corner. (Laughter.) He won't discover it there. There was a time when I searched for it there myself (laughter), but that was before I accomplished what each one of you men regardless of how young or how old, how poor or how wealthy (a faint ripple of satirical laughter), can achieve. It was before I discovered—myself!

"Now I wonder if any of you men know what a 'Heart Talk' is. A 'Heart Talk' is a small book that I began writing about five years ago, where I recorded what I had discovered to be the main reasons for a man's failure and the main reasons for a man's success—from John D. Rockefeller back to John D. Napoleon (laughter), and even further back, to the days when Esau sold his birthright for a bowl of stew. There are now one hundred of these

'Heart Talks.' Those of you who are genuine, who are interested in our offer, and especially those who are unhappy with how things are currently going for you, will receive one to take home with you as you leave through that door this afternoon."

"Right now in my pocket, I'm carrying four letters I just received about 'Heart Talks.' These letters bear signatures from names that are recognized in every household across the United States. Listen to this one from Detroit:"

Dear Mr. Carleton:

"I want to order three thousand more copies of 'Heart Talks' to distribute among my sales team. These books have been more effective at motivating my employees than any bonus program we've ever tried. I read them myself regularly, and I want to sincerely congratulate you on addressing the core of the most significant challenge facing our generation today—the challenge of salesmanship. The foundation upon which our country is built rests on the challenge of salesmanship. With warm congratulations I am

Yours very cordially,

"Henry W. Terral.

He announced the name with three long, booming declarations of triumph, pausing between each one to let the magical effect sink in. Then he read two additional letters, one from a vacuum cleaner manufacturer and another from the president of the Great Northern Doily Company.

"And now," he continued, "I'm going to explain in a few words the proposition that will benefit those of you who approach it with the right attitude. Simply put, it's this: 'Heart Talks' has been established as a corporation. We're going to distribute these small pamphlets to every major business organization, every salesperson, and every person who knows—I don't say 'believes,' I say 'knows'—that he can sell! We are making some of the stock of the 'Heart Talks' company available on the market, and to ensure the distribution reaches as many people as possible, and also to provide a living, concrete, real-world example of what salesmanship is, or rather what it can be, we're going to give those of you who are genuine professionals an opportunity to sell that stock. Now, I don't care what you've attempted to sell before or how you've tried to sell it. It doesn't matter whether you're old or young. I only want to know two things—first, do you desire success, and second, are you willing to work for it?

"My name is Sammy Carleton. Don't call me 'Mr.' Carleton— just Sammy will do. I'm a straightforward, down-to-earth guy without any pretentious airs. I want you to call me Sammy.

"Now this is all I'm going to tell you today. Tomorrow I want those of you who have considered it and have read the copy of 'Heart Talks' that will be handed to you at the door to return to this same room at this same time, and then we'll explore the proposal further and I'll explain what I've discovered the principles of success to be. I'm going to make you believe that you and you and you can sell!"

Mr. Carleton's voice echoed through the hall for a moment before fading away. As many feet stamped around him, Anthony found himself pushed and shoved along with the crowd as they moved out of the room.

Further Adventures With "Heart Talks"

With ironic laughter as his soundtrack, Anthony recounted to Gloria the tale of his business venture. However, she listened without finding any of it amusing.

"You're going to give up again?" she asked coldly.

"Why—you don't expect me to—"

"I never expected anything of you."

He hesitated.

"Well—I can't see any benefit in laughing myself sick over this kind of situation. If there's anything more outdated than the old story, it's the new twist."

It took an incredible amount of moral strength for Gloria to pressure him into coming back, and when he showed up the next day, feeling somewhat discouraged after reading through the tired old platitudes cheerfully presented in "Heart Talks on Ambition," he discovered that only fifty people remained from the original three hundred who were waiting for the dynamic and persuasive Sammy Carleton to appear. This time, Mr. Carleton used his powers of energy and persuasion to explain that brilliant business strategy—the art of selling. Apparently, the proper technique was to present your proposal and then avoid saying "So, will you buy?"—that wasn't the right approach—absolutely not!—instead, the correct method was to present your proposal and then, after wearing down your opponent until they were completely exhausted, to hit them with the ultimate demand: "Now listen here! You've used up my time while I explained this whole thing to you. You've agreed with all my points—all I'm asking is how many do you want?"

As Mr. Carleton stacked claim after claim, Anthony started to develop a kind of revolted trust in him. The man seemed to understand what he was discussing. Clearly successful, he had climbed to a role where he taught others. It never crossed Anthony's mind that the kind of person who achieves business success rarely understands how or why, and, as with his grandfather's situation, when he provides explanations, those explanations are usually wrong and ridiculous.

Anthony observed that among the many older men who had responded to the initial advertisement, only two had come back, and that out of the thirty or so who gathered on the third day to receive actual sales training from Mr. Carleton, only one person with gray hair could be seen. These thirty individuals were enthusiastic converts; they moved their lips along with Mr. Carleton's words; they rocked back and forth in their chairs with excitement, and during breaks in his presentation they whispered to each other with intense approval. However, among the select group who, as Mr. Carleton put it, "were determined to get those rewards that rightfully and truly belonged to them," fewer than half a dozen possessed even a basic level of personal presentation skills along with that valuable quality of being a "go-getter." Nevertheless, they were assured that they were all natural go-getters—they simply needed to believe with an almost fierce intensity in the product they were selling. He even encouraged each person to purchase some stock themselves, if they could afford it, in order to strengthen their own conviction.

On the fifth day, Anthony ventured out onto the street feeling like a fugitive being hunted by law enforcement. Following the advice he'd been given, he chose a towering office building so he could take the elevator to the top floor and work his way down, visiting every office that displayed a nameplate on its door. However, at the crucial moment, he wavered. Maybe it would be wiser to ease himself into the cold reception he anticipated by testing the waters at a few offices on Madison Avenue first. He entered a shopping arcade that appeared only moderately successful, and spotting a sign that read Percy B. Weatherbee, Architect, he courageously pushed open the door and stepped inside. A stern-looking young woman glanced up with a questioning expression.

"Can I see Mr. Weatherbee?" He wondered if his voice sounded shaky.

She hesitantly placed her hand on the telephone receiver.

"What's your name, please?"

"He wouldn't—ah—know me. He wouldn't know my name."

"What do you want with him? Are you an insurance agent?"

"Oh, no, nothing like that!" Anthony quickly denied. "Oh, no. It's a—it's a personal matter." He wondered if he should have said this. It had all sounded so simple when Mr. Carleton had instructed his congregation:

"Don't let yourself be shut out! Show them you're determined to speak with them, and they'll pay attention."

The girl was charmed by Anthony's attractive, melancholy expression, and within moments the door to the back room swung open, revealing a tall man with flat feet and slicked-back hair. He walked toward Anthony with barely hidden irritation.

"You wanted to see me about something personal?"

Anthony shrank back in fear.

"I wanted to talk to you," he said defiantly.

"About what?"

"It'll take some time to explain."

"Well, what's it about?" Mr. Weatherbee's voice showed growing irritation.

Then Anthony, struggling with every word and syllable, started speaking:

"I'm not sure if you've ever come across a collection of booklets called 'Heart Talks'—"

"Good grief!" exclaimed Percy B. Weatherbee, Architect, "are you trying to touch my heart?"

"No, it's business. 'Heart Talks' has been incorporated and we're putting some shares on the market—"

His voice gradually trailed off, worn down by the steady, scornful gaze of his reluctant target. For another minute he pressed on, growing more self-conscious, getting caught up in his own words. His confidence drained away from him in violent, wrenching waves that felt like pieces of himself being torn away. Almost as an act of mercy, Percy B. Weatherbee, Architect, brought the interview to an end:

"Good grief!" he burst out in disgust, "and you call that a personal matter!" He spun around and marched into his private office, slamming the door behind him. Not daring to look at the stenographer, Anthony somehow managed to get himself out of the room in a shameful and mysterious way. Sweating heavily, he stood in the hallway wondering why they didn't come and arrest him; in every hurried glance he saw unmistakably a look of contempt.

After an hour and with the help of two strong whiskies, he gathered the courage to try again. He walked into a plumber's shop, but as soon as he explained why he was there, the plumber started hurriedly putting on his coat, roughly stating that he needed to go to lunch. Anthony politely observed that it was pointless to try to sell someone anything when they were hungry, and the plumber wholeheartedly agreed.

This incident gave Anthony hope; he attempted to convince himself that if the plumber hadn't been heading off to lunch, he would have at least heard him out.

Walking past several gleaming and intimidating marketplaces, he went into a grocery store. A chatty owner explained that he planned to wait and see how the armistice would impact the market before purchasing any inventory. This struck Anthony as almost unjust. In Mr. Carleton's ideal world of salesmanship, the only excuse potential customers ever offered for not buying merchandise was their uncertainty about whether it would be a profitable investment. Clearly, a person in that mindset was ridiculously vulnerable prey, easily conquered simply by skillfully presenting the right sales arguments. But these people—well, they genuinely weren't thinking about making any purchases whatsoever.

Anthony had several more drinks before approaching his fourth target, a real estate agent. Despite this, he was completely overwhelmed by a blow as decisive as a logical argument. The real estate agent mentioned that he had three brothers working in the investment business. Seeing himself as someone who destroys families, Anthony apologized and left.

After another drink, he came up with the brilliant idea of selling the stock to bartenders along Lexington Avenue. This took several hours, since he needed to have a few drinks at each establishment to put the owner in the right mood for business discussions. However, every single bartender argued that if they had money to buy bonds, they wouldn't be working as bartenders. It seemed as if they had all gotten together and agreed on that exact response. As the dark and dreary five o'clock hour approached, he discovered they were becoming even more irritating by brushing him off with jokes.

At five o'clock, he made a tremendous effort to focus and decided he needed to add more variety to his sales approach. He chose a medium-sized delicatessen and walked inside. It suddenly became clear to him that he should work his magic not just on the store owner, but on all the customers too—maybe through group psychology and herd mentality, they would all buy from him as one amazed and instantly persuaded crowd.

"Good afternoon," he began in a loud, thick voice. "I've got a little proposition for you."

If he had wanted silence, he certainly got it. A kind of reverence fell over the half-dozen women who were shopping and over the gray-haired old man who was wearing a cap and apron while slicing chicken.

Anthony pulled a stack of papers from his worn briefcase and waved them enthusiastically.

"Buy a bond," he suggested, "good as a liberty bond!" The phrase pleased him and he expanded on it. "Better than a liberty bond. Every one of these bonds is worth two liberty bonds." His mind took a break and jumped to his concluding speech, which he delivered with fitting gestures, though these were somewhat hindered by the need to grip the counter with one or both hands.

"Listen here. You've wasted my time. I don't want to know why you won't buy. I just want you to tell me why. I want you to say how many!"

At this moment, they should have come up to him holding checkbooks and fountain pens. When Anthony realized they must have missed their cue, his actor's instincts kicked in, so he went back and performed his closing scene again.

"Now listen here! You've taken up my time. You followed the proposition. You agreed with the reasoning? Now, all I want from you is, how many liberty bonds?"

"Look here!" interrupted a new voice. A heavy-set man whose face was decorated with matching curls of blond hair had emerged from a glass office at the back of the store and was approaching Anthony aggressively. "Look here, you!"

"How many?" the salesman repeated firmly. "You've wasted my time—"

"Hey, you!" shouted the owner, "I'll have you arrested by the police."

"You most certainly won't!" Anthony shot back with bold defiance. "All I want to know is how many."

From various spots throughout the store, small bursts of chatter and complaints rose into the air.

"How terrible!"

"He's completely insane."

"He's disgracefully drunk."

The owner grabbed Anthony's arm firmly.

"Get out, or I'll call a policeman."

Some remnants of clear thinking prompted Anthony to nod and awkwardly put his bonds back in the case.

"How many?" he repeated with doubt in his voice.

"Use every available force if we have to!" his opponent roared, his yellow mustache quivering with rage.

"Sell them all a bond."

With that, Anthony turned around, bowed solemnly to his former listeners, and staggered out of the store. He found a taxi at the corner and rode home to the apartment. There he fell into a deep sleep on the sofa, and that's how Gloria discovered him, his breath filling the air with a sharp, unpleasant smell, his hand still gripping his open briefcase.

Except when Anthony was drinking, his ability to feel and experience things had become weaker than that of a healthy elderly man, and when prohibition began in July, he discovered that among those who had the money for it, there was more drinking happening than ever before. A host would now bring out a bottle for the smallest reason. This urge to show off alcohol was an expression of the same impulse that drove a man to adorn his wife with jewelry. Having liquor was something to brag about, almost a symbol of social standing.

In the mornings Anthony woke up exhausted, anxious, and troubled. The peaceful summer evenings and the cold purple dawn both failed to stir any feeling in him. Only for a brief moment each day, when the warmth and revitalizing effect of his first drink kicked in, would his thoughts drift to those shimmering dreams of future happiness—the shared inheritance of both the blessed and the cursed. But this lasted only a short time. As he became more intoxicated, the dreams would fade and he turned into a bewildered ghost, wandering through strange corners of his own consciousness, filled with unpredictable schemes, harshly scornful at his best moments and sinking to sodden and dejected lows. One evening in June he had gotten into a fierce argument with Maury over something completely insignificant. He vaguely recalled the next morning that it had been about a broken pint bottle of champagne. Maury had told him to get sober and Anthony's pride had been wounded, so in an attempt at maintaining his dignity he had stood up from the table and grabbed Gloria's arm, half guiding and half forcing her into a taxi outside, abandoning Maury with three ordered dinners and opera tickets.

This kind of half-tragic disaster had become so common that when these incidents happened, he no longer felt motivated to make things right. If Gloria complained—and lately she was more inclined to retreat into scornful silence—he would either launch into an angry defense of his actions or storm out of the apartment in misery. Not once since what happened on the train platform at Redgate had he struck her in anger—though he was often held back only by some instinct that made him shake with fury. Just as he still loved her more than any other person, he also hated her with greater intensity and frequency.

So far, the judges of the Appellate Division hadn't issued a ruling, but following yet another delay, they eventually upheld the lower court's decision—with two justices disagreeing. Edward Shuttleworth received a notice of appeal. The case was heading to the highest court, and they faced another endless wait. Six months, maybe a year. The whole situation had become incredibly surreal to them, as distant and uncertain as heaven itself.

Throughout the previous winter, one small issue had been a subtle and constant source of irritation—the matter of Gloria's gray fur coat. During that time, women wrapped in long squirrel coats could be spotted every few yards along Fifth Avenue. The women were transformed into the shape of spinning tops. They appeared pig-like and vulgar; they looked like mistresses in the concealing luxury, the feminine wildness of the clothing. Still— Gloria wanted a gray squirrel coat.

Discussing the matter—or more accurately, arguing about it, since even more than during their first year of marriage, every conversation turned into a heated argument filled with phrases like "absolutely," "completely ridiculous," "that's how it is, anyway," and the overly forceful "no matter what"—they decided they couldn't afford it. And so slowly it started to represent their increasing money worries.

To Gloria, the shrinking of their income was an extraordinary occurrence, without explanation or precedent—that it could happen at all within five years seemed almost like deliberate cruelty, planned and carried out by a mocking God. When they got married, seventy-five hundred a year had seemed plenty for a young couple, particularly when combined with the prospect of many millions. Gloria had failed to understand that it was declining not only in total amount but in buying power until paying Mr. Haight's retaining fee of fifteen thousand dollars made this fact suddenly and shockingly clear. When Anthony was drafted, they had estimated their income at over four hundred a month, with the dollar already losing value at that time, but when he returned to New York they found an even more troubling situation. They were getting only forty-five hundred a year from their investments. And although the lawsuit over the will continued ahead of them like an ongoing mirage and the financial warning point appeared in the immediate future, they discovered, nonetheless, that living within their income was not possible.

So Gloria had to do without the squirrel coat, and every day as she walked down Fifth Avenue, she became increasingly aware of her worn-out, half-length leopard skin coat that was now completely out of style. Every couple of months they would sell a bond, but after paying their bills, what remained was barely enough to cover their immediate living expenses. Anthony's financial calculations revealed that their money would last approximately seven more years. This made Gloria deeply resentful, especially since during one week of wild, excessive partying—where Anthony impulsively stripped off his coat, vest, and shirt in a theater and had to be escorted out by several ushers—they spent double what the gray squirrel coat would have cost.

It was November, more like Indian summer actually, and the night was warm and balmy—though such warmth wasn't needed anymore, since summer's work had already been completed. Babe Ruth had shattered the home run record for the first time, and Jack Dempsey had fractured Jess Willard's cheekbone out in Ohio. Across the Atlantic in Europe, the typical number of children suffered from bloated bellies due to hunger, while diplomats carried on with their usual practice of making the world ready for fresh conflicts. In New York City, the working class was being "brought into line," and the betting odds on Harvard were commonly set at five to three. Peace had truly arrived, marking the start of a new era.

In the bedroom of the apartment on Fifty-seventh Street, Gloria lay on her bed, tossing restlessly from side to side. She sat up periodically to push away an extra blanket and at one point asked Anthony, who was lying awake next to her, to get her a glass of ice water. "Make sure you put ice in it," she said firmly. "It's not cold enough straight from the tap."

Looking through the thin curtains, she could see the full moon hanging above the rooftops and beyond it in the sky, the yellow glow from Times Square—and as she watched these two mismatched lights, her mind wrestled with a feeling, or more accurately a tangled web of feelings, that had consumed her thoughts throughout the day, and the day before that, and stretching back to the last time she could recall thinking clearly and logically about anything—which must have been when Anthony was serving in the army.

She would turn twenty-nine in February. The month took on a threatening and unavoidable importance—causing her to question, during these hazy, half-feverish hours, whether she had ultimately squandered her slightly worn beauty, whether there was any purpose for a quality limited by cruel and certain death.

Years earlier, when she was twenty-one, she had written in her diary: "Beauty should only be admired, only to be loved—to be gathered carefully and then offered to a chosen lover like a bouquet of roses. It appears to me, as far as I can see clearly at all, that my beauty ought to be used in that way...."

And now, throughout this entire November day, this bleak and desolate day beneath a grimy white sky, Gloria had been wondering if perhaps she had made a mistake. To protect the purity of her first romantic experience, she had stopped searching for love altogether. When that initial passion and euphoria had faded, dimmed, and finally disappeared, she had started preserving—but what exactly? It confused her that she could no longer identify precisely what she was trying to preserve—whether it was just a sentimental memory or some deep and essential principle of honor. She was now questioning whether there had ever been any moral principle at stake in the way she chose to live her life—to move through the world carefree and without regret along the most joyful of all possible paths, maintaining her dignity by always staying true to herself and doing whatever seemed beautiful for her to do. From the very first little boy in an Eton collar who had called her his "girl," all the way to the most recent casual acquaintance whose eyes had become sharp and admiring when they looked at her, all that was required was that incomparable honesty she could put into a glance or express through a seemingly random comment—because she had always spoken in incomplete sentences—to create around herself boundless illusions, boundless distances, boundless radiance. To awaken souls in men, to generate exquisite joy and exquisite anguish, she had to remain deeply proud—proud to stay untouchable, but also proud to be yielding, to be passionate and completely surrendered.

She understood that deep down, she had never truly desired children. The physical reality, the raw earthiness, the overwhelming emotions that came with bearing children, and the threat to her beauty—all of this had horrified her. She wished to live only as a self-aware flower, extending and maintaining its own existence. Her emotional nature could hold tightly to her own fantasies, but her cynical spirit reminded her that motherhood was simply another trait shared with female baboons. Therefore, her fantasies involved only phantom children—the pure, flawless representations of her pure and flawless love for Anthony.

In the end, her beauty was the one thing that never let her down. She had never encountered beauty that matched her own. Any ethical or aesthetic meaning paled in comparison to the stunning reality of her pink-and-white feet, the flawless perfection of her body, and the childlike mouth that seemed like the physical embodiment of a kiss.

She would turn twenty-nine in February. As the endless night slowly faded, she became intensely aware that she and her beauty were going to make the most of these next three months. Initially, she wasn't certain what for, but the question gradually resolved itself into the familiar pull of the movie screen. She was serious now. No financial need could have driven her the way this fear drove her. Never mind Anthony, Anthony the spiritually impoverished, the weak and shattered man with bloodshot eyes, for whom she still felt occasional moments of affection. It didn't matter. She would turn twenty-nine in February—a hundred days, so many days; she would go to Bloeckman tomorrow.

With the decision came relief. It lifted her spirits to know that somehow the illusion of beauty could be maintained, or maybe preserved on film after the real thing had disappeared. Well—tomorrow.

The following day she felt weak and sick. She attempted to go outside, and prevented herself from fainting only by grabbing onto a mailbox near the entrance. The elevator operator from the Martinique helped her upstairs, and she lay on the bed waiting for

Anthony to come back without the strength to unfasten her brassiere.

For five days she was sick with the flu, which, right as the month shifted into winter, developed into double pneumonia. In her feverish mental wanderings, she roamed through a house of cold, dark rooms searching for her mother. All she desired was to be a little girl again, to be properly cared for by some gentle yet stronger force, less complicated and more reliable than herself. It appeared that the only lover she had ever truly wanted was one that existed only in a dream.

"I Hate the Common Crowd"

One day while Gloria was sick, something strange happened that left Miss McGovern, the professional nurse, confused for quite a while afterward. It was midday, but the room where the patient was resting remained dark and peaceful. Miss McGovern stood beside the bed preparing some medication when Mrs. Patch, who seemed to have been sleeping deeply, suddenly sat up and started speaking with great intensity:

"Millions of people," she said, "swarming like rats, chattering like apes, smelling like all hell ... monkeys! Or lice, I suppose. For one really exquisite palace ... on Long Island, say—or even in Greenwich ... for one palace full of pictures from the Old World and exquisite things—with avenues of trees and green lawns and a view of the blue sea, and lovely people about in slick dresses ... I'd sacrifice a hundred thousand of them, a million of them." She raised her hand feebly and snapped her fingers. "I care nothing for them—understand me?"

The expression she directed at Miss McGovern when she finished speaking was strangely mischievous and strangely focused. Then she let out a brief laugh that gleamed with contempt, and rolling backward, she drifted off to sleep once more.

Miss McGovern felt confused. She found herself wondering what those hundred thousand things were that Mrs. Patch would give up for her mansion. Money, she assumed—though it hadn't sounded quite like money when Mrs. Patch said it.

The Movies

It was February, seven days before her birthday, and the heavy snow that had packed the side streets like dirt filling cracks in floorboards had melted into slush and was being washed toward the gutters by the street-cleaning department's hoses. The wind, no less harsh despite its random gusts, swept through the open living room windows, carrying the grim odors from the courtyard and clearing the stale cigarette smoke from the Patch apartment with its cold, cheerless flow.

Gloria, wrapped in a warm kimono, entered the cold room and picked up the telephone receiver to call Joseph Bloeckman.

"Are you referring to Mr. Joseph Black?" asked the telephone operator at "Films Par Excellence."

"Bloeckman, Joseph Bloeckman. B-l-o—"

"Mr. Joseph Bloeckman has changed his name to Black. Do you want him?"

"Why—yes." She nervously recalled that she had once called him "Blockhead" directly to his face.

His office was reached through two additional female voices; the final one was a secretary who took her name. Only when his own familiar but slightly impersonal tone came through the phone did she realize that three years had passed since they had last met. And he had changed his name to Black.

"Can you see me?" she asked casually. "It's really about business. I'm finally getting into the film industry—if I can make it happen."

"I'm really happy about that. I've always thought you would enjoy it."

"Do you think you can get me a trial?" she demanded with the arrogance that belongs to all beautiful women, to all women who have ever at any point believed themselves to be beautiful.

He promised her that it was simply a matter of when she preferred to schedule the trial. Any time would work? Well, he would call later that day and inform her of a suitable hour. The conversation ended with typical pleasantries exchanged by both parties. Then from three o'clock to five she remained near the telephone—but received no call.

But the next morning brought a note that both satisfied and thrilled her:

My dear Gloria:

Just by chance, something came to my attention that I believe would be perfect for you. I'd love to see you begin with a role that would get you noticed. At the same time, if a stunning girl like you were placed directly in a scene alongside one of those rather worn-out stars that every studio seems to have, people would definitely start talking. However, there's a "flapper" role in a Percy B. Debris production that I think would be ideal for you and would certainly get you the attention you deserve. Willa Sable stars opposite Gaston Mears in what's essentially a character role, and I believe your part would be playing her younger sister.

Anyway, Percy B. Debris, who is directing the movie, says that if you come to the studios the day after tomorrow (Thursday), he will run a screen test for you. If ten o'clock works for you, I will meet you there at that time.

With all good wishes
Ever Faithfully

Joseph Black.

Gloria had decided that Anthony shouldn't know anything about this until she had secured a definite position, so she got dressed and left the apartment the next morning before he woke up. Her mirror had told her, she believed, much the same story as always. She wondered whether there were any remaining signs of her illness. She was still a bit underweight, and she had imagined, a few days earlier, that her cheeks were slightly thinner—but she felt these were just temporary conditions and that on this specific day she looked as fresh as ever. She had purchased and put on her account a new hat, and since the day was warm she had left the leopard skin coat at home.

At the "Films Par Excellence" studios, she was announced over the phone and informed that Mr. Black would come down right away. She glanced around the area. A short, heavy-set man in a coat with slanted pockets was giving two girls a tour, and one of the girls had pointed to a pile of slim packages stacked chest-high against the wall that stretched for about twenty feet.

"That's studio mail," the heavy-set man explained. "Pictures of the stars who are with 'Films Par Excellence.'"

"Oh."

"Each one's signed by Florence Kelley or Gaston Mears or Mack Dodge—" He winked knowingly. "At least when Minnie McGlook out in Sauk Center receives the picture she requested, she believes it's personally autographed."

"Just a stamp?"

"Absolutely. It would take them a solid eight-hour workday just to sign autographs for half of those letters. They say Mary Pickford's fan mail costs her studio fifty thousand dollars a year."

"Say!"

"Absolutely. Fifty thousand dollars. But it's the best kind of advertising you can get—"

They moved away until their voices could no longer be heard, and almost right away Bloeckman showed up—Bloeckman, a dark, smooth gentleman, elegantly in his mid-forties, who welcomed her with polite warmth and said she hadn't changed at all in three years. He guided her into an enormous hall, as big as a military armory and filled throughout with active film sets and blazing rows of strange lighting equipment. Every piece of the scenery bore large white lettering that read "Gaston Mears Company," "Mack Dodge Company," or simply "Films Par Excellence."

"Have you ever been in a studio before?"

"Never have."

She enjoyed it. There wasn't the suffocating heaviness of stage makeup or the smell of dirty, cheap costumes that had disgusted her years earlier when she worked backstage at a musical comedy. This job took place during fresh mornings, and everything seemed luxurious, beautiful, and brand new. On a set decorated cheerfully with Manchu tapestries, a flawless Chinese actor performed a scene following the director's shouted instructions while the massive, gleaming camera captured an age-old moral story meant to educate the American public.

A red-haired man walked up to them and spoke with the familiar respect he showed to Bloeckman, who replied:

"Hello, Debris. I'd like you to meet Mrs. Patch.... Mrs. Patch wants to get into the movie business, as I mentioned to you.... Alright then, where do we go from here?"

Mr. Debris—the great Percy B. Debris, Gloria thought—led them to a set that depicted the inside of an office. Several chairs had been arranged around the camera, which was positioned in front of the set, and the three of them took their seats.

"Have you ever been in a studio before?" Mr. Debris asked, giving her a look that was clearly the height of sharp attention. "No? Well, I'll tell you exactly what's going to happen. We're going to do what we call a screen test to see how your face looks on camera and whether you have natural stage presence and how you react to direction. There's no reason to feel nervous about it. I'll just have the cameraman shoot a few hundred feet of film using a scene I've marked here in the script. We can figure out pretty much everything we need to know from that."

He handed her a typed script and explained the scene she would be performing. The story revealed that a woman named

Barbara Wainwright had secretly married the junior partner of the company whose office was being portrayed. One day, she accidentally entered the empty office and was naturally curious to see where her husband worked. The phone started ringing, and after hesitating for a moment, she decided to answer it. Through the call, she discovered that her husband had been hit by a car and killed instantly. She was devastated. Initially, she couldn't accept what she had heard, but eventually the reality sank in, and she collapsed unconscious on the floor.

"That's exactly what we're looking for," Mr. Debris concluded. "I'll stand right here and give you a rough idea of what to do, but you should act as if I'm not even present and just handle it in your own style. Don't worry about us being too critical in our evaluation. We just want to get a basic sense of how you come across on screen."

"I see."

"You'll find makeup in the room behind the set. Go easy on it. Use very little red."

"I see," Gloria said again, nodding her head. She nervously touched her lips with the tip of her tongue.

The Test

As she entered the set through the genuine wooden door and shut it gently behind her, she felt unexpectedly unhappy with her outfit. She should have purchased a "misses" dress for this event—she could still fit into them, and it would have been a smart choice if it had highlighted her youthful lightness.

Her attention suddenly focused on the crucial present moment when Mr. Debris's voice emerged from the blazing white lights ahead.

"You look around for your husband.... Now—you don't see him ... you're curious about the office...."

She became aware of the steady sound of the camera. It made her anxious. She looked toward it without meaning to and questioned whether she had applied her makeup properly. Then, with deliberate effort, she compelled herself to move—and she had never experienced her body's movements as so ordinary, so clumsy, so lacking in elegance or refinement. She wandered around the office, picking up objects here and there and examining them mindlessly. Then she studied the ceiling, the floor, and carefully examined an unimportant pencil on the desk. Finally, because she couldn't think of anything else to do, and even less to convey, she forced a smile.

"All right. Now the phone rings. Ring-ring-ring! Hesitate, and then answer it."

She paused—and then, faster than she should have, she realized, she grabbed the phone.

"Hello."

Her voice sounded hollow and artificial. The words echoed through the empty stage like the meaningless utterances of a spirit. She was horrified by how ridiculous their demands were—Did they really think she could instantly transform herself into this absurd and mysterious character without any explanation?

"... No ... no.... Not yet! Now listen: 'John Sumner has just been hit by a car and killed instantly!'"

Gloria let her baby mouth fall slowly open. Then:

"Now hang up! With a bang!"

She followed his instructions, gripping the table tightly while her eyes remained wide open and fixed. Eventually, she began to feel a bit more hopeful and her self-assurance grew stronger.

"My God!" she cried. Her voice sounded strong, she thought. "Oh, my God!"

"Now faint."

She fell forward onto her knees and threw her body down on the ground, lying there without breathing.

"All right!" called Mr. Debris. "That's enough, thank you. That's plenty. Get up—that's enough."

Gloria stood up, gathering her composure and dusting off her skirt.

"Awful!" she said with a cold laugh, even though her heart was pounding wildly. "Terrible, wasn't it?"

"Did it bother you?" asked Mr. Debris with a gentle smile. "Did it feel difficult? I won't be able to tell you anything about it until I have it printed."

"Of course not," she agreed, attempting to find some deeper significance in what he had said—but coming up empty. It was exactly the kind of comment he would make when he was deliberately trying not to give her false hope.

A few moments later she left the studio. Bloeckman had promised that she would hear the results of the test within the next few days. Too proud to push for any specific feedback, she felt a confusing uncertainty, and only now when the step had finally been taken did she realize how the possibility of a successful film career had been lingering in the back of her mind for the past three years. That night she tried to review all the factors that might work for or against her. Whether or not she had worn enough makeup troubled her, and since the role was that of a twenty-year-old girl, she wondered if she had been just a little too serious. About her acting she was least satisfied of all. Her entrance had been terrible—in fact, not until she reached the phone had she shown any composure—and then the test had been finished. If only they had understood! She wished that she could attempt it again. A wild idea to call in the morning and request a new audition took hold of her, and just as quickly disappeared. It seemed neither strategic nor courteous to ask another favor of Bloeckman.

The third day of waiting left her in an extremely anxious state. She had chewed the inside of her mouth until it was raw and stinging, burning terribly when she rinsed it with Listerine. She had argued so relentlessly with Anthony that he had stormed out of the apartment in icy anger. But since he was unnerved by her unusual coldness, he phoned an hour later, offered his apologies, and mentioned he was having dinner at the Amsterdam Club, the sole establishment where he maintained his membership.

It was past one o'clock and she had eaten breakfast at eleven, so she decided to skip lunch and headed out for a walk in the Park. The mail would arrive at three. She would return by then.

It was an afternoon that felt like spring had arrived early. Water was evaporating from the sidewalks, and in the park, little girls were seriously pushing white doll carriages back and forth beneath the slender trees while their uninterested nannies walked behind them in pairs, sharing with one another those enormous secrets that only nannies seem to know.

Two o'clock according to her small gold watch. She deserved a new watch, one crafted in platinum with an oblong shape and encrusted with diamonds—but those cost even more than squirrel fur coats and naturally they were beyond her means now, like everything else—unless maybe the right letter was waiting for her ... in approximately an hour ... fifty-eight minutes to be precise. Ten minutes to arrive there left forty-eight ... forty-seven now ...

Little girls seriously pushing their strollers along the wet, sunlit pathways. The nannies chatting in pairs about their mysterious secrets. Scattered throughout, a shabby man sat on newspapers spread across a bench that was drying out, connected not to the bright and wonderful afternoon but to the grimy snow that lay tired in hidden corners, waiting to be cleared away....

Ages later, entering the dimly lit hall, she spotted the Martinique elevator operator standing oddly out of place in the glow from the stained-glass window.

"Is there any mail for us?" she asked.

"Corset stays, madam."

The phone system made terrible screeching sounds, and Gloria waited while he dealt with the telephone. She felt nauseated as the elevator creaked its way upward—the floors went by like centuries slowly passing, each one threatening, condemning, and meaningful. The letter, like a white diseased mark, sat on the grimy tiles of the hallway.

My dear Gloria:

We ran the test yesterday afternoon, and Mr. Debris felt that for the role he was considering, he needed a younger woman. He mentioned that the acting wasn't bad, and that there was a small character part meant to be a very arrogant wealthy widow that he thought you might——

Feeling utterly dejected, Gloria lifted her eyes and gazed out across the courtyard. However, she discovered she couldn't make out the wall on the other side because her gray eyes were brimming with tears. She entered the bedroom with the letter crushed tightly in her grip and dropped to her knees in front of the full-length mirror that stood on the wardrobe floor. Today marked her twenty-ninth birthday, and everything around her seemed to be dissolving before her very eyes. She attempted to convince herself that it was just her makeup causing the problem, but her feelings ran too deep, too intense for such a simple explanation to provide any real comfort.

She squinted hard until she could feel the skin on her temples stretching forward. Yes—her cheeks were just slightly thinner, and small wrinkles lined the corners of her eyes. Her eyes looked different. Why, they really were different! ... And then all at once she realized how exhausted her eyes felt.

"Oh, my beautiful face," she whispered, filled with passionate grief. "Oh, my beautiful face! Oh, I can't bear to live without my beautiful face! Oh, what has happened to me?"

Then she moved toward the mirror and, just like during the test, collapsed face-down onto the floor—and remained there crying. It was the first clumsy movement she had ever made.

Chapter III: No Matter!

Within another year, Anthony and gloria had become like actors who had lost their costumes, lacking the pride to keep playing their tragic roles—so when Mrs. And miss Hulme from Kansas city completely ignored them at the plaza one evening, it was simply because Mrs. And miss Hulme, like most people, despised seeing reflections of their own primitive selves.

Their new apartment, which cost them eighty-five dollars each month, was located on Claremont Avenue, just two blocks away from the Hudson River in the upper numbered streets. They had been living there for a month when Muriel Kane visited them late one afternoon.

It was a perfect twilight on the warm side of spring. Anthony lay on the couch gazing up One Hundred and Twenty-seventh Street toward the river, where he could barely make out a single cluster of bright green trees that promised the artificial shade of Riverside Drive. Beyond the water rose the Palisades, topped by the unsightly steel structure of the amusement park—but soon darkness would fall and those same metal frameworks would become magnificent against the sky, a magical palace suspended above the gentle glow of what seemed like a tropical waterway.

The streets around the apartment, Anthony discovered, were the kind where children played—streets that were somewhat nicer than the ones he used to walk through on his way to Marietta, but essentially the same type, with the occasional hand organ or hurdy-gurdy, and when evening brought cooler air, many pairs of young girls would stroll down to the corner drugstore for ice cream sodas while dreaming endless dreams beneath the expansive sky.

The streets were growing dark now, with children playing outside, calling out jumbled, joyful words that grew faint near the open window—and Muriel, who had come looking for Gloria, was talking to him from the shadowy darkness on the other side of the room.

"Why don't we turn on the lamp?" she suggested. "It's getting eerie in here."

With a weary motion he got up and complied; the gray windowpanes disappeared. He stretched his body. He felt heavier now, his belly hung like dead weight against his belt; his body had grown soft and thick. He was thirty-two years old and his mind was a barren and chaotic ruin.

"Would you like a little drink, Muriel?"

"Not me, thanks. I don't use it anymore. What are you doing these days, Anthony?" she asked curiously.

"Well, I've been quite busy dealing with this legal case," he replied with little interest. "It's moved up to the Court of Appeals—should be resolved one way or another by fall. There's been some dispute about whether the Court of Appeals actually has authority over this issue."

Muriel clicked her tongue and tilted her head to one side.

"Well, you tell them! I've never heard of anything taking so long."

"Oh, they all do," he replied without energy; "all will cases do. They say it's unusual to have one resolved in less than four or five years."

"Oh..." Muriel boldly shifted her approach, "why don't you go to work, you lazy person!"

"At what?" he asked suddenly.

"Why, at anything, I suppose. You're still a young man."

"If that's supposed to be encouragement, I really appreciate it," he replied sarcastically—and then with sudden exhaustion: "Does it especially bother you that I don't want to work?"

"It doesn't bother me—but it does bother a lot of people who claim—"

"Oh, God!" he said with a broken voice, "it feels like for three years all I've heard about myself are crazy stories and moral lectures. I'm exhausted by it. If you don't want to see us, then leave us alone. I don't bother my old friends. But I don't need any charity visits, and I don't need criticism dressed up as helpful advice—" Then he added with an apologetic tone: "I'm sorry—but honestly, Muriel, you can't talk like some social worker even if you are visiting the lower middle class." He turned his bloodshot eyes toward her with reproach—eyes that had once been a deep, clear blue, but were now weak, strained, and half-destroyed from reading while he was drunk.

"Why do you say such terrible things?" she objected. "You talk as if you and Gloria were middle class."

"Why pretend we're not? I hate people who claim to be great aristocrats when they can't even keep up the appearances of it."

"Do you think someone needs to have money to be aristocratic?"

Muriel ... the horrified democrat ...!

"Why, of course. Aristocracy is simply an acknowledgment that certain qualities we consider admirable—courage, honor, beauty, and things like that—can be best cultivated in a supportive environment, where you're not distorted by ignorance and hardship."

Muriel bit her lower lip and shook her head from side to side.

"Look, all I'm saying is that people from good families are always decent. That's your problem, you and Gloria. You think that just because things aren't working out for you right now, all your old friends are trying to stay away from you. You're being too sensitive—"

"Actually," Anthony said, "you don't understand it at all. For me, it's just a question of pride, and for once Gloria is sensible enough to agree that we shouldn't go places where we're not welcome. And people don't want us there. We're too much like the perfect examples of what not to do."

"Nonsense! You can't park your pessimism in my little sun parlor. I think you ought to forget all those morbid speculations and go to work."

"Here I am, thirty-two years old. Let's say I did start working at some mindless job. Maybe in two years I could work my way up to fifty dollars a week—if I'm lucky. That's assuming I could even find a job at all; there's a tremendous amount of unemployment out there. Well, let's say I did make fifty a week. Do you think I'd be any happier? Do you think that if I don't get this inheritance from my grandfather that life will be bearable?"

Muriel smiled with satisfaction.

"Well," she said, "that might be clever, but it's not common sense."

A few minutes later, Gloria walked in, appearing to carry with her some mysterious dark shade that was both indefinable and unusual. Though she didn't say much, she was genuinely pleased to see Muriel. She acknowledged Anthony with a simple "Hi!"

"I've been discussing philosophy with your husband," exclaimed the unstoppable Miss Kane.

"We covered some basic concepts," Anthony said, a slight smile crossing his pale face, made even paler by two days of stubble.

Unaware of his sarcasm, Muriel repeated her argument. When she finished, Gloria said quietly:

"Anthony's right. It's no fun to go around when you have the sense that people are looking at you in a certain way."

He interrupted with a sorrowful plea:

"Don't you think that when even Maury Noble, who was my best friend, won't come to see us it's time we stopped calling people?" Tears welled up in his eyes.

"That was your fault about Maury Noble," Gloria said coolly.

"It wasn't."

"It most certainly was."

Muriel quickly stepped in:

"I met a girl who knew Maury the other day, and she says he doesn't drink anymore. He's becoming pretty cautious."

"Doesn't?"

"Hardly at all. He's making tons of money. He's kind of different since the war. He's planning to marry some girl in Philadelphia who's worth millions, Ceci Larrabee—at least, that's what Town Tattle reported."

"He's thirty-three," Anthony said, voicing his thoughts. But it seemed strange to picture him getting married. Anthony had always considered him so brilliant.

"He was," Gloria whispered, "in a way."

"But brilliant people don't settle down in business—or do they? Or what do they do? Or what becomes of everybody you used to know and have so much in common with?"

"You drift apart," Muriel suggested with the appropriate dreamy look.

"They change," said Gloria. "All the qualities that they don't use in their daily lives get covered in cobwebs."

"The last thing he told me," Anthony remembered, "was that he planned to keep working just so he could forget there wasn't anything worth working for."

Muriel seized on this immediately.

"That's exactly what you should do," she declared with triumph. "Naturally, I wouldn't expect anyone to want to work without pay. But it would give you something to occupy your time. What do you two do with yourselves, anyway? No one ever sees you at Montmartre or anywhere else for that matter. Are you trying to save money?"

Gloria laughed with contempt, shooting Anthony a sideways glance.

"Well," he demanded, "what are you laughing at?"

"You know what I'm laughing at," she answered coldly.

"At that case of whiskey?"

"Yes"—she turned to Muriel—"he paid seventy-five dollars for a case of whiskey yesterday."

"What if I did? It's cheaper that way than buying it by the bottle. You don't need to pretend you won't drink any of it."

"At least I don't drink in the daytime."

"That's a fine distinction!" he shouted, jumping to his feet in feeble anger. "What's more, I'll be damned if you can throw that at me every few minutes!"

"It's true."

"It's not! And I'm tired of you constantly criticizing me in front of guests!" He had become so agitated that his arms and shoulders were clearly shaking. "Anyone would think everything was my fault. Anyone would think you hadn't pushed me to spend money—and spent far more on yourself than I ever did."

Now Gloria stood up.

"I won't let you talk to me that way!"

"All right, then; by Heaven, you don't have to!"

In a hurried manner, he rushed out of the room. The two women could hear his footsteps echoing in the hallway, followed by the sharp sound of the front door slamming shut. Gloria collapsed back into her chair. In the soft glow of the lamp, her face appeared beautiful, calm, and impossible to read.

"Oh—!" Muriel cried out in distress. "Oh, what's wrong?"

"Nothing particularly. He's just drunk."

"Drunk? Why, he's perfectly sober. He talked——"

Gloria shook her head.

"Oh, no, he doesn't let it show anymore unless he can barely stay on his feet, and he speaks normally until he gets worked up. He actually speaks much better than when he's sober. But he's been sitting here drinking all day—except for the few minutes it took him to walk to the corner to buy a newspaper."

"Oh, how awful!" Muriel was genuinely touched. Her eyes welled up with tears. "Has this been happening often?"

"You mean drinking?"

"No, this—leaving you?"

"Oh, yes. Frequently. He'll come in about midnight—and weep and ask me to forgive him."

"And do you?"

"I don't know. We just go on."

The two women sat there in the lamplight and looked at each other, both feeling helpless in their own ways when faced with this situation. Gloria was still beautiful, as beautiful as she would ever be again—her cheeks were glowing and she was wearing a new dress that she had bought—recklessly—for fifty dollars. She had hoped she could convince Anthony to take her out tonight, to a restaurant or even to one of the magnificent, spectacular movie theaters where there would be a few people to see her, people she could stand to look at in return. She wanted this because she knew her cheeks were glowing and because her dress was new and attractively delicate. Only very rarely, now, did they receive any invitations. But she did not share these thoughts with Muriel.

"Gloria, sweetheart, I really wish we could have dinner together, but I made a promise to someone and it's already seven-thirty. I have to run."

"Oh, I couldn't do that anyway. First of all, I've been sick all day. I couldn't eat anything."

After walking Muriel to the door, Gloria returned to the room, switched off the lamp, and rested her elbows on the windowsill to gaze out at Palisades Park, where the bright spinning circle of the Ferris wheel resembled a shivering mirror reflecting the moon's golden light. The street had grown quiet; the children had gone inside—across the way, she could see a family eating dinner. Without reason or logic, they stood up and moved around the table; viewed from this distance, everything they did seemed absurd—as if they were being manipulated carelessly and without purpose by unseen wires from above.

She glanced at her watch—it was eight o'clock. She had felt happy for part of the day—during the early afternoon—while walking along that Broadway of Harlem, One Hundred and Twenty-fifth Street, with her nose picking up various scents, and her thoughts stirred by the remarkable beauty of some Italian children. It struck her in an odd way—just as Fifth Avenue had once affected her, back when, with the calm assurance that comes with beauty, she had understood that everything belonged to her, every store and everything inside it, every grown-up plaything sparkling in a display window, all hers simply for the taking. Here on One Hundred and Twenty-fifth Street there were Salvation Army bands and rainbow-shawled elderly women sitting on stoops and sweet, gooey candy clutched in the dirty hands of glossy-haired children—and the evening sun beating down on the walls of the towering apartment buildings. Everything felt abundant and vibrant and flavorful, like a meal prepared by a resourceful French chef that you couldn't help but savor, even though you suspected the ingredients were likely leftovers....

Gloria suddenly shuddered as a river siren wailed over the darkening rooftops, and leaning back until the pale curtains slipped from her shoulder, she switched on the electric light. The evening was getting late. She knew she had some loose change in her purse, and she wondered whether she should go downstairs to get coffee and rolls where the elevated subway created a thundering tunnel beneath Manhattan Street, or simply eat the devilled ham and bread in her kitchen. Her purse made the decision for her. It held only a nickel and two pennies.

After an hour, the quiet in the room had become too much to bear, and she noticed her gaze drifting from her magazine up to the ceiling, which she stared at blankly. All at once she got to her feet, paused briefly while chewing on her finger—then walked to the pantry, pulled a bottle of whiskey from the shelf and fixed herself a drink. She topped off the glass with ginger ale, and settling back into her chair completed reading an article in the magazine. The piece was about the final surviving revolutionary widow, who as a young woman had wed an elderly veteran of the Continental Army and had passed away in 1906. Gloria found it both peculiar and strangely romantic that she and this woman had lived during the same era.

She flipped to the next page and discovered that a congressional candidate was facing accusations of atheism from a political rival. Gloria's shock disappeared when she realized the allegations were unfounded. The candidate had simply questioned the miracle of the loaves and fishes. When pressed, he acknowledged that he completely believed in the walking on water.

After finishing her first drink, Gloria poured herself a second one. She put on a negligée and settled comfortably on the lounge, then realized she felt miserable as tears streamed down her face. She wondered whether these were tears of self-pity and tried determinedly not to cry, but this hopeless, joyless existence weighed heavily on her, and she continued shaking her head back and forth, the corners of her mouth trembling downward, as if she were rejecting some statement made by someone, somewhere. She had no idea that this gesture of hers was older than recorded history itself, that for countless generations of people, unbearable and relentless sorrow has made that same gesture—one of rejection, of objection, of confusion—toward something deeper and more powerful than any God created in humanity's image, and before which that God, if he existed, would be just as helpless. This truth lies at the core of all tragedy: this force never provides explanations, never gives answers—this force as intangible as air, yet more certain than death itself.

Richard Caramel

Early that summer, Anthony gave up his membership at his final club, the Amsterdam. He had barely visited it twice each year, and the membership fees had become a constant financial strain. He had joined when he returned from Italy because it had been his grandfather's club and his father's before him, and because it was the type of club that, when given the chance, one unquestionably joined—but in reality he had always preferred the Harvard Club, mainly because of Dick and Maury. Still, as his financial situation worsened, it had seemed like an increasingly valuable status symbol to hold onto.... In the end, he let it go with some sadness....

His group of friends had grown to an odd dozen people. He had met several of them at a place called "Sammy's" on Forty-third Street, where you had to knock on the door and get approval from someone behind a metal screen before you could enter and sit around a large round table drinking decent whiskey. It was there that he met a man named Parker Allison, who had been exactly the wrong kind of party-goer at Harvard and was burning through a massive inheritance from the yeast business as quickly as he could. Parker Allison's idea of being impressive involved driving a loud red-and-yellow race car up Broadway with two flashy, cold-eyed women sitting next to him. He was the type who preferred dining with two women instead of one—his mind was nearly incapable of keeping up a conversation with just one person.

Besides Allison there was Pete Lytell, who wore a gray derby tilted to one side of his head. He always had money and was usually cheerful, so Anthony spent many summer and fall afternoons having rambling, lengthy conversations with him. Anthony discovered that Lytell not only spoke but also thought in catchphrases. His entire philosophy consisted of a collection of these sayings, picked up randomly throughout his busy, unreflective life. He had standard phrases about Socialism—the age-old ones; he had sayings about whether God existed—something involving a railroad accident he'd once been in; and he had ready responses about the Irish question, the kind of woman he admired, and why prohibition was pointless. The only time his talk ever rose above these confused fragments of thought, which he used to make sense of the most elaborate events in what had been an unusually eventful life, was when he discussed the concrete details of his most basic physical needs: he knew with remarkable precision exactly which foods, drinks, and women he preferred.

He was simultaneously the most ordinary and the most extraordinary result of civilization. He represented nine out of ten people you encounter walking down a city street—yet he was also a hairless ape equipped with only two dozen simple behaviors. He served as the protagonist in countless stories of life and art—while also being essentially a fool, carrying out steadily but ridiculously a sequence of complex and endlessly amazing adventures throughout seventy years of existence.

With men like these two, Anthony Patch would drink and talk, then drink some more and debate. He enjoyed their company because they knew absolutely nothing about him, because they lived in the moment and had no understanding whatsoever of life's inevitable flow and continuity. They weren't sitting in front of a movie with scenes that connected to each other, but rather watching some dusty, old-fashioned travel documentary where everything was presented in stark black and white, making all the deeper meanings jumbled and unclear. But they themselves weren't confused at all, because there was nothing inside them that could become confused—they switched their favorite sayings from one month to the next just as easily as they changed their ties.

Anthony, who was courteous, subtle, and perceptive, found himself drunk every day—at Sammy's with these men, in the apartment reading some familiar book, and very rarely with Gloria, who had begun to take on the unmistakable characteristics of a quarrelsome and unreasonable woman in his view. She was certainly not the Gloria of the past—the Gloria who, if she had been ill, would have chosen to make everyone around her miserable rather than admit she needed sympathy or help. She wasn't above complaining now; she wasn't above feeling sorry for herself. Every night as she got ready for bed, she covered her face with some new cream that she irrationally hoped would restore the radiance and freshness to her fading beauty. When Anthony was drunk, he mocked her for this. When he was sober, he treated her politely, sometimes even tenderly; he seemed to display for brief periods a hint of that former quality of understanding too deeply to judge—that quality which represented the best part of him and had worked quickly and relentlessly toward his destruction.

But he despised being sober. Sobriety forced him to become aware of the people surrounding him, of that atmosphere of struggle, of hungry ambition, of hope more degrading than despair, of the constant movement up or down the social ladder, which in every major city shows itself most clearly through the unstable middle class. Since he couldn't live among the wealthy, he believed his second choice would have been to live among the extremely poor. Anything would have been preferable to this mixture of sweat and tears.

The feeling of life's vast, sweeping panorama, which had never been particularly strong in Anthony, had grown faint to the point of nearly disappearing entirely. Only occasionally now would some event or one of Gloria's movements catch his attention—but the dull, gray curtains had truly descended upon him. As he aged, those moments became even more distant—and after that, there was only wine.

There was something gentle and warm about being drunk— an indescribable shine and allure it brought, like memories of brief and faded nights. After several cocktails, there was enchantment in the towering, glowing Arabian night of the Bush Terminal Building—its top a summit of pure magnificence, golden and dreamlike against the unreachable sky. And Wall Street, the crude, the ordinary—once again it became the victory of gold, a magnificent living display; it was where the great rulers stored the money for their battles....

The fruit of youth or of the grape, the fleeting magic of the short journey from darkness to darkness—the ancient illusion that truth and beauty were somehow connected.

As he stood outside Delmonico's lighting a cigarette one evening, he noticed two horse-drawn carriages parked close to the sidewalk, waiting for any intoxicated passenger who might need a ride. The outdated cabs looked worn and grimy—the cracked shiny leather was wrinkled like an elderly person's skin, the seat cushions had faded to a dull brownish-purple color; even the horses appeared old and tired, just like the gray-haired drivers who sat up high, snapping their whips with an absurd pretense of charm. A remnant of bygone celebration!

Anthony Patch walked away feeling suddenly depressed, thinking about how bitter it was when such things lingered on. It seemed that nothing became stale as quickly as pleasure did.

On Forty-second Street one afternoon, he ran into Richard Caramel for the first time in many months—a successful, increasingly heavy Richard Caramel, whose face was growing fuller to complement his distinguished Bostonian forehead.

"I just arrived from the coast this week. I was planning to call you, but I didn't have your new address."

"We've moved."

Richard Caramel observed that Anthony was wearing a dirty shirt, that his cuffs were somewhat but noticeably worn, that his eyes were surrounded by half-moon shadows the color of cigar smoke.

"I figured as much," he said, locking eyes with his friend using his bright yellow gaze. "But where is Gloria and what's her situation? My God, Anthony, I've been hearing the most incredible stories about you two all the way out in California—and when I return to New York I discover you've completely disappeared from view. Why don't you get your act together?"

"Listen," Anthony said shakily, "I can't handle a lengthy speech right now. We've lost money in countless ways, and of course people have been gossiping—because of the legal case, but the matter will reach a final resolution this winter, certainly—"

"You're speaking so quickly that I can't understand you," Dick interrupted calmly.

"Well, I've said everything I'm going to say," Anthony snapped. "Come and visit us if you want to—or don't!"

With that, he turned around and began walking away into the crowd, but Dick caught up to him right away and grabbed his arm.

"Listen, Anthony, don't lose your temper so quickly! You know Gloria is my cousin, and you're one of my oldest friends, so it's only natural that I'd be concerned when I hear you're going downhill—and dragging her down with you."

"I don't want to be preached to."

"Well, then, all right—How about coming up to my apartment and having a drink? I've just gotten settled in. I bought three cases of Gordon gin from a tax officer."

As they walked along, he continued with a sudden outburst of frustration:

"And what about your grandfather's money—are you going to get it?"

"Well," Anthony replied with resentment, "that old fool Haight appears optimistic, particularly since people are fed up with reformers at the moment—you know it could make a small difference, for example, if some judge believed that Adam Patch made it more difficult for him to obtain alcohol."

"You can't get by without money," Dick said matter-of-factly. "Have you tried writing anything recently?"

Anthony shook his head without saying a word.

"That's funny," Dick said. "I always thought you and Maury would become writers someday, and now he's turned into some kind of penny-pinching aristocrat, and you're—"

"I'm the bad example."

"I wonder why?"

"You probably think you understand," Anthony said, trying to focus his thoughts. "Both those who fail and those who succeed believe deep down that they see things clearly—the successful person because they've achieved their goals, and the one who failed because they've experienced defeat. The person who succeeds advises their child to learn from their father's good luck, while the person who fails tells their child to learn from their father's errors."

"I don't agree with you," said the author of "A Shave-tail in France." "I used to listen to you and Maury when we were young, and I was impressed because you were both so consistently cynical, but now—well, honestly, which of the three of us has embraced the intellectual life? I don't want to sound boastful, but it's me, and I've always believed that moral values exist, and I always will."

"Well," Anthony objected, finding himself rather entertained by the discussion, "even if we accept that point, you realize that in real life, situations are never presented to us in such clear-cut terms, are they?"

"It does to me. There's nothing I'd violate certain principles for."

"But how do you know when you're breaking them? You have to make educated guesses just like everyone else does. You have to weigh the values when you reflect on things. You complete the portrait at that point—filling in the details and adding the shadows."

Dick shook his head with arrogant stubbornness. "Same old pointless cynic," he said. "It's just a way of feeling sorry for yourself. You don't take action—so nothing has any meaning."

"Oh, I'm perfectly capable of feeling sorry for myself," Anthony admitted, "and I'm not saying that I'm enjoying life as much as you are."

"You say—at least you used to—that happiness is the only thing worthwhile in life. Do you think you're any happier because you're a pessimist?"

Anthony let out a harsh grunt. His enjoyment of the conversation started to fade. He felt anxious and desperately wanted a drink.

"Oh my goodness!" he exclaimed, "where do you live? I can't keep walking forever."

"Your endurance is all in your head, isn't it?" Dick shot back. "Well, I live right here."

He walked into the apartment building on Forty-ninth Street, and within a few minutes they found themselves in a spacious, newly furnished room featuring an open fireplace and four walls completely covered with bookshelves. An African American butler brought them gin rickeys, and an hour passed pleasantly as they slowly finished their drinks while enjoying the warmth of a gentle mid-autumn fire.

"The arts are very old," Anthony said after a moment. After a few drinks, the tension in his nerves eased and he discovered he could think clearly again.

"Which art?"

"All of them. Poetry is dying first. It will be absorbed into prose sooner or later. For example, the beautiful word, the colorful and sparkling word, and the beautiful comparison belong in prose now. To get attention poetry has to reach for the unusual word, the harsh, earthy word that has never been beautiful before. Beauty, as the combination of several beautiful parts, reached its highest point in Swinburne. It cannot go any further—except in the novel, perhaps."

Dick cut him off impatiently:

"You know these new novels wear me out. My God! Everywhere I go some foolish girl asks me if I've read 'This Side of Paradise.' Are our girls really like that? If it reflects real life, which I don't believe, the next generation is headed for ruin. I'm tired of all this cheap realism. I think there's a place for the romantic writer in literature."

Anthony tried to recall what he had recently read by Richard Caramel. There was "A Shave-tail in France," a novel titled "The Land of Strong Men," and several dozen short stories that were even more terrible. It had become standard practice among young and sharp-witted critics to reference Richard Caramel with a contemptuous smile. They referred to him as "Mr." Richard Caramel. His reputation was shamefully torn apart in every literary review section. He was charged with amassing a huge fortune by producing garbage for the film industry. As literary tastes changed, he was becoming practically synonymous with disdain.

While Anthony was thinking about this, Dick had stood up and appeared to be hesitating before making a confession.

"I've collected quite a few books," he said suddenly.

"So I see."

"I've put together a comprehensive collection of excellent American literature, both classic and contemporary. I'm not talking about the typical Longfellow-Whittier selections—actually, most of it consists of modern works."

He walked over to one of the walls and, realizing it was expected of him, Anthony stood up and followed.

"Look!"

Under a printed label marked "Americana," he showcased six lengthy rows of books that were beautifully bound and clearly selected with great care.

"And here are the contemporary novelists."

Then Anthony spotted the joker. Squeezed between Mark Twain and Dreiser sat eight odd and out-of-place volumes, the complete works of Richard Caramel—"The Demon Lover," which was decent enough... but also seven other books that were absolutely terrible, lacking any sincerity or grace.

Reluctantly, Anthony looked at Dick's face and noticed a hint of doubt in his expression.

"I've included my own books, naturally," Richard Caramel said quickly, "although a couple of them aren't quite up to par—I'm worried I wrote too hastily when I had that magazine deal. But I don't believe in fake humility. Certainly some of the reviewers haven't given me as much notice since I became established—but, in the end, it's not the critics who matter. They're nothing but followers."

For the first time in so long that he could barely remember, Anthony experienced a hint of the familiar, satisfying disdain for his friend. Richard Caramel went on:

"My publishers, you know, have been promoting me as the American Thackeray—because of my New York novel."

"Yes," Anthony managed to say, "I suppose there's a lot of truth in what you're saying."

He understood that his contempt made no sense. He realized that he would have switched places with Dick without a second thought. He had done his best to write insincerely himself. Well, then—how can someone dismiss their life's work so easily? ...

That night, while Richard Caramel worked intensely at his desk, constantly hitting the wrong keys and squinting his tired, mismatched eyes as he struggled with his writing well into those bleak early morning hours when the fire burns low and his head spins from extended focus, Anthony lay completely intoxicated, stretched out across the back seat of a taxi heading to his apartment on Claremont Avenue.

The Beating

As winter drew near, it appeared that Anthony was gripped by a kind of madness. He would wake up in the morning so anxious that Gloria could feel his body shaking in bed before he could gather enough energy to stumble to the pantry for a drink. He had become unbearable now unless he was under the influence of alcohol, and as she watched him deteriorate and grow coarse before her very eyes, Gloria's spirit and body recoiled from him; when he stayed out all night, which happened several times, she not only didn't feel sorry but actually experienced some relief. The following day he would show mild remorse, and would comment in a rough, ashamed way that he supposed he was drinking a bit too much.

For hours at a time he would sit in the large armchair that had been in his apartment, lost in a kind of daze—even his interest in reading his favorite books seemed to have vanished, and though constant arguing went on between husband and wife, the one topic they ever truly discussed was the progress of the will case. What Gloria hoped in the dark depths of her soul, what she expected that great gift of money to accomplish, is hard to imagine. She was being shaped by her surroundings into a twisted version of a housewife. She who until three years earlier had never made coffee, now prepared sometimes three meals a day. She walked extensively in the afternoons, and in the evenings she read—books, magazines, anything she found within reach. If now she longed for a child, even a child of the Anthony who came to her bed completely drunk, she neither said so nor showed any sign or indication of interest in children. It is questionable if she could have made it clear to anyone what it was she wanted, or indeed what there was to want—a lonely, beautiful woman, thirty now, withdrawn behind some unbreachable barrier born and existing alongside her beauty.

One afternoon when the snow had turned dirty again along Riverside Drive, Gloria returned from the grocery store to find Anthony pacing back and forth across their apartment floor in an extremely agitated state. The feverish eyes he turned toward her were streaked with small pink lines that made her think of rivers on a map. For a moment she got the distinct impression that he had suddenly and unmistakably become old.

"Do you have any money?" he asked her suddenly.

"What? What do you mean?"

"Exactly what I said. Money! Money! Can't you understand English?"

She ignored him completely and brushed past him into the pantry to put the bacon and eggs in the refrigerator. Whenever his drinking had been particularly heavy, he was always in a whining mood. This time he followed her and, standing in the pantry doorway, kept pressing her with his question.

"You heard what I said. Do you have any money?"

She turned away from the refrigerator and faced him.

"Anthony, you must be out of your mind! You know I don't have any money—just a dollar in change."

He made a sudden turn and went back to the living room, where he started pacing again. It was clear that something important was weighing on his mind—he clearly wanted her to ask what was wrong. Following him a moment later, she sat down on the long couch and began letting down her hair. It was no longer cut short, and over the past year it had changed from a beautiful gold with hints of red to a dull light brown. She had purchased some shampoo and planned to wash it now; she had thought about adding some peroxide to the rinse water.

"—Well?" she conveyed without speaking.

"That awful bank!" he said with a shaky voice. "They've had my account for more than ten years—ten years. Well, it turns out they have some dictatorial rule that you need to keep over five

415

hundred dollars there or they won't keep you as a customer. They sent me a letter a few months ago telling me I'd been running too low. Once I wrote two bad checks—remember? that night at Reisenweber's?—but I covered them the very next day. Well, I promised old Halloran—he's the manager, the greedy Irishman—that I'd be more careful. And I thought I was doing fine; I kept the stubs in my checkbook fairly regularly. Well, I went in there today to cash a check, and Halloran came up and told me they'd have to close my account. Too many bad checks, he said, and I never had more than five hundred in my account—and that only for a day or two at a time. And my God! What do you think he said then?"

"What?"

"He said this was a good time to do it because I didn't have a damn penny in there!"

"You didn't?"

"That's what he told me. Apparently I had written the Bedros people a check for sixty dollars for that last case of liquor—but I only had forty-five dollars in my bank account. Well, the Bedros people deposited fifteen dollars into my account and then withdrew the entire amount."

In her lack of understanding, Gloria imagined a terrifying vision of being locked away and publicly shamed.

"Oh, they won't do anything," he reassured her. "Bootlegging is too dangerous a business. They'll send me a bill for fifteen dollars and I'll pay it."

"Oh." She thought for a moment. "—Well, we can sell another bond."

He laughed with sarcasm.

"Oh, yes, that's always simple. When the handful of bonds we own that are actually earning any interest are only valued at fifty to eighty cents per dollar. We end up losing roughly half the bond's value each time we sell."

"What else can we do?"

"Oh, we'll sell something—as usual. We've got paper worth eighty thousand dollars at face value." Once again he laughed in an unpleasant way. "Would bring in about thirty thousand on the open market."

"I didn't trust those ten percent investments."

"No way you did!" he said. "You pretended you did, so you could blame me if things fell apart, but you wanted to take the risk just as much as I did."

She stayed quiet for a moment, as if she was thinking it over, then:

"Anthony," she suddenly exclaimed, "two hundred dollars a month is worse than having nothing at all. Let's sell every single bond and deposit the entire thirty thousand dollars in the bank—and if we end up losing the case, we can go live in Italy for three years, and then simply die." As she spoke with growing excitement, she became conscious of a subtle wave of emotion stirring within her, the first genuine feeling she had experienced in many days.

"Three years," he said nervously, "three years! You've lost your mind. Mr. Haight will demand much more than that if we don't win. Do you really believe he's doing this work for free?"

"I forgot that."

"—And here it is Saturday," he went on, "and I've only got a dollar and some change, and we have to make it last until Monday, when I can get to my broker's.... And there's not a single drink in the house," he added as a meaningful afterthought.

"Can't you call Dick?"

"I did. His assistant says he's traveled down to Princeton to speak at a literary club or something like that. He won't be back until Monday."

"Well, let's see—Don't you know some friend you might go to?"

"I tried reaching a few people. Couldn't find anyone home. I wish I had sold that Keats letter like I was planning to do last week."

"What about those guys you play cards with at that place called Sammy's?"

"Do you think I would ask them?" His voice was filled with righteous horror. Gloria flinched. He would rather watch her obvious discomfort than feel his own skin crawl from asking for an inappropriate favor. "I thought about Muriel," he suggested.

"She's in California."

"Well, what about some of those men who treated you so well while I was serving in the military? You'd think they might be happy to do you a small favor."

She looked at him with contempt, but he didn't pay any attention.

"Or what about your old friend Rachael—or Constance Merriam?"

"Constance Merriam has been dead for a year, and I wouldn't ask Rachael."

"Well, what about that man who was so eager to help you once that he could barely control himself, Bloeckman?"

"Oh—!" He had finally hurt her, and he wasn't too dense or too thoughtless to notice it.

"Why not him?" he insisted callously.

"Because—he doesn't like me anymore," she said with difficulty, and then when he didn't respond but simply looked at her with cynicism: "If you want to know why, I'll tell you. A year ago I went to Bloeckman—he's changed his name to Black—and asked him to get me into the movies."

"You went to Bloeckman?"

"Yes."

"Why didn't you tell me?" he asked in disbelief, his smile disappearing from his face.

"Because you were probably off drinking somewhere. He had them give me a test, and they decided that I wasn't young enough for anything except a character part."

"A character part?"

"The whole 'woman of thirty' stereotype. I wasn't thirty, and I didn't think I looked thirty either."

"Why, damn him!" Anthony shouted, defending her fiercely with a strange contradiction of feelings, "why—"

"Well, that's why I can't go to him."

"What incredible nerve!" Anthony declared anxiously, "what incredible nerve!"

"Anthony, that doesn't matter now; what matters is that we need to get through Sunday and all we have in the house is a loaf of bread, half a pound of bacon, and two eggs for breakfast." She gave him everything from her purse. "There's seventy, eighty, a dollar fifteen. Combined with what you have, that comes to about two and a half dollars total, right? Anthony, we can make it work with that amount. We can buy plenty of food with that money— more than we could ever eat."

Rattling the coins in his palm, he shook his head. "No. I need a drink. I'm so incredibly anxious that I'm trembling." An idea occurred to him. "Maybe Sammy would cash a check. Then on Monday I could hurry down to the bank with the cash." "But they've shut down your account."

"That's right, that's right—I'd forgotten. I'll tell you what: I'll go down to Sammy's and I'll find somebody there who'll lend me something. I hate asking them though...." He snapped his fingers suddenly. "I know what I'll do. I'll pawn my watch. I can get twenty dollars for it, and get it back Monday for sixty cents extra. It's been pawned before—when I was at Cambridge."

He had put on his overcoat, and after a quick goodbye, he headed down the hallway toward the front door.

419

Gloria stood up. She had suddenly realized where he would most likely head first.

"Anthony!" she called out to him, "wouldn't it be better if you left two dollars with me? You'll only need money for the car fare."

The front door slammed shut—he had acted as if he couldn't hear her. She remained there for a moment, watching where he had gone; then she walked into the bathroom with all her melancholy beauty products and started getting ready to wash her hair.

Down at Sammy's, he discovered Parker Allison and Pete Lytell seated by themselves at a table, sipping whiskey sours. It was shortly after six o'clock, and Sammy, or Samuele Bendiri as he had been baptized, was sweeping a pile of cigarette butts and shattered glass into a corner.

"Hi, Tony!" Parker Allison called out to Anthony. Sometimes he would call him Tony, other times he'd use Dan. In Parker's mind, every Anthony had to go by one of these nicknames.

"Sit down. What'll you have?"

On the subway, Anthony counted his money and discovered he had nearly four dollars. He could afford two rounds at fifty cents per drink, which meant he would have six drinks total. After that, he would head over to Sixth Avenue and exchange his watch for twenty dollars and a pawn ticket.

"Well, troublemakers," he said cheerfully, "how's the life of crime?"

"Pretty good," Allison said. He winked at Pete Lytell. "Too bad you're a married man. We've got some really good stuff planned for around eleven o'clock, when the shows get out. Oh, boy! Yes, sir—too bad he's married—isn't that right, Pete?"

"'Such a shame."

At seven-thirty, after they had finished their sixth round, Anthony realized his good intentions were losing out to his cravings. He felt happy and upbeat now—having a great time. The story Pete had just wrapped up struck him as incredibly funny and deeply amusing—and he concluded, as he did every day around this time, that these were "damn fine guys, for sure!" who would go further for him than anyone else he could think of. The pawnshops would stay open late on Saturday nights, and he sensed that just one more drink would lift him to a wonderful, rosy euphoria.

Skillfully, he searched through his vest pockets, pulled out his two quarters, and looked at them as if he was surprised to find them there.

"Well, I'll be darned," he protested in an upset tone, "here I've come out without my wallet."

"Need some cash?" Lytell asked casually.

"I left my money on the dresser at home. And I wanted to buy you another drink."

"Oh—forget about it." Lytell dismissed the suggestion with a wave of his hand. "I think we can buy a good guy all the drinks he wants. What do you want—the same thing?"

"I tell you," Parker Allison suggested, "how about we send Sammy across the street to get some sandwiches and have dinner here."

The other two agreed.

"Good idea."

"Hey, Sammy, would you do something for us..."

Just after nine o'clock Anthony struggled to his feet and, mumbling a slurred good night to them, walked unsteadily toward the door, slipping Sammy one of his two quarters as he left. Once outside on the street he paused uncertainly and then headed toward Sixth Avenue, where he recalled having often walked past several pawn shops. He passed a newsstand and two pharmacies— and then he realized he was standing in front of the place he was looking for, and that it was closed and locked up. Undeterred he kept going; another one, half a block down, was also shut—as were two more across the street, and a fifth one in the square below. Noticing a dim light in the last one, he started knocking on the glass door; he stopped only when a security guard appeared at the back of the shop and gestured angrily for him to move along. With increasing disappointment, with increasing confusion, he crossed the street and walked back toward Forty-third. On the corner near Sammy's he stopped undecided—if he returned to the apartment, as his body seemed to demand, he would expose himself to harsh criticism; yet, now that the pawn shops were closed, he had no idea where to get the money. He finally decided that he might ask Parker Allison, after all—but he approached Sammy's only to discover the door locked and the lights turned off. He checked his watch; nine-thirty. He started walking.

Ten minutes later, he came to a halt without purpose at the corner of Forty-third Street and Madison Avenue, positioned diagonally across from the illuminated yet almost empty entrance to the Biltmore Hotel. At this spot he paused briefly, then lowered himself with effort onto a wet plank among the scattered remnants of construction work. He remained there for nearly thirty minutes, his thoughts drifting in constantly changing patterns across the surface of his consciousness, the most prominent of which were his need to secure some money and return home before he became too intoxicated to navigate his way back.

Then, looking over toward the Biltmore, he spotted a man standing right beneath the bright lights of the hotel entrance next to a woman wearing an ermine coat. As Anthony observed, the pair stepped forward and waved down a taxi. Anthony recognized through that unmistakable way of identifying someone that comes from knowing how a friend walks that it was Maury Noble.

He stood up.

"Maury!" he shouted.

Maury glanced his way, then turned back to the girl just as the taxi pulled up to the curb. With the frantic thought of borrowing ten dollars, Anthony started running as fast as he could across Madison Avenue and down Forty-third Street.

As he approached, Maury was standing next to the wide-open door of the taxi. His companion turned around and looked at Anthony with curiosity.

"Hello, Maury!" he said, extending his hand. "How are you doing?"

"Fine, thank you."

Their hands fell to their sides and Anthony paused uncertainly. Maury didn't make any effort to introduce him, instead just standing there watching him with an unreadable, cat-like quiet.

"I wanted to see you—" Anthony started hesitantly. He didn't feel comfortable asking for money with the girl standing just four feet away, so he stopped mid-sentence and made a noticeable gesture with his head, as if trying to signal Maury to step aside with him.

"I'm in quite a rush, Anthony."

"I know—but can you, can you—" Once more he paused.

"I'll see you some other time," said Maury. "It's important."

"I'm sorry, Anthony."

Before Anthony could decide to voice his request, Maury had already turned calmly to the girl, assisted her into the car, and with a courteous "good evening," climbed in behind her. When he acknowledged Anthony with a nod through the window, it appeared to Anthony that his facial expression hadn't altered in the slightest. Then with an irritating rattle, the taxi drove away, leaving Anthony standing there by himself beneath the streetlights.

Anthony walked into the Biltmore Hotel without any particular purpose other than the fact that the entrance was right there, and after climbing the broad staircase, he found a place to sit in a small alcove. He was intensely conscious that he had been snubbed; he felt as hurt and furious as he could possibly feel in his current state. Even so, he remained stubbornly focused on the urgent need to get some money before returning home, and once more he counted on his fingers the people he knew whom he might possibly ask for help in this crisis. Eventually, he decided that he could try approaching Mr. Howland, his stockbroker, at his residence.

After waiting for a long time, he discovered that Mr. Howland wasn't in. He went back to the operator, leaning across her desk and fidgeting with his quarter as if he was reluctant to leave without getting what he came for.

"Call Mr. Bloeckman," he said suddenly. His own words caught him off guard. The name had emerged from some intersection of two thoughts in his mind.

"What's the number, please?"

Barely aware of his actions, Anthony searched for Joseph Bloeckman in the phone book. He couldn't locate anyone by that name and was ready to shut the directory when he suddenly remembered that Gloria had said something about a name change. It took just a moment to locate Joseph Black—then he stood in the phone booth waiting while the operator connected the call.

"Hello there. Is Mr. Bloeckman—I mean Mr. Black—in?"

"No, he's out this evening. Is there any message?" The accent was cockney; it brought back memories of the rich vocal courtesies of Bounds.

"Where is he?"

"Why, ah, who is this, please, sir?"

"This is Mr. Patch. It's a matter of vital importance." "Well, he's with a party at the Boulevard Saint-Michel, sir."

"Thanks."

Anthony pocketed his five cents in change and headed toward the Boul' Mich', a well-known dance club on Forty-fifth Street. Though it was almost ten o'clock, the streets remained dark and nearly empty, waiting for the theaters to release their crowds an hour later. Anthony was familiar with the Boul' Mich' since he had visited there with Gloria the previous year, and he recalled that the establishment required patrons to wear formal evening attire. He decided he wouldn't go upstairs—instead, he would have someone fetch Bloeckman and wait for him in the lobby downstairs. For a brief moment, the entire plan seemed perfectly reasonable and appropriate to him. In his confused state of mind, Bloeckman had transformed into just another one of his longtime friends.

The entrance hall of the Boul' Mich' was warm. Bright yellow lights hung overhead, illuminating a thick green carpet below, and from its center, a white staircase led up to the dance floor.

Anthony spoke to the hallboy:

"I want to see Mr. Bloeckman—Mr. Black," he said. "He's upstairs—have him paged."

The boy shook his head.

"'Sagainsa rules require him to be paged. Do you know which table he's at?"

"No. But I have to see him."

"Wait and I'll get you a waiter."

After a brief moment, a head waiter emerged, carrying a card that displayed the table reservations. He shot a cynical glance at Anthony—though it missed its mark. They both leaned over the cardboard together and easily located the table—a party of eight, belonging to Mr. Black himself.

"Tell him Mr. Patch. Very, very important."

Again he waited, leaning against the railing and listening to the jumbled melodies of "Jazz-mad" that drifted down the staircase. A coat-check girl nearby was singing:

"Out in—the shimmy sanitarium"
The jazz enthusiasts live there.
Out in the shimmy sanitarium
I left my blushing bride.
She went and shook herself until she lost her mind.
So let her shiver back again—

Then he spotted Bloeckman coming down the stairs, so he stepped forward to greet him and shake his hand.

"You wanted to see me?" the older man said coolly.

"Yes," Anthony replied with a nod, "it's a personal matter. Could you just step over here?"

Watching him closely, Bloeckman followed Anthony to a curved section of the staircase where they couldn't be seen or overheard by anyone coming into or going out of the restaurant.

"Well?" he asked.

"I wanted to talk to you."

"What about?"

Anthony just laughed—a foolish laugh; he meant for it to sound casual.

"What do you want to discuss with me?" Bloeckman asked again.

"What's the hurry, old man?" He tried to lay his hand in a friendly gesture upon Bloeckman's shoulder, but the latter drew away slightly. "How've you been?"

"Alright, thanks.... Listen, Mr. Patch, I have guests upstairs. They'll think I'm being rude if I'm gone too long. What did you want to talk to me about?"

For the second time that evening, Anthony's thoughts suddenly shifted direction, and the words that came out of his mouth were completely different from what he had planned to say.

"I understand you kept my wife out of the movies."

"What?" Bloeckman's reddish face grew darker as shadows fell across it in parallel lines.

"You heard me."

"Listen here, Mr. Patch," said Bloeckman, calmly and without changing his expression, "you're drunk. You're disgustingly and insultingly drunk."

"I'm not too drunk to talk to you," Anthony insisted with a sneer. "First of all, my wife wants nothing whatsoever to do with you. She never did. Do you understand me?"

"Be quiet!" the older man said angrily. "I would think you'd have enough respect for your wife not to drag her into this conversation given the circumstances."

"Don't worry about what I expect from my wife. One thing's for sure—you stay away from her. Go to hell!"

"Look here—I think you're a little crazy!" Bloeckman shouted. He moved two steps forward as if he was going to walk past, but Anthony blocked his path.

"Not so fast, you goddamn Jew."

For a moment they stood looking at each other, Anthony swaying gently from side to side, Bloeckman almost shaking with rage.

"Be careful!" he shouted in a tense voice.

Anthony might have recalled at that moment a particular expression Bloeckman had given him at the Biltmore Hotel years earlier. But he remembered nothing, nothing——

"I'll say it again, you God——"

Then Bloeckman lashed out with all the power in his well-trained forty-five-year-old arm, striking Anthony directly in the mouth. Anthony crashed backward against the staircase, steadied himself, and threw a wild, drunken punch at his attacker, but Bloeckman, who exercised daily and had boxing experience, easily deflected it and hit him twice in the face with two quick, devastating blows. Anthony let out a small groan and collapsed onto the green velvet carpet, discovering as he went down that his mouth was filled with blood and felt strangely loose at the front. He fought his way back to his feet, gasping and spitting blood, and as he lunged toward Bloeckman, who stood several feet away with his fists clenched but lowered, two waiters who had appeared out of nowhere grabbed his arms and restrained him, leaving him powerless. Behind them, a dozen onlookers had somehow materialized.

"I'll kill him," Anthony shouted, thrashing and struggling from side to side. "Let me kill——"

"Throw him out!" Bloeckman commanded with excitement, just as a small man with a scarred face shoved his way quickly through the crowd of onlookers.

"Any trouble, Mr. Black?"

"This loser tried to blackmail me!" said Bloeckman, and then, his voice rising to a slightly shrill note of pride: "He got what he deserved!"

The small man turned to a waiter.

"Call a policeman!" he commanded.

"Oh, no," Bloeckman said quickly. "I can't be bothered with this. Just throw him out onto the street.... Ugh! What a disgrace!" He turned around and walked toward the restroom with deliberate dignity just as six strong hands grabbed Anthony and hauled him toward the door. The vagrant was thrown forcefully onto the sidewalk, where he hit the pavement on his hands and knees with a sickening slapping noise and slowly rolled over onto his side.

The shock left him stunned. He remained there for a moment, experiencing sharp pain throughout his body. Then the discomfort concentrated in his stomach, and he came back to consciousness to find that a large foot was poking him.

"You need to keep moving, you bum! Keep moving!"

The large doorman was speaking. A town car had pulled up to the curb and its passengers had gotten out—or rather, two of the women were standing on the sidewalk, waiting with dignified offense until this vulgar obstruction would be cleared from their way.

"Move on! Or I'll throw you on!"

"Here—I'll get him."

This was a different voice; Anthony sensed that it was somehow more understanding, more kindly inclined than the first

428

one. Once again arms wrapped around him, half carrying, half pulling him into a blessed patch of shade four doors down the street and leaning him against the stone facade of a hat shop.

"Thanks a lot," Anthony mumbled weakly. Someone shoved his soft hat down on his head and he flinched.

"Just sit still, buddy, and you'll feel better. Those guys sure give you a bump."

"I'm going back to kill that dirty—" He tried to stand up but fell backward against the wall.

"You can't do anything now," came the voice. "Get them some other time. I'm telling you straight, aren't I? I'm helping you."

Anthony nodded.

"And you better go home. You dropped a tooth tonight, buddy. You know that?"

Anthony ran his tongue around his mouth, confirming what had been said. Then, with considerable effort, he lifted his hand and found the empty space.

"I'm going to get you home, friend. Where do you live—"

"Oh, my God! My God!" Anthony burst out, his hands clenched into tight fists with fierce intensity. "I'll show those filthy scoundrels. Help me put them in their place and I'll make it worth your while. My grandfather is Adam Patch, from Tarrytown"—

"Who?"

"Adam Patch, by God!"

"Do you want to go all the way to Tarrytown?"

"No."

"Well, you tell me where to go, friend, and I'll get a cab."

Anthony could see that his Good Samaritan was a short, broad-shouldered person who looked rather worn down by life.

"Where do you live?"

Soaked and rattled as he was, Anthony realized that his speech would be weak backing for his reckless bragging about his grandfather.

"Get me a taxi," he ordered, checking his pockets.

A taxi pulled up. Once again Anthony tried to get up, but his ankle hung loosely, as if it were broken in two pieces. The Good Samaritan had to help him get in—and then climbed in after him.

"Listen here, buddy," he said, "you're drunk and you're beaten up, and you won't be able to get into your house unless someone carries you in, so I'm coming with you, and I know you'll make things right with me. Where do you live?"

With some hesitation, Anthony provided his address. As the taxi pulled away, he rested his head against the man's shoulder and slipped into a hazy, uncomfortable stupor. When he came to, the man had carried him out of the taxi in front of the apartment building on Claremont Avenue and was attempting to help him stand.

"Can you walk?"

"Yes—sort of. You better not come in with me." Once again he searched through his pockets without success. "Listen," he went on, speaking apologetically while swaying unsteadily on his feet, "I'm afraid I don't have any money on me."

"Huh?"

"I'm completely broke."

"Hey! Didn't I hear you promise you'd take care of this with me? Who's going to pay the taxi fare?" He turned to the driver for confirmation. "Didn't you hear him say he'd handle it? All that stuff about his grandfather?"

"Actually," Anthony muttered carelessly, "you were the one doing all the talking; but if you stop by tomorrow—"

At this point the taxi driver leaned out from his cab and said aggressively:

"Oh, hit him once, the dirty cheapskate. If he wasn't a bum they wouldn't have thrown him out."

In response to this suggestion, the Samaritan's fist shot out like a battering ram and sent Anthony crashing down against the stone steps of the apartment building, where he lay motionless while the tall buildings swayed back and forth above him....

After a long time, he woke up and realized it had become much colder. He tried to move but his muscles wouldn't respond. He felt strangely eager to know what time it was, so he reached for his watch, only to discover his pocket was empty. Without thinking, his lips shaped an ancient phrase:

"What a night!"

Surprisingly, he was nearly sober. Without turning his head, he gazed upward to where the moon hung suspended in the middle of the sky, casting its light down onto Claremont Avenue like it was illuminating the depths of a vast and unexplored chasm. There was no indication or noise of life except for the constant ringing in his ears, but after a brief moment Anthony broke the quiet himself with a clear and strange sound. It was the noise he had repeatedly tried to produce back at the Boul' Mich', when he had stood face to face with Bloeckman—the unmistakable sound of bitter laughter. And coming from his torn and bloodied lips, it resembled a pathetic heaving of the spirit.

Three weeks later, the trial reached its conclusion. The seemingly endless web of legal bureaucracy that had stretched over four and a half years suddenly came to an abrupt halt. Anthony and Gloria, along with Edward Shuttleworth and a group of beneficiaries on the opposing side, gave testimony, told lies, and generally conducted themselves poorly in varying degrees of greed and desperation. One morning in March, Anthony woke up realizing that the verdict would be delivered at four o'clock that afternoon, and at this thought he climbed out of bed and started getting dressed. Mixed with his intense anxiety was an unreasonable optimism about the result. He was convinced that the lower court's decision would be overturned, if only because of the backlash against reforms and reformers that had recently emerged due to excessive prohibition. He placed more faith in the personal attacks they had directed at Shuttleworth than in the purely legal elements of the case.

Fully dressed, he poured himself a glass of whiskey and walked into Gloria's room, where he discovered her completely awake. She had been confined to bed for a week, indulging herself, Anthony believed, although the doctor had advised that she should not be bothered.

"Good morning," she whispered, without a smile. Her eyes appeared remarkably large and dark.

"How do you feel?" he asked reluctantly. "Better?"

"Yes."

"Much?"

"Yes."

"Do you feel well enough to come down to court with me this afternoon?"

She nodded.

"Yes. I want to. Dick said yesterday that if the weather was nice he would come up in his car and take me for a ride in Central Park—and look, the room's filled with sunshine."

Anthony automatically looked out the window and then sat down on the bed.

"God, I'm nervous!" he exclaimed.

"Please don't sit there," she said quickly.

"Why not?"

"You smell of whiskey. I can't stand it."

He stood up without really thinking about it and walked out of the room. A short while later she called out to him, so he went outside and picked up some potato salad and cold chicken from the deli for her.

At two o'clock, Richard Caramel's car pulled up at the door, and when he called up to the apartment, Anthony escorted Gloria down in the elevator and walked with her to the curb.

She told her cousin that it was thoughtful of him to take her riding. "Don't be naive," Dick replied dismissively. "It's nothing."

But he didn't mean that it was meaningless, and this was strange. Richard Caramel had forgiven many people for countless wrongs. However, he had never forgiven his cousin, Gloria Gilbert, for something she had said just before her wedding seven years earlier. She had told him that she had no intention of reading his book.

Richard Caramel remembered this—he had kept it clearly in his mind for seven years.

"What time should I expect you back?" asked Anthony.

"We won't come back," she replied, "we'll meet you down there at four."

"All right," he muttered, "I'll meet you."

When he went upstairs, he discovered a letter waiting for him. It was a mimeographed notice that used patronizingly casual language to encourage "the boys" to pay their American Legion dues. He tossed it irritably into the trash can and sat down with his elbows resting on the windowsill, staring down unseeing into the bright street below.

Italy—if the verdict went their way, it meant Italy. The word had transformed into a kind of magical charm for him, representing a place where life's unbearable worries would drop away like worn-out clothing. They would visit the resort towns first and lose themselves among the vibrant, lively crowds, forgetting the dull shadows of hopelessness. Wonderfully refreshed, he would stroll once more through the Piazza di Spagna at dusk, moving among that drifting collection of dark-haired women and tattered beggars, of serious, barefoot monks. The idea of Italian women awakened something faint within him—when his wallet grew heavy once more, even romance might return to settle upon it—the romance of blue waterways in Venice, of the golden green hills of Fiesole after rainfall, and of women, women who transformed, faded, melted into other women and disappeared from his life, but who remained forever beautiful and forever young.

But he felt there should be a change in how he approached things. Every bit of anguish he had experienced, all the grief and suffering, had come from women. It was something they inflicted on him in various ways, without awareness, almost carelessly—perhaps sensing his sensitivity and fear, they destroyed the parts of him that threatened their complete control.

Turning away from the window, he faced his reflection in the mirror, staring sadly at his pale, sickly face, his eyes marked with a network of lines that looked like dried blood streaks, and his hunched, soft body whose very drooping posture told the story of his laziness. He was thirty-three years old—but he looked forty. Well, things were going to change.

The doorbell rang suddenly and he jumped as if someone had struck him. Pulling himself together, he walked into the hallway and opened the front door. It was Dot.

The Encounter

He backed away from her into the living room, understanding only scattered words from the steady stream of sentences that flowed from her lips, one following another in an unrelenting, flat tone. She was dressed respectably but worn—a rather sad little hat decorated with pink and blue flowers covered and concealed her dark hair. He pieced together from her words that a few days earlier she had spotted a news item about the lawsuit, and had gotten his address from the clerk at the Appellate Division. She had phoned the apartment and had been informed by a woman that Anthony wasn't home, though she had declined to provide her name to this woman.

In a living room he stood by the door watching her with a kind of stunned horror as she kept talking.... His main feeling was that

434

all the civilization and social customs around him seemed strangely artificial.... She was working at a hat shop on Sixth Avenue, she told him. It was a lonely existence. She had been ill for quite some time after he departed for Camp Mills; her mother had traveled down and brought her back home to Carolina.... She had arrived in New York with the intention of locating Anthony.

She was devastatingly serious. Her violet eyes were bloodshot from crying; her gentle voice was broken by small, breathless sobs.

That was all. She had never changed. She wanted him now, and if she couldn't have him she must die....

"You need to leave," he finally said, his voice strained with agonizing intensity. "Don't I have enough problems to deal with right now without you showing up here? My God! You have to get out!"

Sobbing, she sat down in a chair.

"I love you," she cried; "I don't care what you say to me! I love you."

"I don't care!" he nearly screamed; "get out—oh, get out! Haven't you caused me enough damage? Haven't—you—done—enough?"

"Hit me!" she begged him—frantically, foolishly. "Oh, hit me, and I'll kiss the hand you strike me with!"

His voice grew louder until it reached nearly a screaming pitch. "I'll kill you!" he shouted. "If you don't leave I'll kill you, I'll kill you!"

There was madness in his eyes now, but Dot wasn't intimidated and stood up, taking a step toward him.

"Anthony! Anthony!—"

He made a small clicking noise with his teeth and pulled back as if he was about to leap at her—but then, shifting his intention, he looked frantically around the floor and walls.

"I'll kill you!" he gasped in short, ragged breaths. "I'll kill you!" He seemed to clamp down on each word as if trying to make it real through sheer force. Finally alarmed, she stopped moving forward, but when she met his wild eyes, she took a step back toward the door. Anthony began pacing frantically back and forth on his side of the room, continuing to shout his single, furious threat. Then he spotted what he'd been looking for—a heavy oak chair sitting next to the table. With a harsh, broken cry, he grabbed it, lifted it over his head, and hurled it with all his violent fury straight at the pale, terrified face on the other side of the room... then a dense, impenetrable darkness descended upon him and wiped out all thought, anger, and madness at once—with an almost audible snap, the world before his eyes completely transformed....

Gloria and Dick arrived at five o'clock and called out his name. When no one responded, they walked into the living room and discovered a chair with its back broken lying in the doorway, and they saw that the entire room was in disarray—the rugs were bunched up, and the pictures and decorative objects were scattered across the coffee table. The air was thick with the cloying scent of inexpensive perfume.

They discovered Anthony sitting in a sunny spot on his bedroom floor. In front of him lay his three large stamp albums, opened wide, and when they walked in, he was running his fingers through a huge pile of stamps he had poured out from the back of one of the books. When he looked up and saw Dick and Gloria, he tilted his head thoughtfully to one side and gestured for them to step back.

"Anthony!" Gloria shouted with intense excitement, "we've won! They overturned the decision!"

"Don't come in," he said weakly, "you'll mess them up. I'm organizing, and I know you'll step on them. Everything always gets ruined."

"What are you doing?" Dick asked in amazement. "Are you going back to being a child? Don't you understand that you've won the lawsuit? They've overturned the lower court's ruling. You're worth thirty million dollars!"

Anthony only looked at him with reproach.

"Close the door when you leave." He spoke like a cheeky child.

With a growing sense of dread appearing in her eyes, Gloria stared at him—

"Anthony!" she shouted, "what's wrong? What's happening? Why didn't you show up—what is it?"

"Listen," Anthony said quietly, "you two need to leave—right now, both of you. Otherwise, I'll tell my grandfather."

He lifted a handful of stamps and allowed them to float down around him like falling leaves, multicolored and brilliant, spinning and dancing brightly in the sunlit air: stamps from England and Ecuador, Venezuela and Spain—Italy....

Together with The Sparrows

That beautiful divine irony which has documented the death of countless generations of sparrows undoubtedly records the most delicate spoken nuances of the passengers on ships like The Berengaria. And undoubtedly it was listening when the young man in the plaid cap walked quickly across the deck and spoke to the pretty girl in yellow.

"That's him," he said, pointing to a bundled figure seated in a wheelchair near the rail. "That's Anthony Patch. First time he's been on deck."

"Oh—that's him?"

"Yes. He's been acting a bit unstable, people say, ever since he came into his inheritance four or five months ago. You see, the other man, Shuttleworth, the devout one, the one who didn't receive the money, he barricaded himself in a hotel room and shot himself—

"Oh, he did—"

"But I suppose Anthony Patch doesn't care much. He's got his thirty million. And he's brought his personal doctor along in case he doesn't feel quite right about it. Has she been on deck?" he asked.

The attractive young woman in yellow glanced around carefully.

"She was just here a moment ago. She was wearing a Russian sable coat that probably cost a fortune." She frowned and then said with conviction: "I really can't stand her, you know. She seems kind of—kind of artificial and dirty, if you understand what I'm saying. Some people just give off that impression whether they actually are or not."

"Of course, I understand," the man wearing the plaid cap replied. "She's actually quite attractive, though." He stopped speaking for a moment. "I wonder what's going through his mind—probably his finances, I suppose, or perhaps he feels guilty about that guy Shuttleworth."

"Probably...."

But the man in the plaid cap was completely mistaken. Anthony Patch, seated near the railing and gazing out at the ocean, wasn't thinking about his wealth, since he had rarely in his life been truly obsessed with material vanity, nor was he thinking about Edward Shuttleworth, because it's better to focus on the positive aspects of such matters. No—he was absorbed in a sequence of memories, much like a general might reflect on a victorious campaign and examine his triumphs. He was contemplating the difficulties, the unbearable ordeals he had endured. They had attempted to make him pay for the errors of his youth. He had been subjected to merciless suffering, his very desire for romance had been punished, his friends had abandoned him—even Gloria had turned against him. He had been alone, completely alone—confronting it all.

Just a few months earlier, people had been pressuring him to give up, to accept mediocrity, to find a job. However, he had understood that his lifestyle was justified—and he had persevered with determination. Indeed, the very friends who had treated him most harshly had eventually come to respect him, recognizing that he had been right from the beginning. Hadn't the Lacys and the Merediths and the Cartwright-Smiths visited Gloria and him at the Ritz-Carlton just a week before their departure?

Great tears filled his eyes, and his voice shook as he whispered to himself.

"I showed them," he was saying. "It was a tough fight, but I didn't give up and I made it through!"

THE END

Thank You For Reading

You've Just Read a Piece of the Greatest Library Ever Rebuilt

Thank you for reading.

This book is one of thousands we're restoring, reimagining, and translating as part of the **Modern Library of Alexandria** — a global movement to preserve and share humanity's most important ideas.

What was once lost to fire and time is now rising again — not just as memory, but as living, breathing knowledge, freely accessible to all.

What You Can Do Next:

- **Keep Reading.**

  Discover more legendary works — in beautiful print, audiobook, or digital form — at LibraryofAlexandria.com.

- **Build Your Own Library.**

  Every title is available as a paperback, hardcover, or collectible boxset — at true printing cost. Craft a personal library worthy of display.

- **Spread the Light.**

  Share this book. Tell others about the movement. Help us translate every timeless work into every language, so no reader is ever left behind.

By finishing this book, you've already taken part in something extraordinary.

Join us at LibraryofAlexandria.com

Together, we're rebuilding the greatest library the world has ever known.

With appreciation,

The Modern Library of Alexandria Team

Visit:
www.libraryofalexandria.com
Or scan the code below: